#MeToo and the Po

"This collection makes an intervention into the theory and politics of sexual violence post #MeToo. Bringing together a range of different contributors and perspectives, it draws out some of the complexities surrounding the issue of sexual violence. Although the collection resists an over-arching message, the theme of inclusion/exclusion is prominent, and it includes a number of more marginalised voices. Overall, this book situates #MeToo and the feminist movement against sexual violence within broader questions about intersectionality, feminist activism and social change. Its final question, inspired by #MeToo founder Tarana Burke, is the right one: 'where to from here?'"

—Alison Phipps, *Professor of Gender Studies, University of Sussex, UK*

"This fresh, erudite and eclectic collection invites readers to meditate on sexual violence politics and activism within and beyond the #MeToo Movement. It explores debates about the significance of #MeToo within feminist history as well as digital activism and social movements more broadly. It is a must-read for anyone who cares about violence and inequality."

—Nicola Henry, *Associate Professor and Principal Research Fellow, Social and Global Studies Centre, RMIT, Australia*

Bianca Fileborn • Rachel Loney-Howes
Editors

#MeToo and the Politics of Social Change

palgrave
macmillan

Editors
Bianca Fileborn
University of Melbourne
Parkville, VIC, Australia

Rachel Loney-Howes
University of Wollongong
Wollongong, NSW, Australia

ISBN 978-3-030-15212-3   ISBN 978-3-030-15213-0   (eBook)
https://doi.org/10.1007/978-3-030-15213-0

Cover illustration: Arthimedes / shutterstock.com

This Palgrave Macmillan imprint is published by the registered company Springer Nature Switzerland AG
The registered company address is: Gewerbestrasse 11, 6330 Cham, Switzerland

For survivors.

Foreword

For over 40 years, feminist scholars and activists have struggled to eliminate the highly injurious behaviors that exist on what Liz Kelly (1987, 1988) refers to as the 'continuum of sexual violence', ranging from non-physical acts to physical ones such as rape. Although the idea of the continuum is often used to portray movement from least serious to most serious, to scholars like Kelly (1988) and many adult female survivors of sexual assault, all these behaviors are serious and have a 'basic common character'. They are all means of 'abuse, intimidation, coercion, intrusion, threat and force' used mainly to control women (p. 76). No behavior on the continuum is automatically considered more harmful than another, and, as Kelly states, women's experiences 'shade into and out of a given category such as sexual harassment, which includes looks, gestures and remarks as well as acts which may be defined as assault or rape' (p. 48).

What progress has been made? There are many answers to this question—one of which is that today, the general public, government agencies, the mass media and academics are much more knowledgeable about the amount and consequences of various types of violence against women. Meanwhile, fictional and nonfictional stories of the abuse of women are commonplace in the media; national, local and international surveys have been conducted; and thousands of academic journal articles and hundreds of scholarly books like Bianca Fileborn and Rachel Loney-Howes' path-breaking anthology have been published. In fact, advances in the social scientific study of various forms of woman abuse have been faster paced than some of the major developments in the physical sciences.

Given the persistence of patriarchy and the ongoing anti-feminist backlash, these are amazing achievements. Still, Claire Renzetti (2018, p. 4), editor of the widely read and cited journal *Violence Against Women*, reminds us that 'it is astounding that we are still fighting some of the same battles as we were 25—even 40—years ago, and that there is still so much work to be done'. The people and behaviors uncovered by the #MeToo social media movement are key indicators of this. On the other hand, for many people, this recent development offers much hope and the possibility of major social change. Indeed, as Fileborn and Loney-Howes correctly point out in their introduction to this volume (see Chap. 1), the #MeToo movement 'was a highly successful one' and 'has generated tangible action'. Nevertheless, they, and other contributors to this book, also sensitize us to the fact there are some serious problems with this campaign. For example, in Chap. 10, Jess Ison makes explicit the heteronormativity of the #MeToo campaign. As well, in Chap. 8, Tess Ryan directs our attention to #MeToo's exclusion of Aboriginal women. More important issues related to the politics of inclusion are covered in other chapters included in Part 2 and those mentioned here should not be deemed to be more important than those not briefly discussed. To again quote Fileborn and Loney-Howes, '#MeToo was championed (at least initially) by wealthy, white, heterosexual women with prominent public profiles, access to capital and thus political, social and economic freedoms that many women around the world do not have'.

We should also keep in mind that the voices of many, if not most, poor white women have been excluded. One low-income, white female bartender in Morgantown, West Virginia, is an example that immediately comes to mind. She told me, 'I would never be hired anywhere else here in town if I named my boss and I am barely getting by as it is'. An even longer list of people left out of the #MeToo movement could easily be provided. This volume, then, is a powerful reminder to always think about others who are not in the room with us when we design and implement progressive strategies aimed at reducing sexual assault. We need to learn from the pitfalls of the #MeToo movement because we don't want to repeat what Fileborn and Loney-Howes note in Chap. 1: 'reinforce assumptions about "real" rape victims who are young, white, heterosexual, able-bodied and not engaged in "risky" sexual behaviors that might make them "responsible" for their sexual victimization'.

Will #MeToo become successful if it overcomes the problems raised in this book? Of course, this is an empirical question that can only be answered empirically, but we definitely know that one strategy alone will not make much of a difference. For years, feminists have emphasized the importance of avoiding simplistic solutions and the value of engaging in a multipronged approach. This is not to say, though, that this book portrays the #MeToo movement as simplistic. In the words of Loney-Howes and Fileborn (see Chap. 20), 'the #MeToo movement is a deeply complex and multi-faced one, brimming with points of tension, contradiction and polarization'. This claim is strongly supported by all the contributions to this book.

There is much more that can, and will, be said about *#MeToo and the Politics of Social Change*. I invite you to read this useful collection because it will energize you and stimulate new feminist ways of thinking about sexual violence.

Anna Deane Carlson Endowed Chair of   Walter DeKeseredy
Social Sciences, Director of the Research
Center on Violence, and Professor of Sociology,
West Virginia University, Morgantown, WV, USA

References

Kelly, L. (1987). The continuum of sexual violence. In J. Hanmer & M. Maynard (Eds.), *Women, violence and social control* (pp. 46–60). Atlantic Highlands, NJ: Humanities Press International.

Kelly, L. (1988). *Surviving sexual violence*. Minneapolis, MN: University of Minnesota Press.

Renzetti, C. M. (2018). Editor's introduction to 25th anniversary special issue 1. *Violence Against Women, 25*(1), 3–5.

Acknowledgments

We would like to thank and acknowledge our wonderful contributors for working with us on this endeavor and for producing such fantastic, critical work under incredibly tight timelines. To Walter DeKeseredy: we are honored that you were able to write the Foreword to this book. Thanks to Josie Taylor and Liam Inscoe-Jones from Palgrave for your enthusiastic support of this collection. A huge thanks to Tanya Serisier, Natalia Hanley and Alyce McGovern, who kindly offered their expertise and feedback on earlier versions of some chapters. Special thanks to Grant for being our last-minute research assistant.

We acknowledge that this book was edited on land that was stolen and sovereignty never ceded, predominantly that of the Bedegal, Dharawal and Wurundjeri peoples.

Bianca would like to thank her family and friends for putting up with me (you know who you are!), particularly during the final stages of editing. I'd like to acknowledge my colleagues at the University of New South Wales (UNSW), where I was based for much of the work on this book, particularly Alyce McGovern and Phillip Wadds, and my wonderful research students Elena Cama and Sophie Hindes for the chats on #MeToo throughout the year. Thanks to Grant for being quietly supportive and endlessly patient as always, and to Bella for the cuddles and writing companionship. And, finally, thank you to Rachel for working with me on this project—I couldn't have asked for a better co-editor.

Rachel would also like to thank her family and friends for their support and patience during the final editing processes of this book. In particular, I'd like to thank my colleague Natalia Hanley at the University of Wollongong, who provided critical feedback on my own work included in this collection. Thank you to Peter Siminski for your generosity and the stimulating conversations we have had relating to this project. Lastly, thank you to Bianca for being such a wonderful co-editor. Your passion and dedication is inspiring, and it is a privilege to work alongside you.

Contents

Notes on Contributors

Rob Cover is an Associate Professor at the School of Social Sciences, The University of Western Australia. He is a chief investigator on an Australian Research Council project (2015–2018) examining the history, conditions and frameworks of lesbian, gay, bisexual, transgender/transsexual, queer/questioning (LGBTQ) youth sexuality support and belonging and another (2018–2020), investigating the role of gender and sexual diversity on Australian screen in promoting social change. Recent books include: *Queer Youth Suicide, Culture and Identity: Unliveable Lives?* (2012), *Vulnerability and Exposure: Footballer Scandals, Masculinity and Ethics* (2015), *Digital Identities: Creating and Communicating the Online Self* (2016) and *Emergent Identities: New Sexualities, Gender and Relationships in a Digital Era* (2018).

Leah Cowan is the Policy and Communications Coordinator at Imkaan, a UK-based national Black feminist organization dedicated to addressing violence against women and girls. Leah is also the Politics Editor at *galdem*, a magazine written by women of color and nonbinary people of color. She has organized with SOAS Detainee Support, a grassroots initiative which works in solidarity with people incarcerated in the UK's immigration detention estate. She writes, speaks and lectures on race, gender, and border and state violence. Her 2018 TEDx talk explored the relationship between emotional labor and capitalism.

Cyndi Darnell holds an MHSc, an MNT, a Grad. Dip. C&HS and a BEd, and is a sex and relationship therapist, spearheading progressive sex and relationships workshops for adults that change people's lives.

She is a reviewer and contributor to academic journals *Sex Education* (UK), *Porn Studies* (UK), and *Sex & Relationship Therapy* (UK). In 2015 she released *The Atlas of Erotic Anatomy and Arousal*, a pioneering educational video series designed to give upfront adult information about sex, the body and, most importantly, pleasure! Her approach spans the clinical to the esoteric and she's working on her first book about unpacking the nature of eroticism to enrich libido. A regular in the Australian media she has appeared on TV, radio and print, besides being a principal consultant and advisor on Northern Pictures' *Luke Warm Sex* (on ABC & Netflix). She counsels individuals and couples, offers training to professionals on sex and the human condition, and offers insight into the quandaries of the erotic to transform fear into freedom.

Bianca Fileborn is Lecturer in Criminology at the School of Social and Political Sciences, University of Melbourne. Her research examines the intersections of space/place, identity, culture and sexual violence, and justice responses to sexual violence. Fileborn was awarded an Australian Research Council *Discovery Early Career Researcher Award* in 2019 to examine justice responses to street harassment. Other recent projects include an examination of safety and sexual violence at Australian music festivals, sexual violence in licensed venues, and LGBTIQ+ young people's involvement in family violence. She is the author of *Reclaiming the Night-Time Economy: Unwanted Sexual Attention in Pubs and Clubs* (Palgrave Macmillan).

Michael Flood is Associate Professor of Sociology at the Queensland University of Technology (QUT). He is a highly regarded researcher on violence against women and its prevention, and he has an extensive record of community and professional engagement. Flood has made significant contributions to scholarly and community understanding of men's and boys' involvements in preventing and reducing violence against women and building gender equality, and to scholarship and programming regarding violence against women and its prevention. Flood is the lead editor of *Engaging Men in Building Gender Equality* (2015) and *The International Encyclopedia of Men and Masculinities* (2007). Flood also is a trainer and community educator, with a long involvement in community advocacy and education focused on men, gender and violence. He has contributed to social change campaigns, worked with sporting and military organizations, participated in international expert meetings and shaped national prevention frameworks.

Mary Anne Franks is Professor of Law at the University of Miami School of Law, where she teaches First Amendment law, criminal law and procedure, family law, and law and technology. She is also the President of the Cyber Civil Rights Initiative, a nonprofit organization that uses the power of law, policy and technology to protect equal rights. She is the author of *The Cult of the Constitution* (2019). Her scholarship has appeared in the *Harvard Law Review, California Law Review*, and *UCLA Law Review*, among others. Franks holds a JD from Harvard Law School, along with a doctorate and a master's degree from Oxford University. Franks previously taught at the University of Chicago Law School as a Bigelow Fellow and Lecturer in Law and at Harvard University as Lecturer in Social Studies and Philosophy.

María Cecilia Garibotti is a visiting professor at Universidad Torcuato Di Tella and Universidad de Palermo, in Argentina. She is a political scientist (Universidad de San Andrés) and a lawyer (Universidad de Buenos Aires) and holds a JSM from Stanford Law School. Her main interests are public law, administration and social mobilization.

Jessamy Gleeson is based at the Royal Melbourne Institute of Technology (RMIT) University and is working on an Australian Research Council-funded project on image-based sexual abuse. Her PhD and recent publications have focused on how social media platforms can be used by feminist campaigns to challenge representations of women in the mainstream media. Outside of her academic life, Jess works as a feminist wrangler and manager who organizes a slew of vibrant feminists. She has previously assisted in the organization of *SlutWalk* Melbourne, Girls On Film Festival and *Cherchez la Femme*.

Bridget Haire is a National Health and Medical Research Council (NHMRC) early-career fellow at the Kirby Institute, University of New South Wales (UNSW) Sydney, and lectures in public health and medical ethics. Bridget is the President of the Australian Federation of AIDS Organizations and worked in the field of HIV and sexual and reproductive health for more than 20 years as a journalist, editor, policy analyst and advocate. Her research focuses on ethical issues in infectious disease control, with an emphasis on underserved or marginalized populations, gender, and sexual and reproductive health.

Cecilia Marcela Hopp is a visiting professor at Universidad de Buenos Aires (UBA) and Universidad Torcuato Di Tella (UTDT), in Argentina. She is a lawyer (UBA) and a specialist in criminal law (UTDT), holds an LLM from New York University School of Law and is a PhD candidate at Universidad de Buenos Aires. Her main interests are criminal law and procedure, with a focus on gender issues and sexual and reproductive rights.

Jess Ison is a PhD candidate at La Trobe University. She is the representative for the Institute for Critical Animal Studies (ICAS) in Oceania, the co-convenor of the La Trobe Animal Studies Association (LASA) and an editor for the journal *Writing from Below*. Jess lives on Wurundjeri land, where she writes on the intersections of queer theory and animal studies.

Huda Jawad is a SAFE Communities project coordinator at Standing Together Against Domestic Violence, a charity working to end domestic violence in London and nationally. SAFE Communities is a project that works with grassroots faith and minoritized communities in London. Huda is a trustee of End Violence Against Women Coalition, a leading coalition of specialist women's support services, researchers, activists, survivors and NGOs working to end violence against women and girls in all its forms. Huda is also a member of Musawah, the global movement for equality and justice in the Muslim family.

Neha Kagal is Research and Development Coordinator at Imkaan, a UK-based, national, Black feminist organisation dedicated to addressing violence against women and girls. Her latest research focuses on understanding the gaps in intersectional VAWG (violence against women and girls) service-delivery for minoritised women and girls across the Western Balkans and Turkey. Kagal has worked with groups of minoritised women in India, particularly HIV positive women, wastepickers and sex workers, on issues relating to rights-based advocacy, livelihoods and VAWG. She also lectures on gender, identity, intersectionality and human rights.

Rachel Loney-Howes is Lecturer in Criminology at the School of Health and Society, University of Wollongong, Australia. A critical socio-legal studies scholar, her research explores the nature, history and scope of anti-rape activism, with a particular focus on the relationship between activism, support services and law reform.

Heidi Matthews is an assistant professor and a co-director of the Nathanson Centre on Transnational Human Rights, Crime and Security, Osgoode Hall Law School, York University. Her work theorizes contemporary shifts in the practice and discourse of the global legal regulation of political violence, with particular attention to history and gender, as well as to political, critical and aesthetic theory. She is working on a research and documentary film project that examines narratives of Allied sexual violence perpetrated against German women at the end of World War II.

Kaitlynn Mendes is Associate Professor of Media and Communication at the University of Leicester, UK. Her research falls in the field of feminist media studies, with developed expertise in representations of feminism, feminist activists and feminist activists in mainstream news media, feminist online media and social media. Her recent research has examined the ways that feminists are using online spaces to challenge misogyny, sexism and rape culture, as evidenced by the recent *SlutWalk* movement, and how this activism is bringing feminism to the public's attention once more. She is the author or editor of five books, including *Digital Feminist Activism: Women and Girls Fight Back Against Rape Culture*.

Christy E. Newman is an Associate Professor at the Centre for Social Research in Health, University of New South Wales (UNSW) Sydney. Drawing on her background in health sociology and cultural studies, Christy examines both experiences and representations of health, sexuality and relationships across a range of collaborative, interdisciplinary projects. She is particularly interested in the way contemporary ideas about inclusivity and diversity are promoted and problematized in health policy and practice, especially in the fields of sexual and reproductive health and blood-borne virus prevention and care.

Nickie Phillips is Associate Professor of Criminal Justice at St. Francis College, Brooklyn Heights, New York. She is the author of *Beyond Blurred Lines: Rape Culture in Popular Media* and co-author of *Comic Book Crime: Truth, Justice, and the American Way*.

Jessica Ringrose is Professor of the Sociology of Gender and Education at the UCL Institute of Education, University College London. Her recent research projects include 'Documenting Digital Feminist Activism: Mapping Feminist Responses to New Media Misogyny and Rape Culture' and 'Adolescent Girls Negotiating Sexualization'. Jessica's work also considers youth feminism and teen's digital gender and sexual cultures, including uses of social media. She is the author of over 60 journal articles and book chapters, editor of 4 special issues of journals and editor or author of 4 books.

Lauren Rosewarne is a senior lecturer at the School of Social and Political Sciences, University of Melbourne, Australia. She teaches in the areas of political science and gender studies, and writes, comments and speaks on a wide variety of topics, including gender, sexuality, public policy, social media, pop culture and technology. Lauren has authored nine books, as well as journal articles, book chapters and hundreds of opinion pieces. Lauren is a co-host on ABC Radio National's *Stop Everything!* pop culture program. More information can be found on her website: www.laurenrosewarne.com.

Kathryn Royal is a PhD researcher based at the Centre for Research into Violence and Abuse (CRiVA), Durham University in the northeast of England. Her research explores media representations of sexual violence and how this affects women who have experienced rape. She is also an active and committed volunteer for her local Rape Crisis Centre, with over five years of experience of supporting women on its helpline.

Tess Ryan is a proud Biripi woman who completed her PhD at the University of Canberra on the topic of Indigenous women and leadership in Australia. Tess is currently located at the Australian Catholic University in Melbourne, Australia. Her work has featured in outlets include *The Conversation, IndigenousX, The Guardian* and *SBS News.*

Michael Salter is an Associate Professor, a Scientia Fellow and a criminologist at the University of New South Wales. He has published widely on violence against women and children, including technologically facilitated forms of abuse. He is the author of *Organised Sexual Abuse* (2013) and *Crime, Justice and Social Media* (2017).

Breanan Turner is a Melbourne-based PhD candidate researching women's experience of feminist activism on social media. She uses a unique performance methodology to investigate under-researched areas and produce shows that provoke, educate and advocate for social change. Bree refers to herself as an 'accidental academic' and often wonders how she has got this far, referencing Beyoncé in most, if not all, of her essays. When Bree isn't trying to dismantle the ivory tower from the inside, she can be found writing or speaking about sexuality and gender. Her podcast, *Glory Whole*, explores ways in which girls and women come to educate themselves about sex, sexuality and womanhood (available in all good podcast apps).

Jing Zeng is a senior research and teaching associate at the Institute of Communication Science and Media Research, University of Zurich. Jing completed her PhD at the Digital Media Research Center of Queensland University of Technology and also holds an MSc degree in Social Science of the Internet from the University of Oxford. Jing's research interests include online activism, digital misinformation and Internet censorship.

1

Introduction: Mapping the Emergence of #MeToo

Bianca Fileborn and Rachel Loney-Howes

Sexual violence is an incredibly polarizing subject. On the one hand, sexual violence can incite outrage and moral indignation from the public and politicians alike. On the other hand, survivors who speak out about sexual violence routinely face scrutiny from their friends, family, police and the public. Many are accused of lying about their experiences, and others for not being 'authentic' victims or traumatized enough. Some are blamed for being assaulted: that they were 'asking for it'.

At the same time, feminist activists have long sought to challenge these views, along with the assumption that rape, sexual assault and sexual harassment are the products of the random acts of individual men who are regarded as 'sick' or 'social deviants' and unknown to their victims. Instead, many feminists argue that these acts are a reflection of a 'rape culture', a highly contested term that refers to the social, cultural and

B. Fileborn (✉)
University of Melbourne, Parkville, VIC, Australia
e-mail: biancaf@unimelb.edu.au

R. Loney-Howes
University of Wollongong, Wollongong, NSW, Australia
e-mail: rlhowes@uow.edu.au

© The Author(s) 2019
B. Fileborn, R. Loney-Howes (eds.), *#MeToo and the Politics of Social Change*,
https://doi.org/10.1007/978-3-030-15213-0_1

1

political processes that condone violence against women but also blame women (and all other victim-survivors) if and when violence is perpetrated against them (Buchwald, Fletcher, & Roth, 1993). The flood of participation in #MeToo reaffirmed publicly just how widespread sexual assault and harassment actually are; that most victim-survivors know the offender; and, significantly, that these experiences are *routine* and *normalized*, in short, confirming many feminist arguments about 'rape culture'.

Millions of individuals around the world used the #MeToo hashtag on social media within 24 hours of Alyssa Milano's call to arms on 15 October 2017, generating a significant and overwhelming response in support of survivors of sexual harassment and violence. Yet, as contributors to this collection demonstrate, #MeToo also faced swift backlash and accusations of having gone 'too far'. The testimony of Dr. Christine Blasey Ford, who, in September 2018, accused the now associate justice to the Supreme Court of the United States of sexually assaulting her when they were teenagers, further demonstrates our polarized responses to victim-survivors. The public and political backlash against Ford illustrated the depth of hostility and trepidation that remains within the American public toward survivors who speak out against powerful men. Such a response was indicative of the continued failure to hear and take seriously survivors when they speak out. This occurred despite the seemingly significant impact of the #MeToo movement and alongside Ford's experience and testimony being heralded as credible and 'believable' (see Rosewarne, this collection). The backlash against Dr. Ford is reflective of the long-standing struggles, challenges and complexities within feminist activism and justice claims regarding sexual violence that have been prevalent since at least the 1970s. These challenges, intricacies and polarizing discourses that the #MeToo movement has once again given rise to are precisely what this edited collection seeks to address.

In this introductory chapter, we discuss the emergence of and responses to the #MeToo movement, placing it in dialogue with historical critiques of feminist efforts to raise awareness about sexual harassment and violence. Our intention here is to establish a critical framework through which to examine the #MeToo movement—and feminist activism and justice efforts to address sexual violence more broadly—and consider the potentials, limitations, complexities and necessities of social, cultural, political and legal changes.

#MeToo as a Moment of Reckoning

In October 2017, the hashtag 'MeToo' exploded on social media. In the wake of a string of sexual harassment and assault allegations against high-profile Hollywood producer Harvey Weinstein, broken by journalists Meghan Twohey and Jodi Kantor in *The New York Times*, actress Alyssa Milano took to Twitter, encouraging women to share their own experiences of sexual violence using #MeToo.

'If you've been sexually harassed or assaulted write 'me too' as a reply to this tweet,' Milano posted through her Twitter account accompanied by the following text:

Me Too. Suggested by a friend: "If all the women who have been sexually harassed or assaulted wrote 'Me too' as a status, we might give people a sense of the magnitude of the problem."

The response, arguably, was nothing short of phenomenal with millions of survivors across the globe using the hashtag to disclose their own experiences of sexual harassment and violence. Some disclosed incidents and their aftermath in intimate detail; others simply marked themselves as survivors: 'me too' (see Gleeson & Turner; Mendes & Ringrose, this collection). With the hashtag used 12 million times in the first 24 hours, the 'magnitude of the problem' of sexual violence in women's (and others') lives was all too apparent.

The social media campaign quickly evolved across local contexts: French women used the #BalanceTonPorc ('name your pig') hashtag; #RiceBunny was used in China (see Zeng, this collection); Italian actress Asia Argento tweeted #QuellaVoltaChe ('that time when…'), encouraging other Italian women to come forward with their stories of sexual harassment; and Spanish women joined in using the hashtag #YoTambien (Di Caro, 2017). Argentine women took advantage of the momentum of #MeToo to further advance the goal of legalizing abortion put on the agenda by the earlier #NiUnaMenos ('not one woman less') campaign (see Garibotti & Hopp, this collection). The movement generated substantive and sustained global media coverage and public debate (see Newman & Haire; Royal, this collection). Months of intensive media reporting culminated in the women who spoke out about Weinstein and others—the 'Silence Breakers'—being named *TIME*'s people of the year in 2017.

Lest the social media campaign be viewed as all talk and no action, #MeToo drove the development of more tangible activist movements and support for those experiencing sexual harassment and violence, particularly in the workplace. Notably, the #TimesUp project, driven (at least initially) by Hollywood actresses, aimed to address 'the systemic inequality and injustice in the workplace that have kept underrepresented groups from reaching their full potential' by providing resources and legal support to women experiencing workplace harassment (Times Up Now, 2017). Similar efforts were established internationally, including the NOW campaign in Australia, spearheaded by journalist Tracey Spicer. In the wake of the movement, France passed new legislation to address public sexual harassment, with lawmakers passing a bill that outlawed catcalling in August 2018 (Masri, 2018). As we began preparing this collection, the Australian Human Rights Commission announced the first national inquiry into workplace sexual harassment.

At the time of writing, Weinstein had been accused of sexual assault by over 70 women, and in May 2018 he surrendered himself to police after being charged with rape, sexual misconduct, sexual abuse and committing a sex act against two women (ABC, 2018). Many other high-profile men were outed and publicly shamed as perpetrators, with varying degrees of consequence, including Louis C.K., Charlie Rose, Matt Lauer and Kevin Spacey. While the movement was initially focused on Hollywood, it quickly proliferated across other industries and contexts. One report estimated that more than 400 men (and a small number of women) across a range of industries spanning far beyond Hollywood had been 'brought down' by the movement (Green, 2018).

The Politics of Social Change

On the face of it, our brief overview suggests that the #MeToo movement was a highly successful one: an act of solidarity with and between survivors arguably on a scale that has not been witnessed before, a movement that has generated tangible action and consequences for some perpetrators, and driven substantive public debate on sexual violence. In addition, the use of social media was instrumental in spearheading discussion in new and nuanced ways.

Yet, to stop here would lead to an overly optimistic and simplistic rendering of the campaign. As the chapters in this edited collection highlight, a much more nuanced and critical unpacking of the movement in dialogue with broader discussions relating to gender, sexuality, race, geography, law, politics and history, is needed in order to understand the disruptive potential (and limits) of #MeToo and indeed question whether we can expect anything to change or be different moving forward (Alcoff & Gray, 1993). The development and circulation of #MeToo brought to a head a series of questions regarding *who* is able to speak and be heard, *what* constitutes sexual violence, *whose* experiences are included and perceived as worthy of redress, and *how* activist communities should go about the 'business' of generating change. Moreover, is it possible to conceptualize #MeToo in and of itself as a social movement, and is it capable of driving substantive change, and change for whom?

Importantly, many of the perceived issues and critiques of the movement are by no means limited to #MeToo, with the movement reproducing many historically problematic features of public feminism and anti-rape activism, which is discussed further in several of the chapters in this collection (see Loney-Howes; Ryan, this collection). It is vitally important that the movement be situated within a broader context and across the multiple histories and trajectories of anti-sexual violence activism and justice efforts. This collection seeks to complicate, critique and contextualize the #MeToo movement within this 'bigger picture' view of feminist agitation: we aim to examine the movement in its own right, while connecting it to what has come before and what may follow.

Situating #MeToo: Trajectories of Feminist Anti-rape Activism

In writing this introductory chapter (and in the chapters that follow) we are strongly reminded, and indeed echo the work, of Tanya Serisier (2007), who has convincingly outlined the complexities and contradictions of the mythology of 'speaking out' about rape. American second-wave feminists and scholars invested in the idea that speaking out about rape and sexual assault could reveal the 'truth' regarding the causes of violence (see Brownmiller, 1975; Estrich, 1987; Griffin, 1971). However, Serisier (2007) highlights that the ways in which survivors have been encouraged to speak their truths about rape, sexual assault and sexual harassment assume a shared commonality among women that erases complex and marginalized sociopolitical histories, subject positions and experiences.

The anti-sexual violence movement has a long, fractured and contentious history, and many of the criticisms aimed at the movement—and at feminism more broadly—have manifested in the wake of #MeToo. For example, in the 1970s, when women began actively and collectively organizing groups and campaigns to highlight the prevalence of sexual violence, public attention was exclusively given to the experiences of white, middle-class women, neglecting the distinctive experiences of women of color and other marginalized groups (Bevacqua, 2000).

This silencing of the experiences, voices and activism of women of color was reflected, at least initially, in the way the #MeToo hashtag was co-opted by Alyssa Milano—however unintentional this may have been (see Ryan, this collection). Generally speaking, the work of anti-rape activists and support services receives lukewarm support from the public at the best of times. However, the work of Indigenous women, African American women, Latino women and other women of color around the world is regularly overlooked or not afforded the recognition it deserves. While #MeToo has generated awareness and support for the work Tarana Burke has been undertaking for decades with African American survivors in disadvantaged communities, it was only when 'me too' was uttered by a privileged white woman that her efforts were acknowledged.

Although the 1980s saw a growing media interest in the representation of sexual violence in film and print media (Serisier, 2018), the late 1980s and early 1990s also saw a backlash against the anti-rape movement. Efforts to highlight the prevalence of sexual violence in the 1970s through consciousness-raising sessions and public 'speak-outs' resulted in responses claiming that the statistics were overinflated or that women 'cry' rape when they have just had a 'bad' or 'regretted' sexual experience (see Roiphe, 1993; Paglia, 1992). Others suggested that women were 'playing the victim' (Wolf, 1993) and in doing so were preventing 'real' victims of violence, such as women in developing countries, from receiving public support (Sommers, 1994). Significantly, such critiques have hardly been limited to conservative political discourse, with feminist scholars also raising concerns regarding the essentialist or totalizing tendencies of (some) anti-rape scholarship and activism (Alcoff, 2018; Matthews, this collection; Serisier, 2007).

We are beginning to see similar forms of backlash and critique in the era of #MeToo, although these conversations have expanded from debating the legitimacy of claims of sexual violence to encompass the ethics of naming and shaming perpetrators online and the misappropriation of #MeToo for political, financial and personal purposes (see Haire, Newman & Fileborn; Salter, this collection) and the potential for #MeToo to feed into conservative sexual agendas (see Matthews, this collection). Some commentators have suggested the movement has gone 'too far' and that the flow-on effect of #MeToo may lead to the criminalizing of men for failing to be 'mind readers' or for engaging in 'normal' acts of flirtation or seduction, even if clumsily executed (see Fileborn & Phillips, this collection). Notably, French actor Catherine Deneuve, along with nearly 100 other French academics, writers and performers, wrote an open letter denouncing the so-called witch hunt against high-profile Hollywood men, suggesting that legal responses to #MeToo may result in increased restrictions on sexual freedoms (*The Guardian*, 2018).

The question of #MeToo having gone 'too far' was further reflected in the controversy that arose following a story reported by the website Babe. net in early 2018, in which Aziz Ansari (a popular comedian and TV star) was all but accused of raping a young woman named 'Grace'. Although Grace did not call her experience rape, she implied that there were non-consensual elements to her experience. This public naming and shaming of Ansari resulted in him making a formal apology, but the response to Grace outing Ansari was mixed. Megan Garber wrote in *The Atlantic* that the story revealed 'the thinness of the line between romantic pursuit and something more predatory', pointing to the so-called gray area that exists within cultural discourses about what 'counts' as rape and sexual assault. Considerable concerns were also raised regarding the arguably unethical journalistic practices of Babe.net in soliciting Grace's story, an issue taken up further by Michael Salter in this collection.

While Grace's story might reflect the gray areas of sexual violence and consent, her story demonstrates the social and cultural permissions afforded to men as sexual subjects and agents and women as sexually passive objects (see Darnell, this collection). In this sense, the suggestion that #MeToo has gone 'too far' reduces the space for nuanced discussion, reflection and exploration of the complexities, potential ambiguities and 'messiness' of sexual violence and consent (Alcoff, 2018; see Darnell; Fileborn & Phillips; Rosewarne, this collection). It closes off avenues for examining the ways in which our sexual agency and decision-making are situated within and shaped by broader norms pertaining to sex, sexuality, gender and consent and for interrogating the ways in which these curtail (or, conversely, open up) our potential for action (Alcoff, 2018; Gavey, 2005; Darnell; Matthews, this collection).

Me Too, but Not You: Accounting for Who can Speak and be Heard

Efforts to construct a 'universal' account of sexual violence are inevitably 'complicit in erasing crucial differences around race, class and sexuality… [acting] to prevent other stories from being told' (Serisier, 2007, p. 85). In a similar vein to the overt focus on white women's experiences of sexual victimization in anti-sexual violence politics and activism, #MeToo has largely been taken up by, and therefore reflects, the experiences of young, cisgender, heterosexual women. Subsequently, the particular experiences, needs and dynamics of sexual violence within and against those from differentially situated communities remained marginalized, if not entirely absent, within #MeToo. Largely obscured from the discussion generated by #MeToo were the experiences of LGBTIQA+ communities (see Ison, this collection), sex workers, women of color, women from the Global South (see Garibotti & Hopp; Kagal, Cowan & Jawad; Ryan, this collection), women with disabilities, older women (Gilmore, 2018) and women from lower socioeconomic backgrounds. Their erasure from the movement serves to reinforce assumptions about 'real' rape victims who are young, white, heterosexual, able-bodied and not engaged in 'risky' sexual behaviors that might make them 'responsible' for their sexual victimization.

Moreover, the consequences for speaking out may generate additional challenges in a globalized world that relies heavily on social media for the sharing of experiences and generating support for campaigns like #MeToo. As scholars such as Michael Salter (2013) and Bianca Fileborn (2017) note, acquiring a digital mouthpiece does not necessarily mean that individuals and groups will be seen or heard. The affordances of social media mean certain survivors are better positioned than others to share their experience(s) in a way that ensures they are heard, believed and validated by others. While online platforms have provided a powerful platform for many in speaking out, seeking solidarity and securing validation (see Gleeson & Turner; Mendes & Ringrose, this collection), the ability to do so is not shared equally among all survivors. Digital justice seeking is limited and partial at best (Fileborn, 2017).

Beyond the issue of who has access to digital platforms lies the question of *who* is actually able to speak at all and under what conditions? Certain privileges and access to resources enable some survivors to speak out about their experiences and in certain instances even name their perpetrators (though this is of course still a courageous and risky act). Yet even the most seemingly privileged survivors are routinely denied recognition, as was evident when Dr. Christine Blasey Ford spoke out about Brett Kavanaugh. If survivors who do have access to resources are subjected to such backlash, how feasible is it then for less privileged individuals and minority groups to speak out (see Kagal, Cowan & Jawad, this collection)? Can, for example, the undocumented migrant woman publicly 'name and shame' a perpetrator she relies upon for work? Can she even acknowledge her experience as sexual violence given the nature of her situation? Would anyone listen if she did speak out?

Combined, these critiques illustrate that the same challenges that have undermined historical attempts to 'speak out' about rape and sexual violence are also hindering contemporary efforts to broaden understandings about whose experience matters. UK-based feminist scholar Fiona Vera-Gray (2018, p. 74) has likewise noted that movements such as #MeToo can provide important opportunities for women to speak out and act in solidarity. However, she also highlights how the often-individualized nature of online and contemporary activism runs the risk of minimizing 'how difficult speaking is given the consistency in women's early lives of the message to do the exact opposite'. That is, the expectation that survivors speak out deflects attention from a cultural context that actively discourages women to speak up and routinely downplays, minimizes and excuses sexual violence, actively silencing survivors and causing many to doubt the veracity or nature of their own lived experience(s). This expectation to speak eclipses the extent to which those who have experienced sexual violence continue to be blamed or disbelieved if and when they do speak out or for their credibility to still be regularly called into question (Alcoff, 2018). It further fails to recognize the ways in which survivors are differentially located in terms of their ability to speak, and be heard and believed, an issue we have touched on already and will further examine throughout this collection.

Are We Listening Now?

The final question we would like to ask is: what is different about the #MeToo campaign? We have been here before. Not only have there been decades of feminist activism, law reform projects and bodies of research documenting the nature and extent of sexual violence, but there have also been previous iterations of #MeToo. For instance, in 2011 numerous Twitter hashtags, such as #WhatIWasWearing and #BeenRapedNeverReported, emerged in response to a Toronto police officer's comments that if women wanted to avoid being raped they should stop dressing like 'sluts' (see Mendes, 2015). These precursor hashtags to 'Me Too', which led to the development of the *SlutWalk* movement, also garnered a strong public response. However, the impact of these forms of hashtag activism and *SlutWalk* more broadly is questionable. Mendes (2015) argued that *SlutWalk* not only drew sexual assault to the global media's attention, but also sought to demonstrate the relationship between the personal and the political (see Loney-Howes, this collection). Yet *SlutWalk* was also criticized for failing to take an intersectional approach to understanding sexual violence and therefore privileging (again) white women's voices (Mendes, 2015). In light of decades of feminist activism on sexual violence, if #MeToo has provided a 'watershed' moment for victim-survivors to speak out and be heard, we may well ask: *why weren't we listening before?* And: *What is significant about this moment in time?*

In addition, there are challenges involved in sustaining movement momentum, which social movement scholars have long reflected on. Inevitably, social movements go through cycles sustained by formal and informal networks of activists who are able to mobilize support when needed. But the ultimate goal must be finding ways to translate the expressive and emotional power of movements, such as #MeToo, into genuine structural, social and cultural change (see Cover; Flood, this collection). What space—if any—does #MeToo open up for future activism?

Certainly, some developments in the wake of the campaign (outlined earlier in this Introduction) do point toward the potential for longer-term, structural and cultural change. However, given the relatively early stage of the movement it is difficult at this point to make any definitive claims about the 'success' of the movement or otherwise. Indeed, we should also question what success looks like for a diffuse movement that does not necessarily have a set of definitive aims or shared goals (see Rosewarne, this collection). Likewise, is it possible for one movement to achieve some sense of justice in response to the broad and diverse needs and experiences of victim-survivors?

Outline of the Book

The points raised in this introductory chapter depict a deeply conflicted, contradictory movement and moment in time, and suggest that many of the questions interrogated throughout the collection are not 'either/or' in nature, nor are they easily resolvable. While the #MeToo movement is itself a phenomenon worthy of investigation, these complexities also situate it within a series of much bigger questions around feminist politics, activism, social change and justice, which this edited collection aims to address. In order to interrogate these complexities, the book is organized around the following thematic areas.

The Politics of Speaking Out and Consciousness-Raising

The anti-sexual violence movement emerged as a subset of second-wave feminism, and it was through the grassroots practices of consciousness-raising and speak-outs that sexual violence came to prominent public attention. Recent feminist scholarship has claimed that social media and other forms of digital technologies have enabled consciousness-raising on a global scale in ways that are more nuanced and diverse than consciousness-raising sessions in the 1970s—what has been referred to as 'Consciousness Raising 2.0' (see, e.g. Wood, 2008).

In this section, contributors reflect on the ways #MeToo ignited a renewed consciousness about sexual violence among survivors. Specifically, Rachel Loney-Howes considers the history of anti-rape activism in dialogue with #MeToo and other recent forms of web-based consciousness-raising and speak-outs. Drawing on research conducted with individuals who participated in #MeToo, Kaitlynn Mendes and Jessica Ringrose reflect on the lived experiences of engaging in online activism. In doing so, they challenge assumptions about 'slacktivism' by examining the ways that participating in #MeToo was transformative for some participants. Following this, Jessamy Gleeson and Breanan Turner investigate the performative nature of consciousness-raising online through an analysis of

#MeToo tweets. Jing Zeng's chapter turns to the ways in which Chinese women have sought to carve out their own #MeToo movement in the face of social media censorship in China, highlighting the innovative ways Chinese women are harnessing social media in order to speak out. Lastly, Mary Anne Franks interrogates the transformative potential of women's transgressive speech acts in relation to sexual violence, given the long history of disbelief surrounding women who challenge men's knowledge and power.

Whose Bodies Matter? #MeToo and the Politics of Inclusion

While digital media and technologies may provide a networked and diverse platform to speak out and engage in consciousness-raising, the #MeToo movement emerged in the Global North. Moreover, #MeToo was championed (at least initially) by wealthy, white, heterosexual women with prominent public profiles, access to capital and thus political, social and economic freedoms that many women and survivors around the world do not have. As noted earlier in this chapter, the movement likewise faced considerable pushback for having gone 'too far' in relation to the 'types' of sexual violence it brought to the fore.

This section therefore seeks to understand the politics of inclusion within anti-sexual violence activism and the potential (or limitations) of #MeToo to broaden the parameters of inclusion and recognition beyond the white, heteronormative, US-centric fold. Authors in this section not only critically interrogate histories of racism, classism and heterosexism, but also reflect on the particular political freedoms that create the conditions for individuals to be able to speak out about experiences of sexual harassment and assault. Bianca Fileborn and Nickie Phillips begin by unpacking the notion that #MeToo has gone 'too far'. Drawing on post-structuralist feminist scholarship, they illustrate the ways in which dominant understandings of sexual violence expand and contract throughout #MeToo, arguing that we must seek to further destabilize what 'counts' as sexual violence. Tess Ryan comments on the representation of Aboriginal women in Australia, discussing the ways in which lingering colonial discourses continue to sexualize black women's bodies and the impact this has on their ability to speak out about sexual violence. While Aboriginal women have been excluded from #MeToo, Ryan points to the ways in which Indigenous women have *already* been speaking out about violence, highlighting the need to recognize their strength and resilience. Neha Kagal, Leah Cowan and Huda Jawad ask what happens if and when minoritized women say 'me too'? The authors explore the ways in which #MeToo excludes the experiences of black and minoritized women through its narrow framing of violence and focus on the formal workplace and through a failure to recognize the ways in which racist rhetoric shapes the experiences of Muslim women if and when they disclose. The exclusion of the LGBTIQA+ community in the #MeToo movement is discussed by Jess Ison, who articulates some of the challenges associated with the heteronormative assumptions underpinning sexual violence. While #MeToo must make space for queer communities, Ison argues that we must also acknowledge that queer perspectives have much to offer anti-sexual violence activism and responses to sexual violence.

Not All That Glitters Is Gold: #MeToo, the Entertainment Industry and Media Reporting

#MeToo initially emerged from the media and entertainment industries in response to the actions of high-profile, powerful men dubbed 'shitty media men'. In the days and weeks following the allegations of sexual harassment and assault perpetrated by Harvey Weinstein, it became clear that his behavior was actually Hollywood's worst kept secret. Indeed, it was also confirmed, as feminist scholars have long argued, that attitudes and behaviors, such as those espoused by Weinstein, are widespread and institutionalized, leaving women with very few avenues to address the toxic masculinity that has 'normalized' sexual harassment and assault in the media industry. The apparent 'newsworthiness' of the movement likewise generated substantive and ongoing media reporting in both 'traditional' and online news media.

Given the origins of #MeToo, Lauren Rosewarne questions whether the movement can successfully translate out of its Hollywood base. While the movement witnessed an outpouring of personal stories, Rosewarne argues that the diffuse and poorly defined nature of the movement means it lacks the ability to generate substantive change. In contrast, María Cecilia Garibotti and Cecilia Marcela Hopp outline how feminist activists in Argentina were able to harness the media storm whipped up in response to #MeToo as an opportunity to advance a pre-standing agenda to legalize abortion, with local celebrities and journalists playing a central role in this movement. Bridget Haire, Christy E. Newman and Bianca Fileborn examine the politics of naming and shaming 'shitty media men', delving into informal justice responses from women working within the media industry. While #MeToo resulted in expansive media discussion, Kathryn Royal's analysis of media reporting on Harvey Weinstein illustrates that the news media continue to depict sexual violence in problematic ways that fail to adhere to available ethical guidelines. Christy E. Newman and Bridget Haire's analysis of sex advice post-#MeToo suggests that online and 'new' media were perhaps more attuned to the nuance and complexities surrounding discussions of sexual consent and violence, with the role of the sex advice columnist being reconfigured through the process of discussing the movement.

Ethical Possibilities and the Future of Anti-sexual Violence Activism

The last section considers the implications of #MeToo for sexual violence activism and how the movement may (or *should*) develop moving forward. Contributors to this section likewise reflect on the potentials for developing ethical relations and practices. Sex therapist Cyndi Darnell considers the opportunities #MeToo has created for rethinking understandings about, and the negotiation of, sexual consent. Darnell argues that our narrow focus on sexual violence and 'yes/no' framings of sexual consent ultimately detracts from the conversations we need to be having about pleasure and desire. Heidi Matthews demonstrates how the dominant discourses surrounding #MeToo constitute a 'sex panic' and serve to reinforce conservative sexual politics. Matthews argues the need to extend understandings of consent beyond the legalistic 'yes-no' binary and to account for the roles of pleasure and danger in experiences of sex. Michael Flood examines the extent to which #MeToo has generated change in men's responses to and understandings of sexual violence and articulates the continued need to challenge the frameworks of structural masculinities that legitimate violence against women. Building on this, Rob Cover explores the potential for the concept of vulnerability to produce more ethical gender and sexual relationalities, particularly in traditionally male-dominated environments such as Hollywood. Finally, Michael Salter proposes the necessity of developing ethical practices in seeking justice via online platforms given the ease with which movements like #MeToo can be so easily co-opted for political and personal gain.

Contributors to this collection include academics, activists and practitioners (with some contributors spanning all of these roles). While the chapters that follow are scholarly in nature, they also aim to be accessible to a broader audience. In doing so, it is our hope that we can engage in a much broader dialog on the #MeToo movement and, ultimately, contribute toward the broader conversation that can and must occur in working toward the elimination of sexual violence.

References

ABC. (2018, May 26). Harvey Weinstein charged with rape and sex abuse against two women, authorities say. Australian Broadcasting Corporation. Retrieved July 28, 2018, from http://www.abc.net.au/news/2018-05-25/harvey-weinstein-charged-with-rape-sex-abuse/9802058.

Alcoff, L. (2018). *Rape and resistance*. Oxford: Polity Press.

Alcoff, L., & Gray, L. (1993). Survivor discourse: Transgression or recuperation? *Signs, 18*(2), 260–290.

Bevacqua, M. (2000). *Rape on the public agenda: Feminism and the politics of sexual assault.* New England: Northeastern University Press.

Brownmiller, S. (1975). *Against our will: Men, women and rape.* London: Secker & Warburg.

Buchwald, E., Fletcher, P., & Roth, M. (1993). *Transforming a rape culture.* Minneapolis: Milkweed Editions.

Di Caro, B. (2017, October 18). #MeToo, #Balancetonporc, #YoTambien: Women around the world lash out at harassment. World Economic Forum. Retrieved July 20, 2018, from https://www.weforum.org/agenda/2017/10/metoo-balancetonporc-yotambien-women-around-the-world-lash-out-at-harassment/.

Estrich, S. (1987). *Real rape.* Cambridge, MA: Harvard University Press.

Fileborn, B. (2017). Justice 2.0: Street harassment victims' use of social media and online activism as sites of informal justice. *The British Journal of Criminology, 57*(6), 1482–1501.

Gavey, N. (2005). *Just sex? The cultural scaffolding of rape.* London and New York: Routledge.

Gilmore, J. (2018, January 31). "That's not sexual harassment, is it?" The untold stories of abuse. *The Sydney Morning Herald.* Retrieved July 28, 2018, from https://www.smh.com.au/lifestyle/thats-not-sexual-harassment-is-it-the-untold-stories-of-abuse-20180131-h0r2z1.html.

Green, J. (2018, June 27). #MeToo has snared more than 400 high profile people. *The Sydney Morning Herald.* Retrieved July 9, 2018, from https://www.smh.com.au/lifestyle/life-and-relationships/metoo-has-snared-more-than-400-high-profile-people-20180627-p4zo5q.html.

Griffin, S. (1971). Rape: The all-American crime. *Ramparts Magazine, 26*–35.

Masri, L. (2018, August 2). Sexual harassment outlawed on the streets of France, following viral video of recent violent attack in Paris. *ABC News.* Retrieved December 20, 2018, from https://abcnews.go.com/International/sexual-harassment-outlawed-streets-france-viral-video-recent/story?id=56986287.

Mendes, K. (2015). *SlutWalk: Feminism, activism, media.* London: Palgrave Macmillan.

Paglia, C. (1992). *Sex, art and American culture.* New York: Vintage Books.

Roiphe, K. (1993). *The morning after: Sex, fear and feminism.* New York: Little, Brown and Company.

Salter, M. (2013). Justice and revenge in online counter-publics: Emerging responses to sexual violence in the age of social media. *Crime Media Culture, 9*(3), 225–242.

Serisier, T. (2007). Speaking out against rape: Feminist (her)stories and anti-rape politics. *Lilith, 16*, 84–95.

Serisier, T. (2018). Speaking out, and beginning to be heard: Feminism, survivor narratives and representations of rape in the 1980s. *Continuum: Journal of Media and Cultural Studies, 32*(1), 52–61.

Sommers, C. H. (1994). *Who stole feminism? How women have betrayed women.* New York: Simon & Schuster.

The Guardian. (2018, January 10). Catherine Deneuve says men should be 'free to hit on' women. *The Guardian*. Retrieved July 28, 2018, from https://www.theguardian.com/film/2018/jan/09/catherine-deneuve-men-should-be-free-hit-on-women-harvey-weinstein-scandal.

Times Up Now. (2017). Our mission. Retrieved July 28, 2018, from https://www.timesupnow.com/#ourmission-anchor.

Vera-Gray, F. (2018). *The right amount of panic: How women trade freedom for safety.* Bristol: Polity Press.

Wolf, N. (1993). *Fire with fire: The new female power and how it will change the 21st Century.* New York: Random House.

Wood, E. (2008). Consciousness-raising 2.0: Sex blogging and the creation of a feminist sex commons. *Feminism and Psychology, 18*(4), 480–487.

Part I

The Politics of Speaking out and Consciousness-Raising

2

The Politics of the Personal: The Evolution of Anti-rape Activism From Second-Wave Feminism to #MeToo

Rachel Loney-Howes

Introduction

When second-wave feminists declared that 'the personal is political', they were doing at least two things: they were exposing the previously concealed reality of a political economy based on the subjugation of women, and they were announcing a radical feminist politics that would change the meaning of what it means to be political. This agenda for social change is nowhere clearer—or more complicated—than within the anti-rape movement, a sub-movement of second-wave feminism.[1] On the one hand, anti-rape activists have sought to highlight the deeply political

---

[1] In this chapter, I use the terms rape and sexual violence interchangeably. I acknowledge that legally rape refers to the very specific act of forced penetration of the vagina or anus, whereas sexual violence refers to a range of behaviours and experiences that are not necessarily penetrative but are nonetheless sexual and equally harmful. The literature describes the "anti-rape movement" as encompassing a broad spectrum of sexually violent experiences (see Bevacqua 2000).

R. Loney-Howes (✉)
University of Wollongong, Wollongong, NSW, Australia
e-mail: rlhowes@uow.edu.au

B. Fileborn, R. Loney-Howes (eds.), *#MeToo and the Politics of Social Change*,
https://doi.org/10.1007/978-3-030-15213-0_2

nature of sexual violence as a product of women's social, cultural and legal subordination, and to use this knowledge to facilitate institutional reforms. On the other hand, activist projects have also attempted to provide space for the recognition of personal experiences and an opportunity to articulate the impact of sexual violence. Both of these perspectives have suffered from backlash and criticism, and in this chapter, I seek to demonstrate how this oscillation between the personal and the political within anti-rape activism has been playing out since the 1970s and where it manifests within the #MeToo movement.[2]

The history discussed in this chapter is neither complete nor comprehensive, and it draws predominantly on the perspectives of white, heterosexual women and events that have taken place in North America. While this is a significant limitation in my discussion, it nonetheless makes a contribution to our understanding of the diversity, complexity and blindness embedded in anti-rape activist projects, and proceeds in four parts. The first part surveys the historical trajectory of the anti-rape movement from the 1970s to the 1990s. I then turn to explore the resurgence of public discourse concerning rape in the 2010s, aided by the use of digital media to connect local struggles to global issues. In the third section, I discuss the emergence of the #MeToo movement and its impact on the precarious relationship between the personal and the political. I conclude by commenting on the challenges this changing public-private dynamic poses for developing a collective agenda for social, cultural and institutional changes.

A Radical Agenda for Change

In 1973, the National Organisation of Women (NOW) in the United States passed a resolution to form the NOW Rape Task Force to push for legislative reforms, improvements in institutional responses to sexual violence and challenges to attitudes and beliefs that created and supported

---

[2] Scholars have questioned whether the #MeToo movement meets the criteria of a true social movement (see Rosewarne, this collection). For simplicity, I refer to the '#MeToo movement' throughout this chapter, although I acknowledge that this approach is uncritical and problematic. I also acknowledge that the relationship between 'feminism' and #MeToo is highly complex and nuanced—something that I do not specifically address in this chapter.

'rape culture'.[3] The task force emerged in response to the radical feminist initiatives of consciousness-raising and public speak-outs, and demonstrated the potential for grassroots activism and the sharing of personal experiences to feed into political action and institutional change (Bevacqua, 2008).

The first consciousness-raising sessions began in the late 1960s in the United States and the United Kingdom, quickly spreading to other parts of the world. Consciousness-raising sessions addressed a wide range of topics. However, by far the most common thread discussed was men's unbridled access to women's bodies (Echols, 1989). Subsequently, as New York radical feminists in 1974 highlighted, rape emerged as *the* issue of second-wave feminism, not because it was a designated topic on the consciousness-raising agenda (see Connell & Wilson, 1974, p. 3). Rather, rape, sexual violence and sexual harassment became the focal point of feminist activism in the 1970s because of how pervasive these experiences were and how fundamental they were to the struggle over the ownership and control of women's bodies.

Consciousness-raising sessions brought to light the pervasive experiences of 'little rapes', such as unwanted sexual advances, sexual harassment, unwanted sexual contact—and rape (see Kelly, 1988). The collective sharing of experiences eroded the assumption that sexual violence was typically physically violent, rare and perpetrated by a stranger outside the presumed safety of the private sphere. In particular, they revealed that rape was perpetrated predominantly by husbands, partners or family members (Estrich, 1987), and therefore these experiences were 'not exotic, quite legal and unavoidable for too many of us' (Barker, 1978, p. 1). The institution of marriage and women's economic dependence on their husbands thus became a significant point of discussion among some activist collectives, who redefined this patriarchal social institution as the means for creating and sustaining the conditions of sexual violence (Barker, 1978).[4] Through the collective sharing of personal experiences

---

[3] Broadly speaking, 'rape culture' refers to social attitudes, policies and laws that normalize and trivialize sexual violence or blame women for their own sexual victimization (see Buchwald, Fletcher, & Roth, 1993).

[4] This is a more nuanced argument than that posed by Susan Brownmiller (1975), who famously (and controversially) stated, 'When men discovered they could rape, they proceeded to do it'.

women highlighted the systematic and institutionalized nature of their subordination, gesturing towards the deeper structural inequalities that position women as lesser human beings than men, whose social role was to be available for sex 'on demand'. Women therefore sought to alter the terms through which rape was socially and legally understood, given that at the time rape in marriage was not recognized as a criminal offence in most, if not all, Western jurisdictions.

Consciousness-raising sessions became the impetus for speak-outs, in which women publicly shared their experiences of sexual violence. The idea of 'breaking the silence' has been a ubiquitous strategy of the anti-rape movement and 'speak-outs' have been, and continue to be, considered the best strategy to educate society about the personal costs of violence (Alcoff, 2018). Simultaneously, speaking out was perceived as an opportunity to publicly demonstrate that the experience of sexual violence was at once deeply personal and intrinsically political; a product of underlying patterns of gender inequality rather than an individual, isolated experience (Alcoff, 2018).

Women and community members also began organizing 'Take Back the Night' marches, to highlight the extent to which the threat of rape and harassment were deployed as mechanisms for controlling or restricting women's movement in public. Language used by early activists captured not only a fighting response but also a militaristic one. For example, radical feminists described themselves as being at 'WAR'—a purposeful acronym to describe 'women against rape' collectives in the United Kingdom. Terms such as 'disarm rapists' and 'smash sexism' were prominent slogans in underground feminist magazines in the United States, and anecdotes from women themselves in these publications describe the physical fighting responses women can perform when 'under attack' (Bevacqua, 2000, p. 103; Gavey, 2009, pp. 100–101). By encouraging women to learn self-defence and fight back against their attackers, anti-rape activists challenged assumptions about women's physical weakness and sexual passivity and men's physical aggression, strength and sexual agency (Gavey, 2009; Marcus, 1992).

This fighting spirit, while radical, seemed to undermine the efforts of consciousness-raising and speak-outs that sought to erode popular perceptions about sexual violence. Subsequently, assumptions about rape as something physically violent and perpetrated by deviant strangers—and as women's responsibility to resist—were (inadvertently) reinforced. This undoing of the politicization of personal experiences was compounded by the increased focus on victimization leading to a backlash against the victim—and therefore personal—politics of anti-rape activism, to which I now turn.

Personalizing Victimization

Feminist activists were rewarded for some of their efforts for speaking out about rape and sexual violence during the 1970s. For one thing, rape in marriage became a criminal offence in most Western jurisdictions during the late 1970s and 1980s. Another significant gain was the development of rape crisis centres and other sexual assault support agencies. Initially staffed by volunteers, increased financial support from the state enabled services to professionalize and victim-survivors were able to access confidential counselling and therapy at little to no cost (Bevacqua, 2000).

The focus on the trauma of rape and sexual violence was significantly enabled by the incorporation of post-traumatic stress disorder (PTSD) in the *Diagnostics and Statistics Manual* in 1974 (see Herman, 1997) and the development of rape trauma syndrome (see Burgess & Holmstrom, 1974). The upshot of this approach was a shift away from the radical claims of gender inequality towards a focus in activism on the 'interiority'—or personalization—of violence (Mardorossian, 2002). Whereas speak-outs in the 1970s had sought to frame the personal experience of sexual violence in political terms, by the late 1980s anti-rape politics began to focus more narrowly on the personal and emotional costs of sexual violence (Mardorossian, 2002).

However, this focus on the intrapersonal impact of sexual violence culminated in a backlash within the movement against the ways in which victims of rape were positioned as suffering from 'wounded attachments'—the process through which individuals became the sum of their victimized identities (see Brown, 1995)—and positioned women as victims 'through and through' (Heberle, 1996; see also Matthews, this collection). Prominent public commentators in the United States subsequently published scathing reviews of the victim politics of the anti-rape movement in the early to mid-1990s. For instance, Katie Roiphe (1993) in her infamous book *The Morning After* suggested that the numbers of women who claimed to have experienced rape were inflated and that the focus on 'date rape'[5] detracted attention from the 'real' victims of rape, namely, victims of physically violent stranger rapes. In addition, Roiphe suggested that women cry rape at what was just 'bad sex' and that they 'play the victim' rather than take responsibility for their own safety and actions (see Fileborn & Phillips, this collection, for a critique of these positions). Naomi Wolf took aim at the 'victim' politics of feminism more broadly, arguing that while the focus on sexual victimization was useful for getting rape on the public agenda initially, such tactics are 'getting in our way' for true social and political transformation (1993, p. xvi). For Wolf, the presentation of collective victimization stymies individual agency and autonomy, positioning women as powerless and incapable of response.

These public forms of backlash were echoed within debates about the appropriateness of law reform as a political strategy for preventing rape and sexual violence and addressing personal experiences. Colloquially referred to as the 'sex wars', debates erupted between feminist scholars who were concerned with the 'carceral creep', in which the criminal justice system was being increasingly employed to respond to crime in ways that problematically regulated social behaviours and heavily punished offenders from marginalized social and economic backgrounds (see Wacquant, 2009). In relation to sexual violence, there was concern that taking such an approach would lead to the criminalizing of 'risky' sexual behaviour (Bumiller, 2008), rather than addressing the political and social contexts that created the conditions for violence to occur (Bevacqua, 2000). Utilizing the law further reduced the political to the personal, it was claimed, because it reinforced women's victimization or 'wounded attachments' (as described above), tethering them to the state and criminal law as the site of paternalistic and individual redress (Brown, 1995).

---

[5] 'Date rape' became a popular term in the late 1980s and 1990s following the publication of a study undertaken by Mary Koss and her colleagues (1987) about incidences of sexual assault on college campuses in the United States. Their findings revealed that one in four women had experienced sexual violence and that young men they were on dates with predominantly perpetrated these assaults—hence the term 'date rape'.

Returning to the Political

Second-wave activists had sought to subvert restrictions placed on women's movements in public, to expose the systemic blaming of women for their victimization and to critique mainstream narratives that keep women in a constant state of fear. In the 2000s these strategies were reactivated following the backlash against the victim politics of the 1980s and 1990s. In 2008, for instance, in response to poor police practices to address a serial rapist in the Garneau neighbourhood in the city of Edmonton, Canada, anti-rape activists sought to counter the dominant, state-sponsored, safety-conscious, personal responsibilizing rhetoric. Police declared that women should avoid being alone in public if they did not want to get raped, thereby perpetuating assumptions about women's inherent vulnerability to sexual violence (Gotell, 2012) and their victimized subjectivities—positioning them, in the words of academic Sharon Marcus, as 'already raped or inherently rapeable' (Marcus, 1992, p. 387).

The tendency of law and order narratives and policing practices to systematically conceal the political nature of sexual violence, and the subsequent reinforcement of victim-blaming attitudes, was further reflected in 2011, when a Toronto police officer caused a global stir among women after positing that if women wanted to avoid being raped they should stop dressing like sluts (Mendes, 2015). The response to his 'suggestion' led to the development of the *SlutWalk* movement, which quickly spread from Canada, establishing collectives around the world where millions of women engaged in protest to challenge victim-blaming attitudes and reclaim the derogatory language used to undermine victim-survivors' experiences and deny them recognition (Mendes, 2015).

Online communication technologies were instrumental in internationalizing *SlutWalk*, as well as becoming new forums for victim-survivors to speak out about their experiences (Mendes, 2015). While *SlutWalk* faced a significant amount of criticism for, at least publicly, overly representing the voices of white, young heterosexual, urban women (Mendes, 2015), it nonetheless demonstrated the power and potential of digital communications technologies, particularly social media, to instigate a global consciousness about sexual violence. Following *SlutWalk*, Twitter hashtags in particular became popular ways of marking oneself as a survivor of sexual violence, showing support for victim-survivors and affording them recognition, and the ability to talk back to rape culture (Rentschler, 2014)—with a particular emphasis on addressing the impact of victim-blaming. Hashtags such as #BeenRapedNeverReported, #RapeCultureIsWhen, #WhyWomenDon'tReport, #Ibelieveher and #YesAllWomen were among Twitter's top-ranking hashtags in 2014 (Maxwell, 2014). Significantly, these social media spaces became new sites of consciousness-raising (Keller, Mendes, & Ringrose, 2018).

This reinvigoration of consciousness-raising in public, semi-public and counter-public spaces online brought (some) experiences of sexual violence out into the open to be witnessed (see Salter, 2013). However, the increased focus on sexual violence during this time also resulted in backlash and an increased polarization of public opinion on the topic similar to arguments put forward in the 1990s discussed above (Gotell, 2015). The use of social media for engaging in political conversations about personal experiences is therefore a 'double-edged sword': an opportunity to speak out and connect with other victim-survivors, yet, survivors' stories are simultaneously held up to public scrutiny and vilification (Alcoff, 2018, p. 1). In addition, as Michael Salter discusses in this collection, the use of digital media for speaking out about sexual violence is increasingly being misappropriated for political and personal agendas. Speaking out and creating platforms for victim-survivors to speak from are clearly fraught with risks in seeking to make the personal political, which #MeToo brought to the fore.

#MeToo in the Activist Canon

As outlined earlier in the chapter, when women started speaking out in the 1970s about sexual violence, they highlighted the political nature of their personal experiences through consciousness-raising and public speak-outs. During the late 1980s and early 1990s, the emphasis on the political shifted towards the personal, with representations of sexual violence and activism focusing on the emotional impact of the experience.

Conclusion

Sexual violence emerged on the public agenda in the 1970s for the same reason that enabled #MeToo to generate such a widespread response, namely, sexual violence against women is pervasive. Second-wave feminist activists set themselves the goal of ending rape in their lifetime (Bevacqua, 2000, p. 76). However, the prevalence of sexual violence and harassment, as well as the institutional cover-ups of a few men 'behaving badly' exposed by the #MeToo movement in 2017, indicates that the work begun in the 1970s is far from complete.

I have suggested in this chapter that the #MeToo movement, and the subsequent ways in which an agenda for change has been developed, illustrates a curious intertwining of the personal and the political. On the one hand, it reveals the necessity of understanding the ways in which victim-survivors variously engage with, take up and/or resist the available language and thereby renegotiate permissible ways of speaking about sexual violence and trauma. On the other hand, engagement with institutions as sites of reform and political change runs the risk of reaffirming the power of those institutions to appropriate, redirect and contain activism and to systematically conceal the social, cultural and political conditions that enable sexual violence. This engagement may fail to take cognizance of the very ways in which those very institutions enable perpetrators to behave in violent ways and the extent to which those institutions profit from the subordination of women and anyone outside the white, heteronormative, masculine fold. Therefore, in seeking to make the personal political, anti-rape activist projects must be careful in developing an agenda for change, lest they inadvertently reinforce the frameworks and foundations they are seeking to disrupt.

References

Alcoff, L. (2018). *Rape and resistance*. Oxford: Polity Press.
Barker, C. (1978). *Women at W.A.R.: Women against rape London and Bristol*. London: Falling Wall Press.

Bevacqua, M. (2000). *Rape on the public agenda: Feminism and the politics of sexual assault.* New England: Northeastern University Press.

Bevacqua, M. (2008). Reconsidering violence against women: Coalition politics in the anti-rape movement. In S. Gilmore (Ed.), *Feminist coalitions: Historical perspectives on second-wave feminism in the United States* (pp. 163–177). Chicago: University of Illinois Press.

Brown, W. (1995). *States of injury: Power and freedom in late modernity.* Princeton: Princeton University Press.

Brownmiller, S. (1975). *Against our will: Men, women and rape.* Harmondsworth: Penguin Books.

Buchwald, E., Fletcher, P., & Roth, M. (1993). *Transforming a rape culture.* Minneapolis: Milkweed Editions.

Bumiller, K. (2008). *In an abusive state: How neoliberalism appropriated the feminist movement against sexual violence.* Durham and London: Duke University Press.

Burgess, A., & Holmstrom, L. (1974). Rape trauma syndrome. *The American Journal of Psychiatry, 131*(9), 981–986.

Connell, N., & Wilson, C. (1974). *Rape: The first sourcebook for women by New York Radical Feminists.* New York: Plume Books.

Echols, A. (1989). *Daring to be bad: Radical feminism in America, 1967–1975.* Minneapolis: University of Minnesota Press.

Estrich, S. (1987). *Real rape.* Cambridge, MA: Harvard University Press.

Gavey, N. (2009). Fighting rape. In R. Heberle & V. Grace (Eds.), *Theorizing sexual violence* (pp. 96–124). New York: Routledge.

Gill, R., & Orgad, S. (2018). The shifting terrain of sex and power: From the 'sexualization of culture' to #MeToo. *Sexualities*, online first.

Gotell, L. (2012). Third wave anti-rape activism on neoliberal terrain: The mobilisation of the Garneau Sisterhood. In E. Sheehy (Ed.), *Sexual assault in Canada: Law, legal practice and women's activism* (pp. 243–265). Ottawa: University of Ottawa Press.

Gotell, L. (2015). Reassessing the place of the critique of carceral feminism. In A. Powell, N. Henry, & A. Flynn (Eds.), *Rape justice: Beyond the criminal law* (pp. 53–71). London: Palgrave Macmillan.

Heberle, R. (1996). Deconstructive strategies and the movement against sexual violence. *Hypatia, 11*(4), 63–76.

Herman, J. (1997). *Trauma and recovery: The aftermath of violence—From domestic abuse to political terror.* New York: Basic Books.

Keller, J., Mendes, K., & Ringrose, J. (2018). Speaking "unspeakable things": Documenting digital feminist responses to rape culture. *Journal of Gender Studies, 27*(1), 22–36.

Kelly, L. (1988). *Surviving sexual violence.* Cambridge: Polity Press.

Koss, M., Gidycz, C., & Wisniewski, N. (1987). The scope of rape: Incidence and prevalence of sexual aggression and victimization in a national sample of higher education students. *Journal of Consulting and Clinical Psychology, 55*(2), 162–170.

Loney-Howes, R. (2018). Shifting the rape script: "coming out" online as a rape victim. *Frontiers: A Journal of Women Studies, 39*(2), 26–57.

Marcus, S. (1992). Fighting bodies, fighting words: A theory and politics of rape prevention. In J. Butler & J. Scott (Eds.), *Feminists theorize the political* (pp. 385–403). New York: Routledge.

Mardorossian, C. (2002). Toward a new feminist theory of rape. *Signs: Journal of Women in Culture and Society, 27*(3), 743–775.

Maxwell, Z. (2014, March 27). Rape culture is real. *Time.* Retrieved February 15, 2017, from http://time.com/40110/rape-culture-is-real/.

Mendes, K. (2015). *SlutWalk: Feminism, activism, media.* London: Palgrave Macmillan.

Rentschler, C. (2014). Rape culture and the feminist politics of social media. *Girlhood Studies, 7*(1), 65–82.

Roiphe, K. (1993). *The morning after: Sex, fear and feminism.* New York: Little, Brown and Company.

Salter, M. (2013). Justice and revenge in online counter-publics: Emerging responses to sexual violence in the age of social media. *Crime Media Culture, 9*(3), 225–242.

Serisier, T. (2007). Speaking out against rape: Feminist (her)stories and anti-rape politics. *Lilith, 16,* 84–95.

Serisier, T. (2018). *Speaking out: Feminism, rape and narrative politics.* London: Palgrave Macmillan.

Wacquant, L. (2009). *Punishing the poor: The neoliberal government of social insecurity.* Durham: Duke University Press.

Wolf, N. (1993). *Fire with fire: The new female power and how it will change the 21st Century.* New York: Random House.

3

Digital Feminist Activism: #MeToo and the Everyday Experiences of Challenging Rape Culture

Kaitlynn Mendes and Jessica Ringrose

The world should know that we face harassment everywhere.
—MeToo Survey Respondent

In October 2017, we as a research team were moved by the flood of experiences and messages of support, solidarity, sadness, anger, and outrage that emerged around #MeToo through our own social media accounts. Although initially surprised by the global attention garnered by the #MeToo movement, the fact that survivors took to social media to share experiences of sexual violence and engage in a 'call-out culture' resonated strongly with our ongoing research. Since 2014, we have been studying the broad terrain of 'digital feminist activism' and the public's growing

K. Mendes (✉)
School of Media, Communication and Sociology, University of Leicester,
Leicester, UK
e-mail: km350@le.ac.uk

J. Ringrose
UCL Institute of Education, University College London, London, UK
e-mail: j.ringrose@ucl.ac.uk

© The Author(s) 2019
B. Fileborn, R. Loney-Howes (eds.), *#MeToo and the Politics of Social Change*,
https://doi.org/10.1007/978-3-030-15213-0_3

37

willingness to engage with resistance and challenges to sexism, patriarchy, and other forms of oppression via feminist uptake of digital communication (see, for instance, Mendes, Ringrose, & Keller, 2019). Although there is much research under way on the #MeToo movement and other forms of digital feminist activism (see Fischer, 2016; Fotopoulou, 2016), few to date have collected empirical data from participants in these movement themselves. In this sense, while there has been a growth of scholarship examining *how* feminists are using digital media technologies, little is known about the complexities inherent in *doing* digital feminist activism, which may be overlooked, hidden, or invisible via textual media analyses alone (for exceptions, see Fileborn, 2017, 2018; Keller, Mendes, & Ringrose, 2018; Ringrose & Mendes, 2018).

Drawing on a thematic analysis of original empirical data gathered from 117 qualitative surveys responses from #MeToo users, as well as further in-depth interviews with six of these respondents, this chapter interrogates the everyday experiences of those who have participated in the #MeToo campaign. In doing so, we unpack the complex range of motivations underpinning participation in this media event, drawing attention to issues of power and privilege in the ways certain testimonies are listened to, ignored, or (dis)believed (see also Kagal, Cowan & Jawad; Ryan; Ison, this collection). Throughout the chapter, we challenge generalizations that engaging in digital activism is easy and banal, or a form of 'low-intensity' activism, and instead highlight the often traumatic, emotionally exhausting, and affective nature of this work. We conclude by pointing to the ways that involvement in digital feminist campaigns such as #MeToo transforms many of our participants' lives in both tangible and hard-to-measure ways.

As a qualitative study with a relatively small sample size, we are highly cognizant that our findings in no way speak for all, or even many, #MeToo users. That being said, the data below nonetheless presents an important starting point for researchers wishing to explore the experiential accounts of contemporary Western digital feminism. We recognize the ways further attention is needed to collect the voices of traditionally marginalized groups such as gender non-confirming communities, LBGTQ+, and BAME women, which, despite the visibility of #MeToo, are often silenced, unrecognized, or ignored (see Cole, 2015; Geisler, 2018).

'The World Should Know That We Face Harassment Everywhere': Being Moved Into Action

To understand the experience of participants, one of the key questions we asked in both the open-ended web survey and follow-up interviews was why they participated in the #MeToo movement. Here, our participants shared a variety of reasons for taking part, from a desire to educate boys and men on the harms of sexual violence ('To raise awareness of the blindness to toxic masculinity'), to make rape culture visible ('The world should know that we face harassment everywhere'), to express solidarity with others ('Because…. metoo…. We need to support each other, or else we are all alone against it') and to locate sexual violence as a political issue ('I recognized the potential to use a deceptively simple message to illustrate to society writ large that sexism/misogyny/violence against women is not an individual problem or isolated issue but a systemic/ubiquitous one'). What emerged in many of these responses was the way many were seemingly *compelled* to add their voice and often literally felt 'moved' into doing so from outrage, anger, and a desire to be heard and spark social change. These motivations fit well with the work of social movement scholars who have been influenced by the 'affective turn' in social media scholarship (Papacharissi, 2015), in particular, those who recognize the ways anger and outrage can be productive emotions when trying to instigate social change and are critical in forging 'affective counter-publics' (McCosker, 2015), what we have elsewhere called 'networked feminist counter-publics' (Mendes et al., 2019). These counter-publics are both public in some senses that they are online and visible but also 'intimate' (Dobson, Robards, & Carah, 2018) and forged through feelings of intimacy such as personal sharing, meaningful resonance with others, and mutual recognition common to feminist consciousness-raising (see Mendes et al., 2019). They are counter-publics also because they are resistant subcultures that go against social norms and forming new languages, vocabularies, and communicative modes or vernaculars of engagement and resistance (see also Ringrose & Mendes, 2018).

Social movement research suggests most people will only become 'open to the possibility of protest' in response to a 'moral shock' or something truly upsetting or disturbing (Jasper, 1997) and this idea of critical breaks and ruptures has also informed research on feminist pedagogy and learning (Ringrose, 2007). More recently, we've found Sara Ahmed's concept of a 'feminist snap' or critical breaking point useful for understanding participant involvement in affective ways that consider sudden jolts of awareness that are significant and 'glow' for participants in particular ways (Ringrose & Renold, 2014). As one woman shared after joining the #MeToo hashtag: 'It felt like it was the tipping point for me. I could no longer just stand by and do nothing.' We also witnessed this at many points in our observations of posts in our personal network—a compulsion to respond, that was experienced in a range of ways. This affective sense of an inability to remain silent—or an obligation to speak and join in—was reiterated throughout the surveys and follow-up interviews and, importantly, was experienced in positive but complex and conflicting ways.

#MeToo therefore represented a 'breaking point' for some, and this was articulated in a range of ways. For example, one spoke about how she joined because of an 'inner sense of conviction' that was sparked by public, networked posts. Still another wrote about how she felt she had a 'moral obligation to speak against a culture of violence toward women.' Providing no further context, one participant simply stated that she felt at that moment that sharing her story 'was the right thing to do.' The prevalence of coming or standing together discourses demonstrates how adding their voices to #MeToo was not simply about individual empowerment, but was done because of the recognition that 'nothing will change until we act collectively.' These posts are temporally marked by a sense of urgency and immediacy, which are generated via a sense of an avalanche of responses and chiming in with a wave of discussion.

Understanding more about the motivations and feelings about participants' responses helps challenge critiques that movements such as #MeToo are simply narcissistic endeavors used to attain a supposedly 'coveted status' of victimhood (Will, 2014). Instead, these movements demonstrate how the public creatively use digital technologies to build networks of feminist solidarity, support, and identity (see Fileborn, 2017; Loney-Howes, 2018; Mendes et al., 2019). Rather than simply joining into a celebrity-driven movement to gain visibility and attention, as a range of conservative news media detractors have positioned these debates, #MeToo could be regarded as enabling the 'construction of knowledge, communities and identities' which has long played a central role in feminist practice (Mohanty, 2003, p. 528). Furthermore, these practices simultaneously focus on 'individual and collective experiences of oppression and exploitation and of struggle and resistance' (Mohanty, 2003, p. 522). We see this reflected with one participant, who shared how seeing others open themselves up and 'putting themselves out there, made me want to do the same thing and join in in the movement.' In this sense, many articulated how adding their voice to #MeToo was about more than simply sharing an individual experience, but about simultaneously building a political analysis of structural violence (Drueke & Zobl, 2016) and wider communities of care.

Two important elements needed to build counter-publics, which operate also as communities of care, are practices of listening and recognition. While some may be doubtful that this type of community is possible in the capitalized and profit-driven social media environments such as Twitter (Dean, 2009), we argue that caring relations do emerge out of these platforms. Academic Leah Bassel (2017, p. 6) has discussed the importance of listening as a political project and how it can be a crucial form of recognition 'that counters vicious exclusions that combine race, gender, class and means of rendering people socially abject (Tyler, 2013) and… unheard.' Although women have been speaking out against sexual violence for decades (see Loney-Howes, this collection; Serisier, 2007), the difference with #MeToo as a networked movement across continents isn't that the silence has finally been broken, but due to perhaps volume and mass of response, the wider public are beginning to *listen* and take seriously what (some) victims are saying. There is a multipronged dynamic where both the tactics and modes of communicating are changing, but also these new strategies are enabling *recognition* of their stories. The potential of having experience recognized by others using the hashtag was particularly important for some participants, given the shame, stigma, and disbelief levelled toward those who disclose experiences of sexual violence. This is the result of a wider rape culture, which normalizes sexual violence and has a whole repertoire of discourses to blame victims rather than perpetrators (see Alcoff, 2018). One participant explained that sharing her story to #MeToo was her way of countering the ways she had been 'silenced and ashamed about my own experience.' Presumably it was the recognition of her experience that helped to counter shame experienced through the forced secrecy and silence of victims in rape culture climates. In this sense, some participants deliberately used the hashtag to take control over their own storytelling and in doing so, challenge dominant 'scripts' around sexual violence, particularly those which blame the victim (see Loney-Howes, 2018).

Yet, while it is true that survivors are more likely to be listened to and heard than perhaps ever before, not everyone is likely to have their experience recognized, believed, or supported in equal measures (see Fileborn, 2017; Loney-Howes, 2018; Mendes et al., 2019). To date, scholars have highlighted how diversity continues to remain a problem within (popular) feminist digital spaces, which are often dominated by white, middle-class, cisgender women (Fileborn, 2017; Fotopoulou, 2016; Kagal, Cowan & Jawad; Ryan, this collection). We needn't look beyond the #MeToo movement for evidence of this. As stated in the Introductory chapter, despite originally being coined by African American activist Tarana Burke in 2006, the widespread and systemic nature of sexual violence was not *recognized* until a white, Hollywood actress took up the cause. Some of our participants demonstrated an awareness of the role power and privilege played in disclosing experiences of sexual violence, using #MeToo as a unique opportunity to bring often hidden experiences to the mainstream. Lisa, a 30-year-old queer doctoral student in the UK, explained in her interview that she used #MeToo to share her experience of sexual violence in gay clubs both because she wanted to raise visibility of violence in those spaces and because as a queer woman, she wanted her experiences 'to be counted.' In this sense, Lisa seeks to discursively challenge entrenched rape myths which render LGBTQ+ communities as unrapeable or as unworthy or less understandable as legitimate victims in a heteronormative context (see also Guadalupe-Diaz, 2015; Ison, this collection).

And while anyone who shares their experiences of sexual violence online risks having their 'testimony contested or challenged, overlooked, or dismissed' (Loney-Howes, 2018, p. 45)—what Loney-Howes terms 'negative witnessing' (p. 28)—scholars have noted the ways this is particularly true for gender non-conforming individuals, members of the LGBTQ+ communities, and those who challenge standards of perceived feminine 'respectability' and 'credibility' and whose experiences challenge traditional rape scripts (see Mendes et al., 2019). As a result, while we celebrate the broader visibility #MeToo brings to sexual violence, we are aware that its uptake and potential is simultaneously 'problematic and limited' (Fileborn, 2017, p. 1485).

An Easy, Banal, or "Low-Intensity" Form of Activism?

In recent years, there have been many critiques of the supposedly easy, banal, and low-intensity nature of digital engagement (see Gladwell, 2010; Morozov, 2011). Being dismissed as 'meaningless' forms of 'armchair activism,' 'slacktivism,' or 'clicktivism,' some scholars and pundits alike ignore very real differences between forms of online activism or the emotional and affective labor spent participating in a hashtag such as #MeToo. As Papacharissi (2016, p. 312) argued:

> We assume that social media use will have the same results for all types of movements or publics—it does not. There are similarities, but there are also important differences in how the digital aspect of a movement unfolds online, and across different platforms.

As quotes from our participants have already shown, rather than being 'easy' or low level, many articulated the various challenges and difficulties they experienced in the run-up and aftermath of participating in #MeToo. Several described the experience as 'traumatic' and described a powerful range of emotions, from anger, outrage, fear, and anxiety—which were not simply contained to digital spaces but spilled over from online practices to offline contexts. In this sense, our research contributes to a growing body of scholarship that problematizes simplistic binaries between 'online' and 'offline' life (Ringrose & Harvey, 2017) and showcases the slippage of experiences across domains. Exploring affect is one way to show the impact of experiences of digital activism in ways that are not containable to online engagements.

Take the experiences of Britt, a 35-year-old Dutch woman, who explained how she first saw news of #MeToo on Facebook but took two days before she added her story. As she recalled, she only participated in the movement after being 'seriously angry' about public conversations around the hashtag, reading comments about how women were 'exaggerating, and that the movement had gone too far' and that 'one couldn't even smile at a woman without it being taken out of context.' Sharing her story thus served as a way to 'talk back' (Hooks, 1989) to those who 'weren't understanding' the hashtag or who dismissed experiences of street harassment as trivial. Drawing from Sara Ahmed (2010, 2017), we can see Britt's response as that of a willful, disobedient subject, who enacts the figure of the 'feminist killjoy' (Ahmed, 2010) by refusing to remain silenced or allowing these experiences to be dismissed. This is also a powerful example of how the feminist counter-public emerges through an affective politics of support and refutation through targeted posts, debate, and prolonged combative engagement with those who are disputing the severity and implications of gender and sexual violence.

Yet despite feeling very angry about public response to the movement, Britt did not immediately share her own personal experiences on #MeToo. As she explained:

> [I]t took me two days to write my story. So, I wrote it for myself first. I wrote it on my phone in the notes app on iPhone…I was in a hotel with my husband and I was reading about #MeToo online and it was midnight, and I couldn't sleep because I kept thinking about it, and thinking about my own experiences. And how I deal with things is I write it down, and then it's out. And so, I did that to get it off my chest and then I started reading more Facebook posts, and that night I read my post again and I edited it again, and after writing it I showed my husband first. And that was an emotional moment because of the stories and hearing all about it… After I showed it to him, I sent it to my brother and said should I put this on Facebook? And he said yes.

It is clear from the excerpt above that contributing her story to the #MeToo hashtag was neither meaningless, easy, nor banal for Britt, who not only agonized for several days over whether to share her story, seeking encouragement from her husband and family, but spent time 'curating' it (Fileborn, 2018). This curation is a complex online-offline negotiation where she clears her story with the immediate men in her intimate life—her husband and brother. It is important that it is a supportive offline family context that enables her post, which may not be possible if these conditions were different. Indeed, it is striking that she sought their permission or acceptance in order to proceed. This alerts us to the complex gendered power dynamics at work in engaging with and using #MeToo and digital activism against sexual violence and the difficulty of personal disclosure (see also Mendes et al., 2019). Hers is just one example of why scholars must attend not only to the unique formations of various digital feminist campaigns (Papacharissi, 2016), but to the highly complex, differentiated, and varied experiences of those who contribute to them. Drawing from bell hooks (1989, p. 18), scholars must not forget the way speaking can be a radical act:

> When we dare to speak in a liberatory voice, we threaten even those who may initially claim to want our words. In the act of overcoming our fear of speech, of being seen as threatening, in the process of learning to speak as subjects, we participate in the global struggle to end domination.

Indeed, feminist scholars have written about the importance of 'discursive activism' and how in the fight to transform power relations and social structures, attention and resources must be spent on speech acts which change the ways people think (see Keller et al., 2018; Mendes, 2015; Shaw, 2012). Thus, we argue it is important to push back against broad claims that digital activism in general, and hashtag activism specifically, is necessarily easy or meaningless simply because it is done online. As we also discuss below, the potential of a movement such as #MeToo can contribute to dramatic personal changes, which are necessarily connected to the possibility of broader social transformations, if we are attentive to the relationship of the affective and the personal and social as entangled in ways that must be mapped out.

The Transformative Potential of #MeToo

As we have written about in more detail elsewhere regarding other formations of digital feminist activism (Mendes, Ringrose, & Keller, 2018; Mendes et al., 2019), we are generally optimistic about the power and potential of popular feminist movements such as #MeToo for bringing about 'real-world' changes and transforming our participants' lives. From both our wider data set and that focusing specifically on #MeToo, participants shared a range of changes in their everyday lives, actions, mindsets, and beliefs. While some of the changes discussed are tangible, such as one victim who went on to report her rape to her campus police, many are seemingly ephemeral, take place on micro-levels, and are difficult to measure. These include the ways participants became 'more vocal' in calling out sexist practices and behaviors, to another who ended a friendship with someone because of the way he harassed women.

Indeed, from participants' perspectives, the vast majority were adamant that #MeToo has had a significant impact, either on themselves, people in their lives, or society more broadly. As one participant wrote: 'I think it has (at least on a personal level) and will do in the future.' Many survey respondents used exclamation marks to further emphasize their agreement with this statement ('Yes! It means that for the first time we generally assume that victims tell the truth') or words such as 'definitely' or 'I know it has.' While many survey participants simply affirmed that #MeToo had some form of impact, others provided more details, such as the ways it has opened up new conversations: 'Yes, for example we talked about it in my family, both with my male and female family members.' Another noted how it has made people become 'more conscious in work environments.' Several participants also mentioned how #MeToo has resulted in widespread conversations, protests, and discussion about the need for consent and better sex education in the curriculum. Although it's unclear what these conversations will lead to, consciousness-raising has always remained an important tenet of feminist activism for decades and has been shown to have material consequences on women's lives (Shaw, 2012).

While the impact discussed above may be taking place at a micro-level and may not be easily quantified, other participants identified measurable results. One participant in Sweden credited #MeToo for spurring forward 'new laws regarding consent. I think laws in turn will effect people's viewpoints.' Another participant from Northern Ireland noted the ways #MeToo inspired many to take part in 'mass protests' and 'subsequent discussions to alter rape laws and consent education.' One Australian participant shared: 'Certainly, in Australia we've seen the introduction of NOW, to provide legal support to women who've experienced sexual harassment in the workplace (similar to the US Time's Up campaign).' Significantly, our survey was live just as Bill Cosby was found guilty for aggravated sexual assault, and several participants specifically identified this verdict as tangible evidence of change. As one wrote: 'Yes. Look at Cosby verdict. I believe that's influenced by #metoo.'

While we are heartened to see participants identifying changes, it would be disingenuous to claim all participants were optimistic about #MeToo's impact or potential, as some doubted its ability to foster longer-term, broader social or cultural change. Yet even among these responses, there were clear articulations of *hope* that it would, with variations of 'I hope so but I'm not sure.' Here, many noted that while #MeToo had started very important conversations around sexual violence, consent, and rape culture, 'there's a very long way yet to go.' Rather than looking forward to the future, several looked back to the past noting, 'I hope so, although if the past is anything to go by, I'm not overly optimistic. But I hope I'm wrong.' Another participant articulated the importance of cultural change, noting how this is 'harder to instil than legislation,' which is why it is vital that the public 'continue to talk about it.' As we have also made clear, it is this intimate counter-public (Dobson et al., 2018) experience of talking, sharing, and creating shared awareness and the capacity for dissent that is so salient in understanding the processes of social transformation. Our affective lens is important for enabling a discussion of these micro-politics of experiences of digital activism, which transform individuals and possibly their relational contexts in profound ways as yet uncharted.

Conclusion

Drawing from empirical data gathered from 117 real-life #MeToo users via surveys and semi-structured interviews, this chapter explored some of the motivations and experiences of participating in this digital feminist phenomenon. Influenced by the affective turn in scholarship, the chapter sought to demonstrate how one 'deceptively simple message' moved many into participation. Participants shared a range of reasons why they added their voice to the hashtag—from a sense of anger and outrage at the pervasiveness of rape culture, to a desire to challenge rape myths that deny recognition for many victims, to a desire to build structural analysis of sexual violence, to generating communities of care. Throughout the chapter, we have shown how the varied reasons for contributing to and joining in the hashtag are the flesh and bones of an emergent feminist counter-public. Although these tangible experiences have not yet been charted, they show the force and relevance of these experiences in our participants' lives. In a sense, the chapter highlights why it is so important not merely to investigate what people are contributing to the hashtag, but their practices and experiences of participation. As scholars, we must also be mindful of which voices are absent, and in this chapter we have attempted to draw attention to issues of power and privilege which shape the ways certain testimonies are listened to, ignored, or (dis)believed. Further work is necessary to theorize the limits and constraints of forging feminist counter-publics in terms of what discourses and experiences fit, or are recognized and legitimated in relation to sexual violence, and what do not (Powell, 2015).

Moreover, in privileging the voices and experiences of our participants, our chapter is also strongly challenging problematic generalizations that engaging in digital activism is easy and banal, or a form of 'low-intensity' activism (Gladwell, 2010; Morozov, 2011), and instead highlights the affectively charged, often traumatic nature of this work. Digital feminist campaigns such as #MeToo have transformed many of our participants' lives in both tangible and hard-to-measure ways, but fleshing out experience moves us to a different register in understanding how social transformation happens. Finally, we also strongly refute the notion that participating in #MeToo is simply about empowering the self in any individualizing way—as many of our participants stressed that its power lies firmly in the *collective* act of speaking out against sexual violence and knowing there was 'strength in numbers.' We must firmly understand #MeToo as a digitally networked phenomenon which has enabled mass participation, connectivity, and consciousness-raising. Therefore, while #MeToo alone will not end sexual violence, it is part of the combat and battle that chips away at normative gender and sexual power relations offering new possibilities; it therefore plays a critically important role in making visible the 'structural connections of sexism and violence' (Drueke & Zobl, 2016, p. 50) which are becoming increasingly harder to ignore.

References

Ahmed, S. (2010). Killing joy: Feminism and the history of happiness. *Signs, 35*(3), 571–594.

Ahmed, S. (2017). *Living a feminist life*. Durham and London: Duke University Press.

Alcoff, L. M. (2018). *Rape and resistance*. London: Polity Press.

Bassel, L. (2017). *The politics of listening: Possibilities and challenges for democratic life*. Basingstoke: Palgrave Macmillan.

Cole, K. K. (2015). 'It's like she's eager to be verbally abused': Twitter, trolls, and (en)gendering disciplinary rhetoric. *Feminist Media Studies, 15*(2), 356–358.

Dean, J. (2009). *Democracy and other neoliberal fantasies*. Durham: Duke University Press.

Dobson, A., Robards, B., & Carah, N. (2018). *Digital intimate publics & social media*. London: Palgrave Macmillan.

Drueke, R., & Zobl, E. (2016). Online feminist protest against sexism: The German-language hashtag #aufschrei. *Feminist Media Studies, 16*(1), 35–54.

Fileborn, B. (2017). Justice 2.0: Street harassment victims' use of social media and online activism as sites of informal justice. *British Journal of Criminology, 57*(6), 1482–1501.

Fileborn, B. (2018). Naming the unspeakable harm of street harassment: A survey-based examination of disclosure practices. *Violence Against Women*, online first.

Fischer, M. (2016). #Free_CeCe: The material convergence of social media activism. *Feminist Media Studies, 16*(5), 755–771.

Fotopoulou, A. (2016). *Feminist activism and digital networks: Between empowerment and vulnerability*. Basingstoke: Palgrave Macmillan.

Geisler, C. (2018). *The voices of #MeToo: From grassroots activism to a viral roar*. International Communication Association, Prague. 24–28 May.

Gladwell, M. (2010, October 4). Why the revolution will not be tweeted. *The New Yorker*. Retrieved December 20, 2018, from https://Www.Newyorker.Com/Magazine/2010/10/04/Small-Change-Malcolm-Gladwell.

Guadalupe-Diaz, X. (2015). Same sex victimization and the LGBTQ community. In T. N. Richards & C. D. Marcum (Eds.), *Sexual victimization: Then and now* (pp. 173–192). Thousand Oaks, London & New Delhi: Sage.

Hooks, B. (1989). *Talking back: Thinking feminist, thinking black*. Toronto: Between the Lines.

Jasper, J. M. (1997). *The art of moral protest: Culture, biography and creativity in social movements*. Chicago and London: University of Chicago Press.

Keller, J., Mendes, K., & Ringrose, J. (2018). Speaking unspeakable things: Documenting digital feminist responses to rape culture. *Journal of Gender Studies, 27*(1), 22–36.

Loney-Howes, R. (2018). Shifting the rape script: 'coming out' online as a rape victim. *Frontiers: A Journal of Women's Studies, 39*(2), 26–57.

McCosker, A. (2015). Social media activism at the margins: Managing visibility, voice and vitality affects. *Social Media + Society, 1*(2), 1–11.

Mendes, K. (2015). *SlutWalk: Feminism, activism & media*. Basingstoke: Palgrave Macmillan.

Mendes, K., Ringrose, J., & Keller, J. (2018). #MeToo and the promise and pitfalls of challenging rape culture through digital feminist activism. *European Journal of Women's Studies, 25*(2), 236–246.

Mendes, K., Ringrose, J., & Keller, J. (2019). *Digital feminist activism: Girls and women fight back against rape culture*. Oxford: Oxford University Press.

Mohanty, C. T. (2003). "Under western eyes" revisited: Feminist solidarity through anticapitalist struggles. *Signs, 28*(2), 499–535.

Morozov, E. (2011). *The net delusion: The dark side of internet freedom*. New York: Public Affairs.

Papacharissi, Z. (2015). *Affective politics: Sentiment, technology, and politics*. Oxford: Oxford University Press.

Papacharissi, Z. (2016). Affective publics and structures of storytelling: Sentiment, events and mediality. *Information, Communication & Society, 19*(3), 307–324.

Powell, A. (2015). Seeking rape justice: Formal and informal responses to sexual violence through technosocial counter-publics. *Theoretical Criminology, 19*(4), 571–588.

Ringrose, J. (2007). Successful girls? Complicating post-feminist, neoliberal discourses of educational achievement and gender equality. *Gender and Education, 19*(4), 471–489.

Ringrose, J., & Harvey, L. (2017). Digital mediation, connectivity and affective materialities. In *Routledge handbook of physical cultural studies*. New York & London: Routledge.

Ringrose, J., & Mendes, K. (2018). Mediated affect and feminist solidarity: Teens' using Twitter to challenge 'rape culture' in and around school. In T. Sampson, D. Ellis, & S. Maddison (Eds.), *Affect and social media*. London: Rowman and Littlefield.

Ringrose, J., & Renold, E. (2014). F**k rape!': Mapping affective intensities in a feminist research assemblage. *Qualitative Inquiry, 20*(6), 772–780.

Serisier, T. (2007). Speaking out against rape: Feminist (her)stories and anti-rape politics. *Lilith, 16*, 84–95.

Shaw, F. (2012). "Hottest 100 women": Cross-platform discursive activism in feminist blogging networks. *Australia Feminist Studies, 27*(74), 373–387.

Will, G. (2014, June 6). Colleges become the victims of progressivism. *Washington Post*. Retrieved December 19, 2018, from https://www.washingtonpost.com/gdpr-consent/?destination=%2fopinions%2fgeorge-will-college-become-the-victims-of-progressivism%2f2014%2f06%2f06%2fe90e73b4-eb50-11e3-9f5c-9075d5508f0a_allComments.html%3f&utm_term=.3f1b4ecfcbbd.

4

Online Feminist Activism as Performative Consciousness-Raising: A #MeToo Case Study

Jessamy Gleeson and Breanan Turner

Introduction

Consciousness-raising has been formally employed as a feminist campaign tactic since at least the initial suffragette movement (Ryan, 1992). The broader motivation for consciousness-raising groups stemmed from the concept that the 'personal is political' (Hanisch, 1970) and that these groups can in turn create spaces in which women would become conscious of their own personal and private oppressions, and subsequently seek political reparation (see Loney-Howes, this collection).

Contemporary feminist research contends that feminist activism and discussion in online spaces can be conceptualized as a form of consciousness-raising (Clark, 2015; Martin & Valenti, 2012). However, others have problematized this practice, arguing that engaging with men in online spaces can lead to an obstruction of feminist organizing online and cases of harassment and abuse (Long, 2015; Megarry, 2017).

J. Gleeson (✉) • B. Turner
RMIT University, Melbourne, VIC, Australia
e-mail: jess@jessamygleeson.com; breanan.turner@rmit.edu.au

© The Author(s) 2019
B. Fileborn, R. Loney-Howes (eds.), *#MeToo and the Politics of Social Change*,
https://doi.org/10.1007/978-3-030-15213-0_4

This chapter argues that feminist activism and discussion in social media spaces are a valid and worthwhile form of contemporary consciousness-raising, and further contends that this practice is a specific, and valuable, way of performing identity and activism. Firstly, the chapter examines the importance of feminist activism in social media spaces by using #MeToo as a case study.

Secondly, we move to conceptualizing participation in online feminist campaigns, such as the #MeToo campaign on Twitter, as a specific type of performance—one in which actors can move into and out of the audience's eye by choice. Sociologist and environment theatre practitioners Schechner and Schuman (1976) argued there is little difference between theatre and ordinary life and says of the two that they are an arrangement of space and bodies in places and that the differences lie in how conscious all players are, or can be, of the conventions, the rules that define the games—and how these rules can change. This idea of space as a player, something that can be performed, or that performs you, as well as deciphering theatre and social interactions according to consciousness or context (whether you are in a theatre or online) is significant when considering #MeToo as a performance of consciousness-raising. Performers of #MeToo are conscious of a specific audience, the platform (or space) they perform it in, and the general script that is delivered. As women speak out about their respective assaults, abuse, harassments, and rapes, the public, their audience, is invited to participate by either joining the chorus of #MeToo's or to simply bear witness. This type of personal storytelling as a way to unburden, enlighten, and oftentimes empower mirrors that of what we have seen as consciousness-raising throughout history.

As a practice, consciousness-raising can be understood to have grown beyond its first- and second-wave origins. By expanding our view of consciousness-raising to have crossed offline borders and moved into online spaces, and to resultantly have feminist actors engage with people that fall outside understandings of the label 'woman', we view the performance of consciousness-raising (which is to say the performance of a particular feminist identity, gender, and personal storytelling) to hold continued value and relevance in contemporary feminism. Consciousness-raising as a performance of feminist identity in turn may involve an expression of one's feelings, a sharing of lived experiences, and an evaluation and reinforcement of others' stories.

Consciousness-Raising Across the Waves

Ryan (1992, p. 46) has argued that consciousness-raising groups[1] initially served to 'explore women's common gender experiences'. The formation of consciousness-raising groups across feminism's second wave was designed as a way for women to learn about patriarchal structures of domination, but they also served as a way for women to 'unleash pent-up hostility and rage about being victimized' (Hooks, 2000, p. 8). The practicalities of consciousness-raising groups were straightforward: according to Pilcher and Whelehan (2004, p. 28), women 'should regularly collect in small groups over an agreed period of time and give accounts of their own lives and how they "became" a "woman"'. To this, Loss (2011, p. 288) adds that the recounting of these 'personal and group histories could serve as a powerful wellspring for political mobilization'.

Consciousness-raising groups therefore laid the foundation for broader actions and movements; they acted, as hooks argues, as 'sites of conversion' (2000, p. 8). The groups included 'organizers who encouraged each woman to contribute her own experiences… [and] then discussed forms of resisting oppression, actions, and organising new consciousness-raising groups' (Sowards & Renegar, 2004, p. 535). Kathie Sarachild's programme for consciousness-raising in the second wave contained the following outline of what she envisioned the groups to aspire to:

1. Ongoing consciousness expansion

    • Personal recognition and testimony

---

[1] Consciousness-raising has never been an activity exclusive to feminists alone. Liberal movements of the 1960s also encompassed consciousness-raising as a tactic, including gay men's organizations (Weeks, 2007) and civil rights campaigns (Behrent, 2013; Evans, 1979; Lasch-Quinn, 2002). The use of consciousness-raising more broadly can be seen as a consequence of the structural nature of oppression and disempowerment: although the experiences of women, gay men, and people of colour were different in nature, they each owed their oppressions to structures of domination, violence, and discrimination.

- Recalling and sharing our bitter experiences
- Expressing our feelings about our experiences both at the time they occurred and at present
- Expressing our feelings about ourselves, men, and other women
- Evaluating our feelings

Although Sarachild described her proposed programme for consciousness-raising as a 'hunch of what a theory of mass consciousness-raising would look like' (1968, p. 79), it holds many commonalities with the wider #MeToo movement: specifically, the sharing of 'bitter experiences' and the personal testimonies recounted by participants. Campbell (1999) challenges the view of consciousness-raising as taking place in small group interactions, and instead points to the aforementioned features as also occurring in essays and speeches—and adds that these stylistic features are 'public and political rather than private and personal' (1999, p.130). Sowards and Renegar (2004) have also noted that third-wave feminism used popular culture as a viable forum to communicate feminist ideas and that there were numerous instances of the practice taking place within more public settings. Although the two did not clearly identify online activities as a feature of more contemporary forms of consciousness-raising, they did state that third-wave approaches to consciousness-raising had 'adapted to the changing cultural climate [by seeking] to address larger and more public audiences' (2004, p. 547).

Consequently, it can be understood that contemporary consciousness-raising has grown beyond our understanding of its second-wave forms. This chapter uses both Sarachild's (1968) and Campbell's (1999) descriptions of consciousness-raising to draw similarities between second-wave practice and contemporary feminist activism on social media platforms. In particular, it contends that this practice is a specific, and valuable, way of performing identity and activism.

We are not alone in making this contention: recent research has turned to consider how hashtags can be used to raise consciousness. Anderson and Grace's 2015 article examines feminist consciousness-raising within a digital motherhood community and how an online Facebook group assisted mothers in performing feminist activism and provided a space for them to carry out their feminist identity through consciousness-raising practices. Rentschler and Thrift (2015) argue that the sharing and experience of feminism in an online space provided a form of consciousness-raising in which women felt that they belonged to a wider feminist community. Ultimately, Rentschler and Thrift (2015, p. 341) suggest that the result of online consciousness-raising has led to feminists in virtual spaces producing, curating, and deploying:

> Their capacity to respond to sexist statements and misogynist practices in the political sphere and popular culture, remixing those practices toward feminist ends. In the process, they help build a larger networked feminist public.

In particular, the analysis of feminist hashtags has dominated much of the recent literature. Feminist researchers have published pieces examining the use of hashtags for campaigns such as #YesAllWomen (Thrift, 2014), #BringBackOurGirls (Loken, 2014), and #KadınKatliamıVar (translated as 'there is a massacre of women' in Turkish) (Altinay, 2014). Laura Portwood-Stacer and Susan Berridge note that feminist hashtags have the ability to be 'taken up by newspapers, television, and other media outlets as stories of collective public opinion and, sometimes, further action' (2014, p. 1090).

Researchers also have observed the ability of the hashtag to assist campaigners in promoting broad feminist attitudes. For example, in a 2017 article, Kangere, Kemitare, and Michau share the story of the Gender-Based Violence (GBV) Prevention Network and their efforts to use social media campaigns and hashtags to 'populariz[e] feminism' and undertake 'feminist consciousness-raising' (Kangere, Kemitare, & Michau, 2017, p. 900). Elsewhere, Rentschler (2017, p. 6) also notes that the Black feminist hashtag #YouOkSis? 'does the labour of consciousness-raising about the problems with carceral answers to street harassment'. Finally, Mendes, Ringrose, and Keller have also argued that the #MeToo hashtag has allowed the public to engage with 'resistance and challenges to sexism, patriarchy and other forms of oppression' who otherwise might not have been interested in engaging with feminist ideas (2018, p. 237).

The evolution outlined above—one of consciousness-raising efforts shifting from their occurrence within closed groups to also taking place online and in public discussions—is a key feature of contemporary feminist practice. By *publicly* discussing *personal* stories of sexual harassment, the #MeToo hashtag participants undertake visible consciousness-raising and highlight misogyny and sexism within online and offline spaces. Furthermore, the use of a hashtag to perform consciousness-raising is useful for uniting many conversations and disparate users within a single community (Mendes et al., 2018). #MeToo acts as a chorus of sorts, when one person shares their experience and then tags it with #MeToo: in turn, this call and response technique transforms one person's story into a wider non-individualized testimony (see Mendes & Ringrose, this collection).

Hashtags are therefore an effective way of quickly and collectively engaging in activist discourse (Williams, 2015). Hashtags are searchable, quantifiable, and contagious. When we use a hashtag, we are publicly participating in a specific discourse and are in effect saying 'search this #, and you will find me'. It is with this concept of people using hashtags as a way to have their story seen and heard that we argue that an individual's use of the #MeToo hashtag in turn engages them in a specific and conscious performance.

Performing #MeToo, Identity, and Public Participation

Within the first 24 hours of Alyssa Milano's tweet (see Introduction), the #MeToo hashtag had spawned over 500,000 tweets and 12 million separate Facebook comments, posts, or reactions, with Facebook estimating that 45% of its US users had a friend who had posted 'me too' (CBS, 2017). Due to the sheer volume of these contributions, we have narrowed our focus to particular individual contributions to the #MeToo movement and how participation in #MeToo can be conceptualized as a form of contemporary consciousness-raising and a type of performance.

This chapter takes a qualitative approach to the data generated by the #MeToo hashtag and relies on Foucauldian discourse analysis to uncover the blatant and latent meanings attached to those who participated in the initial hashtag. Discourse analysis 'examines how language and representation fuse together to produce meaning, with particular attention paid to how the intersections of representation, meaning, power, identities, and subjectivities all create relationships with each other' (Harp, Grimm, & Loke, 2018, p. 6). In this chapter, discourse analysis is applied to a series of tweets posted in the #MeToo hashtag stream, in order to further understand the efforts of consciousness-raising performed by contributors in this particular social media space.

In a similar approach to that previously used by Rentschler (2017), we avoid drawing on techniques of web-scraping and large-scale data mining of the tweets that mentioned #MeToo. Instead, we have sought to analyse how individual Twitter users produced and shared their experiences through the hashtag. Although the #MeToo hashtag quickly spread from Twitter to other social media platforms, we chose to restrict our analysis to Twitter hashtags. In line with other research-examining hashtags (Brown, 2018; Harp et al., 2018; Kim, 2017), we collected a series of initial tweets from the #MeToo hashtag from October 15 to October 16, 2017. Further search parameters included the requirements that the tweets could be in any language, from any country, and with Twitter's quality filter (designed to filter out spam) turned off. The tweets then selected for discussion within this chapter were gathered from what Twitter had deemed to be the 'top' tweets within the #MeToo hashtag that were sent during this time period. Twitter has previously outlined that that it considers 'top' tweets to be those that 'are the most relevant tweets for your search', contingent on the user's specific search terms, and are determined through an algorithm (Twitter, 2018a).

What is evident from examining #MeToo is the level at which women publicly shared their personal stories. Women who have held onto their trauma for decades are speaking out by the millions (CBS, 2017); and although the movement was initially anticipated by some to 'fade into the background again' (Renkl, 2017), its subsequent longevity leads us to highlight its importance. Why this hashtag? Why now? Although some answers may lie in the initial news reports of widespread sexual harassment across celebrated and prominent industries such as entertainment (Ricker, 2018; USA Today, 2018), a broader understanding can also be drawn from the power of performing a story.

We can conceptualize Twitter as an online 'stage' of sorts: the platform is the space where the performance occurs; the performer is the author of the tweet; and the performance is the conscious and considered script that they construct and perform in 140–280 characters. Extending this conceptualization, a performer's 'audience' can be further gathered by way of the hashtag. A performer can assemble an audience by using a specific hashtag in their tweets. A person's use of a hashtag may also indicate their knowledge of a certain audience and how their tweet may subsequently be received: people rarely post things on public online forums such as Twitter without considering the reception and how they will be perceived as most people are conscious of upholding a certain perceived identity (Shreffler, Hancock, & Schmidt, 2016). Engaging with a particular hashtag is an indication of a sense of awareness or knowledge of a particular issue and its affected audience: thus anyone who uses this hashtag may have already considered how it will be received.

J.L. Austin first theorized performativity as to say something is to do something (1955). Since then, performativity theory has been taken elsewhere to help us understand our identities, our social personas, and impression management (Goffman, 1959), as well as how even our gender is socially constructed and performed (Butler, 1999). We contend that when women participate in a space such as Twitter by sharing their stories, their performance is subsumed within performativity—the language they use to express themselves and share their experiences is both performative and a performance for a broader audience (Gregson & Rose, 2000). There are many intersections that can be considered when analysing this specific type of performance—gender, the online space as a player,[2] power, public participation, and identity. By saying #MeToo, a person is *doing* an action. They are participating in political discourse, joining an ensemble of women and other victim/survivors, using an online (public) tool, and some are identifying as a feminist (however

---

[2] 'The online space as a player' merges both Richard Schechner's and Mady Schuman's (1976) performance theory concept (that posits we must consider the affect of space/environment when analysing performance and performativity) and Michel Callon (1986) and Bruno Latour's (1999) actor network theory (which asserts that everything in the social and natural worlds exist in constantly shifting networks of relationship). We contend that platforms like Twitter shape what people say and disclose: not necessarily deliberately but even an element such as a character limit actively affects what is said and how it is said.

broadly they may interpret that identity), allies, a victim-survivor, (most likely) a woman, and an activist. The idea of space as a player is important to consider, as Gregson and Rose extrapolate:

> Specific performances bring these spaces into being. And since these performances are themselves articulations of power, of particular subject positions, [...] we need to think of spaces too as performative power relations. (2000, p. 441)

So how big a part does Twitter or Facebook actually play in the #MeToo performance? Returning to the work of Schechner and Schuman (1976), when we consider social media as the game or theatrical space, the performers play with a certain level of consciousness. They use the hashtag to ensure visibility and participation and to attempt to establish an audience. They tell their story in as many characters as the platform allows and they employ the language they have been socialized to use when sharing their story of abuse. Language such as 'you are not alone', 'speak your truth', and 'don't give up' are common idioms and phrases that apply to many scenarios. However, when used in this context the terms conjure feelings of solidarity and empowerment. Twitter also encourages audience participation by replying, re-tweeting, or favouriting the tweet—the performer is then notified on how their performance was received, a favourite or a re-tweet is like an applause or endorsement, validation. A reply could mean someone is actively listening, are saying 'me too' in addition to you, or in the worst-case scenario 'boo-ing' your performance by trolling and/or dismissing your testimony. Not only are the authors of these tweets being judged on how well they are performing victimhood (or survivorship), but additionally, both their feminist identity (if they identify as such) and the way they orient their claim are also open for critique.

#MeToo Storytelling as Consciousness-Raising

Milano's initial tweet posed the scenario of what would happen if 'all the women who have been sexually harassed or assaulted wrote "Me too"' (Milano, as cited in Renkl, 2017). A large number of tweets within the responses followed this narrative, with users adding the #MeToo hashtag to their tweet. Some were fairly straightforward: a number of people chose to simply copy Milano's tweet and added 'Me too' above or below it, such as this simple tweet[3]:

Me too #MeToo

However, a number of users also chose to add descriptions of their experience (or experiences) of sexual harassment, assault, or rape. These varied from relatively vague accounts of experiences to explicit descriptions:

I'm fortunate enough to have escaped when he pushed me into an empty room #MeToo

I was made to grovel for forgiveness, and lie about the incident so the person wouldn't be exposed. Young and scared, I conformed #MeToo

I will never forget the first time I was 5 years old. The sitter's husband was my first abuser but not my last #MeToo

Raped at 6 by someone I admired. He stole my innocence, but not my spirit. I was determined to be a better person than he was and now I am #MeToo

I suffer from #PTSD as a result of being raped. I want every one who also hurts to know you are not alone. It is still harrowing. #MeToo

Molested by a family member. Raped as a kid and an adult. Became a drug addict, then overcame. Don't ever give up. I'm here. #Metoo

Others still found that there wasn't enough room within Twitter's platform to adequately share their stories:

#MeToo Too many instances for 140 characters

The number of times I can fit #MeToo into 140 characters, or even 280, won't come close to the number of times I have been touched by strange men.

---

[3] Each of the tweets used in this chapter was gathered in accordance with the ethical guidelines of the Association of Internet Researchers (2012).

Within these tweets, none of the users explicitly declared their particular motivations for describing their experiences of sexual harassment, assault, or rape. Indeed, Milano's initial tweet did not ask women to describe their experiences: instead, it simply asked them to write 'me too' as a status update. This therefore leads to the question of why users felt compelled to share their stories, rather than simply posting the #MeToo hashtag alongside Milano's initial tweet.

However, the sharing of these stories can be framed as a crucial element of consciousness-raising groups. Previous accounts of second- and third-wave consciousness-raising practices make specific mention of the recounting of personal experiences; indeed, Sarachild (1968) labels them the recollection and sharing of 'bitter experiences'. The Red Stockings Collective argues that the sharing of personal testimonies was an essential step in consciousness-raising groups and that this allowed women to 'relate to one another and generalize experiences' (Sowards & Renegar, 2004, p. 535). Without the disclosure of collective narratives—those that were thought to be 'personal deficiencies and individual problems' (Campbell, 1999, p. 128)—consciousness cannot be raised. It is, as Dubriwny (2005, p. 396) argues, the situation in which 'individual experiences make possible a reframing of one's understanding of the world'. The need to hear other stories is articulated by others within the tweets examined for this research:

Always tell your story: you never know who may need to hear it. #MeToo
It breaks my heart, but it also warms my heart. I grew up in a time when #MeToo was outlawed. We are all shouting it at once, and that's progress
Hearing stories from other courageous women has made my decision to speak up so much easier, and made me feel SO MUCH less alone #MeToo
We can't let them silence us. Speak your truth even if your voice shakes and in moments of doubt, remember that you're not alone. #MeToo
You're not alone, and despite what you've been told, you'll never be alone. Listening to them isolates you but speaking empowers you. #MeToo
To all survivors of sexual violence: shame belongs to the perpetrator and not to you. Please remember that you are not alone. #MeToo

For these users, the decision to share their stories was prompted by hearing others' experiences. Indeed, the last tweet of these three specifically identifies that her experience was made 'easier' by hearing from others first.

During consciousness-raising meet ups in second-wave feminism, when one woman shared her lived experience of everyday sexism or disclosed her abuse, she was often met with a chorus of women sharing similar stories (Bruley, 2013). Although these women were not punctuating their stories with a hashtag, they were still declaring 'me too'. Vulnerability encourages others to be vulnerable with us: it invites others in to sit with us in our pain, discomfort, or confusion (Brown, 2007). It gives those who bear witness to our stories permission to share theirs, and when our stories are met with a resounding 'me too', it qualifies our experience and raises consciousness.

There is an element of safety and accountability in face-to-face consciousness-raising groups that cannot be recreated online. When we move consciousness-raising online, we accept that our stories may no longer be private, nor ephemeral, and that our performance is open for a mixed audience. Depending on the affordances of the platform we use for consciousness-raising, at any time someone could screen shot our words or react in an aggressive manner. However, by tagging our posts on Twitter with #MeToo, a person is not the first to share their story: they are both comforted and protected by the words of others. Every time a person uses the #MeToo hashtag, they in turn make it easier for others to share their stories and feel less alone. This solidarity creates a sense of safety for women to share their stories, and it is the knowledge that they are not alone that reassures and (potentially) empowers them.

A common response within the tweets discussed within this chapter was that of empathy, support, and advice: both for survivors specifically and the public more broadly. Although direct responses to tweets were not analysed for this research, a number of tweets captured pointed to specific resources and links for both survivors and the general public more broadly:

It's powerful to see so many come forward and share their #MeToo experiences of sexual assault and harassment. This is a thread[4] of key resources.

Dudes! In the wake of #MeToo you will be hearing things that should horrify you. DON'T ask survivors for next steps.

Dear survivors—there [are] so many posts online about #MeToo—please do take care, and tune out if need be. You are important.

Bearing in mind that each of the above tweets (alongside others that fell into this category) were what Twitter had deemed to be 'popular', their resultant reach can be understood to be reasonably broad. Although the people who shared their stories using the #MeToo hashtag may not have done so in order to visibly and knowingly employ a form of consciousness-raising, their actions nonetheless fall into line with these broader practices. Our analyses of these tweets points to a wider need to share stories and unite experiences. Further tweets then reinforce the importance and impact that the disclosure of experiences has had on the user and how this has in turn led them to share their own stories. In framing these tweets as a form of consciousness-raising, we can also see evidence of impacts of this process. The *raising* of consciousness itself requires, as Eisenstein (2001) points out, a personal change. And it is this personal change that is often followed by the next step of consciousness-raising: how individuals can resist oppression through further actions (Sowards & Renegar, 2004).

Concluding Thoughts

In concluding the previous section with Sowards and Renegar's thoughts on *action* as a further resistance (2004), we are left with the question of 'what next?' This is despite any signs that the #MeToo movement is slowing down: indeed, one year on, since Alyssa Milano's tweet sent #MeToo viral and over a decade since Tarana Burke first started to use 'me too' to raise our consciousness on sexual assault and abuse, it is *still* relevant.

---

[4] A 'thread' on Twitter has been defined by the platform as 'a series of connected Tweets from one person…[designed to] provide additional context, an update, or an extended point' (Twitter, 2018b).

Perhaps somewhat idealistically, we hope that there is a time 'beyond' #MeToo—that women, alongside other oppressed people, are consistently and continuously encouraged and supported to speak up and speak out. In envisioning social media spaces as a type of stage, and the telling of these stories as a performance, we must also ask how we can best invite the audience in, to bear witness, and how both we, as the audience, can then continue to enact change. How do we move from telling our past to speaking our future? We suggest that in further shifting the #MeToo discussion from what our stories were, to what our stories can be, we can continue to highlight intersecting oppressions and further our understandings of how change is both highly diverse and highly contextual. By using the same platforms that we have currently facilitated to further debate and discuss our future stories perhaps we can take the next step towards a more effective, more powerful, performance.

References

Altinay, R. E. (2014). 'There is a massacre of women': Violence against women, feminist activism, and hashtags in Turkey. *Feminist Media Studies, 14*(6), 1102–1103.

Anderson, W. K. Z., & Grace, K. E. (2015). "Taking mama steps" toward authority, alternatives, and advocacy: Feminist consciousness-raising within a digital motherhood community. *Feminist Media Studies, 15*(6), 942–959.

Association of Internet Researchers. (2012). Ethical decision making and internet research 2.0: Recommendations from the AoIR ethics working committee. Retrieved December 20, 2018, from https://aoir.org/reports/ethics2.pdf.

Austin, J. (1955). *How to do things with words* (2nd ed., William James lectures; 1955). Oxford: Clarendon Press.

Behrent, M. (2013). When the personal became political: First-person fictions and second-wave feminism. Dissertation. University of New York. Retrieved from https://search-proquest-com.ezproxy.lib.rmit.edu.au/indexinglinkhandler/sng/au/Behrent,+Megan/$N?accountid=13552.

Brown, B. (2007). *I thought it was just me (but it isn't): Making the journey from 'what will people think?' to 'I am enough'.* New York, NY: Avery.

Brown, J. A. (2018). #wheresRey: Feminism, protest, and merchandising sexism in Star Wars: The Force Awakens. *Feminist Media Studies, 18*(3), 335–348.

Bruley, S. (2013). Consciousness-raising in Clapham: Women's liberation as 'lived experience' in South London in the 1970s. *Women's History Review, 22*(5), 717–738.

Butler, J. (1999). *Gender trouble feminism and the subversion of identity.* New York: Routledge.

Callon, M. (1986). The sociology of an actor-network: The case of the electric vehicle. In M. Callon, J. Law, & A. Rip (Eds.), *Mapping the dynamics of science and technology: Sociology of science in the real world* (pp. 19–34). Houndmills, UK: Macmillan.

Campbell, K. K. (1999). The rhetoric of women's liberation: An oxymoron. *Communication Studies, 50*(2), 125–137.

CBS. (2017). More than 12M 'MeToo': Facebook posts, comments, reactions in 24 hours. *CBS.* Retrieved June 27, 2018, from https://www.cbsnews.com/news/metoo-more-than-12-million-facebook-posts-comments-reactions-24-hours.

Clark, C. (2015). *#TrendingFeminism: The impact of digital feminist activism.* Masters dissertation. The George Washington University.

Dubriwny, T. N. (2005). Consciousness-raising as collective rhetoric: The articulation of experience in the Redstockings' abortion speak-out of 1969. *Quarterly Journal of Speech, 91*(4), 395–422.

Eisenstein, H. (2001). Raising consciousness, eyebrows, and hell. *Science & Society, 65*(1), 145–147.

Evans, S. M. (1979). *Personal politics: The roots of women's liberation in the civil rights movement and the new left.* New York, NY: Vintage Books.

Goffman, E. (1990/1959). *The presentation of self in everyday life.* New York, NY: Penguin Books.

Gregson, N., & Rose, G. (2000). Taking Butler elsewhere: Performativities, spatialities and subjectivities. *Environment and Planning D: Society and Space, 18*(4), 433–452.

Hanisch, C. (1970). The personal is political. In S. Firestone & A. Koedt (Eds.), *Notes from the second year: Women's liberation* (pp. 76–77). New York, NY: New York Radical Women.

Harp, D., Grimm, J., & Loke, J. (2018). Rape, storytelling and social media: How Twitter interrupted the news media's ability to construct collective memory. *Feminist Media Studies, 18*(6), 979–995.

Hooks, B. (2000). *Feminism is for everybody: Passionate politics.* Cambridge: South End Press.

Kangere, M., Kemitare, J., & Michau, L. (2017). Hashtag activism: Popularizing feminist analysis of violence against women in the Horn, East and Southern Africa. *Feminist Media Studies, 17*(5), 899–902.

Kim, J. (2017). #iamafeminist as the 'mother tag': Feminist identification and activism against misogyny on Twitter in South Korea. *Feminist Media Studies, 17*(5), 804–820.

Lasch-Quinn, E. (2002). Liberation therapeutics: Consciousness-raising as a problem. *Society, 39*(3), 7–15.

Latour, B. (1999). On recalling ANT. In J. Law & J. Hassard (Eds.), *Actor network theory and after* (pp. 15–25). Malden, MA: Blackwell.

Loken, M. (2014). #BringBackOurGirls and the invisibility of imperialism. *Feminist Media Studies, 14*(6), 1100–1101.

Long, J. (2015). The oppression that dare not speak its name? Silences around heterosexuality in contemporary feminism. In M. Kiraly & M. Tyler (Eds.), *The freedom fallacy: The limits of liberal feminism* (pp. 145–152). Ballarat: Connor Court Publishing.

Loss, C. P. (2011). 'Women's studies is in a lot of ways—Consciousness raising': The educational origins of identity politics. *History of Psychology, 14*(3), 287–310.

Martin, C. E., & Valenti, V. (2012). #FemFuture: Online revolution. *New Feminist Solutions, 8*, 1–34.

Megarry, J. (2017, October 30). Why #metoo is an impoverished form of feminist activism, unlikely to spark social change. *The Conversation*. Retrieved June 27, 2018, from https://theconversation.com/why-metoo-is-an-impoverished-form-of-feminist-activism-unlikely-to-spark-social-change-86455.

Mendes, K., Ringrose, J., & Keller, J. (2018). #MeToo and the promise and pitfalls of challenging rape culture through digital feminist activism. *European Journal of Women's Studies, 25*(2), 236–246.

Pilcher, J., & Whelehan, I. (2004). *50 key concepts in gender studies*. London: Sage Publications.

Portwood-Stacer, L., & Berridge, S. (2014). Introduction. The year in feminist hashtags. *Feminist Media Studies, 14*(6), 1090.

Renkl, M. (2017, October 19). The raw power of #MeToo. *New York Times*. Retrieved June 27, 2018, from https://www.nytimes.com/2017/10/19/opinion/the-raw-power-of-metoo.html.

Rentschler, C. A. (2017). Bystander intervention, feminist hashtag activism, and the anti-carceral politics of care. *Feminist Media Studies, 17*(4), 565–584.

Rentschler, C. A., & Thrift, S. C. (2015). Doing feminism in the network: Networked laughter and the 'Binders Full of Women' meme. *Feminist Theory, 16*(3), 329–359.

Ricker, D. (2018). #MeToo movement spurs national legal response. *ABA Journal, 104*(3), 10–11.

Ryan, B. (1992). *Feminism and the women's movement: Dynamics of change in social movement ideology, and activism.* New York, NY: Taylor and Francis.

Sarachild, K. (1968). A program for feminist consciousness raising. *First National Women's Liberation Conference.* Retrieved June 27, 2018, from http://rhetoricalgoddess.wikia.com/wiki/Kathie_Sarachild:_%22A_Program_for_Feminist:_Consciousness_Raising%22.

Schechner, R., & Schuman, M. (1976). *Ritual, play, and performance: Readings in the social sciences/theatre.* New York, NY: Seabury Press.

Shreffler, M., Hancock, M., & Schmidt, S. (2016). Self-presentation of female athletes: A content analysis of athlete avatars. *International Journal of Sport Communication, 9*(4), 460–475.

Sowards, S. K., & Renegar, V. R. (2004). The rhetorical functions of consciousness-raising in third wave feminism. *Communication Studies, 55*(4), 535–552.

Thrift, S. C. (2014). #YesAllWomen as feminist meme event. *Feminist Media Studies, 14*(6), 1090–1092.

Twitter. (2018a). Sign up. Retrieved June 27, 2018, from https://twitter.com/i/flow/signup.

Twitter. (2018b). How to create a thread on Twitter. Retrieved December 4, 2018, from https://help.twitter.com/en/using-twitter/create-a-thread.

USA Today. (2018, February 20). How common is sexual assault in Hollywood? *USA Today.* Retrieved October 25, 2018, from https://www.usatoday.com/story/life/people/2018/02/20/how-common-sexual-misconduct-hollywood/1083964001/.

Weeks, J. (2007). Gay left: An overview by Jeffrey Weeks. Retrieved October 25, 2015, from http://gayleft1970s.org/intro.asp.

Williams, S. (2015). Digital defense: Black feminists resist violence with hashtag activism. *Feminist Media Studies, 15*(2), 1–3.

5

You Say #MeToo, I Say #MiTu: China's Online Campaigns Against Sexual Abuse

Jing Zeng

Introduction

China's #MeToo campaign has been given the moniker MiTu (米兔) by its supporters—a direct phonetic translation of 'me too', which in Mandarin literally means 'rice bunny'. For this reason, images of bunnies have also become a symbol of China's adaptation of the #MeToo movement. From early 2018, women in China joined the global #MeToo movement to fight sexual harassment and sexual abuse. As of September 2018, over 50 public allegations were made on social media against powerful men in various walks of life, including university professors, media personalities, and NGO founders (Zuo, 2018). Many of the accused have been fired by their respective organizations.

Compared to the US, where the #MeToo movement originated, China's #MiTu campaign has many divergent characteristics. For example, where #MeToo sprung out of the entertainment industry, China's #MiTu first emerged in universities, where numerous renowned professors have been

J. Zeng (✉)
University of Zurich, Zurich, Switzerland

© The Author(s) 2019
B. Fileborn, R. Loney-Howes (eds.), *#MeToo and the Politics of Social Change*,
https://doi.org/10.1007/978-3-030-15213-0_5

accused of sexual harassment by current and former students (Zeng, 2018). Also, in contrast to their Western counterparts, Chinese women's attempts to further expand the campaign into a nationwide movement face strict political obstacles. Chinese authorities routinely exercise high levels of censorship to curtail the growth of activism. Therefore #MiTu supporters are forced to continually adjust their strategies to circumvent censorship and keep the campaign alive. On top of government censorship, the #MiTu campaign also faces societal challenges. For instance, large segments of society, such as the working classes and other marginalized groups, struggle to be heard (see Ryan; Kagal, Cowan & Jawad; Ison, this collection). Meanwhile, embedded power structures mean that men in the higher echelons of government remain 'untouchable'. This chapter aims to critically discuss the particularities of China's #MiTu campaign, focusing on how it emerged, how it operates within China's sociopolitical milieu, and its limitations in generating social change.

University: The Ground Zero

China's participation in the global anti-sexual harassment and anti-sexual assault campaign started on New Year's Day, 2018. On 1 January, Luo Xixi—a former graduate student at Beihang University in Beijing—made an allegation on Chinese social media against her then supervisor, Professor Chen Xiaowu (Denyer & Wang, 2018). According to Luo's post, Chen repeatedly harassed her while she undertook her PhD 12 years ago. Luo's post received millions of views and was widely circulated. The university and education authorities quickly responded to Luo's allegation by sacking Chen. Encouraged by the triumph of Luo's allegations, more women from China broke their silence and shared their own encounters of sexual harassment at the hands of university professors. Within two weeks after Luo made the open allegation, students and alumni from over 50 universities signed online petitions, demanding their schools develop mechanisms to prevent and deal with sexual harassment on campus (Zhou & Zheng, 2018). In solidarity, 56 professors from top universities in China signed a petition calling for educational institutions in China to develop reporting systems for sexual harassment claims (Hu & He, 2018).

It is no coincidence that universities became the ground zero for China's latest fight against sexual harassment. The institutional structure of universities leads to a power imbalance between students and their teachers. In comparison with Western universities, such a power disparity becomes particularly problematic, given the documented corruption and lack of transparency within the Chinese education system (Yang, 2015). As several victims of university sexual harassment revealed, predatory teachers often used coursework scores, scholarships, and even the outcome of their degrees to lure or blackmail them into silence. The power imbalance between university students and their advisors makes the former vulnerable to abuse, but at the same time such abuse is perhaps easier to be exposed. Students' ties to learning institutions are more temporary, and upon graduation they face fewer institutional obstacles if they choose to speak out. By contrast, when women are more permanently tied to a company, or to an industry, the stakes can often be too high for them to make allegations against men in higher positions.

The increasingly international network of Chinese graduate students and alumni is another key factor contributing to universities leading in China's #MiTu campaigns. According to official statistics from the Chinese Ministry of Education, there are millions of Chinese graduates living overseas, including those who are currently enrolled, or who have previously studied, in foreign higher education institutions (MOE, 2018). This international network of Chinese students and alumni, especially those based in North America, became the first force promoting #MeToo in their home country. For example, Luo Xixi, whose allegation sparked the #MeToo campaign in China, lives in the US, where she first learned about and was inspired by the #MeToo movement (Denyer & Wang, 2018). Similarly, some of the most active participants of #MiTu on Chinese social media are Chinese students studying in Canada or the US. These Chinese expats are eager to bring #MeToo China, not only because they are close to the hub of the global #MeToo movement but also because they have witnessed the contrast between Western and Chinese universities with regard to the mechanisms in place to protect students from sexual harassment. As Luo Xixi wrote in an open letter, which she published on New Year's Day, 2018,

During my studies in the U.S., I have seen how American universities pre-vent sexual harassment on campus…97 percent of higher education insti-tutions have implemented anti-sexual harassment regulations… But we do not have it in China yet.[1]

These measures Luo describes have by no means stamped out sexual harassment and assaults on US campuses. However, the higher awareness and intolerance of sexual harassment Chinese students have witnessed in Western institutions have galvanized them to push for change in their homeland.

Social and Governmental Responses

The rigorous #MiTu campaigns in universities have been received posi-tively by Chinese society. In the spirit of #MiTu, an increasing number of women from a variety of sectors have now made allegations of sexual harassment and assault against powerful men, including writers, media personalities, leaders of NGOs, and even high-profile Buddhist monks (Chen, 2018). Supporters of the campaign set up chat groups on social media to share their stories, collect evidence, and give legal advice. Xuanzi, one of these outspoken women, who recently accused one of China's most well-known TV presenters of sexual harassment, made the follow-ing remark in an interview with *Renwu* magazine:

I now realised how the #MeToo movement develops and expands: It does not rely on men, but on women who quickly build solidarity. If you are a woman, and if you grew up in this environment, everyone's body will hold some kind of memory (of sexual abuse), of which you can never be rid. Other women have empathy toward me, because our bodies have shared memory. My mother can understand my story, not because I am her daughter, but because she is also a women and she has had similar experiences.[2]

---

[1] URL to Luo's original Chinese post: https://www.weibo.com/ttarticle/p/show?id=2309404191293831018113.

[2] The original interview was published on *Renwu*'s public WeiChat account in Chinese, but it has been censored. The text provided here is based on the author's own archive of the original post.

Xuanzi's statement implies that sexual harassment of women is ubiquitous in Chinese society, like in most of the world. But #MiTu opens up a space for collective voices and mutual support among women (see also Mendes & Ringrose, this collection). Arguably, in Chinese society, women's awareness to speak out about sexual harassment and fight for justice is already a great achievement. As indicated in prior studies (e.g., Dussich, 2001; Feldman-Summers & Ashworth, 1981; Mori, Bernat, Glenn, Selle, & Zarate, 1995), underreporting of sexual violence is much more common among Asian women than their Western counterparts, partially due to cultural factors. For example, the Confucian teaching of not challenging seniority (e.g., in terms of age or position at work), as well as the traditional value of chastity as a woman's main virtue, can contribute to Chinese women's reluctance to speak out about their experiences of sexual harassment. However, when more and more women make public allegations of sexual harassment and sexual assault, they are not just overcoming personal reservations but challenging conservative social norms as well.

Faced with the growing popularity of the #MiTu campaign, Chinese authorities have a dilemma. Rhetorically, the Communist Party of China (CPC), who places 'building a harmonious society' at the top of their agenda, has to respond positively to the university students' sincere advocacy. Therefore, in the wake of sexual harassment scandals from a number of top Chinese universities, both the Ministry of Education and state media have published official statements condemning inappropriate teacher behavior and have acknowledged the importance for educational institutions to build response mechanisms (Kan, 2018). At the same time, however, authorities carefully moderate the online campaign to prevent it from spreading out of control, causing 'social unrest' or threatening the government's legitimacy (Zeng, 2018). Even though at this stage those exposed by the #MiTu movement are mostly non-political figures, such as university professors, it is not hard to imagine that the campaign could escalate and begin to implicate those in positions of political power.

Subsequently, in response, despite the rhetoric from Chinese authorities expressing support for the #MiTu movement, there has been tight control over the flow of information related to the campaign from the

Chinese State. For example, on China's two major social media platforms—Weibo and WeChat—'MeToo' and 'sexual assault' (性侵) have become sensitive words, and a large number of related posts have been censored. Also, shortly after '#MeTooinChina' began trending on Weibo in January 2018, the entire hashtag was blocked, and many posts under this hashtag have been removed (Lim, 2018). Blocking hashtags is a crucial strategy used by the Chinese authorities to undermine the impacts of the campaign because it prevents supporters from assembling. Under the CPC's ruling, demonstrations and gatherings are strictly controlled, as are many forms of online collective action that seek to mobilize large swathes of participants. As #MiTu supporters can use hashtags as a proxy to identify and assemble fellow activists (see also Gleeson & Turner, this collection), hashtags are now also used as a shortcut to crack down on any attempt to organize collective action online.

The Cat and Mouse Game

The social and governmental responses to #MiTu discussed above highlight the tension between campaigners and the authorities, which results in the unique dynamic of China's anti-sexual harassment and anti-sexual assault campaign: a push and pull of silencing and voicing, censorship and circumvention. In order to evade the government's attempts at cracking down on the social media campaign, #MiTu supporters have exhibited creativity and persistence. In fact, the name of the campaign itself—MiTu—is an act of clever circumvention. As mentioned earlier, the first dominant hashtag related to the campaign—#MeTooinChina—was removed from Weibo after it began trending widely. In response to this, Weibo users launched an alternative hashtag #MiTuInChina (Rice Bunny In China) to evade authorities. As a result, MiTu, or rice bunny, became the new symbol for China's #MeToo campaign. Other attempts to avoid censorship of the hashtag include using emojis (of rice bowls and bunny heads) and local dialects. Two examples of the latter are *laozi yeshi* and *an yeshi*, which means 'I also', in Sichuan and northern dialects, respectively.

In April 2018, this cat and mouse game escalated to a new level, following a renewed online outrage of a decades-old case of sexual assault at one of China's most prestigious universities: Peking University (PKU). A female student from PKU—Gao Yan—committed suicide in 1998 after making allegations against her professor—Shen Yang. PKU fired Shen after the incident, but the University's investigation on Gao Yan's allegation was never revealed to the public. Twenty years later, as #MiTu sweeps across higher education institutions in China, a group of students at PKU have revisited the case and are seeking justice on Gao's behalf, calling for PKU to reopen its investigation of Gao Yan's case to a public hearing (Hernández, 2018). The petition was rejected by University authorities, but one of the students initiating the petition, Yue Xin, revealed on social media how she was pressured and threatened by the University to stop her petition. Yue's open letter was widely shared online, before it was eventually removed from all platforms.

In order to combat the authorities' attempts to prevent the circulation of Yue Xin's letter, supporters have come up with innovative ways to trick the system. For example, in order to prevent the screenshots of Yue's letter from being deleted from social media, people have been rotating the image to trick the platform's detection algorithms. One anonymous supporter of Yue even added her letter to a tamper-proof blockchain, to escape Chinese Internet censorship. On 23 April 2018, an unidentified user of Ether—a cryptocurrency—sent himself/herself an empty transaction and attached Yue's letter to the transaction record. Because the letter is now permanently documented in Ethereum's public blockchain, anyone with the URL to this transaction can read it. Other tech-savvy supporters of Yue Xin also archived her deleted social media posts on GitHub,[3] an open-source repository hosting service where programmers share and manage code.

China has developed arguably the world's most robust systems for controlling online information flows, but in doing so, it has inadvertently inspired some of the most sophisticated 'online rebels' to become increasingly innovative in their methods to combat government censorship. The

---

[3] This is an example of such page: https://github.com/sikaozhe1997/Xin-Yue/blob/master/letter.md.

irony of this situation may also be seen in Chinese women's fight for a more equal and safer society. The #MeToo movement did not initiate the anti-sexual harassment campaign in China. Chinese activists have launched various campaigns in recent years, predating #MeToo, to raise the public's and government officials' awareness of the issue of sexual harassment. In 2013, activist Xiao Meili walked from Beijing to Guangzhou, a distance of over 2000 km, to collect signatures for a petition calling for the establishment of anti-sexual harassment mechanisms in Chinese education systems (Xiao, 2015). In 2015, five women—Li, Zhen, Wu, Wei, and Wang—organized protests against sexual harassment on public transport, and in 2017, Zhang Leilei attempted to crowdfund a nationwide anti-sexual harassment advertising campaign (Wong, 2015). Even though most of these women ended up being prosecuted for their activities,[4] they still carry on their activism online. For instance, in this year's #MiTu campaign, some of these women were the most vocal activists.

The Limitations of the Current Campaign

China's #MiTu campaign may not be able to develop into a nationwide movement, not merely due to the authorities' crackdown discussed above, but also due to the limitations of the campaign itself. First of all, the individuals involved in the campaign are almost exclusively 'elites', on both the accuser and accused sides. For instance, at the time of writing, most of the women who have made public allegations against sexual predators are highly educated and media savvy. A certain amount of 'social capital' is required to be considered as a credible victim, worthy of receiving wider media attention (see also Rosewarne, this collection). By contrast, little media and public attention has been paid to commonplace sexual harassment in the workplace or that inflicted upon more marginalized social groups, such as those based in rural China or low-income workers. For instance, in early 2018, a worker at Foxconn published an

---

[4] Li, Zhen, Wu, Wei, and Wang were detained for weeks, and Zhang was asked by Guangzhou authorities to leave the city.

open letter asking the company to introduce systematic safeguards to prevent the sexual harassment of female workers. As one of Apple's major suppliers, Foxconn often receives media attention, which helped the news story appear in domestic and international media. But, ultimately, this was an isolated case, which failed to receive official response or inspire more female factory workers to follow suit. The problem of 'inclusion' and 'diversity' has become a critique of the #MeToo movement in America. For instance, activists have raised concern that the plight of marginalized women risks being sidestepped by the #MeToo movement's focus on Hollywood (Scott, 2017; Strike, 2018). Similarly, there are many marginalized groups within Chinese society who are vulnerable to sexually violent crimes, such as low-income workers and youths living in rural areas; however, their voices are yet to be heard. Therefore, China's #MiTu campaign will be more fruitful if 'elite women' can use their resources to grow the campaign so that it reaches a wider social sphere.

China's #MiTu campaign is not merely limited in its ability 'reach down', to influence less-privileged sectors of society, it also faces challenges in 'reaching up' to affect men in higher political positions. When compared to making allegations against university professors, the stakes involved in accusing politicians are far higher. There are few examples of sexual allegations against politicians appearing in China's #MiTu campaigns, and all existing allegations target low-level government officials. In China's current media environment, direct accusations against high-profile officials remain one of the most sensitive topics. Therefore, to implicate a high-ranking politician in the #MiTu campaign would risk a complete crackdown on the campaign. In other words, if the political power structure does not change, the 'untouchables' will remain untouchable.

Furthermore, as much as China needs a campaign like #MiTu to shift social attitudes toward sexual harassment and unify women, the country also needs top-down efforts to improve China's legislation and law enforcement regarding sexual harassment and sexual assault. China's legislation regarding such issues is in its infancy when compared to most Western democracies. For example, China's current civil code does not mention 'sexual harassment' (性骚扰). Only recently the Chinese legislation authorities began to draft a new section on this topic, which is expected to be completed around 2020 (Cao, 2018). Moreover, as a number of China's #MiTu stories show, some individuals who experienced sexual violence did report the case to local authorities, but ended up being asked by law enforcement officers to withdraw the allegation in order to protect the reputation of accused individuals or organizations (Wang, 2018). Such flawed legislation and enforcement pushed women in the country to pursue justice through 'alternative channels', such as social media (see also Haire, Newman, & Fileborn, this collection). However, to change policy and legislation, there are no 'alternative channels': impetus must come from the top. Therefore efforts need to be maintained and increased to persuade the government to institute tangible change.

Conclusion

The #MiTu campaign is the story of a collection of resilient Chinese women battling socially ingrained harassment as well as resistant social and political forces. The campaign was sparked by a group of college students, inspired by the #MeToo movement, who made public allegations of sexual harassment against university professors, and it has blossomed from there. Although #MiTu has received positive response from the community and inspired women from more sectors of Chinese society to speak out, it has also faced resistance from an authoritarian system opposed to social activism. Consequently, supporters of the campaign have needed to constantly adapt to the political and media systems. Like the international #MeToo movement, #MiTu has its limitations. Despite some early successes, the movement has so far failed to expand its scope to include more marginalized voices or generate enough momentum to pressure the government to implement a top-down approach to improving legislation and law enforcement around sexual abuse.

For #MiTu to accomplish more requires deeper cultural reflection from within Chinese society, especially with regard to gender equality. The rate at which China is closing its gender gap lags far behind that of its economic growth. In the World Economic Forum's 2017 global gender gap index, for instance, China dropped for a ninth year in a row and is currently ranked 100 out of 144 nations (WEF, 2017). Gender inequality in China has deep historical roots. The most dominant Chinese gender norms have long highlighted the differences between men and women and have valued the balance between 'strong men and weak women'. In modern China, such stereotypical gender norms are no longer promoted by official rhetoric, but they still exert great influence (Li, 2004). However, more educated, financially independent, and media-savvy Chinese women have begun to challenge traditional gender norms, as showcased in the case of #MiTu. For now, the story of #MiTu is merely one of the many stories of Chinese women fighting for a safe and equal society. These courageous women, as well as their solidarity, are the key to making change in a rapidly evolving China.

References

Cao, Y. (2018, August 28). Civil code draft backs the victims of sexual harassers. *China Daily*. Retrieved December 20, 2018, from www.chinadaily.com.cn/a/201808/28/WS5b849044a310add14f3880f1.html.

Chen, A. H. (2018, August 16). China's top Buddhist Monk has resigned amid sexual harassment allegations. *Time Magazine*. Retrieved December 20, 2018, from www.time.com/5367775/china-monk-metoo-sexual-harassment/.

Denyer, S. & Wang, A Z. (2018, January 9). Chinese women reveal sexual harassment, but #MeToo movement struggles for air. *The Washington Post*. Retrieved December 20, 2018, from https://www.washingtonpost.com/world/asia_pacific/chinese-women-reveal-sexual-harassment-but-metoo-movement-struggles-for-air/2018/01/08/ac591c26-cc0d-4d5a-b2ca-d14a7f763fe0_story.html?utm_term=.16014655696c.

Dussich, J. P. (2001). Decisions not to report sexual assault: A comparative study among women living in Japan who are Japanese, Korean, Chinese, and English-speaking. *International Journal of Offender Therapy and Comparative Criminology, 45*(3), 278–301.

Feldman-Summers, S., & Ashworth, C. D. (1981). Factors related to intentions to report a rape. *Journal of Social Issues, 37*(4), 53–70.

Hernández, J. C. (2018, April 9). China's #MeToo: How a 20-year-old rape case became a rallying cry. *The New York Times*. Retrieved December 20, 2018, from https://www.nytimes.com/2018/04/09/world/asia/china-metoo-gao-yan.html.

Hu, R., & He, L. (2018, January 22). 56 Weio Jiaoshi Shiming Changyi Jianquan Xiaoyuan Fanxingsaorao Jizhi. *The Paper*. Retrieved December 20, 2018, from www.chinanews.com/sh/2018/01-22/8429917.shtml.

Kan, F. (2018, January 16). Jiaoyubu Zaidu Huiying Xiaoyuan Xingsaorao. *China News*. Retrieved December 20, 2018, from www.chinanews.com/gn/2018/01-16/8425137.shtml.

Li, M. (2004). To be a woman successful in career is not as good as to be a woman successful in marriage? Some thoughts on the gender outlook of contemporary Chinese college girls. *Collection of Women's Studies, 4*(20), 25–30.

Lim, L. (2018, March 2). China's #MeToo censorship bypassed through netizens' creative use of language. *South China Morning Post*. Retrieved December 20, 2018, from https://www.scmp.com/magazines/post-magazine/short-reads/article/2134847/chinas-metoo-censorship-bypassed-through.

Ministry of Education. (2018). 2017 sees increase in number of Chinese students studying abroad and returning after overseas studies. *Ministry of Education*. Retrieved December 20, 2018, from en.moe.gov.cn/News/Top_News/201804/t20180404_332354.html.

Mori, L., Bernat, J. A., Glenn, P. A., Selle, L. L., & Zarate, M. G. (1995). Attitudes toward rape: Gender and ethnic differences across Asian and Caucasian college students. *Sex Roles, 32*(7–8), 457–467.

Scott, E. (2017, December 7). The marginalized voices of the #MeToo movement. *The Washington Post*. Retrieved December 20, 2018, from https://www.washingtonpost.com/news/the-fix/wp/2017/12/07/the-marginalized-voices-of-the-metoo-movement/?utm_term=.8d22f7a0d64d.

Strike, A. W. (2018, March 8). Disabled women see #MeToo and think: What about us? *The Guardian*. Retrieved December 20, 2018, from https://www.theguardian.com/commentisfree/2018/mar/08/disabled-people-metoo-womens-movement-inclusion-diversity.

Wang, Y. (2018, September 3). As MeToo unnerves China, a student fights to tell her story. *Associated Press*. Retrieved December 20, 2018, from https://www.apnews.com/188ddcd956c94cb58af5b260463fe69f.

Wong, E. (2015, April 13). China releases 5 women's rights activists detained for weeks. *The New York Times*. Retrieved December 20, 2018, from https://www.nytimes.com/2015/04/14/world/asia/china-releases-3-of-5-detained-womens-rights-activists.html.

World Economic Forum. (2017). *The global gender gap report 2017*. Switzerland: World Economic Forum.

Xiao, M. (2015, May 13). China's feminist awakening. *The New York Times*. Retrieved December 20, 2018, from https://www.nytimes.com/2015/05/14/opinion/xiao-meili-chinas-feminist-awakening.html.

Yang, R. (2015). Corruption in China's higher education: A malignant tumour. *International Higher Education, 39*, 18–20.

Zeng, J. (2018, February 6). From #MeToo to #RiceBunny: How social media users are campaigning in China. *The Conversation*. Retrieved December 20, 2018, from https://theconversation.com/from-metoo-to-ricebunny-how-social-media-users-are-campaigning-in-china-90860.

Zhou V., & Zheng S. (2018, January 16). Chinese students use #MeToo to take fight against sexual harassment to elite universities. *South China Morning Post*. Retrieved December 20, 2018, from https://www.scmp.com/news/china/society/article/2128341/chinese-students-use-metoo-take-fight-against-sexual-harassment.

Zuo, M. (2018, July 27). China's #MeToo revival: Famed activists, TV host and writer named. *South China Morning Post*. Retrieved December 20, 2018, from https://www.scmp.com/news/china/society/article/2157204/well-known-activists-among-accused-metoo-campaign-gathers-pace.

6

A Thousand and One Stories: Myth and the #MeToo Movement

Mary Anne Franks

Introduction

Women telling stories—particularly stories about the abuses of men—is at the heart of the #MeToo movement.[1] The founder of the movement, Tarana Burke, recounts how #MeToo began with a 13-year-old girl's attempt to tell Burke the story of being abused by her stepfather: a story that Burke, burdened by her own untold, all-too-similar story, could not bear to hear at the time (Fessler, 2018). #MeToo can be described as an unleashing of women's stories, a wave of women's voices rushing to speak painful truths, to bear witness, to demand justice.

In one sense, then, the #MeToo movement is fundamentally a movement about speech. One might expect it to be praised as such, especially

---

[1] Of course, #MeToo is not solely about women's voices and not solely about male abuses. But the movement began with women speaking up about rape and sexual harassment at the hands of men, and this theme has continued to be predominant.

M. A. Franks (✉)
University of Miami School of Law, Coral Gables, FL, USA
e-mail: mafranks@law.miami.edu

© The Author(s) 2019
B. Fileborn, R. Loney-Howes (eds.), *#MeToo and the Politics of Social Change*,
https://doi.org/10.1007/978-3-030-15213-0_6

given that it unfolded at a historical moment when free speech, especially provocative free speech, was widely and energetically valorized by prominent figures across the political spectrum in the United States and elsewhere. But while there was widespread support for the movement's first phase, when women were simply stating 'me too' or sharing stories mostly devoid of identifying details, this support began to wane once women started to name names. This was especially true when the men named were powerful or popular.

While few voices were raised in defense of men like Harvey Weinstein, criticism of the #MeToo movement increased as stories emerged involving more sympathetic figures and less lurid conduct. This was particularly the case with stories involving alleged or confirmed sexual misconduct that fell short of rape, such as those that surfaced about Louis C.K., Al Franken, and Aziz Ansari, and stories that were viewed as threatening the career trajectories of powerful men, such as Brett Kavanaugh.

The litany of complaints against the #MeToo movement is by now familiar: it has become a 'witch hunt'; men are no longer allowed to flirt or make jokes about sex; men's lives can now be ruined forever over mere allegations. Influential individuals on both the right and the left have criticized #MeToo for being too extreme, for not being subtle or careful enough, for being harmful to men. Based on the intensity of the criticism of #MeToo, one might easily be led to believe that the movement had triggered violent vigilante justice or severe criminal penalties. But the reality is that the #MeToo movement has to date remained, for better or worse, primarily about speech and not action. Its leaders and proponents have not advocated violence or even, in most cases, specific consequences for egregious conduct. Many #MeToo stories have neither been intended to nor have in fact resulted in legal repercussions; only a few of them have had reputational or financial consequences, which may prove to be short-lived. That is, the supposed harm caused by #MeToo is not only largely intangible, but also largely speculative.

The backlash against #MeToo is, in essence, a backlash against speech. This backlash exposes a disturbing truth about free speech fundamentalism: like religious fundamentalism, it is highly selective, often hypocritical, and primarily intended to serve patriarchal interests. While the harms of offensive speech have been trivialized and dismissed when the targets are women, speech that offends men—whether it is offense directed at their egos, their reputations, or their sensibilities—is treated as a deadly serious matter. The #MeToo backlash demonstrates how quickly the swaggering, politically incorrect façade of self-proclaimed free speech defenders melts away in the heat of women's speech. Women's speech against men is treated as dangerous and harmful in a way that virulent misogyny, anti-Semitism, white supremacy, and other forms of common bigotry are not.

In some ways, the backlash against #MeToo is a very old story. Women's speech, and especially women's speech perceived to undermine men's interests, has been feared and suppressed for centuries. From the scold's bridle to (actual) witch hunts to the violent suppression of women's suffrage, history is replete with attempts to keep women quiet and in their place. Men's silencing of women, particularly spurred by women's sexual decisions or actions, is also a prominent theme in the mythology and folk tales of multiple cultures. As myths represent some of our deepest and oldest fears and desires, these stories serve as rich sources of illustration and illumination in understanding the relationship between men's sexual rage and the suppression of women's speech.

The stories of three mythical women—Cassandra, Philomela, and Scheherazade—offer insights into the interaction of male sexual rage and women's speech that shed light on the #MeToo movement and the backlash it has inspired.

Cassandra

What most people remember about the myth of Cassandra is that she was the prophetess that no one would believe. Less well known are the circumstances that led Cassandra to suffer from this particular fate. According to several sources, the god Apollo gave Cassandra the gift of prophecy after becoming transfixed by her beauty and attempting to have sex with her. Upon her refusal, Apollo cursed Cassandra so that no one would ever believe the truth that she would foretell.

Cassandra was condemned to spend her life warning the people around her of impending destruction and tragedy, to no avail. The ability to foresee the future but never be believed tormented Cassandra, and she was often imprisoned or restrained for what seemed to other people to be mad ravings. In one particularly dramatic example, Cassandra attempted to warn the Trojan people of the Greek soldiers hiding in the giant horse that arrived at their gates. In response, the Trojans mocked and insulted her, decrying her lack of 'maiden modesty' for her speech (Quintus Smyrnaeus, 1913). Determined to expose the treachery of the Greeks, Cassandra ran toward the horse with a battle-axe in one hand and a burning torch in the other, but the crowd set upon her and flung her aside. Troy was then destroyed by the Greeks. As Troy fell, Cassandra sought shelter in Athena's temple, where she was violently raped by Ajax the Lesser. Cassandra was later given to Agamemnon as a spoil of war, and eventually murdered along with him by Agamemnon's wife, Clytemnestra.

The story of Cassandra is a story, first, about men's excessive sensitivity to sexual rejection. Apollo is not just a particularly powerful and privileged male but a literal god with divine powers. And yet the sexual rejection by a mortal woman—the denial of one momentary pleasure—sends him into such a rage that he devises a devastatingly cruel revenge to make Cassandra suffer every single moment for the rest of her life. The story of Cassandra suggests that the more powerful the man, the frailer his sexual ego.

Cassandra's tale is also about the particularly effective method of punishment that Apollo inflicts upon Cassandra. Rather than taking away her ability to speak altogether, or depriving her of the gift of prophecy, Apollo turns her own truthful, powerful speech against her, rendering her literally unbelievable. Cassandra's fate is moreover not hers alone; entire populations suffer and die because of the refusal to heed her words.

But Cassandra's story is also about the bravery of women's speech and the perils of ignoring it. Cassandra continued to warn those around her about impending death and destruction, even as they mocked, beat, and imprisoned her for doing so. Such was Cassandra's concern for the fate of her people that she instructed her twin brother, Helenus, in prophecy, knowing that he would be believed where she would not.

Philomela

As told by Ovid (1998) in *The Metamorphoses*, Procne asks her husband Tereus, King of Thrace, to allow her sister Philomela to visit her. Tereus travels to Athens to escort Philomela to Thrace, but on the way he takes her to a cabin in the woods and rapes her. He warns Philomela to never tell anyone what he has done. Defiantly, Philomela informs Tereus that she will not keep silent. In Ovid's version of the story, Philomela vows,

> …my revenge shall take its proper time,
> And suit the baseness of your hellish crime.
> My self, abandon'd, and devoid of shame,
> Thro' the wide world your actions will proclaim;
> Or tho' I'm prison'd in this lonely den,
> Obscur'd, and bury'd from the sight of men,
> My mournful voice the pitying rocks shall move,
> And my complainings echo thro' the grove.
> Hear me, o Heav'n! and, if a God be there,
> Let him regard me, and accept my pray'r. (Ovid, 1998)

Enraged by her words, Tereus cuts out Philomela's tongue and abandons her in the cabin. But Philomela finds another way to speak. She weaves a tapestry that tells the story of what Tereus has done and sends it to her sister. In revenge, Procne kills their son and serves his flesh to an unwitting Tereus. After he eats his meal, Procne reveals what she has done and Tereus seizes an axe to attempt to kill both Philomela and Procne. But the two women pray to the gods to be turned into birds so that they may escape his violence. Procne is turned into a swallow, and Philomela into a nightingale.

Like Apollo, Tereus believes himself to be entitled to women's bodies, and like Apollo, he turns to cruelty when a woman defies his will. One can read the myth of Philomela as a harsher version of Cassandra's story: Philomela is not only threatened with rape but is raped, and is deprived not only of the credibility of her speech but of speech itself. So fearful and enraged is Tereus at the prospect of Philomela telling the truth that he resorts to extraordinarily cruel violence.

But Philomela is also the story of a woman refusing to be silenced. Even with her tongue cut out, Philomela finds a way to communicate what has been done to her. Her story is also one of female solidarity: when Philomela's sister discovers what her husband has done, Procne makes no attempt to excuse his behavior or blame her sister. Rather, she orchestrates bloody vengeance against her husband, though at the expense of her own son. Philomela's story suggests that women's cunning and solidarity can prevail over men's sexual violence.

Scheherazade

As told in *A Thousand and One Nights* (Anonymous, 2008), Shahryar, the King of the realm, discovers that his wife has been unfaithful to him with a slave. He is so enraged that he has her killed. But this is not enough to satisfy his fury, as he is convinced that all women are unfaithful and all should be punished. He decides he will marry a new virgin every night, sleep with her, and then have her executed in the morning, thus depriving her of any opportunity to be unfaithful. As the population of young women in the kingdom dwindles, Scheherazade, the daughter of the vizier, volunteers to marry the king.

On their wedding night, Scheherazade asks the king if she could be allowed to say farewell to her sister, who has been instructed to request that Scheherazade tell her one last story. Scheherazade begins a suspenseful, action-packed story that reaches its most exciting point as the morning dawns. Scheherazade breaks off, and the king asks her to finish the story. Scheherazade says she cannot, as the time has come for her execution. But the king is desperate to hear the end of the story, so he grants Scheherazade one more night to finish it. The next night, Scheherazade finishes the story, but begins an even more exciting story before dawn breaks. Once again, when it is morning, the king spares her life for one more night so that she can finish the story. This goes on for 1001 nights, until the king finally tells Scheherazade that he will not ever have her put to death, nor will he have any other woman put to death.

The king's cruelty in response to sexual rage in this myth surpasses even that of Apollo and Tereus. His anger at one woman's sexual betrayal triggers what is in essence a serial campaign of rapes followed by executions. Like the stories of Cassandra and Philomela, the story of Scheherazade speaks to men's sexual frailty and the extreme sadism it provokes.

But even more so than the other two myths, the story of Scheherazade is ultimately a story of the power of women's speech. Scheherazade's speech literally saves not only her life, but also the lives of all the surviving women in the realm. Only Scheherazade's words had the power to restrain the most powerful man in the kingdom from continuing his extermination campaign against women. Scherherazade's story, like that of Philomela, is one of sisterly solidarity; it also echoes Cassandra's willingness to sacrifice herself for the sake of the larger good. Whereas Cassandra is thwarted in her attempts to save the Trojans from destruction, Scheherazade succeeds in saving the women of her kingdom from rape and murder.

Myth and the Modern Day

The myths of Cassandra, Philomela, and Scheherazade offer important insights that can illuminate both the #MeToo movement and the backlash it has triggered. The first insight is just how *dangerous* women's speech is perceived to be and the lengths to which men will go to punish or silence women who have triggered any form of male sexual rage, from denial of sexual access (Cassandra) to threatening to reveal sexual assault (Philomela), to anticipated sexual betrayal (Scheherazade). These retaliatory measures range from the destruction of credibility (Cassandra), physical mutilation (Philomela), to execution (Scheherazade). All of these measures are reflected in the modern reality of male abuse of women. Victims of sexual assault and harassment are routinely discredited, portrayed as promiscuous, crazy, or simply unreliable. Many victims endure the threat of physical assault or death as a means to keep them quiet; far too many experience the fulfillment of these threats.

A second insight is the variation in the purposes of women's speech. Cassandra seeks to warn; Philomela seeks to testify; and Scheherazade seeks to save her life and the lives of others. Cassandra never seeks to hold Apollo accountable for his attempted rape, nor does Scheherazade seek retribution for the king's gynocide. Only in Philomela's story does personal vengeance play a role, and even there, it is not the sole motivation: Philomela also seeks to tell the truth about what Tereus has done, to let the gods hear of his crime and of her suffering. In the backlash to #MeToo, women's stories have often been treated as a monolith. The most reductive criticism of #MeToo treats these stories as motivated primarily by hostility to men and assumes that their inevitable and intended result is to 'ruin men's lives,' whether through jail sentences, reputational damage, or loss of employment opportunities. But women have multiple motivations for telling their stories of abuse and assault, most of which have little or nothing to do with formal penalties.

Some, like Philomela, do want to name their abuser and his crime and see him brought to justice. Others simply want to say out loud what they have kept secret for so long. Still others, like Cassandra, want to educate and warn: to foretell impending disasters so that they can be stopped. And some, like Scheherazade, recognize the power of storytelling to make women's humanity visible, to protect them from future harm.

Shades of all three myths can be seen in the real-life, modern-day example of Dr. Christine Blasey Ford. In September 2018, Ford testified before a heavily male-dominated Senate committee that Judge Brett Kavanaugh, President Trump's nominee to replace retiring Justice Anthony Kennedy, had attempted to rape her when the two were teenagers. Ford testified that while attending a party in 1982, when she was 15 years old, she had suddenly found herself being pushed into a bedroom where rock music was playing loudly. According to her account, an intoxicated 17-year-old Kavanaugh held her down on a bed, tried to pull her clothes off, and covered her mouth with his hand to stifle her screams. She managed to escape when Kavanaugh's friend Mark Judge, who was watching the incident and egging Kavanaugh on, fell on top of them. She fled to a bathroom and locked herself in, waiting until she heard the two boys going down the stairs before leaving the house.

Before and after her testimony, Ford was subjected to intense efforts to undermine her credibility. Republican supporters of Judge Kavanaugh, including President Donald Trump, attempted to portray Ford as a liar, mentally unstable, and/or a paid Democratic operative. President Trump, himself accused of sexual misconduct by more than a dozen women, mocked Ford at a campaign rally for her failure to recall details of the night of the alleged assault.

By the time Ford testified, her private information had been posted online, her email had been hacked and used to send out messages in her name recanting her allegation, and she had received death threats that forced her and her husband and sons to leave their home. According to a statement issued by her lawyers a few days before her testimony, 'Despite actual threats to her safety and her life, Dr. Ford believes it is important for senators to hear directly from her about the sexual assault committed against her' (Stolberg & Fandos, 2018). For several months, she was not able to return to her home or her job as a university professor (North, 2018). Like Cassandra, Ford felt compelled to speak the truth even though she knew she would not be believed. Faced with credible threats of physical harm, including death, Ford nonetheless chose, like Philomela, to testify about the violence she suffered at the hands of a powerful man. Like Scheherazade, Ford's storytelling held the power to save other women.

Conclusion

On February 7, 2018, then-House Minority Leader Nancy Pelosi spoke for eight hours, uninterrupted, in an effort to convince House Republicans to allow a vote on an immigration bill to protect Dreamers, undocumented young people who were brought to the United States as children, from deportation (Gambino, 2018). It was the longest speech in House history. Pelosi used most of the time to read from letters from Dreamers, telling their stories of their childhoods, their hopes for the future, their love of America. Pelosi's speech did not achieve its desired aim, but the image of the 77-year-old Pelosi, standing in four-inch stiletto heels, taking no breaks and speaking without interruption for eight straight hours, earned widespread media coverage. Only a day before, #MeToo founder Tarana Burke gave an interview to *Quartz* magazine in which she stated, 'Sometimes we have to tell our stories to help other people and give them permission to tell theirs, right? Sometimes we have to tell our stories for ourselves, or in service of other people' (Fessler, 2018). Though Burke was speaking of the #MeToo movement, her words apply equally to Nancy Pelosi's historic speech and many modern-day Scheherazade moments: women harnessing the power of speech to elicit humanity from their audience, both on their own behalf and on behalf of others.

Men have always tried to silence women. Women's speech has been both feared and hated throughout history, and with good reason: women's speech has the power to testify, to warn, and, perhaps most importantly, to change the world as we know it. This is especially true of women's speech about the abuses of men. From witch hunts to angry anti-suffragist mobs to online harassment campaigns, men have made their animosity towards women's speech clear. Even as free speech absolutism has become cultural and legal orthodoxy, one form of speech has been consistently treated as too frightening, too provocative, too injurious to tolerate: women's speech about men's abuses. Because although women's speech about sexual abuse has never encouraged armed protesters to march through peaceful towns waving swastikas and Confederate flags, or promoted the murder of people of color or religious minorities as they gather in their places of worship, or prompted anyone to send bombs to people whose political views they disagree with, it nonetheless poses a threat that some consider even greater than all of these: a world in which women are equals to men.

The myths of Cassandra, Philomela, and Scheherazade do more than underscore the suffering women endure for speaking truth to power. They also demonstrate that women will not, in the end, remain silent and that suppressing women's speech comes at great cost to us all. Tereus' violent attempt to silence Philomela ultimately fails, and the repeated refusal of the Trojans to heed Cassandra's warnings leads to the destruction of the world as they knew it. #MeToo signifies women's defiance of the violent attempts to suppress and discredit their speech. Whatever else the #MeToo movement teaches us, it is that there are thousands of

Cassandras, Philomelas, and Scheherazades in the world—telling stories to bear witness, to warn of danger, or to save their lives—and that we ignore them at our collective peril.

References

Anonymous. (2008). *Arabian nights*. (M. C. Lyons & U. L. Lyons, Trans.). London: Penguin.

Fessler, L. (2018, February 6). Tarana Burke, creator of Me Too, believes you don't have to sacrifice everything for a cause. *Quartz*. Retrieved December 20, 2018, from https://qz.com/work/1193569/me-too-movement-creator-tarana-burke-says-you-dont-have-to-sacrifice-everything-for-a-cause/.

Gambino, L. (2018, February 8). Nancy Pelosi's eight-hour speech: An attempt to persuade GOP on immigration. *The Guardian*. Retrieved December 20, 2018, from https://www.theguardian.com/us-news/2018/feb/08/nancy-pelosi-gives-record-eight-hour-speech-on-dreamers.

North, A. (2018, November 8). Christine Blasey Ford has a security detail because she still receives threats. *Vox*. Retrieved December 20, 2018, from https://www.vox.com/2018/11/8/18076154/christine-blasey-ford-threats-kavanaugh-gofundme.

Ovid. (1998). *Metamorphoses* (J. Dryden, Trans.). Ware: Wordsworth Editions.

Quintus Smyrnaeus. (1913). *The fall of troy* (A. S. Way, Trans.). Cambridge, MA: Harvard University Press.

Stolberg S., & Fandos, N. (2018, September 23). Christine Blasey Ford reaches deal to testify at Kavanaugh hearing. *New York Times*. Retrieved December 20, 2018, from https://www.nytimes.com/2018/09/23/us/politics/brett-kavanaugh-christine-blasey-ford-testify.html.

Part II

Whose Bodies Matter? #MeToo and the Politics of Inclusion

7

From 'Me Too' to 'Too Far'? Contesting the Boundaries of Sexual Violence in Contemporary Activism

Bianca Fileborn and Nickie Phillips

The explosion of #MeToo in late 2017 was arguably a long overdue reckoning and watershed moment in sexual violence activism, not least of all because it opened up space for (some) survivors to share experiences that have all too rarely featured in public discussion. Experiences that had previously remained hidden, minimized, or dismissed—those located within the so-called murky 'gray' area or deemed too 'trivial' to warrant mention—were brought to light via mass, shared disclosures. Importantly, #MeToo provided a context in which, for at least some survivors, these disclosures were taken seriously, validated, and believed (see Mendes & Ringrose, this collection). Yet, simultaneously (and seemingly instantaneously), others have attempted to push back against this expansion of

B. Fileborn (✉)
University of Melbourne, Parkville, VIC, Australia
e-mail: biancaf@unimelb.edu.au

N. Phillips
Sociology & Criminal Justice, American Studies, St. Francis College,
Brooklyn Heights, NY, USA
e-mail: nphillips@sfc.edu

© The Author(s) 2019
B. Fileborn, R. Loney-Howes (eds.), *#MeToo and the Politics of Social Change*,
https://doi.org/10.1007/978-3-030-15213-0_7

'what counts' as sexual violence through claims that the #MeToo movement has gone 'too far'.

In this chapter we examine how various key moments in #MeToo represent a process through which the boundaries of what constitutes sexual violence are destabilized. #MeToo provided a moment of rupture in which definitions of sexual violence are simultaneously opened up and pulled back toward more conservative understandings. Drawing on scholar Liz Kelly's (1988) continuum of sexual violence and poststructuralist accounts of the role of language, we critique claims that the movement has gone 'too far'. Rather, we argue for the need to further open up the parameters of sexual violence in a way that centers victim-survivors' experiences, resists bounded, hierarchical definitions, and accounts for sexual violence in its full complexity and 'messiness'. In short, we argue that rather than having gone 'too far', the #MeToo movement is yet to go far enough in its potential to open up understandings of sexual violence.

From Watershed to Witch Hunt

One of the most consistent findings in research on sexual violence is the historical reluctance of survivors to come forward, to speak out, and report their experiences (Lievore, 2003). This pattern of underreporting is embedded in legal, cultural, and social conditions that reward silence and submission in the service of maintaining the status quo (Alcoff, 2018). In this context, the #MeToo movement is a long overdue reckoning.

Yet, the movement has not been without its critics. To say that the backlash against #MeToo was swift is an understatement. In fact, the discursive arc of #MeToo began to shift almost immediately. Testimonials that initially brought to light institutionalized abuse and patterns of gendered harassment, violence, and exclusion were followed by counterclaims cautioning a moral panic, witch hunt, and mob rule. For instance, on the same day that actress Alyssa Milano encouraged survivors to tweet #MeToo to 'give a sense of magnitude to the problem', prominent Hollywood director Woody Allen (who has himself faced allegations of sexual abuse from his adopted daughter, Dylan Farrow) cautioned against a 'witch hunt atmosphere, a Salem atmosphere, where every guy in an office who winks at a woman is suddenly having to call a lawyer to defend himself' (Chow, 2017).

Following Allen's remarks, claims of a witch hunt, moral panic, and sex panic became relatively commonplace. Between the publication of the initial Weinstein article in October and December 2017, when *Time* magazine's Person of the Year issue featured The Silence Breakers—that is, those who went on the record with their allegations—several mainstream media articles queried whether the movement had 'gone too far'.[1] A focus on survivor claims shifted toward the plight of the accused, confusion around consent and 'flirtation', consequences of informal social sanctions, alarms around the erosion of due process, and warnings of false allegations.

Much of the backlash could be characterized as oppositional rhetoric rooted in anti-feminism. That is, counter-claims were often hyperbolic and gendered, invoking feminist overreach, hysteria, and irrationality (Berlinski, 2017; Sommers, 2017; Shrier, 2018). As the witch-hunt narrative unfolded, the movement was linked to other historical atrocities such as McCarthyism, claims of satanic panic, and other moral panics.[2] For example, political commentator Bill Maher stated, 'I'm down with #MeToo, I'm not down with #MeCarthyism' (Moran, 2018; Young, 2018). Other headlines cautioned, 'Ladies, Let's Be Reasonable About #MeToo Or Nothing Will Ever Be Sexy Again', 'Beware the Long Reach of #MeToo', and 'It's Time to Resist the Excesses of #MeToo' (Editorial Board, 2017; Petri, 2018; Sullivan, 2018).

---

[1] In a search of newspaper commentary and editorials from October 2017 to June 2018, much of the commentary reinforced activists' concerns while about 26% of the commentaries were critical of the movement. In this limited sample, #MeToo was used as a framework for discussing a variety of issues including the difficulty of filing workplace harassment claims, forced arbitration, and the persistent gender pay gap. The discussions extended to the plight of low-wage workers and exposed entrenched systems of enablers in a variety of industries including religious and political institutions. The issue was discussed as both a domestic problem and a global problem implicating human rights violations.

[2] McCarthyism refers to the campaign in the 1950s led by US Senator Joseph McCarthy who, without evidence, falsely accused individuals of being communist and infiltrating the government. His fear-mongering campaign led to blacklists and job losses.

Delineating the 'Boundaries' of Sexual Violence

In counteracting and making sense of these claims that #MeToo has gone 'too far' we need to examine two interrelated concepts. Firstly, what is sexual violence? How do we best define and understand what sexual violence 'is' and whose experiences 'count'? Secondly, we need to examine the role that discourse—that is, the language made available to us via particular social structures and institutions to label, express, and make sense of our experiences—plays in shaping sexual violence.

Dominant understandings of sexual violence tend to frame this behavior in a dualistic way: something either does or does not meet the criteria for 'being' sexual violence. Processes of recognition are likewise mired in structural inequalities, with the experiences of white, middle-class, cisgender, heterosexual women more likely to be constructed as legitimate (something that has arguably been replicated through #MeToo—see Loney-Howes; Ison; Ryan, this collection): 'legitimate' experiences of sexual violence are situated within the interplay between *what* happened and *who* it happened to.

Dualistic constructions of sexual violence were often expressed in #MeToo commentary as a criticism of the movement's tendency to blur the lines, erase distinctions, or trivialize legitimate complaints. For example, political commentator Andrew Sullivan critiqued that #MeToo has 'extended to more ambiguous and trivial cases' where 'righteous exposure of hideous abuse of power had morphed into a more generalized revolution against the patriarchy' (Sullivan, 2018). Similarly, *New York Times* columnist Bari Weiss described 'legitimate' #MeToo complaints as clear cut, such as those involving men forcing themselves on victims or instances such as a 'factory floor supervisor who demanded sex'. She simultaneously encouraged the movement to dismiss experiences of 'lousy romantic encounters' and 'bad sex' (Weiss, 2018).

Public debate over what counts as sexual violence was perhaps most prominently sparked in the aftermath of an article detailing a young woman's date with Aziz Ansari (Bennett, 2018). As detailed in the introductory chapter, when 'Grace's' account of her date with Ansari was published on Babe.net, a flurry of commentary appeared addressing the complexities around sexual consent and coercion. Grace's account was interpreted by some as a simple case of a regretful one-night stand and signaled that women were wielding their 'temporary power' in a dangerous way. For example, journalist Caitlin Flanagan wrote, 'What she felt afterward—rejected yet another time, by yet another man—was regret'. Describing the incident through the lens of a generational divide, Flanagan acknowledged that many contemporary young women reported having experiences that were 'frighteningly and infuriatingly similar' to those of Grace, but dismissed her account as '3,000 words of revenge porn' (Flanagan, 2018).

Others have acknowledged the journalistic shortcomings of the Babe. net article but emphasized that the incident might best be viewed as facilitating a broader discussion of 'sex, male entitlement and misogyny in the bedroom' (Filipovic, 2018). These conversations would lead to greater understandings of how the gendered power dynamics at play in hook-up culture result in women being far more likely than men to feel dissatisfied, if not victimized, in the aftermath of these encounters (Loofbourow, 2018; Wade, 2017).

As some of the commentary surrounding the Ansari incident illustrates, attempting to construct very firm boundaries around what sexual violence 'is' suggests that sexual violence can be easily delineated from non-violence (or, in this case, consensual sexual activity). Under this line of thinking, what sexual violence 'is' tends to be informed by stereotypical notions, often referred to as rape myths. These myths and stereotypes typically paint 'real' sexual violence as requiring the use of physical force or overt violence, as perpetrated by a monstrous stranger and as involving penetration (usually a penis penetrating a vagina). Moreover, 'real' sexual violence requires unambiguous refusal on the victim-survivors' behalf: a clear, verbal 'no' or physical resistance.

However, this way of understanding sexual violence has been thoroughly challenged by feminist scholarship and the nature of victim-survivors' experiences. Liz Kelly's widely used continuum model of sexual violence is particularly useful in drawing out the limitations of dualistic constructions of sexual violence. For Kelly, the continuum is not one of ranking severity or seriousness but rather recognizing the linkage between specific forms of sexual violence to 'more common everyday aspects of male behavior' (1988, p. 75). Kelly emphasized that prevalent forms of everyday harassment and intimidation share underlying mechanisms of coercion, abuse, and force that are extensions of normalized heterosexual behaviors. That is, gendered relations rooted in patriarchy structure our understandings of behaviors ranging from consensual sex to rape. Additionally, seemingly diffuse forms of sexual violence are drawn together by the fact that they all work to deny or circumscribe victim-survivors' sexual and bodily autonomy. Despite this interconnectedness, only a narrow range of these experiences are legitimized as 'real' sexual violence in dominant discourse.

The continuum likewise views sexual violence as a lived *process*, meaning that the ways in which we make sense of experiences can shift over time. Our experiences of individual incidents are shaped by what has come before and what comes after and should not be viewed in an isolated, decontextualized way. As such, claims of #MeToo that highlight experiences involving pressured sex (as opposed to rape allegations) tend to be held up as examples of how the movement has gone too far—despite efforts of feminist scholars to theorize how these behaviors exist along a continuum of harm, to demonstrate the ways in which this array of behaviors are embedded within the social and cultural fabric of our society, and to capture the nuance and complexity of lived experience.

Reconstructing the Boundaries of Sexual Violence

Post-structuralist feminist accounts are likewise productive in challenging dualistic views of sexual violence/non-violence. In particular, such accounts suggest that there is no underlying, stable category of 'sexual violence'. As scholars Heberle and Grace (2009, p. 2) explain, 'there is no singular form that sexual violence can be reduced to even as we seek to make it visible as an unjust and damaging action'. Rather, our understandings of what sexual violence 'is' and what behaviors or experiences 'count' within this category are fluid, shifting, and changing over time to open up (or close down) different ways of understanding.

Indeed, the Ansari case provides an example of this fluidity in action. While there was considerable backlash to the Ansari case, and claims that Grace's experience was merely 'bad sex' rather than sexual violence, we simultaneously witnessed the emergence of public discussion about the complexities of consent, sex, and sexual violence—a discussion that opened up space for experiences such as Grace's to be recognized as a form of sexual harm. The mainstream, public debate dedicated toward the Ansari case represents a moment in which dominant understandings of sexual violence were contested, the boundaries of inclusion shifting, perhaps ever so slightly.

This brings us to the second, related point: the role of discourse or language in shaping lived 'realities' or understandings of sexual violence. As academic Linda Alcoff (2018, p. 3) puts it in her book on *Rape and Resistance*:

> Language itself is part of the practice, part of what makes it possible, part of what makes it meaningful, part of what gives people ideas of what they can do and of what they have just experienced.

In suggesting that discourse shapes our experiences and understandings of sexual violence, this does not mean that language is the only factor informing our reality or that sexual violence is something that is *only* brought into existence through language. The act of sexual violence involves very real things happening '*to, with, and through bodies*', as one of us has argued elsewhere (Fileborn, 2016, p. 9). Rather, as Swedish scholar Lena Gunnarsson (2018) explains, discourse can be understood as co-constructing sexual violence: it is the conversation between language and bodily experience that matters here. While sexual violence involves very tangible things happening to our bodies, how we understand or make sense of these experiences, and whether we recognize and label our experiences as 'counting' as sexual violence, is deeply implicated in the language available to us. The extent to which our experiences 'fit' dominant understandings of sexual violence—such as those constructed through the criminal justice system or through rape myths—may limit our ability to recognize and label our experience as such (Loney-Howes, 2018).

Yet, a mismatch between our lived experience and discourse may equally expose the limitations of these dominant understandings and the language available to express experience (Gunnarsson, 2018): we may well question, why *doesn't* my experience count, or why *doesn't* the language available to me adequately reflect or communicate my experience? While language can be limiting, it can also be contested and resisted. Perhaps most importantly, the language we have to capture and express sexual violence can *change*. Of course, language is not neutral: it typically reflects the interests of particular, powerful groups. The language that has traditionally been available to us in articulating sexual violence has tended to exclude or minimize all but the most unambiguous, 'serious' experiences. As such, it is unsurprising that current dominant accounts of sexual violence tend to exclude many experiences and generally fail to capture Kelly's continuum model.

The notion that sexual violence is clearly defined and bounded, with only certain experiences recognized, works to silence others from coming forward (Alcoff, 2018). Resultantly, not only are particular experiences un(der)recognized, those who perpetrate these actions are not held to account, and the underlying power structures and norms remain unexamined. This suggests that the debate around #MeToo having gone 'too far' can be understood as a site of power struggle and contestation. #MeToo provides a contemporary example of the *processes* through which our language and understandings of sexual violence expand and evolve: sexual violence activism can work to rupture and reform the boundaries of sexual violence. Yet, #MeToo also illustrates the ways in which this process is resisted and contested—our ways of understanding sexual violence *simultaneously* expanding and contracting (see also Rosewarne, this collection).

This process of contestation over what behaviors are considered socially harmful was perhaps most clearly illustrated in an open letter signed by over 100 French women, including renowned actress Catherine Deneuve, academics, writers, and other high-profile individuals. Originally published in the French outlet *Le Monde*, the authors constructed clear boundaries between 'legitimate' acts of sexual violence and 'seduction', with men whose behavior falls within the latter category finding themselves placed 'in the exact same category as sex offenders...when their only crime was to touch a woman's knee, try to steal a kiss...or send sexually-charged messages to women who did not return their interest' (Chiche, Millet, Robbe-Grillet, Sastre, & Shalmani, 2018). The authors collectively defended 'a freedom to *bother* as indispensable to sexual freedom' (original emphasis), especially, the authors claim, given 'we' are capable of distinguishing 'between an awkward attempt to pick someone up and what constitutes a sexual assault' (Chiche et al., 2018). Curiously, the authors argued that acts such as a man rubbing up against a woman on the subway may be considered 'as the expression of a great sexual deprivation, or even as a non-event', while simultaneously acknowledging that such an encounter may be an 'offensive' one (Chiche et al., 2018).

The French letter provides an exemplar of the role of language in shaping sexual violence, with the authors' claims working to close down the expanding boundaries of sexual violence in the #MeToo movement. The letter reframes sexual violence and harassment as 'normal', 'consensual' behavior: a discursive power-play that reaffirms the pre-existing normative boundaries of sexual violence.

Rather than acknowledging the ways in which women experience these unwanted, harassing, or non-consensual encounters as problematic, they are instead positioned as examples of 'seduction', with the right for men to 'bother' women in this way essential to heteronormative sexual encounters. Such reframing minimizes and downplays the harms of these actions, as expressed by countless individuals through #MeToo. It fails to recognize the interconnections between these 'flirtatious' acts and the continuum of sexual violence. In framing such encounters as 'awkward attempts' to initiate a sexual encounter arising from 'sexual deprivation', this evades any critical interrogation of the actions of these men and the power structures underpinning them. Rather, it positions #MeToo as about sexual morality and as 'anti-sex', rather than as concerned with the ways in which 'sex and power intersect' (Gill & Orgad, 2018, p. 5). When such encounters are labelled as a 'non-event', this limits the ability of victims to articulate these admittedly often 'messy' or 'gray' experiences as *harmful* or problematic ones.

Notably, the letter was impactful, in part, because it was penned and signed by women. Like much pushback against #MeToo by self-described feminists, the letter suggests that to consider acts short of rape as harmful is to embrace perpetual victimhood, something second-wave feminists were accused of perpetuating (see Loney-Howes, this collection). Invoking the witch-hunt narrative, the letter warns that the movement has severely curtailed men's 'freedom to offend', subjecting them to a totalitarian climate, mired by guilt and under threat of purge for mere 'inappropriate behavior' (Chiche et al., 2018). The letter lays bare the fractures in feminism around the concept of victimhood and demonstrates how the movement disrupts dominant notions of who may claim victimhood status that are rooted in patriarchal, racialized gender norms and reinforced by persistent rape myths. In the process, the letter raises some interesting questions regarding how the actions of these men *should* be constructed: are they perpetrators or merely 'normal' men attempting to engage in acceptable forms of (hetero)sexual seduction? We turn to this question in the following section.

Rethinking 'Perpetration'

If #MeToo challenges the boundaries of what constitutes sexual violence, it equally follows that we must critically rethink popular notions of who may be considered a perpetrator and in the process confront destructive and dehumanizing myths. For instance, if behaviors that have previously been cast as forms of 'seduction' and 'normal' aspects of heteronormative sexual encounters are being reframed as problematic, this requires us to reconsider the comforting, but inaccurate, myth of the 'monster' predator.

In fact, #MeToo testimonials have shattered this myth by offering widespread recognition that sexual violence is often experienced between and among individuals known to each other (Krebs et al., 2016; Planty, Langton, Krebs, Berzofsky, & Smiely-McDonald, 2013). For example, the most high-profile instances of sexual violence exposed by #MeToo implicate men who have held positions of power and confirm that harms commonly arise not from strangers but from those in close proximity and who wield power over others' social and economic well-being (Johnson,

Widnall, & Benya, 2018). Recognizing this—and taking into account the full continuum of sexual violence, including those forms commonly positioned as 'trivial'—forces us to rethink who perpetrates abuse, how we label those who engage in this behavior, and how we respond to these incidents. Indeed, even in writing this chapter, we struggled to find the appropriate language to capture these actions: in some instances, 'perpetrator' or 'offender' seems too legalistic. Yet, terms such as 'aggressor' or 'transgressor' sometimes fail to adequately convey the harm of these actions. Again, we find ourselves lacking the language to capture and express the full complexity of these experiences.

Other accusations flowing from #MeToo further disrupt stereotypes of who is a 'perpetrator' and who is a 'victim'. These involve accusations against women and other feminist allies who are called out for engaging in harassment, sexual coercion, and sexual assault (see also Cover; Ison; Newman & Haire, this collection). For instance, Italian actress Asia Argento was among the first of many women to speak out against Harvey Weinstein and was considered a prominent figure in the movement (Severson, 2018). However, it was later revealed that Argento herself was accused of committing sexual assault and had paid hundreds of thousands of dollars to silence her male accuser. The sexual assault allegedly occurred in 2013 and the victim was then 17-year-old actor Jimmy Bennett (at the time, underage in California). Argento denies the assault. In his public statement explaining his reluctance to come forward, Bennett echoed one of many social constraints faced by victims of sexual violence:

> At the time I believed there was still a stigma to being in the situation as a male in our society. I didn't think that people would understand the event that took place from the eyes of a teenage boy. (Thomas, 2018)

Research has shown that men, and boys, are reluctant to report claims of sexual assault. As such, they are undercounted and under-researched (Abdullah-Khan, 2008). Rather than view these revelations as a simple gender-flip, they expose how heteronormative scripts and gendered norms limit our ability to recognize and account for a range of social harms. As more men engage with #MeToo, the opportunity increases to examine how, in a patriarchal society, sexual coercion, harassment, and sexual assault are experientially different for men and women (Gavey, 2005).

As the discourse disrupts dominant notions of who is considered a 'victim' and 'perpetrator', the movement reveals widespread and deep ambiguity around appropriate policy responses. While there are, at times, public calls for punitive responses that invoke carceral feminism, for the most part, the #MeToo movement has exposed a long-standing tendency for discourse to devolve into what philosopher Kate Manne calls 'himpathy'—undue sympathy for victimizers that sustains patriarchy by reinforcing gendered norms and expectations (Manne, 2018). Here, the promising future of the accused is at the forefront of discussion, reflecting concern about how allegations cast one's legacy and potential social contributions into doubt.

Despite claims that #MeToo is a 'witch hunt', goes 'too far', and runs the risk of destroying the careers of (supposedly) innocent or otherwise undeserving men, it would seem such fears have not borne out in practice (see also Franks, this collection). In 2018, nominee to the United States Supreme Court, Brett Kavanaugh, was accused of attempted rape by Christine Blasey Ford and sexual misconduct by at least two others. Despite testimony by Ford under oath before the Senate Judiciary Committee (and after the refusal to allow others who would offer corroboration to testify), Senator Mitch McConnell dismissed the allegations and declared to supporters that Kavanaugh will nonetheless be confirmed to the position. He stated, '…don't get rattled by all of this. We're going to plow right through it….' (Collins, 2018). This declaration proved to be accurate, with Kavanaugh successfully appointed.

Indeed, less than a year out of the #MeToo movement, comebacks were on the horizon for other men in prominent positions of power such as Matt Lauer and Charlie Rose, and both Louis C.K. and Aziz Ansari performed 'comeback' comedy sets (Arnold, 2018). Notably, these second chances are available irrespective of whether the accused has expressed remorse. As author Roxane Gay opined in *The New York Times*, it is the victims who are expected to offer a path to redemption, even when those seeking it lack contrition (Gay, 2018). This of course raises a series of difficult questions regarding what consequences these men *should* face in being held to account, particularly for those whose actions fall outside the remit of the criminal law. A detailed discussion of this is, unfortunately, beyond the scope of this chapter. Certainly, we do not intend to promote overly punitive carceral criminal justice responses here, particularly given these are also tied up in a range of oppressive power relations with regard to race and class. Rather, we aim to illustrate the overarching *lack* of consequences for these men in light of fears that they would be excessively punished (see also Rosewarne, this collection).

#MeToo: Not Far Enough

Returning to both Linda Alcoff and Lena Gunnarsson, what all of this suggests is that we need to evolve the language and mainstream concepts available to express and capture the diverse, complex array of sexually violent experiences. While #MeToo has provided a moment of rupture in which understandings of sexual violence have expanded and contracted, many forms of sexual violence continue to be minimized, trivialized, and excused—positioned as outside the bounds of 'real' violence. We echo Alcoff's claim that 'we need to *complexify* our understanding of what counts as sexual violence and move away from simplistic binary categories and simplistic claims' (2018, p. 12). On a similar note, Gunnarsson (2018, p. 6) argues that we require new ways of talking about sex and sexual violence 'that can better do justice to the complexities…and the grey area in between'. We have demonstrated that public discourse is currently in the nascent stages of this process, and it is in this light that we argue #MeToo has not gone far enough.

Throughout this chapter, we documented how the movement simultaneously expands and restricts whose experiences count and what is recognized as sexual violence. In the process, we have shown that despite fears to the contrary, in our patriarchal social order there is a significant amount of 'himpathy' for those who are accused and scarce accountability. We have shown that #MeToo exposed how many individuals continue to maintain a vested interest in reinforcing normative sexual behaviors that delineate sharp boundaries around 'what sexual violence is' for the purposes of benefiting those in positions of power. It is our task to continue to create space that acknowledges and takes seriously experiences that do not sit within dominant accounts of sexual violence but are nonetheless harmful, problematic, or unethical: to open up the boundaries such that all survivors are able to say 'yes, me too'.

References

Abdullah-Khan, N. (2008). *Male rape: The emergence of a social and legal issue.* London: Palgrave Macmillan.

Alcoff, L. (2018). *Rape and resistance.* Oxford: Polity Press.

Arnold, A. (2018, August 21). What's going on with Avital Ronnell, the prominent theorist accused of harassment? *The Cut.* Retrieved September 24, 2018, from https://www.thecut.com/2018/08/avital-ronell-professor-accused-of-harassment-what-to-know.html.

Bennett, J. (2018, February 23). The #MeToo moment: Navigating sex in the 'gray zone'. *New York Times.* Retrieved September 24, 2018, from https://www.nytimes.com/2018/02/23/us/the-metoo-moment-navigating-sex-in-the-gray-zone.html?emc=edit_tnt_20180224&nlid=73413358&tntemail0=y.

Berlinski, C. (2017, December 7). We're on a sexual harassment warlock hunt. *USA Today.* Retrieved September 24, 2018, from https://www.usatoday.com/story/opinion/2017/12/07/sexual-harassment-warlock-hunt-editorials-debates/108413460/.

Chiche, S., Millet, C., Robbe-Grillet, C., Sastre, P., & Shalmani, A. (2018, January 9). Nous défendons une liberté d'importuner, indispensable à la liberté sexuelle. *Le Monde* (Translated by Wordcrunch). Retrieved September 10, 2018, from https://www.worldcrunch.com/opinion-analysis/full-translation-of-french-anti-metoo-manifesto-signed-by-catherine-deneuve.

Chow, A. (2017, October 15). Woody Allen warns of 'witch hunt' over Weinstein, then tries to clarify. *New York Times.* Retrieved September 24, 2018, from https://www.nytimes.com/2017/10/15/movies/woody-allen-harvey-weinstein-witch-hunt.html.

Collins, E. (2018, September 21). McConnell: We're going to 'plow right through' and get Kavanaugh confirmed despite assault allegation. *USA Today.* Retrieved September 28, 2018, from https://www.usatoday.com/story/news/politics/2018/09/21/mitch-mcconnell-were-going-plow-right-through-ford-allegation/1380905002/.

Editorial Board. (2017, November 7). Beware the long reach of #MeToo. *Chicago Tribune*. Retrieved September 24, 2018, from http://www.chicago-tribune.com/news/opinion/editorials/ct-edit-metoo-weinstein-harass-20171102-story.html.

Fileborn, B. (2016). *Reclaiming the night-time economy: Unwanted sexual attention in pubs & clubs*. London: Palgrave Macmillan.

Filipovic, J. (2018, January 17). The poorly reported Aziz Ansari exposé was a missed opportunity. *The Guardian*. Retrieved September 24, 2018, from https://www.theguardian.com/commentisfree/2018/jan/16/aziz-ansari-story-missed-opportunity.

Flanagan, C. (2018, January 14). The humiliation of Aziz Ansari. *The Atlantic*. Retrieved September 24, 2018, from https://www.theatlantic.com/entertainment/archive/2018/01/the-humiliation-of-aziz-ansari/550541/.

Gavey, N. (2005). *Just sex? The cultural scaffolding of rape*. London and New York: Routledge.

Gay, R. (2018, August 29). Louis C.K. and men who think justice takes as long as they want it to. *New York Times*. Retrieved September 28, 2018, from https://www.nytimes.com/2018/08/29/opinion/louis-ck-comeback-justice.html.

Gill, R., & Orgad, S. (2018). The shifting terrain of sex and power: From the 'sexualization of culture' to #MeToo. *Sexualities*, online first.

Gunnarsson, L. (2018). "Excuse me, but are you raping me now?" Discourse and experience in (the grey areas of) sexual violence. *NORA—Nordic Journal of Feminist and Gender Research, 26*(1), 4–18.

Heberle, R. J., & Grace, V. (2009). Introduction: Theorizing sexual violence: Subjectivity and politics in late modernity. In R. J. Heberle & V. Grace (Eds.), *Theorizing sexual violence* (pp. 1–13). New York and Oxon: Routledge.

Johnson, P., Widnall, S., & Benya, F. (Eds.) (2018). *Sexual harassment of women climate, culture, and consequences in academic sciences, engineering, and medicine*. Washington, DC: Committee on the Impacts of Sexual Harassment in Academic Science, Engineering, and Medicine, Committee on Women in Science, Engineering, and Medicine, Policy and Global Affairs, National Academies of Sciences, Engineering, and Medicine. National Academies Press. https://doi.org/10.17226/24994.

Kelly, L. (1988). *Surviving sexual violence*. Cambridge: Polity Press.

Krebs, C., Lindquist, C., Berzofsky, M., Shook-Sa, B., Peterson, K., Planty, M., & Stroop, J. (2016, January 19). *Campus climate survey validation study final technical report*. Washington, DC: RTI International and Bureau of Justice Statistics. Retrieved from http://www.bjs.gov/content/pub/pdf/ccsvsftr.pdf.

Lievore, D. (2003). *Non-reporting and hidden recording of sexual assault: An international literature review*. Canberra: Australian Institute of Criminology.

Loney-Howes, R. (2018). Shifting the rape script: "Coming out" online as a rape victim. *Frontiers: A Journal of Women Studies, 39*(2), 26–57.

Loofbourow, L. (2018, January 25). The female price of male pleasure. *The Week*. Retrieved September 24, 2018, from http://theweek.com/articles/749978/female-price-male-pleasure.

Manne, K. (2018). *Down girl: The logic of misogyny*. Oxford University Press.

Moran, L. (2018, January 20). Bill Maher: 'I'm down with #MeToo, I'm not down with #MeCarthyism'. *Huffington Post*. Retrieved September 24, 2018, from https://www.huffingtonpost.com/entry/bill-maher-me-too-movement_us_5a62ed6ce4b002283002ed73.

Petri, A. (2018, January 13). Ladies, let's be reasonable about #MeToo or nothing will ever be sexy again—The Washington Post. *The Washington Post*. Retrieved September 24, 2018, from https://www.washingtonpost.com/blogs/compost/wp/2018/01/13/ladies-lets-be-reasonable-about-metoo-or-nothing-will-ever-be-sexy-again/?noredirect=on&utm_term=.02545a4a08cd.

Planty, M., Langton, L., Krebs, C., Berzofsky, M., & Smiely-McDonald, H. (2013). *Female victims of sexual violence, 1994–2010*. NCJ 240655. Washington, DC: Bureau of Justice Statistics. Retrieved from http://www.bjs.gov/content/pub/pdf/fvsv9410.pdf.

Severson, K. (2018, August 18). Asia Argento, a #MeToo leader, made a deal with her own accuser. *New York Times*. Retrieved September 24, 2018, from https://www.nytimes.com/2018/08/19/us/asia-argento-assault-jimmy-bennett.html.

Shrier, A. (2018, January 16). #MeToo repels men by infantilizing women with petty complaints. *The Federalist*. Retrieved September 24, 2018, from http://thefederalist.com/2018/01/16/metoo-repels-men-infantilizing-women-petty-complaints/.

Sommers, C. (2017, November 26). A panic is not an answer: We're at imminent risk of turning this #metoo moment into a frenzied rush to blame all men. *New York Daily News*. Retrieved September 24, 2018, from http://www.nydailynews.com/opinion/panic-not-answer-article-1.3651778.

Sullivan, A. (2018, January 12). It's time to resist the excesses of #MeToo. *New York Magazine Daily Intelligencer*. Retrieved September 24, 2018, from http://amp.nymag.com/daily/intelligencer/2018/01/andrew-sullivan-time-to-resist-excesses-of-metoo.html?__twitter_impression=true.

Thomas, M. (2018, August 23). Asia Argento's accuser speaks out. *CNN*. Retrieved September 24, 2018, from https://www.cnn.com/2018/08/23/entertainment/jimmy-bennett-statement/index.html.

Wade, L. (2017). *American hookup: The new culture of sex on campus*. New York, NY: Norton.

Weiss, B. (2018, January 15). Aziz Ansari is guilty. Of not being a mind reader. *New York Times*. Retrieved September 24, 2018, from https://www.nytimes.com/2018/01/15/opinion/aziz-ansari-babe-sexual-harassment.html.

Young, T. (2018, September 20). Ian Buruma and the age of sexual McCarthyism. *Spectator*. Retrieved November 2, 2018, from https://spectator.us/ian-buruma-nyrb-sexual-mccarthyism/.

8

This Black Body Is Not Yours for the Taking

Tess Ryan

Introduction

This Black body is not yours for the taking. It doesn't belong to you. You don't own it, can't co-opt it, and try as you might, can't destroy it. That is the message that needs to be signaled regarding the #MeToo movement in relation to Black Australian women. The #MeToo movement originated as an idea from a strong African American woman and her fight for justice against abuse, harassment, and assault of Women of Color in the United States in 2006. Tarana Burke has since been applauded for her drive for change; however, it needs to be acknowledged that in the beginning Burke was ignored as the instigator for that change. And for the #MeToo movement in Australia, Indigenous women have once again been forgotten.

#MeToo was initiated by a desire to break down the misuse of power and perpetration of sexual violence that is commonplace and ordinary. #MeToo is a response to women having their power taken away from

T. Ryan (✉)
Australian Catholic University, Melbourne, VIC, Australia

B. Fileborn, R. Loney-Howes (eds.), *#MeToo and the Politics of Social Change*,
https://doi.org/10.1007/978-3-030-15213-0_8

117

them—the power of owning one's body, to walk, work, and live safely in the world. It is also about the power to deal with snide comments about our appearance, responses of 'it was just a joke' to our complaints, and denigrations of our character and femininity. We, as Indigenous, Black, Native, Women of Color, need to respond to those attacks that aim to objectify us and rob us of our power.

When '#MeToo' is expressed from the perspective of a Black Woman, it becomes more than a feminist fight for justice over harassment and assault. It becomes a conversation about intersectionality—the illumination of multiple layers of power and oppression. It brings to light arguments around Black versus White feminism that exist because the experiences of Black Women in fighting against male dominance have a different lens to those of White Women, and White feminists are often blind to this difference in lived experience.

In this chapter, I privilege Aboriginal and Torres Strait Islander (and other Black) women's voices as much as possible, for their wisdom and knowledge in encouraging an ongoing discussion, disruption, and intervention into the ways White Women involved in the feminist movement have in large part conducted themselves for many years. This is not to say that there has been radio silence on the differences (both nuanced and dramatic) within feminist ideology (see, e.g., Liddle, 2016; Maguire, 2015), with many such contributions from Indigenous and Black feminists discussed throughout this chapter. Indeed, the digital platforms that enabled #MeToo have likewise provided space for collective Indigenous and Black feminist voices to demonstrate and challenge the power dynamics embedded within White feminism. However, broader Australian society remains deaf and blind to the numerous behaviors contributing to Black Women's oppression by both men and women, including those within feminist and anti-violence movements. Staunch Aboriginal women have publicly been exerting power for many years, and it is the very position and claims they exude that need to be acknowledged and considered when discussing the #MeToo movement in an Australian Indigenous context.

This inability of White dominant culture to see Black Women's struggle and resilience is an issue that must be addressed. It is also part of a larger discussion about Black bodies—the rendering of us as a statistic, disposable and exploited. The gaze upon Black bodies as deviant, dysfunctional, and problematic has been a narrative born from the colonial project used to justify the need for our removal. In this climate of blame culture that permeates Western society, where women are told not to dress inappropriately, not to walk home alone at night, or not to be too open about their sexuality, it appears it is our own fault that we experience violence. For Indigenous women, the past traumas of sexualization through the settler/colonial period remain raw and have influenced the belief in dominant society that we are domicile, vulnerable, or even disposable in modern life.

Black Women take the brunt of a different level of sexualized and racialized scrutiny. With so much to examine relating to power—the erasure of women's voices, the exploitation and subjugation of the Black body—this chapter highlights these issues through a series of case studies to illuminate the impact on Black Women in Australia and how we use our strength, humor, and resilience to address and resist them.

Initial #MeToo Conversations in Australia with Black Women

In the wake of the #MeToo movement, Aboriginal and Torres Strait Islander women commented on their own experiences, calling out the numerous moments women have had where they have felt unsafe, harassed, or minimized by a man's misuse of their power. Strong Aboriginal feminists such as Nayuka Gorrie (2017) and Celeste Liddle (2018) spoke out, suggesting there needs to be a deeper narrative of the removal and erasure of Black Women's voices and experiences within feminist discourses, as well as an overhaul of the ways systems and institutions respond to violence against Aboriginal women. Many women also spoke of the absence of Black Women's voices in this conversation. In particular, they commented on how Tarana Burke herself was left out in both the preliminary stages of the movement and the institutional domains that contribute to the problem of White Women's dominance over Black Women. Some Indigenous women chose to comment on the lack of an appropriate representative voice in these discussions. Nayuka Gorrie, for example, made a comment on the Australian Broadcasting Company's (ABC) Q&A program addressing the impact of the #MeToo movement, stating: 'Hey @QandA surely you could have gotten women of color on your #metoo panel instead of these white dudes? Fucking hell. What a white wash' (2018).

One cannot ignore the numbers in the violence perpetrated against Black Women, which are devastating, leaving an indelible mark on Indigenous Australian society. A 2016 Productivity Commission report states, 'Aboriginal and Torres Strait Islander women reported experiencing physical or threatened violence in the previous 12 months at 3.1 times the rate of non-Indigenous women' (2016, p. 498). A report from Our Watch further illustrated that 'hospitalisation rates for Aboriginal and Torres Strait Islander women due to family violence-related assaults are 32 times the rate for non-Indigenous women' (2018, p. 6). These numbers relate to real people and lives that have been largely affected by a deeper context of cultural trauma that is ongoing for many. Despite this context, the voices of Indigenous women remained largely absent from mainstream #MeToo debate within Australia.

Historical Representations of Black Women

Representation matters, and so regularly we see poor examples of representation in the public sphere that work to render women as fitting into certain stereotypes. The impact of these representations is further compounded for Aboriginal and Torres Strait Islander women, and there have been countless examples of poor and inaccurate representations of Black Women in Australia's history. Since colonization in Australia, Black Women have been viewed as lascivious and manipulative beasts, erotic curios, and domicile victims at the whims of men. In Australia's dark and largely ignored history, Indigenous women have been exploited and misrepresented, from the time of early 'settlement' to the false representations perpetuated in the media of lascivious victims, drug addled and dependent (Humphreys, 2008, p. 2).

However, Indigenous women have been breaking the silence for years—long before the emergence of #MeToo. They have been screaming out in fact, demanding to be heard by dominant Australian society as being more than someone's fetish. This long history crosses borders and territories, and stories of objectification, sexualization, and oppression are littered throughout Indigenous and First Nations women's lives on a global scale. Indigenous women around the world have shared histories of mistreatment functioning as a form of control and domination, and the perpetuation of sexualized stereotypes of Black and Native women, which works to negate Black Women of their power and strength. For the remainder of this chapter, I discuss some of the ways Black Aboriginal Women in Australia have been constructed as disposable and their voices marginalized, highlighting the ongoing erasure of Women of Color in feminist activism.

'Black Velvet' and 'Gin Jockeys'

Historically, there has been a fascination with the Black body as a tool for subjugation and exploitation, and as an objectifying element used by various oppressors in the dismantling of proud identities. The use of derogatory terms and phrases to diminish women is not new, and Aboriginal and Torres Strait Islander women have had to endure this form of violence just as other First Nations and Native women have throughout history.[1] In Australia during the 1900s, the term 'Black Velvet' was used to describe the smooth skin of Aboriginal/Black Women.[2] In using this term, our Aboriginality and womanhood were viewed as sexual objects for the services they could provide to White men, which produced children who were labeled 'burnt corks' during the colonial era. However, this fetishizing of the Black body was not dissimilar to that which occurred throughout the colonial world.

Aboriginal academic Liz Conor states, 'the presence as much as the absence of "Black Velvet" in print demonstrates how colloquial language was a means for white colonizers to boast ownership over Aboriginal

---

[1] Native American women were regularly called 'Squaw,' which has been thought to refer to a Native woman's vagina, although this appears a contentious point, as some references have been made to the term simply meaning 'young native woman.'

[2] Australian laureate Henry Lawson was quite fond of the term, and it's use in everyday conversation (see 'The Ballad of the Rouseabout', 1900), along with others such as 'gins' (Aboriginal women) and 'gin jockeys' (the white men who associated with them) (Pioneers of Love, 2005).

women's bodies' (Conor, 2013, p. 52). The representations used to type-cast Black Women have become part of the discourse associated with power over women, both within legitimate, widespread formats, like the media, and in the colloquial, everyday terms used against them. The term 'Gin' is one such word of weaponry, used to oppress Indigenous women to imply promiscuity. Yet we reframe these words using our humor, we appropriate what has been done to us, and, in so doing, we show a strength and resilience that cannot be diminished. An example of this can be found in Sandra Phillips' article 'Black Velvet: Redefining and Celebrating Indigenous Women in Art.' Showcasing the art of Indigenous woman, Boneta-Marie Mabo, the work Mabo installed 'spoke back to colonial representations of Indigenous womanhood' (2016, p. 1).

These colonial discourses exist to this day, albeit reframed or subtly suggested within the subtexts of the way Black Women are represented within the media. An example of this can be seen in the reporting of Indigenous women, such as the death of Lynette Daley. Ms. Daley was violently raped and murdered by two men on a beach. Media reports suggested that the 'drunk woman died after vigorous "group sex"' (Sydney Morning Herald, 2017). Describing the rape of a woman as wild sex, as well as mentioning her intoxication, demonstrates a framing of lascivious and willing participation. While this article could be considered mere media sensationalism, the tone of it suggests that Black Women in Australia are willing parties in an exchange involving dominance and power; it positions Aboriginal women as sexually available and 'unrapable.'

Deadly Women's Blues

Recent representations of Black Women have added another layer of complexity to the #MeToo movement, specifically through men's erasure of women's stories to render them powerless. An example of Black Australian women being treated in such ways is evident in how they were blatantly misquoted and misrepresented in the 2018 book, *Deadly Woman Blues*, by Clinton Walker. The book was meant to be a celebration of Black Women in the Australian music industry. Walker, however, failed to tell some of the women he was 'celebrating' that they were included as he did not inform them that he was writing the book, nor did he gain consent to use their stories. Not only that, but he misquoted and misrepresented many, with factual errors about some regarding their histories, and used their talents to capitalize and commodify Black Women's voices.

For example, Aboriginal Opera singer, Deborah Cheetham, was misrepresented in the way her family history was written. Walker had removed elements of Cheetham's story regarding the Stolen Generation and altered history concerning her grandmother's experience of walking off Cummeragunja along with her husband James and 200 other Yorta people in 1939. Cheetham at the time emphatically stated:

> For me, the false statement that I was born on Cummeragunja is particularly distressing, as it denies the experience of my mother Monica who gave birth to me in Nowra District Hospital, only to have me taken from her 3 weeks later. (Cheetham, 2018)

The book was very quickly removed from print, with Walker releasing a statement apologizing for the errors. Walker stated:

> I have been devastated to learn that my failure to consult with many of the women in my book Deadly Women Blues has caused such distress and anguish to them and to their friends and families. (NITV, 2018)

The question must be asked, however, as to how these gross misrepresentations were able to occur, particularly during the height of the #MeToo movement, where (some) women's voices were supposedly valued and promoted? Was the further objectifying of a Black Woman at play here an attempt to assert ownership over a story that the author had no official claim to? Are we as Black Women so disposable that the accuracy of our lives need not be important? If you eliminate the issue of proofreading from the publisher, didn't Walker have a responsibility to check his sources? Or did he simply think that his reimagining of Black Women's history was poetic license for him to create great hooks for his stories? This also speaks to the fetishization and romanticism of Aboriginal women's lives. To change our story is to remove us from it, and replacing our lived and at times painful experiences alters historical frames of power and our responses to that power.

The 'Meanjin Debacle' and *Latte* Magazine

You would think that in the areas of the arts and humanities, there would be some understanding of the rich lived realities of Black Women and their connections to the deeply embedded cultural respect for place, language and spirit. Sadly, literary magazine *Meanjin* failed to get the memo regarding this. *Meanjin* is an Aboriginal place name for the Brisbane region, from the Turbal language. Volume 77, issue number 2, of the publication came out with part of the word *Meanjin* crossed out and replaced to read 'MeToo.' Someone thought this idea to be clever: to remove cultural language so important in Indigenous heritage. This in turn removes the voices of Black Women. It once again undermines lived experiences of language and pride in identity, which adversely affects all Indigenous peoples. But as Indigenous writer Karen Wyld wrote, the 'erasure of Aboriginal and Torres Strait Islander women, the co-opting of the Black grassroots #MeToo movement, and ongoing frustrations with exclusionary feminism' brought with it some difficult yet measured conversations that *Meanjin* magazine needed to hear. On Twitter, for instance, Indigenous women critiqued the erasure, with @NoUluruforYou stating:

> The symbolism of Aboriginal words wiped out to be replaced with a word that represents a movement predominantly for white women—yet stolen from a black woman—just screams of colonisation and I don't even know why it surprises me at all. (Twitter, 2018)

All of this was occurring at a time when Aboriginal and Torres Strait Islander women were receiving widespread recognition of their importance and strength in vocalizing the needs of their communities and keeping culture alive. The year 2018, for example, held a concentrated level of acknowledging the power of Black Women with the National Aboriginal and Islander Day of Celebrations (NAIDOC) theme being 'Because of her, we can.' NAIDOC is run every year during July as a celebration of Indigenous Australians, with a theme appointed each year.

'Because of her, we can' acknowledged the 'mothers, our elders, our grandmothers, our aunties, our sisters and our daughters' that play significant roles in society today (NAIDOC, 2018). This theme acknowledged years of influence, mobilization, leadership, and advocacy of Indigenous women who regularly worked without recognition while raising families for many generations.

Black Women in Australia are often doing the heavy lifting in building stronger communities and lead forcefully in advocating for structural and societal change to occur. They are advocating for basic needs such as water or quality education, or they are pushing for institutional change in the health system. These women regularly work on the front lines but largely go unrecognized. Speaking back to power, screaming out against racism, inequality, and discrimination, feels at times part of our genealogy. So why would a society ignore that, why would other feminists be afraid of that strength, and why would feminist media agendas disregard it so easily?

The cover of *Latte* magazine, a periodical published by 'Business Chicks,' came out during 2017 with numerous women gracing the cover with the caption underneath reading 'Tracey Spicer and the women dismantling discrimination.' Journalist Tracey Spicer had started a new campaign to address harassment and assault called NOW Australia in response to the #MeToo movement, and the women surrounding her in the picture were all part of a cohort working toward ending discrimination against women. The cover, however, failed to include any Women of Color. The discussions surrounding this omission were largely held on the Twittersphere, with Indigenous journalist Amy Maguire and social media platform @indigenousx making comments. Indigenous woman Laura La Rosa wrote an article for *Eureka Street*, stating that while the #MeToo movement:

> Was intended to be collective and accessible. By contrast, in Australia we are increasingly seeing a mainstream picture of women's liberation that ignores a longstanding struggle for diversity, genuine inclusiveness and radicalism. Instead, the movement continues to be appropriated by corporate 'feminists' leveraging themes of oppression to gain various forms of capital. (La Rosa, 2018)

She continued to state that the failures of the movement to reach the fringes and empower women of difference are of concern, and the corporatization of such movements—given their emphasis on institutional rather than social reform—further enforces structural oppression. The erasing of these women in the story of dismantling discrimination further situates Aboriginal women as irrelevant, and considering the statistics of Aboriginal women impacted by violence, this erasure contributes to the construction of Black Women's bodies as disposable. The multiple waves of the women's liberation movements positioned in the White middle-class space progressively build on this narrative, promoting that group's experiences as the only real experience. In doing so, it silences the parallel but different lived experiences of other women.

The Curious Case of Trevor Noah

A significant example of Aboriginal Australian women speaking back to power and misogyny is that directed toward comedian Trevor Noah and a 'joke' he made in 2013, which made derogatory mentions of Black Women in Australia. Unearthed in 2018 via YouTube and since removed, Noah told the joke in response to an article stating that White Women were the most attractive in the world.

> Women of every race can be beautiful… And I know some of you are sitting there now going, 'Oh Trevor… I've never seen a beautiful Aborigine.' But you know what you say? You say, 'Yet.' Because you haven't seen all of them, right? It's not always about the looks, Maybe Aborigine women do special things. Maybe they'll just, like, jump on top of you. (2013)

Noah then made a comment about the Didgeridoo, linking it to oral sex. There is no doubt that these comments were disrespectful, salacious, sexualized, and racialized. They were cheap laughs and easy marks toward targets unable to respond, and sadly commonplace rhetoric when discussing Black femininity.

The power that the digital era has given us is in commentary and voice, and women have fully embraced this to weaponize and speak back in the

#MeToo movement (see Mendes & Ringrose, this collection). As mentioned before, some Black Women in Australia have wholeheartedly adopted this weapon of choice. What Noah didn't understand was that Aboriginal women wouldn't stand for that kind of talk. While these comments were made years ago, due to recent pushing back against power and dominance, there was always going to be backlash once this was unearthed. Once again, social media was the weapon of choice for many female Black commentators, and the comments made in retaliation to the joke were vehement. Writer, actress, and commentator Nakkiah Lui stated:

> Yo @Trevornoah, I'm Beautiful BECAUSE I'm Aboriginal. I'm Strong BECAUSE I'm Aboriginal. I'm Loved BECAUSE I'm Aboriginal. I'm Smart BECAUSE I'm Aboriginal. I am surrounded by Beautiful Aboriginal women who aren't punchlines, they're Warrior Goddesses. (Lui, 2018)

Mental health advocate Joe Williams said:

> Hey @Trevornoah, your comments about Aboriginal @IndigenousX in this clip are utterly unacceptable! As a man of colour, you are usually on point with racism & divide—here you are perpetrating & encouraging racial abuse. (Williams, 2018)

It sadly comes as no surprise that Noah made this joke, even though his own blackness has been commented on in previous years. But it is rather curious for Noah to be so blatantly disrespectful of Women of Color, as he has expressed his love and admiration for his Black South African mother in his memoir *Born a Crime: Stories From a South African Childhood* (2016). Noah's own experiences regarding race and representation, as well as his reverence for his mother for her hard work and progressive attitude, denote a comprehension of the difficulties that surround the Black female body: how a Black body is seen, and how it is unseen, ignored, and disrespected.

The pushback against Noah's comments brought yet again more attention to the ways that, even in light of the #MeToo movement stating that enough is enough, there remains an element of neglect when it comes to

Black Women being given the same levels of respect that non-Black Women may receive. To his credit, Noah joined two Indigenous Australian women on community radio to discuss the joke and subsequent fallout. Dr. Chelsea Bond (a prominent Indigenous Australian academic) and Angelina Hurley host 'Wild Black Women' on *98.9FM Brisbane*. They interviewed Noah and discussed the many ways his comments affect Indigenous Australian women. Dr. Bond explained:

> It's the logic that underpinned the joke… In this country, white men have long joked about their entitlements upon sexual violence towards Aboriginal women… There's really offensive terms that are still used in this country that Aboriginal women are not necessarily desirable or attractive, but they are good for something else and that is all. (Bond, 2018b)

Noah did not provide an apology. In not apologizing and excusing comedy from having to be constrained by social sensitivities, he demonstrated a widespread belief where political correctness is perceived as negative and people's differences are permitted to be ridiculed—as long as it is not a ridiculing of one's own cultural differences. Noah refuses to see the similarity between his own lived experience, such as attempting to relate his mother's experiences of apartheid in South Africa, and that of Aboriginal Women in Australia. In only offering an excuse of his behavior, he entrenches the broader lack of appreciation of women's intersectional experiences of sexualization, racialization, power, and abuse perpetuated by a patriarchal, colonial society.

Black and White Feminism

The 'angry Black woman' syndrome is not just an extension of the feminist killjoy that Sara Ahmed and others have mentioned. The added layer of us as Black Women knowing our place is suggested in the argument against us, that we dare to speak out against White women, White men, and institutions that have 'allowed' us to contribute toward society. As Aboriginal feminist academic, Larissa Behrendt notes:

Feminist theory tends to see the struggle for power as being between men and women. Such theories tend to see Black Women as a sub-set of women, creating a model for the power struggle within society. (Behrendt, 1993, p. 31)

Indigenous Australian academic, Dr. Aileen Moreton-Robinson, further discusses this power exercised by White feminists over Black Women, arguing that Black Women's voices are often ignored within feminism. In particular, she states:

White women who dominate feminist discourse today rarely question if their perspective on women's reality is true to the lived experiences of women as a collective group. Nor are they aware of the extent to which their perspectives reflect race and class biases. (Moreton-Robinson, 2000, p. 3)

Feminism has long been subjected to negative connotations surrounding firm and forthright women, from notions of acting 'too masculine' and being a 'killjoy' for speaking up about gender inequality. Sara Ahmed states, 'The "angry black woman" for instance, can be described as a killjoy; she may even kill feminist joy, for example, by pointing out forms of racism within feminist politics' (2010, p. 257). The idea that any woman be deemed as dangerous or 'angry' by society is an issue that feminists have been discussing for many years. Women of Color globally are positioned as angry when speaking back to power within feminist movements and patriarchal structures more broadly, as we are apparently meant to 'know our place.' Indigenous academic Bronwyn Fredericks posits that dissenting Aboriginal women's voices are marginalized and silenced, and the Aboriginal women who raise concerns are positioned as angry or as aggressive (2010, p. 547). And yet, with all that has been presented before you, which is only a small portion of how we as Black Women are misrepresented and diminished, can you be that surprised? As Dr. Chelsea Bond has stated:

Black Women have long been using anger as compost to fertilise our garden. Black Women have long carried the weight of the multiple, intersecting oppressions of race, class and gender, along with the responsibility to make some good from it. (2018a, p. 1)

The apparent anger seen is resistance; it is holding to account those that attempt to usurp, undermine, and misrepresent us, and we hold it close to our hearts to get things done.

The Long Way to Go

Indigenous women in Australia want to be seen. We are women; some of our issues are just the same as other women and some are very different because of the history of oppressive power that has been exercised over us since colonization. In Australia, we are unable to begin discussing this freely before unpacking the denial that exists regarding colonization and the ignored history that has occurred ever since. In connection to the #MeToo movement and the subsequent movements that have arisen from it, Indigenous women in Australia demand to be heard and seen. But then again, we always have, it is just that our voices and our stories continue to be ignored.

Indigenous women understand power plays better than most. We see someone using their power to perform, or corrupt, and we can look at each other with knowing eyes without speaking. But we do something else also. We hold our stare back at that curious gaze we receive from others: that look of us being romanticized, fetishized, and demonized. And we persist—through our struggles we fight. We find other ways to get in there when doors are closed on us, we navigate through our vulnerabilities, and we challenge people and institutions who seek to avoid hearing us speaking back to power.

References

AAP. (2017, July 31). Mother-of-seven Lynette Daley died after violent group sex, court told. *Sydney Morning Herald*. Retrieved November 11, 2018, from https://www.smh.com.au/national/nsw/motherofseven-lynette-daley-died-after-violent-group-sex-court-told-20170731-gxmkl9.html.
Ahmed, S. (2010). Killing joy: Feminism and the history of happiness. *Signs: Journal of Women in Culture and Society, 35*(3), 571–594.

Australian Screen. (2005). *Pioneers of love*. Retrieved August 10, 2018, from https://aso.gov.au/titles/documentaries/pioneers-love/clip1/.

Behrendt, L. (1993). Aboriginal women and the white lies of the feminist movement: Implications for Aboriginal women in rights discourse. *Australian Feminist Law Journal, 1*(1), 27–44.

Bond, C. (2018a). Chelsea bond: The audacity of anger. *IndigenousX*, Retrieved November 28, 2018, from https://indigenousx.com.au/chelsea-bond-the-audacity-of-anger/#.W_4vtuJoQuU.

Bond, C. (2018b, August 24). Wild black women: Trevor Noah. *98.9fm*. Retrieved September 1, 2018, from https://989fm.com.au/podcasts/lets-talk/wild-black-women-22/.

Cheetham, D. (2018, March 6). The Drum. *ABC News*. Retrieved September 1, 2018, from http://www.abc.net.au/news/2018-03-06/the-drum-tuesday-march-6/9519892.

Conor, L. (2013). 'Black Velvet' and 'Purple Indignation': Print responses to Japanese 'poaching' of Aboriginal women. *Aboriginal History Journal, 37*, 51–76.

Fredericks, B. (2010). Reempowering ourselves: Australian Aboriginal women. *Signs: Journal of Women in Culture and Society, 35*(3), 546–550.

Gorrie, N. (2017, November 7). Post-#MeToo: Creating a culture of support. *NITV*. Retrieved November 10, 2018, from https://www.sbs.com.au/nitv/article/2017/11/07/post-metoo-creating-culture-support-1.

Gorrie, N. @Nayuka. (2018, February 12). Hey @QandA surely you could have gotten women of colour on your #metoo panel instead of these white dudes? Fucking hell. What a white wash. [Twitter post]. Retrieved from https://twitter.com/NayukaGorrie/status/963212412382883840.

Humphreys, A. (2008). *Representations of Aboriginal women and their sexuality*. Unpublished Honour's Thesis, University of Queensland.

La Rosa, L. (2018, June 27). Trickle-down feminism doesn't cut it. *Eureka Street*. Retrieved August 30, 2018, from https://www.eurekastreet.com.au/article.aspx?aeid=55977.

Lawson, H. (1900). The ballad of the Rouseabout. *The Bulletin, 21*(1039), 32.

Liddle, C. (2016, March 9). Looking past White Australia and White Feminism. *New Matilda*. Retrieved August 1, 2018, from https://newmatilda.com/2016/03/09/looking-past-white-australia-and-white-feminism/.

Liddle, C. (2018, June 13). Maimed but not dead: Is an Aboriginal rose a rose by another name? *Independent Australia*. Retrieved November 11, 2018, from https://independentaustralia.net/australia/australia-display/maimed-but-not-dead-is-an-aboriginal-rose-a-rose-by-any-other-name,11594.

Lui, N. (2018, July 27). Comedian Trevor Noah in hot water over sexual Aboriginal women 'joke' pressured to apologise. *SBS*. Retrieved October 23, 2018, from https://www.sbs.com.au/nitv/nitv-news/article/2018/07/23/comedian-trevor-noah-hot-water-over-sexual-aboriginal-women-joke-pressured.

Maguire, A. (2015, March 5). All feminists are created equal, but some are more equal than others. *New Matilda*. Retrieved August 1, 2018, from https://newmatilda.com/2015/03/05/all-feminists-are-created-equal-some-are-more-equal-others/.

Moreton-Robinson, A. (2000). *Talkin' up to the white woman*. St. Lucia, QLD: University of Queensland Press.

NAIDOC. (2018). Retrieved September 1, 2018, from https://www.naidoc.org.au/.

Noah, T. (2013). *Born a crime: Stories from a South African childhood*. New York: Spiegel & Grau. (2013). Cited in Donaldson, M. (2017, February 15). Trevor Noah: Why he owes it all to his Mum. *Stuff*. Retrieved September 4, 2018, from https://www.stuff.co.nz/entertainment/tv-radio/87198967/trevor-noah-why-he-owes-it-all-to-his-mum.

NoUluruForYou. (2018, June 4). The symbolism of Aboriginal words wiped out to be replaced with a word that represents a movement predominantly for ww—yet stolen from a black woman—just screams of colonisation and I don't even know why it surprises me at all. [Twitter post]. Retrieved from https://twitter.com/ChewbeckaSolo/status/1003613966331871232.

Our Watch. (2018). *Changing the picture: A national resource to support the prevention of violence against Aboriginal and Torres Strait Islander women and their children*. Melbourne: Our Watch.

Phillips, S. (2016, May 9). Black Velvet: Redefining and celebrating Indigenous Australian women in art. *The Conversation*. Retrieved November 20, 2018, from https://theconversation.com/black-velvet-redefining-and-celebrating-indigenous-australian-women-in-art-56211.

Steering Committee for the Review of Government Service Provision. (2016). *Overcoming indigenous disadvantage: Key indicators 2016*. Canberra: Productivity Commission.

Williams, J. @JoeWilliams. (2018, July 21). Hey @Trevornoah, your comments about Aboriginal @Indigenousx in this clip are utterly unacceptable! As a man of color, you are usually in point with racism & divide—Here you are perpetrating & encouraging racial abuse! [Twitter post]. Retrieved from https://twitter.com/joewilliams_tew/status/1020918115616501761.

Wyld, K. (2018, June 6). Meanjin debacle: Erasing Aboriginal words in order to highlight white women's appropriation. *NITV*. Retrieved August 3, 2018, from https://www.sbs.com.au/nitv/article/2018/06/06/meanjin-debacle-erasing-aboriginal-words-order-highlight-white-womens-1.

9

Beyond the Bright Lights: Are Minoritized Women Outside the Spotlight Able to Say #MeToo?

Neha Kagal, Leah Cowan, and Huda Jawad

When speaking of #MeToo it is important to recognize the origins of the movement. The #MeToo campaign was started by a black activist Tarana Burke in 2006, as a grassroots out-reach movement to support young women who were sexual assault survivors in underprivileged—predominantly African-American—communities. In this sense the 'movement' predates the online 'moment'; grassroots, community-based efforts across the globe have been systematically calling out sexual violence against women and girls for decades. Despite this, it was only when affluent white women and men began to voice their own experiences of sexual violence that social media (and popular news media in general) chose to pay attention. That said, it is also significant to note that at the same time, affluent white women's disclosures of sexual assault work to turn the gaze toward the Global North in a way which reveals itself to be a

N. Kagal (✉) • L. Cowan
Imkaan, London, UK
e-mail: neha@imkaan.org.uk; leah@imkaan.org.uk

H. Jawad
End Violence Against Women Coalition, London, UK
https://muslimfeminist.co.uk/

© The Author(s) 2019
B. Fileborn, R. Loney-Howes (eds.), *#MeToo and the Politics of Social Change*,
https://doi.org/10.1007/978-3-030-15213-0_9

133

space where women are still not granted the very freedoms that the 'West' prides itself on espousing.

For decades, mainstream political narratives of violence against women and girls (VAWG) have been rooted in binaries of East versus West, 'uncivilized' versus 'civilized', and 'us' versus 'them'. It was women of color who always needed to be 'saved' from 'barbaric' men of color whose very nature, according to state policymakers and media commentators alike, inclined them to be violent toward women as a way to exert the power embedded in their misogynistic 'cultures' and 'traditions'. Toxic masculinity had a face, and it was definitely not that of a Harvey Weinstein. What the #MeToo movement has done therefore is to highlight the misogyny and sexism that continues to be rife and excused in white Western society. At the same time, we can ask questions about the accepted victimhood of white women that made this narrative relatable and palatable to (some segments of) a wide audience. What this means is that the campaign is a significant *moment* in a decades-old feminist movement. But also that we still have a long way to go.

Over the last year there have been astute criticisms of the #MeToo movement, most notably its centering of experiences of white, affluent and educated women with access to a significant social media following and offline clout. Activists have rightly pointed out the erasure of poor, informally educated, low-paid, disabled, LGBT and non-urban women of color from the #MeToo movement. Australian-based musician and activist Miss Blanks explains that '#MeToo stories of cisgender white women have been the most amplified so far. Because of white supremacy, white women are more likely to be believed, validated, supported and make worthier victims' (Blanks, 2018). Given this context it is vital to specifically consider if and how the #MeToo movement can be a space for black and minoritized women who are further marginalized within our community. This includes transgender women who are disproportionately subjected to fatal violence (Human Rights Campaign, 2018); indigenous women who are twice as likely to experience violence in comparison to other women (New Zealand Ministry for Women, 2015); and sex workers who face high rates of violence and homicide due to poor working conditions and effective impunity for perpetrators (Sanders, Cunningham, Platt, Grenfell, & Macioti, 2017). American rapper Cardi

B has questioned whether the #MeToo movement is an inclusive space for sex workers to disclose harassment, explaining, 'I bet if one of these women stands up and talks about [sexual harassment], people are going to say, "So what? You're a ho. It don't matter"' (Gonzales, 2018).

Given that the response to the #MeToo movement has predominantly focused on women's experiences of sexual harassment in the workplace, what can we infer about the kinds of violence the #MeToo movement is allowing women to call out? In this chapter we examine who can access the 'space' created by #MeToo in two case studies: the first examining precarious and informal women workers' ability to say #MeToo and the second exploring the specific case of allegations against theologian Tariq Ramadan as a lens for considering Muslim women's ability to disclose violence in France. We use these pertinent examples to explore what kinds of violence are left out of the conversation, and why?

Around the world, normative frameworks define VAWG as comprehensive of a broad spectrum of experiences that constitute discrimination and violence that a woman or girl is subjected to, because she is a woman or girl. The Convention on the Elimination of Discrimination against Women (CEDAW) includes 'gender-based violence' in its definition of discrimination, further defining this violence as 'acts that inflict physical, mental or sexual harm or suffering, threats of such acts, coercion and other deprivations of liberty' (CEDAW, 1979). The Istanbul Convention similarly defines violence against women and girls as 'all acts of gender-based violence that result in, or are likely to result in, physical, sexual, psychological or economic harm or suffering to women […] whether occurring in public or in private life' (Council of Europe, 2011). Articles 32–42 define forced marriage, stalking, female genital mutilation (FGM), forced abortion and sterilization, sexual harassment and so-called honor-based violence as forms of VAWG. Articles 59–61 also detail the particular forms of VAWG that are experienced by migrant women, including border violence such as the threat of detention and deportation. Importantly in the context of this chapter, the Istanbul Convention (along with numerous other international instruments) recognizes 'economic violence' as a form of VAWG. These Conventions represent a seismic shift toward an intersectional understanding of VAWG that recognizes multiple perpetrators of violence, which for minoritized women will often include acknowledgment of the state as the perpetrator.

With this in mind, the #MeToo movement, with its seemingly singular focus on sexual harassment in the workplace, faces critique for being too simplistic. This critique asks the question: whose experiences are represented when a movement only calls out a particular manifestation of violence, without focusing on the structural roots that allow such kinds of violence to thrive? This is pertinent because for minoritized women it is not sufficient to speak of violence only as a gendered phenomenon. Other systems of inequality such as racism, classism, ableism and discrimination based on religion and geographical location need to be taken into account when engaging with the nature of violence that women across the globe face. A nuanced understanding of different women's lived experiences instead explores the ways in which oppressions crash together or 'intersect' to produce specific experiences such as those felt by a person who is both black (such as racism) and a woman (such as sexism or gender-based violence). For millions of women across the globe tackling significant barriers such as poverty, discrimination, insecure housing and lack of access to education, employment and health care is a necessary component of doing work on VAWG. Is it possible then to imagine a #MeToo movement that encapsulates an intersectional understanding of VAWG?

'Our Work Wasn't Recognized as "Work"': What Does #MeToo Mean for Women in the Informal Economy?

As outlined above, VAWG is more often than not compounded by multiple, intersecting inequalities within a broader context of social exclusion and marginalization. 'Intersectionality', a concept defined by black feminist academic Kimberlé Crenshaw, provides a lens for understanding violence against women and girls which demands comprehension of the range of perpetrators that women experiencing different oppressions might face (Crenshaw, 1991). For example, a black migrant woman might face racism, border violence and misogyny, enacted by perpetrators that include state bodies such as police, health-care services, social services and immigration enforcement.

However, the #MeToo movement has almost exclusively drawn attention to sexual harassment and exploitation in the workplace. This is despite the fact that across the globe women constitute only 39% of the 'official' labor force (World Bank, 2018), with some countries in the Global South having even lower rates of female labor force participation. The global economic crisis, characterized by increasing de-regulation, privatization and outsourcing of jobs down the supply chain, is leading to a transformation of employment; from that of formal employment to more informal, precarious employment. A distinguishing feature of the informal sector globally is the disproportionate percentage of women who find work within it. The proportion of women workers in the informal sector exceeds that of men in most countries (ILO, 2002; Chen, 2004) with women forming 'the majority of workers in sub-contracted, temporary or casual work, part-time work and informal occupations' (ILO, 2000, p. 11). Informal employment is generally characterized by hazardous working conditions, lower wages and unorthodox working hours, compounding women's vulnerability to sexual harassment and exploitation. An example that illustrates the precarity of women working in the informal economy is shared by Vijaya, a 29-year-old wastepicker from India (see Kagal, 2017), who stated:

> The security guards wouldn't let us pick waste from the landfill. They would allow some women in, but only those women who slept with them. The rest of us they would treat so badly. They'd call us thieves, abuse us, throw us out. And on days like that we'd have to go hungry. We couldn't complain to the police because our work wasn't recognized as 'work' per se. We were considered to be scavengers and we had to therefore put up with whatever treatment they meted out to us.

For women like Vijaya, who are informally employed, very rarely do mechanisms for redress exist, and women like her are unlikely to be logging on to Twitter accounts to share their tales of abuse and exploitation. The precariousness of their employment status often means that women cannot 'afford' (literally and figuratively) to call out sexual harassment in the workplace. In a country like India where 50% of unorganized women workers are the sole earners of their families (Geetika, Gupta, & Singh, 2011), women's economic dependence on their employer is very high. For wastepickers like Vijaya who have no 'employer', maintaining cordial relationships with men in positions of power, such as security staff and police officers, is critical to their ability to earn a living. This does not leave women with the freedom to call out sexual exploitation, harsh working conditions and low wages. This prompts the question: is the #MeToo movement even relevant to such women? As Ranjana Kumari, women's rights activist and Director of the Centre for Social Research in New Delhi, suggests:

> [The #MeToo movement] has to come down to the level of a village woman who is working in somebody's farms in the field. [It] has to come down to a labour(ing) woman who is trying to work in the construction industry or building the road, and being exploited by the contractor. (Al Jazeera, 2018)

What Kumari is highlighting is the need for the #MeToo movement to find relevance beyond the 'formal sector', thereby encompassing millions of women for whom their nature of employment and employment relations are increasingly being informalized.

The situation is mirrored in the UK where the economy relies heavily on migrant workers, 54% of who are women (FLEX, 2017). Sectors such as hospitality, cleaning, care and domestic work are highly feminized with rates of female participation ranging from 62% in the hospitality sector to 82% in the adult social care sector (FLEX, 2017; Jasiewicz, 2017). Within these sectors the expectation that women be friendly, compliant and subservient directly relates to the significant presence of sexual harassment; research in the hospitality sector has shown that 67% of women report some form of sexual harassment from colleagues, managers, customers and hotel guests (Jasiewicz, 2017).

Work within these sectors is routinely outsourced with informal employment arrangements, precarious work and low wages being the norm. Concerns have been raised about a wide range of abuses within these sectors including payment below minimum wage, wage theft, bogus self-employment, unfair deductions from pay and health and safety breaches. Research suggests that women are subject to routine discrimination, harassment and gender-related abuse and violence, particularly of a sexual nature (FLEX, 2018). A range of barriers to reporting abuse at work compounds this. Women may be reluctant to raise issues of abuse to male colleagues in positions of authority. When they do find the courage to report they often face a culture of disbelief, bullying or intimidation from employers or fellow staff. Migrant women in particular often feel that they won't be believed by authorities and may be reluctant to report abuse because of threats of job loss and even deportation (FLEX, 2018).

'Our Disclosures Are Weaponized': Can Muslim Women in Europe Say #MeToo?

Women are commonly obliged to weigh up a variety of factors when considering disclosing violence: we have explored how fear of unemployment prevents survivors from saying #MeToo in workplace settings. Low socioeconomic status and discrimination in public spaces, employment, education, housing and when accessing public services such as health care and the criminal justice system are a reality for women living at the intersections of different oppressions. For example, Muslim women living in the UK have experienced increased levels of hate crimes, including a 326% rise in Islamophobic incidents in 2015 (Ganesh, Arnold, Anwer, Begum, & Abou-Atta, 2016) and up to 100% rise in attacks following the 2016 EU referendum (Jones & Sharman, 2017). Given that the climate in Europe is increasingly hostile toward Muslim communities, stoked by political and media commentary, what happens when minoritized Muslim women say #MeToo in Western society? In particular what is the response of the white patriarchal establishment to their statements of hurt and demands for justice?

The case of Tariq Ramadan, a renowned and now infamous public figure, academic and theologian from Switzerland, illustrates the fact that while #MeToo has enabled some women in Europe to carve out a space to express and share their experiences, that luxury hasn't been afforded to many Muslim women. The handling of allegations levied against Tariq Ramadan illustrates how racist patriarchy has actively appropriated and weaponized Muslim women's experiences to perpetuate racism and Islamophobia, thereby silencing women, denying them justice and preventing them from accessing help and support.

Tariq Ramadan is one of Europe's most influential Muslim intellectual figures and is well known among European and American Muslims globally. He has a following in both the *banlieues*[1] and the professional classes. In February 2018, he was charged in Paris with two counts of rape, was detained but granted a conditional release nine months later on 15 November by the Paris Appeal Court and at the time of going to print, a date had yet to be set for his trial (The Guardian, 2018). In September 2018, a criminal case against him for rape was opened in Geneva. The case has been marred with delays, questionable practices by the criminal justice system and inconsistencies and contradictions in the testimonies of the plaintiffs (Gabon, 2018). It would be fair to say that Ramadan's treatment by the French legal system and the response by society and the state has been the exception rather than the norm that is offered to white men of his status and professional profile.

The fact that French ministers Gerald Darmanin and Nicolas Hulot, who faced accusations of rape (Gabon, 2018), were given support and solidarity from the French Prime Minister and President shows the extent to which structural racism and Islamophobia has taken hold and impacted access to justice for men of color who are accused of sexual violence. Parliamentarians greeted Darmanin with a standing ovation upon entering parliament as prosecutors opened the case against him. The double standards by which powerful white men and men of color are treated and protected by French society are evident. Muslim women, as with other minoritized groups, are acutely aware of the imbalance of this punitive power dynamic and have therefore been silenced. They are weary of

---

[1] *Banlieue* literally translates to mean 'suburb', but the word is commonly used as a pejorative euphemism for low-income housing projects, many of which have high proportions of migrant residents who face poverty and discrimination in areas such as employment and education.

adding fuel to the fire and for their trauma to be appropriated by racist rhetoric as a weapon against them and their community members.

Racism and Islamophobia have clearly skewed the application of law and the treatment of Tariq Ramadan. The support that prominent right-wing media personalities have given to the women who came forward accusing Ramadan of rape and sexual assault is not an insignificant detail in this saga. Tariq Ramadan was held in solitary confinement despite the deterioration of his neurological disorder and numerous medical examinations advising against detention. The absence of a date being set for his trial nine months on from his arrest (at the time of writing) as well as the recent granting of conditional release are clear and extreme ways of silencing Muslim women who might consider saying #MeToo.

The exploitation of race and ethnicity in reinforcing stereotypes about allegedly inherently violent and dangerous men of color is weaponized to mute survivors of sexual abuse, particularly if they are minoritized victims of minoritized perpetrators. This has been the case with the Ramadan case, in which the criminal prosecution is being handled by Francois Molins, the lead government prosecutor for 'Islamist' terror suspects. This in turn works to feed the racist trope of Muslim men and men of color as being inherently violent and sexually predatory.

White feminism acts as a further toxic factor in repressing the agency and voices of Muslim #MeToo survivors. In response to the allegations levied against Ramadan, Marlene Schiappa, the French Minister for Women's Rights, went on public record praising the power of the #MeToo movement for its 'liberation of women's voices'. However, when charges of rape were made against her two governmental colleagues, she was quick to remind the public that social media platforms are 'echo chambers' that cannot replace courts of justice or tribunals (Gabon, 2018). Schiappa has accused the journalists who broke the story of the allegations against her colleagues of being irresponsible and condemned the media for 'lynching' innocent men. The irony of applying such terms to describe the relatively nuanced media discussions about the conduct of two privileged powerful white men in comparison to the sensationalizing of every aspect of the Ramadan case, his family history, his career and political views and the survivors who have disclosed abuse is not lost on Muslim women.

Stereotypes of the 'worthy' victim and the 'good immigrant' versus the 'bad Muslim' have been a feature of the French response to Ramadan and his survivors. To date, two women have come forward publicly. In interviews, articles and books that have been written about their experiences,[2] sexist-racist tropes about helpless Muslim women who are controlled, covered and coerced by their families, partners and communities have been concocted as key parts of their narratives before and during the time of assault. These same stereotypes have been harnessed to celebrate how their journey since disclosing has led them to liberty, freedom and modernity, inevitably typified by their appearance as glamorous, Westernized and secular Parisian women. The impact of this stereotyping is clear and long-lasting: it adds to Muslim women's labor of expending psychological, emotional and cognitive energy resisting, explaining and disproving these stereotypes in their relationships and interactions outside of their faith and ethnic communities. Muslim women who are survivors of violence are tasked with negotiating gendered Islamophobic tropes, the instrumentalization of their faith and trauma, and feelings of shame and disbelief directed both from non-Muslim commentators as well as from within community networks. Muslim women survivors are forced to reckon with the discomfort of feeling like they are 'flogging' their trauma to their community's oppressor in order to be heard at all. Is it any wonder that for many Muslim women, the stakes of saying #MeToo are simply too high and the possibility of support or healing is minimal?

The Ramadan case clearly outlines the ways in which Muslim women's experiences of sexual assault and violence in the French context have been weaponized and used to further reinforce structural and Islamophobic discrimination. In some contexts, #MeToo has been anything but an empowering movement. The threat of appropriation of survivors' voices and the #MeToo movement by white supremacy and patriarchy is real and present for all women, but with different and multiple impacts for others.

---

[2] Such as Ayaan Hirsi Ali's (2015) book *Heretic: Why Islam Needs a Reformation Now* and articles by Carlotta Gall in *The New York Times* (November 2017) and Laure Lugon in *Le Temps* (October 2017).

How Can #MeToo Find Relevance for Minoritized Women Out of the Limelight?

The fora opened up by #MeToo, both online and offline, broadly purports to provide a space for disclosing sexual harassment and violence. This chapter has explored scenarios in which some women may in fact not be in a position to speak up online or offline and report harassment and violence, let alone pursue legal-judicial redress. This section provides an example of how minoritized women are seeking alternative avenues to have their voices heard. In particular it focuses on women workers in the informal economy and discusses how these marginalized workers have begun creating spaces for themselves where they can proclaim with defiance: '#MeToo':

> The sanghatna (organization) taught us not to be afraid of anyone. They'd tell us, 'If anyone commits an injustice against you, tell us, don't be afraid, we are there behind you.' They'd say, 'If anyone harasses you at work let us know. Don't be afraid. Don't live under the dabaav (pressure) of anyone; not the police, not your husband, not your in-laws. No one'. Pallavi, wastepicker member of KKPKP [Excerpt from Kagal (2017)]

The *sanghatna* (organization) that Pallavi is referring to is the Kagad Kach Patra Kashtakari Panchayat (KKPKP). The KKPKP is a trade union of wastepickers in Pune, India, which has been organizing *informal women* workers based on the principles of gender equality, social justice and human rights for over 20 years. Over the last 25–30 years, countries like India have witnessed the mushrooming of a number of such independent organizations of women in the informal economy, many of which have sprung from spontaneous mobilization of women against oppressive forces, particularly those threatening their livelihoods (Nayak, 2013). Informal workers are organizing in a variety of ways including trade unions, workers' associations outside the formal trade union movement, cooperatives, community-based organizations, local, national and transnational networks and federations (Bonner & Spooner, 2012; Agarwala, 2013). These organizations not only demand rights to livelihoods but also social protection, better conditions of work, regulation and legal protection for their members (Rowbotham & Mitter, 1994; Chen, Jhabvala, Kanbur, & Richards, 2007).

A number of these organizations conceptualize VAWG as including manifestations of structural inequality such as poverty, precarious employment and threats to women's livelihoods. Although they might not address ending VAWG 'directly' through their programs or projects, research has highlighted that membership to labor organizations helps in promoting the collective capabilities of women, providing women with a sense of identity, awareness about decision-making, courage, respect, recognition and dignity (Hill, 2010; Kabeer, Sudarshan, & Milward, 2013; Kagal, 2017). These networks unite women in solidarity, increasing their confidence and creating positions of leverage from which they can assert themselves (Friedemann-Sánchez, 2006; Hill, 2010).

For instance, research into the impact of organizing 8000 women wastepickers in Pune, India, into a trade union (known as KKPKP) has found that membership to the union increases women's bargaining power both within the household and outside it (Kagal, 2017). Since becoming members of KKPKP, women wastepickers reported being able to demand changes in their work environment by negotiating better conditions of work for themselves including freedom from sexual harassment and higher wages. Union members were also able to transform intra-household gender relations; the most visible changes being a reduction in the frequency and intensity of domestic violence and improvements in husbands' financial accountability.

Pathways via which these changes occur are complex but in general membership to KKPKP provided women access to a variety of material, relational and cognitive resources which were used by women to strengthen their *ability* and *willingness* to bargain for better treatment within their homes and work environments (see Kagal, 2017). Over time, women's active engagement with a union led to a transformation in women's understanding of their place in the world, increased confidence, access to information about their rights and an increased capacity to claim these rights. In addition collective bargaining through the union led to higher wages and better conditions of work for women wastepickers. Lastly, the union provided women a sense of solidarity, comfort and inclusion which allowed women wastepickers the opportunity to reflect upon their lives and begin to imagine 'other ways of being' (ibid). Ultimately these changes have translated into women's increased ability to say #MeToo.

Conclusion

In August 2018, Tarana Burke posted a tweet that called for a 'shift from talking about individuals' in order to 'begin to talk about power'. In the context of the case studies explored in this chapter, such a shift would necessitate meaningful recognition and incorporation of the way in which minoritized women globally have and are expanding conversations about and responses to sexual harassment and violence. Vast swathes of women do not have access to formal complaints procedures or human resource departments in their workplaces—indeed daily tasks involve maintaining smooth relationships with powerful individuals in order to do their jobs and sustain their livelihoods. This begs the question: what does solidarity and justice look like in situations where women's disclosures will likely be weaponized against them in the cases provided, either by compounding the precarious nature of their labor or by fueling Islamophobic agendas? In this chapter, we have provided some examples to illustrate some transformative approaches to ending violence against women and girls devised by and for minoritized women. Around the world, women living at the intersections of different oppressions along lines such as race, class or caste organize together to find holistic, supportive strategies for safety, harm reduction and liberation.

It goes without saying that Burke's call for a radical structural analysis of power relations must necessarily move beyond the bright lights of Hollywood. Movement building is long, slow-burning work, and re-shaping conversations around violence against women is unlikely to spin on a hashtag. It remains to be seen whether #MeToo can provide the temporary disruption needed to broaden the viewfinder of public outrage enough to foreground the experiences of minoritized women.

References

Agarwala, R. (2013). *Informal labor, formal politics and dignified discontent in India*. New York, NY: Cambridge University Press.

Al Jazeera. (2018, January 26). Is #MeToo a West-only movement? (2018). *UpFront*. Retrieved December 20, 2018, from https://www.aljazeera.com/programmes/upfront/2018/01/metoo-west-movement-180126112833101.html.

Ali, A. H. (2015). *Heretic: Why Islam needs a reformation now*. New York, NY: Harper.

Blanks, M. (2018, April 19). As a trans woman of colour, my words are met with silence. *The Guardian*. [online]. Retrieved November 19, 2018, from https://www.theguardian.com/commentisfree/2018/apr/19/as-a-trans-woman-of-colour-my-words-are-met-with-silence.

Bonner, C., & Spooner, D. (2012). The only school we have: Learning from the organizing experiences across the informal economy. *WIEGO*. Retrieved December 20, 2018, from http://www.wiego.org/resources/only-school-we-have-learning-organizing-experiences-across-informal-economy.

Chen, M. (2004). Rethinking the informal economy: Linkages with the formal economy and the formal regulatory environment. *EGDI and UNU-WIDER Conference Unlocking Human Potential: Linking the Formal and Informal Sectors. 17–18 September 2004, Helsinki, Finland*. Retrieved December 20, 2018, from http://www.findevgateway.org/sites/default/files/mfg-en-paper-rethinking-the-informal-economy-linkages-with-the-formal-economy-and-the-formal-regulatory-environment-sep-2004_0.pdf.

Chen, M., Jhabvala, R., Kanbur, R., & Richards, C. (2007). *Membership based organizations of the poor*. Oxon: Routledge.

Council of Europe. (2011). *Council of Europe convention on preventing and combating violence against women and domestic violence*. CETS No. 210. Council of Europe. Retrieved November 19, 2018, from https://www.coe.int/en/web/conventions/full-list/-/conventions/treaty/210.

Crenshaw, K. (1991). Mapping the margins: Intersectionality, identity politics, and violence against Women of Color. *Stanford Law Review, 43*(6), 1241–1299.

FLEX. (2017). Women workers and exploitation: The gender pay gap is just the beginning. *Focus on Labour Exploitation*. Retrieved November 16, 2018, from https://www.labourexploitation.org/news/women-workers-and-exploitation-gender-pay-gap-just-beginning.

FLEX. (2018). Flex's five-point plan to combat labour exploitation. (2018): Women in the workplace. *Focus on Labour Exploitation*. Retrieved November 9, 2018, from https://www.labourexploitation.org/sites/default/files/publications/FLEX%205%20Point%20Plan.pdf.

Friedemann-Sánchez, G. (2006). Assets in intrahousehold bargaining among women workers in Colombia's cut-flower industry. *Feminist Economics, 12*(1–2), 247–269.

Gabon, A. (2018). Milestones: Commentary on the Islamic world. *Milestones Journal*. Retrieved December 20, 2018, from https://www.milestonesjournal.net/articles/2018/3/19/the-tariq-ramadan-case-a-comprehensive-review.

Gall, C. (2017). 'I could not forget what happened to me that night with him'. *The New York Times*. Retrieved December 7, 2018, from https://www.nytimes.com/2017/11/03/world/europe/henda-ayari-tariq-ramadan-oxford-muslim-scholar.html.

Ganesh, B., Arnold, J., Anwer, R., Begum, R., & Abou-Atta, I. (2016). The geography of anti-Muslim hatred in 2015: Tell MAMA Annual Report. *TellMAMA*. Retrieved December 20, 2018, from https://www.tellmamauk.org/wp-content/uploads/pdf/tell_mama_2015_annual_report.pdf.

Geetika, T., Gupta, A., & Singh, T. (2011). Women working in the informal sector in India: A saga of lopsided utilization of human capital. *International Conference on Economics and Financial Research (IPEDR), 4*, 534–538.

Gonzales, E. (2018). Cardi B shares her own #MeToo story and stands up for women in hip-hop. *Harper's Bazaar*. Retrieved November 20, 2018, from https://www.harpersbazaar.com/celebrity/latest/a19486392/cardi-b-metoo-story-women-hiphop/.

Hill, E. (2010). *Worker identity, agency and economic development: Women's empowerment in the Indian informal economy*. London: Routledge.

Human Rights Campaign. (2018). Violence against the transgender community in 2018. *Human Rights Campaign*. Retrieved December 20, 2018, from https://www.hrc.org/resources/violence-against-the-transgender-community-in-2018.

International Labour Office. (2000). *World labour report 2000: Income security and social protection in a changing world*. ILO. Retrieved December 20, 2018, from https://www.ilo.org/public/english/standards/relm/gb/docs/gb279/pdf/esp-7.pdf.

International Labour Organization. (2002). *Decent work and the informal economy*. ILO. Retrieved December 20, 2018, from https://www.ilo.org/wcmsp5/

groups/public/%2D%2D-ed_emp/%2D%2D-emp_policy/documents/publication/wcms_210442.pdf.

Jasiewicz, E. (2017). At your service? Migrant women workers in the UK hospitality sector. *Novara Media*. Retrieved November 16, 2018, from https://novaramedia.com/2017/03/10/at-your-service-migrant-women-workers-in-the-uk-hospitality-sector/.

Jones, I. & Sharman, J. (2017). Hate crimes rise by up to 100 per cent across England and Wales, figures reveal. *Independent*. Retrieved December 3, 2018, from https://www.independent.co.uk/news/uk/home-news/brexit-vote-hate-crime-rise-100-per-cent-england-wales-police-figures-new-racism-eu-a7580516.html.

Kabeer, N., Sudarshan, R., & Milward, K. (Eds.). (2013). *Organizing women workers in the informal economy: Beyond the weapons of the weak*. London and New York: Zed Books.

Kagal, N. (2017). "In the union I found myself": The impact of collectivization of informal economy women workers on gender relations within the home. Unpublished. PhD Thesis. SOAS, University of London.

Lugon, L. (2017). Du salafisme à la lumière, la femme qui accuse Tariq Ramadan. *Le Temps*. Retrieved December 20, 2018, from https://www.letemps.ch/suisse/salafisme-lumiere-femme-accuse-tariq-ramadan.

Ministry for Women, New Zealand. (2015). Wāhine Māori, Wāhine Ora, Wāhine Kaha: Preventing violence against Māori women. *Ministry for Women, New Zealand*. Retrieved November 20, 2018, from http://women.govt.nz/sites/public_files/Wahine%20Maori%20wahine%20ora%20wahine%20kaha.pdf.

Nayak, N. (2013). Organizing the unorganized workers: Lessons from SEWA experiences. *The Indian Journal of Industrial Relations, 48*(3), 402–414.

Rowbotham, S., & Mitter, S. (1994). *Dignity and daily bread: New forms of economic organising among poor women in the Third World and the First*. London: Routledge.

Sanders, P., Cunningham, S., Platt, D., Grenfell, P., & Macioti, D. (2017). Reviewing the occupational risks of sex workers in comparison to other 'risky' professions. *Welcome Trust, University of Leicester & London School of Hygiene and Tropical Medicine*. Retrieved November 20, 2018, from https://www2.le.ac.uk/departments/criminology/people/teela-sanders/sex-work-and-homicide.

The Guardian. (2018, November 15). Tariq Ramadan: Oxford professor facing rape charges granted conditional release. *The Guardian*. Retrieved December

20, 2018, from https://www.theguardian.com/world/2018/nov/15/tariq-ramadan-oxford-professor-facing-rape-charges-granted-conditional-release.

UN General Assembly, Convention on the Elimination of All Forms of Discrimination Against Women. (1979, December 18). United Nations, Treaty Series, vol. 1249, p. 13. Retrieved July 8, 2019, from https://www.refworld.org/docid/3ae6b3970.html.

World Bank. (2018). *World Bank.* Retrieved November 16, 2018, from https://data.worldbank.org/indicator/SL.TLF.TOTL.FE.ZS.

10

'It's Not Just Men and Women': LGBTQIA People and #MeToo

Jess Ison

Lesbian, gay, bisexual, transgender, queer, intersex and asexual (LGBTQIA) people have largely been absent from the #MeToo movement. The conversations, and in particular the media reporting, have focused on heterosexual sexual assault where both people are cisgender. There have been some notable exceptions to this focus, albeit often in a very US-centric context, such as articles examining how cis-heterosexual men have assaulted femmes[1] and/or transwomen (e.g., Talusan, 2018). While #MeToo has many complexities, it could, and indeed must, be more inclusive of the issues faced by queer people (Talusan, 2018). As Hale (2017, para. 7) argued:

> Until people as a whole recognize and embrace that a meaningful conversation about sexual assault cannot be constrained to *only* supporting

---

[1] Femme is a queer identity that can relate to a person's sex and/or gender. It does not necessarily or by necessity relate to womanhood or femininity.

J. Ison (✉)
La Trobe University, Melbourne, VIC, Australia
e-mail: J.Ison@ltu.edu.au

B. Fileborn, R. Loney-Howes (eds.), *#MeToo and the Politics of Social Change*,
https://doi.org/10.1007/978-3-030-15213-0_10

151

heterosexual, heteroromantic, cisgender folks, trans and queer people are stuck on the outside.

Hale points to an important element that is rarely discussed: the focus on heteromantic preferences, which can exclude people who engage in non-romantic sex. Hearing #MeToo only within the heterosexual context isolates queer people who have experienced sexual assault not just from outside the community but from other queer people in our communities. Further, LGBTQIA people face many unique issues on account of our gender and sexuality, as well as intersections with other marginalized positions such as race or ability (Burke, 2017).

This chapter addresses the dearth in queer issues relating to the #MeToo campaign. Throughout this chapter, the term 'queer' is used broadly to refer to those who sit outside of the cisgender, heterosexual norm. Yet, this is a hard task from the outset, as I too must utilize 'queer' to mean a broad range of people who all in fact have different stories and who may experience very different effects of queerphobia. However, at some points, specific groups will be distinguished when possible. I apologize for how flawed this approach is and yet how language leaves us so little choice. Even as I address the issues of queer (lack of) inclusion in #MeToo, I must write in exclusionary ways. Most notably, much of what is written and what I write here is impacted by the urban queer context. Nonetheless, this chapter begins a conversation about what queer communities have to offer the campaign.

Before I continue, I want to be open about my own position. I am heavily invested in queer communities, with a strong anti-state political position. I am a survivor of sexual violence perpetrated by heterosexual cisgender men and queers. My gender is femme, something that doesn't fit any box on a form I've ever seen. I am white, living on the land of the Wurundjeri people with ancestors who were complicit in, as well as used and abused by, colonialism, and I therefore exist in a privileged body. My background is working class, yet I live with the complexities of being an academic who can theorize about class while being a broke casual academic who has no money to see a psychologist to deal with any affects I might experience from writing this chapter. But perhaps, most importantly for this chapter, I am staunchly against normative politics. I despise movements for gay marriage or acceptance of LGBTQIA people in the military, so how I write here is very much informed by this position.[2]

Debunking the Cis-hetero Myth

There is a misconception that violence does not happen in queer communities. This is often because of homophobia and heteronormativity. LGBTQIA people, our lifestyles, relationships and sex lives were historically—and often still—seen as illegitimate. The problem then is that if we are not legitimate from the outset, how could the violence we enact be seen? Another reason for this view that we are not violent is that much feminist discourse sees violence as cismale violence perpetrated against a cisfemale. In line with this Mortimer (2018) argues: 'LGBTIQ victims/survivors sit at a nexus between complex and interlocking ideas about sex, sexuality and violence that serve heteronormative, cisnormative and patriarchal interests'. While queer people have to navigate this complexity, we 'are not immune to a systemic culture of rape, for example, simply because we are queer. In fact, we often experience violence *because* of who we are' (Patterson, 2016, p. 7).

Despite this lack of recognition, there is a growing field of data and advocacy examining some ways LGBTQIA people experience sexual assault and violence, which demonstrates that there are similar, and at times higher levels of violence in queer communities compared to heterosexual people (see, e.g., Australian Human Rights Commission, 2017; Fileborn, 2012). According to Fileborn (2012), one of the key causes of abuse is heterosexism, which is the privileging of heterosexuality, and heterosexual relationships, over others.

While the studies in Australia are not yet extensive, there have been many reports conducted in the United States over the last ten years regarding the prevalence of sexual violence in the LGBTQIA community (e.g., National Center for Transgender Equality, 2016; National Sexual

---

[2] This chapter has been read, edited and workshopped by many queer people, in order to queer the act of writing by engaging with the community and incorporating their voices. Particular thank you to Karen Bland, Carolyn D'Cruz and Cee Devlin (in alphabetical order).

Violence Resource Center & Pennsylvania coalition against rape, 2012). These concur with the Australian studies that LGBTQIA people experience high rates of violence, and that these rates are higher for people who also face discrimination in relation to issues such as race and ability.

Across all of these reports, however, there is a reoccurring issue. The focus is on either intimate partner violence or an unidentified perpetrator who appears to be from outside the community. Yet queer people have many and varied relationships, not just intimate partners. There is little specific research on sexual assault that occurs from someone the survivor may know but is not necessarily in a monogamous partnership with. For example, the person may be a casual acquaintance from the community or an occasional sexual partner. This is an oversight in the literature that could be addressed to give a clearer picture of who the perpetrator(s) are and the contexts in which queer sexual violence occurs.

With so little research on sexual assault in queer communities we are forced to rely upon anecdotal evidence. This is not necessarily a negative outcome. Queer communities, as with any marginal community, have modes of operating that are outside of the norms of mainstream society and therefore researchers must draw on the stories of individual community members. This allows for centering personal narratives over statistics that fail to capture the nuance of people's experiences. In light of the focus of #MeToo on hearing personal narratives, the queer history of telling our stories means that we already have an infrastructure for narrative building.

What Can Queers Do When They Are Assaulted Anyway?

I have established that LGBTQIA people experience violence and yet our stories are often not represented in #MeToo. This must lead us to consider how queers are seeking assistance and support in the aftermath of sexual violence. One of the barriers that LGBTQIA people face is accessing services (Fileborn, 2012). Most sexual assault services are for heterosexual cisgender women. This is problematic and exclusionary insofar as it reinforces assumptions about ideal survivors, something already heavily critiqued by feminists, but also perpetuates heteronormativity as the lens through which sexual violence is understood and responded to. In addition, queer people may fear that services will be homophobic and/or transphobic, adding another barrier to access (Todahl, Linville, Bustin, Wheeler, & Gau, 2009). As Patterson states, 'when we expect all survivors to fit the mainstream survivor narrative, we miss opportunities to organize and mobilize in a larger capacity' (2016, p. 6).

In this vein, transgender rights campaigner Sarah McBride aired some of her concerns, saying:

> There's this baseline level of disbelief that survivors of sexual assault writ large face … And then there's this extra unique barrier that transgender people face around this notion that … we are somehow so undesirable that people wouldn't sexually assault us, which is a fundamental misunderstanding of both who transgender people are and how sexual assault works. (As quoted in: Dastagir, 2018)

This must be examined in relation to #MeToo, which advocates for survivors to speak out and the imperative for us to listen to those voices. If LGBTQIA people are silenced from the outset how can they participate? It is likely that someone trying to speak out in relation to queer sexual assault has already had to overcome multiple layers of denial to even consider seeking help. To then be faced with a cis-heterocentric response can shatter a person's ability to speak. This is especially the case where the response provided may express disbelief, based on the misperception that 'same sex' partners are on equal-footing and no power dynamic exists as it does for straight couples, or the transphobic view that only cisbodies are desirable (Hammer & Gossett, 2016).

While queer services do exist, they might not always be a viable option. What if the manager of a queer service is a perpetrator? What if a counselor is a friend of the perpetrator? Similar to the research discussed earlier, queer service providers can also frame sexual violence as something that occurs in the context of ongoing monogamous relationships. For example, two of the largest LGBTQIA health organizations in Australia, *The AIDS Council of NSW (ACON)* and *ThornHarbour Health,* predominately have resources for people experiencing abuse in an intimate partnership. While these resources are no doubt relevant to some members of the queer community, it is nonetheless telling that the intimate relationship is what is centered on rather than a diverse understanding of sexual relationships in the LGBTQIA community.

Another apparent avenue of response in the aftermath of sexual violence is through the criminal justice system. Accessing police services, if that is even something the survivor wants, is much harder for queer people (Langenderfer-Magruder, Walls, Kattari, Whitfield, & Ramos, 2016). There are systemic reasons why LGBTQIA people are distrustful of the police, particularly when this intersects with race, class or other marginalized positions (Bassichis, 2011; Davis, 2005). For example, in Australia we have the highest rate of Indigenous incarceration in the world (Australian Bureau of Statistics, 2018). Indigenous people are more heavily policed, more likely to be incarcerated and more likely to be given a longer sentence than non-Indigenous Australians. Quite simply, prison is a continued tool of colonization. Therefore, engaging with this oppressive system may not be possible or safe for LGBTQIA Indigenous people, and is something non-Indigenous queers should oppose (Mogul, Ritchie, & Whitlock, 2011; Stanley & Smith, 2011).

This disdain and distrust of the criminal (in)justice system is further problematic when the perpetrator is known and part of marginalized communities, where the survivor may not want that person to face jail.[3] Hostility toward police, and indeed the knowledge that attempting to utilize the (in)justice system could lead to the victim being further traumatized, leaves little room for marginalized LGBTQIA people to access services from the state.

---

[3] The biography *Dirty River* by Lakshmi Piepzna-Samarasinha (2016) grapples with this complexity in incredible nuance.

The History of Queer Sex as a Perversion

While rates of violence are similar, if not higher, in LGBTQIA communities, I have shown the issues that exist with service provision. Within some of our communities there have been other responses, such as transformative justice, which I discuss later in this chapter. However, to fully grasp how queer communities deal with sexual violence, we must have an understanding of queer liberation.

Queer history, as with any history, can be told in many ways. Here, I give a brief and incomplete overview about the fears surrounding gay sex in the Australian context, to move away from the well-known US narratives that dominate queer history. In Australia, the first act of violence was the invasion of the land by the British in which the colonialists endeavored to erase the histories and stories of Aboriginal people they saw as gender nonconforming and queer. However, many Indigenous sistergirls and brotherboys and/or queer and/or trans-people have and still are resisting this attempted erasure (see: Clark, 2015; Hodge, 2015). Britain brought anti-sodomy laws to Australia and enforced them where possible. These laws have always operated as a key tool of oppression and worked to construct queer people as deviant. Regardless of the laws and attitudes toward queer people, we have consistently found each other and engaged in sex and community.

In the face of this overt oppression, so the story goes, LGBTQIA people fought back with the first Mardi Gras in Sydney in 1978. Of course, many events actually came before, during and after this, and most of this activism was from radical activists in the face of repression. Unfortunately, much of the earlier types of activism were halted due to the AIDS crisis. While the Australian government was quicker to respond to the crisis than places such as the US, their response was nonetheless homophobic. One needs only to recall the infamous 1987 National Advisory Committee on the AIDS grim reaper advertisement, which showed a grim reaper in a bowling alley, with a voice over saying: 'At first only gays and IV drug users were being killed by AIDS'. It then cuts to a young girl, with blonde hair and a pink dress, crying. After this other acceptable heterosexuals are hit by the bowling ball. Following the male voice advocating the use of condoms, the camera zooms out to show an endless row of grim reapers bowling. This ad was clearly stating that gay men and drug users were infecting the future, that is, the white heterosexual future. The effect of which was to reiterate homosexual sex as something disgusting and perverted.

With governments responding to HIV with homophobia, or simply not responding at all, some people in the LGBTQIA community began championing causes that reflected 'homonormativity'. In brief, homonormativity is:

> A politics that does not contest dominant heteronormative assumptions and institutions—such as marriage, and its call for monogamy and reproduction—but upholds and sustains them while promising the possibility of a demobilized gay constituency and a privatized, depoliticized gay culture anchored in domesticity and consumption. (Duggan, 2003, p. 179)

In reifying heteronormativity,[4] examples of homonormativity include the call for same-sex marriage equality or the acceptance of LGBTQIA persons in the military. Such projects are a deliberate move away from earlier efforts to achieve sexual liberation to a focus on being just like heterosexuals and in doing so reinforce rather than deconstruct social, cultural and institutional discourses that maintain the LGBTQIA community's marginalized status.

Homonormativity and #MeToo

Moreover, this shift toward homonormativity did not address the violence that can occur in queer relationships.[5] To be accepted within the dominant framework of heterosexuality, homonormative people have to be 'straighter than straight', and any discussions of violence or other

---

[4] Heteronormativity, coined by Michael Warner (1993), relates to the systems and norms that enforce heterosexuality as 'natural' and 'normal'.

[5] This issue was addressed as early as Vickers' (1996) article *The Second Closet: Domestic Violence in Lesbian and Gay Relationships: A Western Australian Perspective*. Revisiting this article, one can see that much of the argument is still relevant today.

forms of apparent 'deviance' in the community need to be quashed. This is evidenced in all of the campaigning around gay marriage both in Australia and globally. Looking through the gay marriage material you are lucky to even see a kiss, let alone sex.[6] Instead, these materials predominately show happily married white couples in expensive suits embracing. This non-sexual representation was part of creating us as acceptable minorities, whose sexual practices/preferences, and by extension the violence occurring in those communities, remained hidden from public view.

One of the problems with the enforcement of acceptability in the form of homonormativity is that even the slightest 'failure' is blown out of proportion when it falls outside the norm. Therefore, talking about queer sexual assault in a world obsessed with heterosexuality—a world that can barely talk openly and honestly about queer consensual sex—is risky. The chance of there being consequences for failing at homonormativity can result in queers having to maintain a veneer of respectability, and the consequences of these conversations can, and do, stifle how we respond internally. How can we talk about sexual assault in our communities when the broader society is saying that we are sexually deviant? This is even more complicated when people engage in sexual practices, such as BDSM, given the often-punitive responses to such practices. This is a topic that cannot be covered here but should be addressed in relation to #MeToo, for example, because an examination of BDSM may help to unpack some of the complexities surrounding sexual consent and power (see also Darnell; Newman & Haire, this collection).

This problem of needing to be straighter than straight also manifests when sexual assault perpetrated by a queer person becomes public, in which the media will often respond with queerphobia as well as victim-blaming. Take for example the case of Avital Ronnell, a well-known philosopher and lesbian who was accused of sexual harassment and assault from one of her male gay graduate students. This case became widely discussed within queer circles and academia when the story emerged in August 2018 (for a good overview, see Chu, 2018). Details of the

---

[6] For example, the It's Time campaign from Get Up (2013) ends on the two men hugging each other after a marriage proposal.

victim-survivor's claims, and the university's response, were leaked to the media, which included a particularly harrowing letter signed by a list of esteemed scholars who were supporting Ronnell. To justify her behavior, Ronnell argued that she was in fact acting like all queers, in a camp and fun manner, stating:

> Our communications—which <the victim-survivor>[7] now claims constituted sexual harassment—were between two adults, a gay man and a queer woman, who share an Israeli heritage, as well as a penchant for florid and campy communications arising from our common academic backgrounds and sensibilities…These communications were repeatedly invited, responded to and encouraged by him over a period of three years. (Greenberg, 2018)

The onslaught of media reporting struggled to make sense of this case, with titles such as 'What happens to #MeToo when a feminist is accused' (Greenberg, 2018).[8] Yet, reading across the newspaper articles written on this topic, myself and other queer people I know felt no confusion about the fact that the perpetrator was a lesbian and the survivor was a gay man. For queer people, interrelations across genders and sexualities isn't something new or different, it is our general way of interacting. What was significant (and problematic) was the way Ronnell used queerness to justify her actions, calling on the deviance narrative that has been used to oppress queers who transgress homonormativity. Here, the claiming of queerness that is pathologized and criminalized as a justification for sexual assault appears to be a tactic of the queer abuser.[9]

The Ronnell case points to the larger issue of how many within the queer community have found ourselves in similar situations, where an act of assault or harassment was somehow seen as different or confusing because it involved queer people. This is a key issue that points to an important difference in how queers can relate to the #MeToo campaign.

---

[7] I have chosen to redact the name of the victim-survivor as this information was leaked without his permission. While this is not something he has necessarily asked for, I hope that it stands in solidarity with him and his rights to privacy.

[8] It must be noted, her claims to feminism have been disputed (Chu, 2018).

[9] Something that could be related to the Kevin Spacey case as well.

Within our communities, our relationships to our bodies and others' bodies differ wildly from the norm of heterosexuality. We are seen as excessive, deviant and even abnormal. From this point, it is only a short step to concluding that sexual assault is a part of queer territory or that as a sexual deviant, perhaps the survivor deserved it.

This was underlying much of the Ronell case. In light of this, #MeToo needs to be ever vigilant about excluding us because this can easily reinforce queers as deviant.

Given the issues discussed so far, a queer survivor faces multiple hurdles on top of dealing with the sexual assault. At times, some might not even see it as sexual assault as all of these issues compound, and the dominant heteronormative framing of sexual assault works to render queer experiences invisible. Additionally, queers are not taught about our sexuality from a young age, instead learning about sexuality and consent from within our communities, and often making up relationship 'rules' as we go along. While this can allow queer people to subvert and open up possibilities for ethical and non-violent sexual practices, it can also lead to some problematic situations (e.g., particularly for young queers, who may not have any visible models of 'healthy' queer relationships). Queer communities have responded by developing education, such as safe sex and consent workshops. These are a necessity and must be queer led in order to counteract the contradictory messages that queer people are, on the one hand, perverted and, on the other hand, that sexual violence cannot occur in queer relationships.

Perpetrator-Victim-Perpetrator-Survivor

In light of these complexities, and in the need to build relationships, we often take a reprieve from the mainstream world in more radical queer circles in what we call (sometimes begrudgingly) 'the queer community'. These are spaces that queer people cherish and are incredibly important to many of us for survival. Some of these spaces are small, like having friends over for a cup of tea. Others are bigger, such as performance nights or community meetings. These queer spaces are meant to be safe, and yet, often they too are the sites where we experience violence from those in our community.

Thus, a crucial element to this is that survivors and perpetrators can and do co-exist in small populations and tight-knit communities. This is an issue that extends beyond queer communities, and looking to these other contexts can therefore help shed light on some of the issues facing LGBTQIA people. For instance, a report from the Australian Government's Institute of Family Studies on sexual assault and rural communities 'describes rural communities as having high levels of "acquaintance density", meaning that most people have some level of familiarity with most other people in the community' (2004, p. 12). This can result in women not wanting to report because they do not have anonymity (both with the police and among community members), which is clearly an issue that translates to LGBTQIA communities.

An offshoot of this *acquaintance density* is that perpetrators themselves may be victims. This is complex in small communities, as people tend to know each other's business, histories and stories. Indeed, particularly in queer communities, one might perform their story on stage to an audience or post about it publicly online. Later, one can learn details of this same person being a perpetrator, without perhaps even knowing that person beyond a cursory smile at a queer event. As a result, it is hard to come to terms with this revelation of a person enacting violence after the story they told of the violence enacted on them and the bravery that took. This is not necessarily limited to queer communities, but it is indeed a specific outcome of having a community that values performance and the telling of one's trauma.

In general, violence is also framed as occurring within a victim-perpetrator dynamic. In contrast, Jennifer Patterson argues that we need to 'look at interpersonal sexual violence as being but a part of the larger structural systems of violence like the military and prison industrial complex' (2016, p. 6). By looking at all sexual assault as part of larger issues of violence enacted by the state, we can understand how such violence happens in queer communities. There is no doubt that cis-heterosexual men perpetrate the majority of sexual violence against women. However, by ignoring the complexities that occur in places such as queer communities, we are denying the chance to look beyond just the individual. This is not to detract from how important the individual is, of course. But going forward, #MeToo should consider queer experiences to shed light on how sexual violence is situated within much broader systems of power, with far-reaching consequences. A positive outcome of this may be that we start to hear *all* survivors, not just those who fit the dominant narrative.

What Queers Have to Offer

While it is important that the #MeToo movement opens up to create space for queer experiences, it is also important to recognize there is much to be learned from queer communities. Queer communities have diverse ways of engaging in sex and relationships. One of the key issues with campaigns, such as marriage equality, is that we were positioned as a homogenous group when we are anything but (Ison, 2018). Indeed, I have inevitably fallen into this trap in writing this chapter. We are many and varied and, no doubt, there will be people who vehemently disagree with what I have written here. By focusing on violence perpetrated in normative monogamous-style relationships, we have left out a large number of queer people and subsequently some crucial lessons the queer community has to offer. Many queer people do not support marriage or are part of relationship models that do not follow the heteronormative ideals of monogamy. For example, instead of maintaining a hierarchal relationship, where power is so easily unchecked, S Bear Bergman (2013) explains his relationships as a 'constellation of intimates'—a model that has radical potential. In this, the potential for having a loving community is much higher and this community can support relationships to flourish, but they can also respond when a relationship turns bad and can keep each other informed about others in the community.

Because of our concerns in relation to the criminal (in)justice system, some queers have been responding internally to sexual assault until this point. For example, in Naarm (so-called 'Melbourne', Australia) we have developed transformative justice processes that hold the perpetrators to account while the survivor is supported and cared for. Transformative justice is about working with a perpetrator to rectify harm and heal the victim(s) while challenging our carceral system of punishment. Indeed, transformative justice hopes to challenge violence at its core (The Chrysalis Collective, 2011). There is no doubt that under our current system this model is hard, not least of all because it is time-consuming and our communities are already stretched emotionally and physically. However, it is a model that can be invested in and is a lesson that heterosexuality can learn from us. Perhaps by expanding one's constellation and building stronger communities, we can begin to support survivors and hold perpetrators to account. This is an important first step and one that does not rely on the people involved being heterosexual. Radical inclusivity in the form of a constellation map should be what we consider next for #MeToo.

References

Australian Bureau of Statistics. (2018). Summary of findings: Persons in corrective services. *Corrective Services, Australia*. Retrieved from http://www.abs.gov.au/ausstats/abs@.nsf/mf/4512.0.

Australian Human Rights Commission. (2017). *Change the course: National report on sexual assault and sexual harassment at Australian universities.* Australian Human Rights Commission. Retrieved from https://www.humanrights.gov.au/sites/default/files/document/publication/AHRC_2017_ChangeTheCourse_UniversityReport.pdf.

Australian Institute of Family Studies. (2004). *Responding to sexual assault in rural communities.* Australian Institute for Family Studies. ACSSA Briefing No. 4. Retrieved December 20, 2018, from https://aifs.gov.au/publications/responding-sexual-assault-rural-communities/introduction.

Bassichis, M. (2011). Reclaiming queer & trans safety. In C. I. Chen, J. Dulani, & L. Lakshmi Piepzna-Samarasinha (Eds.), *The revolution starts at home: Confronting intimate partner violence within activist communities.* Brooklyn and Boston: South End Press.

Bergman, S. B. (2013). *Blood, marriage, wine, & glitter.* Vancouver: Arsenal Pulp Press.

Burke, T. (2017, November 9). #MeToo was started for Black and Brown Women and Girls. They're still being ignored. *The Washington Post.* Retrieved December 20, 2018, from https://www.washingtonpost.com/news/post-nation/wp/2017/11/09/the-waitress-who-works-in-the-diner-needs-to-know-that-the-issue-of-sexual-harassment-is-about-her-too.

Chu, A. L. (2018). I worked with Avital Ronell. I believe her accuser. *The Chronicle of Higher Education*. Retrieved December 20, 2018, from https://www.chronicle.com/article/I-Worked-With-Avital-Ronell-I/244415.

Clark, M. (2015). Indigenous subjectivity in Australia: Are we queer? *Journal of Global Indigeneity, 1*(1), 1–5.

Dastagir, A. E. (2018, June 13). She was sexually assaulted within months of coming out. She isn't alone. *USA Today*. Retrieved December 20, 2018, from https://www.usatoday.com/story/news/2018/06/13/sarah-mcbride-gay-survivors-helped-launch-me-too-but-rates-lgbt-abuse-largely-overlooked/692094002/.

Davis, A. Y. (2005). *Abolition democracy: Beyond empire, prisons and torture.* New York: Seven Stories Press.

Duggan, L. (2003). *Twilight of equality?: Neoliberalism, cultural politics, and the attack on democracy.* Boston: Beacon Press.

Fileborn, B. (2012). *Sexual violence and gay, lesbian, bisexual, trans, intersex, and queer communities.* Australian Institute of Family Studies. Retrieved December 20, 2018, from https://aifs.gov.au/publications/sexual-violence-and-gay-lesbian-bisexual-trans-intersex-and-queer-communiti.

GetUp! (2013, 13 May). Marriage equality. It's time. *GetUp!* Retrieved December 20, 2018, from http://www.getup.org.au/campaigns/marriage-equality/twins-tvc/marriage-equality-its-time.

Greenberg, Z. (2018). What happens to #MeToo when a feminist is accused? *The New York Times*. Retrieved December 20, 2018, from https://www.nytimes.com/2018/08/13/nyregion/sexual-harassment-nyu-female-professor.html.

Hale, J. L. (2017). LGBTQ people are also silence breakers. Listen when we say #MeToo. *Bustle*. Retrieved December 20, 2018, from https://www.bustle.com/p/lgbtq-people-are-also-silence-breakers-listen-when-we-say-metoo-7211752.

Hammer, I., & Gossett, R. (2016). Holding the pattern while living our truth: Ida Hammer speaking on violence against trans women, as told to Reina Gossett. In J. Patterson (Ed.), *Queering sexual violence: Radical voices from within the anti-violence movement* (pp. 225–230). New York: Riverdale Avenue Books.

Hodge, D. (2015). *Colouring the rainbow: Black queer and trans perspectives.* Mile End, SA: Wakefield Press.

Ison, J. (2018). Queers against gay marriage: What to do in this postal vote? In Q. Eades & S. Vivienne (Eds.), *Going postal: More than 'yes' or 'no'* (pp. 82–86). Melbourne: Brow Books.

Lakshmi Piepzna-Samarasinha, L. (2016). *Dirty river: A queer femme of color dreaming her way home.* Vancouver: Arsenal Pulp Press.

Langenderfer-Magruder, L., Walls, N. E., Kattari, S. K., Whitfield, D. L., & Ramos, D. (2016). Sexual victimization and subsequent police reporting by gender identity among lesbian, gay, bisexual, transgender, and queer adults. *Violence and Victims, 31*(2), 320–331.

Mogul, J. L., Ritchie, A. J., & Whitlock, K. (2011). *Queer (in)justice: The criminalization of LGBT people in the United States.* Boston: Beacon Press.

Mortimer, S. (2018). "It's just 100 times more difficult to talk about": LGBTIQ people and sexual violence. *Queer Legacies, New Solidarities Conference.* Deakin University, Melbourne 22–24 November 2018.

National Advisory Committee on AIDS. (1987). *Australian Government, Canberra.* Retrieved December 20, 2018, from http://www.youtube.com/watch?v=2zMdWhoFFck.

National Centre for Transgender Equality. (2016). *The report of the 2015 U.S. transgender survey.* National Centre for Transgender Equality. Retrieved December 20, 2018, from http://www.transequality.org/sites/default/files/docs/usts/USTS%20Full%20Report%20-%20FINAL%201.6.17.pdf.

National Sexual Violence Resource Center & Pennsylvania coalition against rape. (2012). *Sexual violence & individuals who identify as LGBTQ.* NSVRC. Retrieved December 20, 2018, from https://www.nsvrc.org/sites/default/files/Publications_NSVRC_Research-Brief_Sexual-Violence-LGBTQ.pdf.

Patterson, J. (2016). *Queering sexual violence: Radical voices from within the antiviolence movement.* New York: Riverdale Avenue Books.

Stanley, E. A., & Smith, N. (2011). *Captive genders: Trans embodiment and the prison industrial complex.* Oakland, CA: AK Press.

Talusan, M. (2018, March 2). Trans women and femmes are shouting #MeToo—But are you listening?' *Them.* Retrieved December 20, 2018, from https://www.them.us/story/trans-women-me-too.

The Chrysalis Collective. (2011). Beautiful, difficult, powerful: Ending sexual assault through transformative justice. In C. I. Chen, J. Dulani, & L. Lakshmi Piepzna-Samarashinha (Eds.), *The revolution starts at home: Confronting intimate violence within activist communities* (pp. 189–206). Brooklyn and Boston: South End Press.

Todahl, J. L., Linville, D., Bustin, A., Wheeler, J., & Gau, J. (2009). Sexual assault support services and community systems: Understanding critical issues and needs in the LGBTQ community. *Violence Against Women, 15*(8), 952–976.

Vickers, L. (1996). The second closet: Domestic violence in lesbian and gay relationships: A Western Australian perspective. *Murdoch University Electronic Journal of Law, 3*(4), 1–27.

Warner, M. (1993). *Fear of a queer planet: Queer politics and social theory.* Minneapolis: University of Minnesota Press.

Part III

**Not All That Glitters Is Gold:
#MeToo, the Entertainment Industry
and Media Reporting**

11

#MeToo and the Reasons To Be Cautious

Lauren Rosewarne

Following the public revelation of the Harvey Weinstein accusations in October 2017, Tarana Burke's MeToo hashtag was popularized as a social media rallying cry for victims of sexual misconduct to share their stories of abuse. On the one hand #MeToo looks as though it's had some tangible success: Weinstein lost his business, and household names like news anchors Matt Lauer and Charlie Rose, actor Kevin Spacey and politicians Al Franken and John Conyers each lost their jobs. If scalps are a measure of success, then we indeed have a handful. There is, however, a president in the White House who has had two-dozen sexual misconduct complaints levelled against him and was still elected. Donald Trump is one of numerous reasons to pause for thought and, in all our excitement about, and enthusiasm for, #MeToo, that we examine the reasons to be cautious.

#MeToo is also discussed in this chapter as a contemporary consciousness-raising movement. While #MeToo is not entirely the same

L. Rosewarne (✉)
School of Social and Political Sciences, University of Melbourne,
Parkville, VIC, Australia
e-mail: lrose@unimelb.edu.au

© The Author(s) 2019
B. Fileborn, R. Loney-Howes (eds.), *#MeToo and the Politics of Social Change*,
https://doi.org/10.1007/978-3-030-15213-0_11

as the radical feminist airing of grievances that transpired in the 1960s and 1970s, nonetheless we have 50 years of data teaching us about the limitations of women 'just' telling their stories.

In this chapter, I examine Donald Trump as testimony to the reality that while the news media may care about exposing stories of sexual misconduct, the general population isn't quite as concerned. The fact that ordinary people—that 'real Americans'—managed to elect a person so widely accused of the very acts that #MeToo exists to shame demonstrates that broader culture still has a way to go before truly believing that sexual misconduct is a problem worth acting on. This latter point nudges another criticism explored: that #MeToo is a problematically diffuse movement. In public policy, to solve a problem that problem needs to be clearly defined. While #MeToo started as a rallying cry against sexual misconduct, in practice it has become a shorthand for anything vaguely feminist. Without clearly defined objectives, such a mission is doomed to struggle.

Also explored is the extent to which the media presents a false idea of impact: celebrity stories are disproportionately reported on, and celebrities still front the campaign. Translating #MeToo *out* of Hollywood and into factories, department stores or restaurants requires more (see also Cover; Kagal, Cowan & Jawad, this collection). The media is also examined because, in their need for newsworthiness, a demand exists for ever-more salacious disclosures, meaning that unless new revelations are 'worse' than what we've already heard, such stories are unlikely to be reported on.

The Trump Testimony

In the US, there's a term to describe a piece of data, a scandal, a well-timed leak, that gets released the month prior to a November election: October surprise. In October 2016, that surprise was *The Washington Post*'s release of the *Access Hollywood* tape: a hot mic recording of a 2005 conversation that Trump had with television host Billy Bush. There on video, with audio, is Trump bragging about his interactions with a 'Nancy'—later exposed as Nancy O'Dell, former host of *Access*

Hollywood—where he claims to have: 'Moved on her like a bitch'. In the tape, Trump says:

> I'm automatically attracted to beautiful... I just start kissing them. It's like a magnet. Just kiss. I don't even wait. And when you're a star they let you do it. You can do anything ... Grab them by the pussy. You can do anything.

Whether Trump was boasting about his prowess as a predator, or merely engaging in some peacocking in front of Bush, the tape was construed by many as testimony to his abhorrent sexual politics.

From polls to pundits, the 2016 election looked like it would be a watershed year with the anticipated first female presidential victory. Even on those occasions when the polls looked close, the *Access Hollywood* tape felt for many like the smoking gun that would end Trump's campaign. Add the tape to the 24 accusations of sexual misconduct against Trump (Jamieson, Jeffery, & Puglise, 2016) and surely nobody who was a woman, or who cared about women, would vote for him.

At 3 am on the morning of Friday, November 10, 2016, Trump delivered his victory speech. He might have lost the popular vote by 3 million, but he won the electoral college: enough Americans—some 63 million of them—knew about the misconduct allegations, had undoubtedly heard the endlessly replayed *Access Hollywood* tape and yet either wholeheartedly endorsed Candidate Trump or did so while holding their noses. Either way, the election outcome demonstrated that over one-third of Americans were able to overlook Trump's treatment of women enough to vote for him. One could stretch that number to include many eligible voters who didn't care enough to actively vote *against* him.

The election of Donald Trump demonstrated that in the gamut of issues Americans care about, sexual misconduct ranks low. The election result set in motion a series of retaliations from women who were revolted by Trump's victory and who positioned themselves to resist. In 2017, the day after Trump's inauguration, millions of people took to the street in what was known as the Women's March. By October that year, momentum built toward a progressive unrest that would, in part, manifest in the #MeToo movement: Trump might be in the White House, but other men who had harassed and assaulted were set to get their comeuppance.

A year on and another October surprise. Judge Brett Kavanaugh was nominated to the Supreme Court in 2018 and, mere days prior to the vote on his confirmation, a confidential letter sent to Senator Dianne Feinstein was leaked. In it, Judge Kavanaugh was named in a sexual assault allegation. Public interest in the story led the Senate to invite the accuser, Christine Blasey Ford, to testify in front of the judicial committee, akin to what transpired when Anita Hill, bearing similar allegations, fronted the same committee in 1991 during the Clarence Thomas confirmation hearings. Mirroring the 1991 hearing in many ways—including down to the presence of three of the same senators, still serving 27 years on—Ford was heard, the Senate voted and the accused Kavanaugh was sworn in as Justice on October 8, 2018.

The Kavanaugh confirmation was a perfect #MeToo-era test case. Here was a victim with accusations that were widely considered credible and yet the alleged perpetrator was still confirmed into the job he'd been earmarked for. Ford's testimony was widely described as powerful, as persuasive, just not enough for any tangible consequences to occur (Rosewarne, 2018a, 2018d).

The confirmation of Kavanaugh came at the one-year #MeToo anniversary, highlighting that while there might be a fervent resistance to Trump and the Trumpian ethos, to frat boy and bully boy culture and to the silencing of women, there actually *hasn't* been the reckoning women had hoped for. On the contrary, it could be suggested that the election of Donald Trump, combined with the Senate's aggressive commitment to Kavanaugh's ascent, is indicative of a *backlash* against women's rights—a statement *against* identity politics and so-called political correctness—and that for all the attention #MeToo received, a counterattack was simultaneously being mounted by conservatives (see also Fileborn & Phillips, this collection). As transpires when any movement seeks to redistribute power, those with the most to lose invariably retaliate. When Trump says of the #MeToo movement that it's a 'scary time for young men in America' (in Diamond, 2018), he's once again giving voice to men—including, undoubtedly, himself, as a serial accused—who simply don't want to lose their stranglehold on power.

The Trump election, the relative stability of polls in the years since and the confirmation of Kavanaugh each demonstrate the limitations of any successful revolt against the sexual political status quo. Throughout this chapter I propose a range of reasons for this, the first being that the movement is stuck at the *consciousness-raising* stage.

#MeToo as a Consciousness-Raiser

In the late 1960s, women who had been highly influenced by first-wave feminist writers like Mary Wollstonecraft and Elizabeth Cady Stanton, and by works like Simone de Beauvoir's *The Second Sex* (1949), broke away from their second-wave sisters, to carve out a new movement that would become known as radical feminism. Another potent influencer on these women were the writings of Mao Zedong, in particular his ideas around 'speaking bitterness'. In practice, this involved women coming together and sharing their stories of violence in marriage, workplace sexual harassment and job discrimination: that is, consciousness-raising. Historically women's problems had been viewed—and dismissed—as private concerns and as separate from the public policy agenda. Through talking to one another women realized that gender-based subordination was endemic to the female experience that no woman was alone in her suffering. From these consciousness-raising sessions two key principles emerged: the personal is political and that sisterhood is powerful (see also Loney-Howes; Gleeson & Turner, this collection). While radical feminism is often viewed as limited in its efficacy—its central goal of dismantling patriarchy has obviously failed—women telling their truths gave important insight into the prevalence of gender-based harassment, violence and abuse, insight that would later prove influential on public policy (Abrar, Lovenduski, & Margretts, 2000).

Flash forward half a century. While we may have moved on from small radical feminist consciousness-raising sessions and wholeheartedly embraced the global platform of social media to broadcast the cause, the principles remain the same. Fifty-odd years on and it's apparently still the job of women to keep telling our stories over and over again in the hope that one day we're believed. That we have to keep reading about each other's hurt to remind ourselves that we're not alone, that it's not just us. In the earliest days of #MeToo I wrote about my fears that the movement's successes would lie in delivering a comprehensive picture of the prevalence of gender-based harassment, violence and abuse but would fall short of moving beyond awareness (Rosewarne, 2017a). Since that time, there have been some examples of outcome. I opened this chapter identifying men who have lost jobs. While I'm not convinced that employment termination is necessarily more than public relations (as I explore later in this chapter), it exists as movement. Similarly, in Australia, the Human Rights Commission has instigated a national inquiry into workplace harassment. While the government funding an Inquiry is testimony to the issue's importance, gleaning a picture of prevalence is, I would contend, merely supplementing what #MeToo has already been successful at accomplishing. My concerns, therefore, remain potent that #MeToo is largely stuck in consciousness-raising.

What happens *after* the stories are told and retold? Where do millions of testimonials and a clear understanding of the extent of such crimes lead us? For Christine Blasey Ford her testimony led to not only her accuser being confirmed to the Supreme Court, but to death threats and public ridicule from the President, each serving, alas, as a cautionary tale to the *perils* of revelation (Rosewarne, 2018b). In terms of evaluating #MeToo as a movement, the picture is more complicated. On one hand it has successfully been baked into social discourse: '#MeToo is now the lens, the vibe, the gossamer overlay on every issue of sexual politics. If we talk women in 2018, invariably we're also using the slogan' (Rosewarne, 2018a). But how does it become *more* than just a public confessional? How are Trump's polls so stable given his many accusations, and how does Ford get 'believed' but not enough to actually thwart Kavanaugh's confirmation? While the backlash is part of the explanation for this, so too is #MeToo being problematically diffuse. #MeToo doesn't look or operate like the political movements that have gone before. It lacks formal leadership, structure and agreed-upon goals and objectives and instead more closely resembles an issues network not yet mobilized to do anything beyond help to shape and perpetuate discourse around sexual misconduct (see Garibotti & Hopp, this collection).

The Policy Challenges for #MeToo

Public policy is the process by which a government administers, prioritizes and funds things like laws, regulations and programs. In most manuals for policymaking—the Australian policy cycle is one such example (Althaus, Bridgman, & Davis, 2018)—the process generally starts with the identification of issues: what is the problem we're trying to address? #MeToo emerged from a call to arms for victims of sexual abuse to tell their story: in mere days it was used millions of times.

In terms of policy definition, #MeToo has aptly demonstrated that there is a widespread prevalence of sexual misconduct committed by men. It's the next parts of the policy cycle that are more complicated: how do we get *beyond* recognition that something is wrong? Furthermore, how do we establish agreement that this is a problem not only *worth* acting on but that the capacity exists to make genuine change? How do we decide *what* constitutes sexual misconduct and *who* is responsible for resolution? Few would disagree that sexual misconduct is a concern or even that something needs to be done. The *what* of this—through education, cultural change, legislation, workplace policies and a dismantling of patriarchy—is far less easy to build consensus around.

Social media campaigns can be very good at agenda-setting: at helping issues get media attention and, occasionally, even onto the radar of policymakers. If the effectiveness of #MeToo is measured purely through use of the hashtag, through media mentions and through public awareness of the problem, then its success is indisputable. If, however, success is measured as working toward the *elimination* of a policy problem, then the movement appears substantially less effective. The movement has been highly effective at creating a repository of testimonials, but it has not yet moved into the policy influence realm.

Criticizing the movement as unable to make change is, of course, premised on the assumption that it ever set out to achieve revolution rather than to exclusively raise consciousness. If, therefore, drawing attention to a problem was its main objective—if getting #MeToo onto the lips of the media and politicians was all that was desired—then the movement can unquestionably be considered a resounding success. But if there is a genuine desire to make change, the movement needs to transition from being geared around confessionals and start to create infrastructure to formulate objectives like targets, funding objectives and policy change. Until a clear picture of the movement's goals emerges, it is impossible to truly evaluate success.

While #MeToo has been highly successful in getting public attention, it's worth noting that the movement has had better success at shedding light on certain kinds of sexual misconduct over others, highlighting that one of the limitations of the movement is its inextricable link to Hollywood.

Media and the Hollywood Limitation

#MeToo was always destined to be the kind of movement that would captivate the attention of the media. The idea of high-profile figures like Harvey Weinstein being accused by high-profile figures like Rose McGowan immediately positioned the story as suitably salacious to summon an enormous amount of press attention. If we think of the faces of #MeToo—the women referred to (if erroneously) by the popular press as the 'leaders' of the movement—our thoughts immediately go to the *celebrity* victims and the *celebrity*-alleged perpetrators. The fact that actress Alyssa Milano got credit for popularizing the hashtag long before Tarana Burke is illustrative of this.

It's not that millions of ordinary women haven't used the hashtag since: they absolutely have. But the platform of an ordinary, non-celebrity victim is limited beyond plugging into a network of similar testimonials. The media, similarly, has no genuine interest in reporting on the harassment of ordinary people. Certainly not when Ronan Farrow can offer us stories involving the titans of Tinseltown.

'Real', non-Hollywood activists did briefly find themselves in the spotlight at the 2018 Golden Globes awards ceremony, when eight activists were the guests of actresses and utilized their time on the red carpet to give airtime to their cause. Burke for example, who started the #MeToo movement and is the Senior Director of the non-profit Girls for Gender Equity, was the guest of actress Michelle Williams. The fact, however, that these real-life activists *only* got attention through the very Hollywood vehicle of an awards ceremony reiterates that the movement is still primarily *Hollywood*: that Hollywood remains the conduit—and perhaps also the *boundary*—for the bulk of media interest, attention and action. While millions of sexual misconduct disclosures have emerged since October 2017, the stories that have received attention are disproportionately ones that impact—or implicate—*celebrities*. Equally—and perhaps most pressingly—it is the distorted view on impact presented by the media that makes the movement appear more successful than it is.

In the introduction of this chapter, I listed several scalps that have been collected across the course of the movement. In a range of cases men have lost their jobs. If all our information on #MeToo is gleaned from the media, it indeed looks like much is happening. It's important, however, to flag here that much of this change is in fact part of the gossamer overlay mentioned earlier, where everyone in the public eye is expected to speak in the language of #MeToo without there being any burden for anyone to create revolution.

When Netflix fired Kevin Spacey from *House of Cards*, when HBO dumped Louis C.K. from their programming, such acts can be construed as change, as a tangible outcome and a demonstration of studio responsiveness. I'm not sure, however, that this is the full story. These responses were *post-fact* and happened only *after* accusations were made *public*. A studio response needs to be distinguished from attempts to genuinely alter culture and to establish infrastructure to help prevent future instances of abuse. One could in fact, argue that firings were responses motivated less about making change and more as a response to public interest in, and outrage about, #MeToo accusations: that studio action was primarily motivated by a desire to prevent the firestorm that *inaction* would create.

It was the #MeToo momentum that placed pressure on *NBC* to get rid of Matt Lauer, for *CBS* to dump Charlie Rose and for Al Franken to leave the US Senate. *NBC*, notably, had received complaints about Lauer long before October 2017 but hadn't done anything (Maddaus, 2018). In the wake of #MeToo, however, Lauer's continued tenure had become a public relations disaster for the network, particularly so in the context of a breakfast news show with a predominantly *female* audience. Following the Kevin Spacey accusations, Sony reshot Spacey's scenes in *All the*

Money in the World with a different actor. The studio can, again, be construed as being responsive, but it's also worth examining the economic motives driving the decision:

> [I]t's worth questioning whether Netflix, Sony and HBO are doing this because they believe and support the victims, or because they are businesses and businesses care, most of all about money.
>
> Was the stink-brand of Kevin Spacey, for example, going to ruin any chances of *All the Money in the World* making a motza at the box office? Was keeping Louis C.K. on air going to make HBO look like abetters? (Rosewarne, 2017b)

If studios are motivated primarily by optics rather than cultural change, the successes of #MeToo are limited to a continued reporting of events *after* they happen, rather than prevention.

The media's starring role in the #MeToo story also dictates the necessity for stories to be consistently salacious. When the *New Yorker* published the tape of Ambra Battilana Gutierrez being harassed by Weinstein, the story was suitably wrenching to command attention. In a movement now *saturated* by such disclosures though, how do new allegations achieve cut-through? Equally, amid the millions of terrible tales told, there now appears an unsubtle ranking of them in terms of egregiousness. Instead of viewing stories as a dataset—as evidence of a gendered public policy problem needing a response—discourse now centers on questioning the degree to which individual accusations are awful or, conversely, unwarranted. For example, was 'Grace's' interactions with comedian Aziz Ansari *just* a bad date (Way, 2018) or, as I have argued elsewhere, testimony to the entrenched, problematic sexual scripts that work to further the messy dynamics between men and women (Rosewarne, 2018c, see also Darnell; Fileborn & Phillips, this collection)? Such stories then become dominated by a semantics debate rather than the broader prevalence of women feeling abused and violated. Finding new ways to keep the story fresh and reportable—and thus on the *public* radar—remains both a challenge and a millstone for the movement if it is to continue and, hopefully, influence tangible change.

The Swinging Pendulum of Politics

In 1992, the phrase 'Year of the Woman' was used to celebrate the high number of female candidates spurred to run in that year's election. Candidates were motivated by factors including the confirmation of Clarence Thomas to the Supreme Court. Flash forward several decades and the same phrase again is being used to describe 2018. The election of Trump and the rise of #MeToo has similarly led to record numbers of women and minority candidates running for office.

Having people interested in making change through elected office is important: the only way for a movement to move on from awareness is through action. But we've been here before (Rosewarne, 2018d). In 1991, Clarence Thomas was beleaguered by sexual misconduct allegations and yet got confirmed to the Supreme Court. In 2018, Brett Kavanaugh was similarly besieged and now gets to call himself Justice. This isn't an observation intended to imply that nothing progressive has happened in the intervening decades—of course it has, including in no small way the rise of social media—but it is also a reminder that motion in the context of politics doesn't always go in one direction. Speaking our bitterness has been a technique with only modest success for feminists, and thus I fear that using the same technique again is likely to get us to the same destination. Also worth factoring in is the inevitable equal and opposite *backlash* that transpires after the success of any social movement. At the end of the second-wave feminist movement in the 1980s, a backlash occurred against the many gender equality strides made during the two decades prior (Faludi, 1991). Two steps forward, one step back. After two terms of a relatively progressive black president, come 2016 and conservatives were salivating for not just a seizing of power but a backlash *against* the progress made over the last decade. Two steps forward, one step back. The rise of #MeToo has prompted a similar backlash where the President claims it's scary out there for men and readily mocks Christine Blasey Ford at a campaign rally, and where conservatives utilize the bugle of social media to assert their own fears of a progressive mob. Here, the backlash responds *disproportionately* to a movement that has, in fact, altered little more than discourse (see also Franks, this collection), potentially setting us even further back.

Invariably when sexual conduct is discussed, the role of the government gets mooted. In terms of legislation, sufficient laws exist in the wealthy, English-speaking countries where most of the #MeToo chatter has transpired. Despite laws though, sex crimes persist. Partly this is because sexual misconduct is a *wicked problem*, a term used in public policy to describe certain social problems that 'are never solved. At best they are only re-solved—over and over again' (Rittel & Webber, 1973, p. 160). Such crimes persist though, in part, because few governments have made addressing them a priority. Until we start talking about harmful manifestations of masculinity (see Flood, this collection), until we have frank conversations about sexual scripts and the complexity of consent, we are unlikely to create the cultural change needed to reduce sexual violence. Of course, there's more to the role of government than leadership. Both Australia and the US, for example, have a tragic problem of thousands of untested rape kits. The resources, apparently, don't exist to conduct the tests, so such kits are 'languishing' in storage facilities (Power, 2018). There's no point questioning all the many reasons women don't report sexual violence (Rosewarne, 2018b), until we address the current situation whereby reports are unlikely ever to lead to prosecution.

To be more than a movement of confessionals, to fight the battles that exist in a political climate that has swung substantially to the right in recent years, activists need an agenda. What would true reform look like in the sexual misconduct space? Until this is unpacked, #MeToo will likely remain an immensely successful way to provoke conversation. And perhaps that's exactly where it should stay with the mantle of leadership taken up by other outlets.

References

Abrar, S., Lovenduski, L., & Margretts, H. (2000). Feminist ideas and domestic violence policy change. *Political Studies, 48*(2), 239–262.

Althaus, C., Bridgman, P., & Davis, G. (2018). *The Australian policy handbook: A practical guide to the policy-making process*. Crows Nest: Allen and Unwin.

Diamond, J. (2018, October 2). Trump says it's 'a very scary time for young men in America'. *CNN*. Retrieved October 13, 2018, from https://edition.cnn.com/2018/10/02/politics/trump-scary-time-for-young-men-metoo/index.html.

Faludi, S. (1991). *Backlash: The undeclared war against women*. London: Vintage.

Jamieson, A., Jeffery, A., & Puglise, N. (2016, October 28). A timeline of Donald Trump's alleged sexual misconduct: Who, when and what. *The Guardian*. Retrieved October 9, 2018, from https://www.theguardian.com/us-news/2016/oct/13/list-of-donald-trump-sexual-misconduct-allegations.

Maddaus, G. (2018, April 26). Ann Curry warned NBC of sex harassment claim against Matt Lauer. *Variety*. Retrieved October 11, 2018, from https://variety.com/2018/tv/news/nbc-matt-lauer-tom-brokaw-1202789751/.

Power, J. (2018, February 24). Untested sexual-assault kits that could catch rapists are languishing in storage. *The New Daily*. Retrieved October 11, 2018, from https://thenewdaily.com.au/news/national/2018/02/24/rape-kits-storage/.

Rittel, H. W. J., & Webber, M. W. (1973). Dilemmas in a general theory of planning. *Policy Studies, 4*(2), 155–169.

Rosewarne, L. (2017a, October 19). #MeToo and modern consciousness-raising. *The Conversation*. Retrieved October 9, 2018, from https://theconversation.com/metoo-and-modern-consciousness-raising-85980.

Rosewarne, L. (2017b, November 11). From public confessions to public trials: The complexities of the "Weinstein Effect". *The Conversation*. Retrieved October 10, 2018, from http://theconversation.com/from-public-confessions-to-public-trials-the-complexities-of-the-weinstein-effect-87265.

Rosewarne, L. (2018a, October 8). Sure we believed Ford. Just not enough. *Meanjin*. Retrieved October 9, 2018, from https://meanjin.com.au/blog/sure-we-believed-ford-just-not-enough/.

Rosewarne, L. (2018b, October 8). Why don't women report alleged abuse? Just look at the Kavanaugh saga. *The Sydney Morning Herald*. Retrieved October 9, 2018, from https://www.smh.com.au/lifestyle/life-and-relationships/why-don-t-women-report-alleged-abuse-just-look-at-the-kavanaugh-saga-20181007-p5089w.html.

Rosewarne, L. (2018c, January 15). Aziz Ansari and the politics of sexual scripts. *Meanjin*. Retrieved October 11, 2018, from https://meanjin.com.au/blog/aziz-ansari-and-the-politics-of-sexual-scripts/.

Rosewarne, L. (2018d, October 14). The problem is, Americans just don't care enough. *The Sydney Morning Herald*. Retrieved October 14, 2018, from https://www.smh.com.au/world/north-america/the-problem-is-americans-just-don-t-care-enough-20181012-p509ab.html.

Way, K. (2018, January 13). I went on a date with Aziz Ansari. It turned into the worst night of my life. *Babe*. Retrieved October 11, 2018, from https://babe.net/2018/01/13/aziz-ansari-28355.

12

Substitution Activism: The Impact of #MeToo in Argentina

María Cecilia Garibotti and Cecilia Marcela Hopp

Introduction

Argentina is a fertile terrain for autochthonous social movements and protests,[1] which should have set an optimistic a priori scenario for the #MeToo uprising. However, the actual story is more nuanced. The path followed by #MeToo was influenced by the local feminist agenda and

---

[1] From protests against human rights violations in the last dictatorship to the *piqueteros*, social movements in Argentina have been a key tool for democratization. See Thalhammer and Branigan (2017) and Bukstein (2012).

M. C. Garibotti (✉)
Universidad Torcuato Di Tella, Buenos Aires, Argentina

Universidad de Buenos Aires, Buenos Aires, Argentina

Universidad de San Andrés, Buenos Aires, Argentina

Stanford Law School, Stanford, CA, USA

C. M. Hopp
Universidad Torcuato Di Tella, Buenos Aires, Argentina

Universidad de Buenos Aires, Buenos Aires, Argentina

New York University, New York City, NY, USA

© The Author(s) 2019
B. Fileborn, R. Loney-Howes (eds.), *#MeToo and the Politics of Social Change*,
https://doi.org/10.1007/978-3-030-15213-0_12

context. In particular, the #MeToo movement was preceded by the #NiUnaMenos ('not one woman less') movement in 2015, with an agenda focused on gender-based violence fueled by the outrage over the increasing number of femicides[2] in the country. #NiUnaMenos, which also started as a hashtag, was launched through social media by journalists and social media personalities who organized a massive protest after a young man murdered his 15-year-old girlfriend (Iglesias, 2015). Initially, these journalists did not identify themselves as feminists, but after the 2015 protest that gathered over 300,000 people who marched across the country, a feminist agenda became more visible and pervasive within the movement. Many feminist organizations joined #NiUnaMenos, and they started to assemble regularly to keep the movement alive by organizing successive marches and compiling the demands of various feminist agendas (Goñi, 2016). While it was femicides that garnered most publicity for #NiUnaMenos, sexual abuse or harassment and the legalization of abortion were also part of the broader claims against women's subordination. These issues remained latent behind the dramatic femicides.

In this chapter, we argue that in its transnationalization, #MeToo—a highly decentralized movement from its inception—created a political opportunity to advance the local feminist agenda centered on historic demands of the Argentine feminist movements, most prominently the legalization of abortion. To provide a dynamic account of the trajectory followed by the Argentine women's movement in this regard, we focus on: firstly, the political and media environment created in the country concomitant to #MeToo, which opened a space for the appearance of new activists—particularly actresses incentivized to raise their voices by their counterparts in North America. Secondly, we explain how feminists who identified with #NiUnaMenos used the opportunity to talk about the Argentine feminist agenda on mainstream media when they were summoned to analyze the #MeToo movement. They were key in substituting the primary message of #MeToo—the sexual assault and harassment of actresses—with the Argentine feminist agenda of abortion, by framing the issue as a form of discrimination and violence against women.

---

[2] The term is attributed to US sociologist Diane Russell and Jane Caputi (1992), and it refers to men's violent killing of women.

As a result, after more than a decade of feminist organizations trying to get Congress to debate a bill that would legalize abortion during the first trimester[3] without success (Bellucci, 2014, pp. 391–392), the Argentine President pushed the legislature to discuss a bill,[4] even though he and most of his party did not support its legalization (Braslavsky, 2018).

The concept of 'political opportunity structure' refers to 'features of regimes and institutions that facilitate or inhibit a political actor's collective action' (Tarrow & Tilly, 2007, p. 440), and research on contentious politics works to explain the timing, dynamics and variance between the dispute, political power and institutions. Among others, political opportunities theory explores how external pressures and the capabilities of local actors to frame issues accordingly can catalyze changes in local contexts. The causal mechanisms that tend to be involved in the dynamics of the contention include relational mechanisms, which specifically affect interpersonal and group networks, and sustain processes of political identity formation.

This literature is useful to gain new insight into the different levels through which #MeToo affected the local context and distinguishes itself from 'traditional' transnational movements.[5] In the latter, social media has also proven to be very useful for transnational politics, as it helps connect political actors and empower them by pushing the same agenda.[6] However, to become a true social movement, a common language that helps members present their claims in a consistent manner within the realm of contentious politics must be developed. The decentralized nature of #MeToo on the one hand prevented this common understanding from developing but, on the other, it presented local movements with the opportunity to re-signify and use the power of #MeToo to advance their own agendas.

---

[3] Argentine law criminalizes abortion as a general rule, but it allows it when pregnancy endangers the life or health of the pregnant woman and when pregnancy is the result of rape.

[4] That would eventually fail to pass the Senate.

[5] Human rights activism (Keck & Sikkink, 1998), labor unions (Tarrow, 2005) and genetically modified organisms (Motta, 2015).

[6] International regimes have been key for the construction of transnational movements that reflect basic understandings of norms and rules and shape the transnational policy discourse (Motta, 2015).

The media and social movements interact in numerous and, sometimes, mutually beneficial ways (Gamson & Wolfsfeld, 1993). The media provide movements with the opportunity to mobilize new people, present activists as legitimate interlocutors and their claims as valid. They help to (re)define how a conflict is framed. At the same time, the media needs social movements as a way to provide new stories, and a story from Hollywood proved especially appealing. Moreover, it helped to activate a previously disorganized group, the Argentine Actresses Association, which did not develop an anti-harassment agenda but was essential to bringing the abortion agenda closer to more people during the legislative debates. In this sense, no new social movement[7] was formed out of #MeToo, but a preexisting movement that built and expanded over the window of opportunity created through #MeToo.

In this chapter, we argue that #NiUnaMenos was able to create a positive synergy with the political opportunity opened by #MeToo to mobilize and further advance their feminist agenda on abortion. We explain the different levels of connections established between the #MeToo anti-rape agenda and feminism in Argentina to show how part of the success in the transnationalization of #MeToo has come about through its re-signification to the local challenges and needs of the feminist movement. #MeToo was 'imported' in a way, but was quickly adapted to reflect the priorities of the local agenda. Even more so, when empowered local actresses raised their voices against harassment brought about by important men in show business, they were mostly met with backlash, threatening the implosion of the Actresses Association, which gained prominence in 2018 during the abortion debate.

---

[7] According to Tarrow (1994), there are four main properties of social movements: (i) they present a collective challenge, (ii) they have a common purpose, (iii) they foster solidarity and (iv) they sustain collective action.

Feminist Agendas in Argentina: Gendered Violence and Abortion

Even though feminist mobilization has existed for at least three decades in Argentina,[8] during the 1980s and 1990s, demands were centered on very basic civil and political rights for women, such as the right to get divorced, shared parental rights and effective political participation. Argentina was in the process of democratization after decades of alternating between democratic governments and dictatorial regimes[9] that precluded any meaningful advancement of women's rights and violently repressed social mobilization (Bellucci, 2014).

However, in the last decade due to the high number of murdered girls and women made increasingly visible by the media, the feminist agenda changed. As public outrage increased, the issue of violence against women started to figure prominently in public debate. On June 3, 2015, the first #NiUnaMenos demonstration—a massive protest against gendered violence—gathered over 300,000 people in the City of Buenos Aires (O'Dwyer, 2016). It was organized through Twitter after the recurrence of news about women who were killed by intimate male partners. As protests spread across the country and even reached Uruguay and Chile, the government was forced to respond to this issue (Adamovsky, 2015).

Unlike other 'spontaneous' nonpartisan social demonstrations that came before #NiUnaMenos, the protest was not aimed at legal reform or more criminalization for perpetrators. The document that was read in the first #NiUnaMenos protest asked for better policies and effective implementation of already existent laws, access to justice and gender-sensitive education for people in general—for example, incorporating subjects in schools and specific training for state agents, such as police officers, prosecutors and judges dealing with gender-based violence. What started as a social media campaign quickly transformed into a fully fledged social

---

[8] Since 1986, feminist movements have organized an annual National Encounter of Women, where women gather to discuss diverse topics that affect women's lives (Bellucci, 2014).

[9] Between 1930 and 1983, Argentina suffered six military coups that imposed dictatorial governments. In 53 years there were only 19 in which the government was elected through democratic elections without fraud. However, during that period, there were two democratic elections in which the majority party was not allowed to run.

movement composed of feminist organizations that joined in periodic assemblies to decide the next steps both in discourse and in action. As previously mentioned, initially, the agenda was strategically limited to issues that would be agreeable for most people, and it avoided more divisive issues, such as the legalization of abortion. However, as a result of increased feminist intervention in its organization, the second #NiUnaMenos manifesto did include the legalization of abortion as one of its demands, although it was not among the most visible ones (Ni Una Menos, 2016).

Including and publicly incorporating the legalization of abortion into the agenda of a massive protest was a great accomplishment for the feminist organizations.[10] Up until that point, the barriers preventing mainstream debates about the issue had led feminist activists to focus on legalization through broadening the interpretation of the Argentine law that only allows abortion for therapeutic reasons and when pregnancy is the result of rape. Feminist lawyers and activists promoted the understanding that risks to health should be read according to the definition of health provided by the World Health Organization (WHO).[11] Another strategy was to help reduce the risks and harms of unsafe abortions by providing information via 'hotlines' (Drovetta, 2015).[12] These approaches

---

[10] Abortion is the primary cause of maternal mortality in Argentina (Ministerio de Salud de la Republica Argentina, 2016).

[11] The World Health Organization (WHO) defines health as 'a state of complete physical, mental and social well-being and not merely the absence of disease or infirmity'.

[12] By 2015, the legalization of abortion had been a central issue for feminist organizations for a decade. In 2005 the National Campaign for the Legalization of Abortion was launched. Its main strategy was to draft a proposal to amend the law on abortion, but all political parties systematically blocked the debate. Since the main aim of the movement was to change a law, lawyers played significant roles. However, the legislative agenda limited the strategy, and younger lawyers, eager to achieve change, developed alternative legal paths centered on increasing the provision of abortion services under the existing law. Firstly, they challenged the restrictive interpretation of the law, which made abortion unattainable even in cases that were legally allowed. Concomitantly, other activists created a parallel strategy, which was to focus on providing information that would make it safer for women to get an abortion outside the formal health system by using misoprostol. This strategy ultimately developed and spread throughout the territory, as feminist organizations founded offices where they could meet face to face with women who needed help to get a safe abortion and they started sharing their experience of medical abortion (Bergallo, 2014, 2016). Legal arguments about the duty of the state to guarantee access to legal abortions were the subject of litigation and reached the Supreme Court in 2012. The Court stated that the Federal and Provincial governments had to ensure women were able to access the practice in the cases contemplated by the

accomplished some success. Decentralized strategies were more effective than traditional attempts to promote legal change. Activism and the use of new technologies were key to transforming the policy landscape of abortion in Argentina. Less visible approaches were able to advance the legal agenda by creating local and ministerial regulations and contesting restrictive interpretations of the existing law. Strategies based on activism and the dissemination of information were discrete but showed great success in reducing the risks and harms derived from criminalization (Alcaraz, 2018). As a result, many women started to have abortions without fear of dying and without the stigma and dangers associated with underground practices.

In this context, #NiUnaMenos contributed to the abortion agenda by making feminist demands visible and understandable for the public. From 2015 on, they were able to increase public debate on other gender issues, especially violence against women. They claimed that lack of access to legal abortion, as well as death and other health problems related to unsafe abortions were examples of gendered violence and discrimination against women. As a result, they channeled social sensitivity regarding gender-based violence into a new understanding about the criminalization of abortion (Alcaraz, 2018). Nevertheless, the reframing of abortion gained almost no traction in the mainstream media in the way that femicide did. Although incredibly successful in generating changes to policy, feminists lacked agenda-setting power in the media.

This focus on abortion is the broader context of feminist activism in which #MeToo arrived in Argentina. In the next sections, we turn to analyze the impact of #MeToo in Argentina, both as an opportunity to advance an agenda on sexual harassment and to further the local feminist agenda on abortion. Specifically, this was achieved by attracting the mainstream media's attention and through the emergence of the Actresses Association, which actively promoted the legalization of abortion, using strategies inspired by the Hollywood actresses' uprising.

---

law. Finally, the information campaign caused the decrease of deaths related with unsafe abortions and transformed the experiences of women who decided to terminate their pregnancies.

#MeToo Arrives in Argentina

#MeToo was initially picked up by gossip shows that usually reinforced sexism and were suddenly confronted by a feminist rebellion in Hollywood (Centera, 2018). With ratings as their primary concern, tabloids and television shows felt the need to address the #MeToo Twitter frenzy. However, they found themselves incapable of analyzing the complexity of the phenomenon with their usual panelists, who were more used to everyday conflicts of television divas and local celebrities.

Subsequently, for the first time since the launch of #NiUnaMenos, feminist activists were invited to speak on gossip programs to explain anti-rape politics and address what was happening in Hollywood. However, these journalists and young feminists, who had been working relatively undercover on abortion, took the opportunity to reframe the #MeToo debates and talk instead about abortion. After appearing on primetime television shows, discussions about feminism became a trending topic on social media, and the economic logic of the media—for once—served the feminist agenda.

Following Hollywood patterns, Argentine actresses were also invited to address the issues brought by #MeToo in the local context. For the first time, actresses were explicitly confronting questions about harassment in the media. Many of these actresses turned to feminist activists for guidance and subsequently gained a deeper insight into their feminist agendas, including the legalization of abortion. The synergy between activists and actresses was so successful that the latter decided to create an association—the Argentine Actresses Association—and became very vocal and active in lobbying for the abortion law reform.

Energizing the Abortion Debate in Argentina

The media's coverage of #MeToo became crucial for abortion to enter everyday discussions (Centera, 2018). In February 2018, the women's movement organized another protest in front of Congress demanding the legalization of abortion. Such protests had become customary by then, and even though the number of attendees had been increasing, no one seriously believed Congress would act upon it.

Surprisingly, on February 22 2018, conservative President Mauricio Macri announced that he would not oppose Congress discussing abortion (Braslavsky, 2018).[13] Considering how influential the President is on determining the legislative agenda (Tsebelis & Aleman, 2005), the announcement was a game changer for the women's movement. As one of the slogans women used during the abortion debate shows, 'We will not shut up anymore'. Abortion in Argentina had been silenced, taboo. In a way, just like #MeToo unveiled sexual harassment, Argentine women brought our abortions to light and started talking about how the criminalization of abortion burdens our sexuality with fear and maternalizes our bodies.[14] For instance, women shouted, 'We won't go back in the closet', and sought to highlight an array of identities that differed from the stereotype of the woman whose only goal in life is to get married and have children (Dillon, 2018). Oppression of our choices and the risks associated with unsafe abortion needed to stop. These slogans used by the women's movement show connections to the core notion of #MeToo, which is not just about anti-rape politics, but also about ensuring women's broader experiences of violence and political oppression are heard and their voices respected.

Ultimately, after a narrow pass in the House of Representatives, the bill on the legalization of abortion lost the vote in the Senate on August 9. However, a new, qualitatively different way of women's political organizing emerged that did not exist before #MeToo, with actresses becoming important spokespeople for the movement.

---

[13] It should be noted that for many years, abortion was considered an issue *piantavotos* (in the local lunfardo dialect, piantavotos means an issue that repels rather than attracts voters) with virtually all political parties excluding it from their agendas. Graciela Fernandez Meijide in 1999 was a well-known pro-choice human rights activist, and she had to face public scrutiny for her position.

[14] Frug (1992, p. 1050) holds that the Law maternalizes women's bodies when it: 'reward(s) women for singularly assuming responsibilities after childbirth and with those that penalize conduct—such as sexuality or labor market work—that conflicts with mothering. Maternalization also occurs through rules such as abortion restrictions that compel women to become mothers and by domestic relations rules that favor mothers over fathers as parents. Another meaning of "female body", then, is a body that is "for" maternity. Legal discourse supports that meaning'.

In the next section, we show the limits of #MeToo in Argentina. Some actresses came forward to talk about their experience of abuse in the workplace and were met with backlash and lack of support both by mainstream media and their colleagues in the Actresses Association.

The Limit to the Anti-rape Agenda

As in other countries, when #MeToo spread in Argentina, some actresses took the chance to publicly denounce situations of harassment and assault they had had to endure while working in show business. However, as efficient and productive as the allegiance was among actresses and feminists on abortion, sexual harassment threatened the stability and unity of the newly formed Actresses Association.

The first case which could be clearly framed as a #MeToo emulation came from Calu Rivero, a young Argentine actress based in New York, who abruptly left her leading role at a primetime TV series as a result of her male costar consistently harassing her by being rough while filming sexually charged scenes. In November 2017, she turned to social media to publicly disclose her experience (Clarin, 2018). Her level of empowerment and capacity to speak out was clearly related to her geographic location, but in the local Argentine context, the message was lost. Under the hashtag #NoEsNo ('No means No'), some actresses quickly joined Rivero in repudiating the alleged conduct. However, Rivero's former costar was (and still is) the leading actor in another successful TV series, and gossip shows gave the episode their usual noncommittal treatment, questioning her motives to share the experience. In addition, her alleged aggressor filed a civil suit against her for defamation.

The most successful story in terms of anti-rape politics came from a video that was leaked showing journalist Ari Paluch grabbing a woman inappropriately, corroborating the disclosures of several women who had complained about his improper behavior, leading him to be fired from the TV network. The key contributing factor in this case was the existence of visual evidence. However, there was no focus within the media on the voices of the women who claimed to have experienced sexual harassment perpetrated by him.

The lack of a fundamental reappraisal of harassment complaints in show business became evident in the middle of the abortion debate, when the Actresses Association was at its strongest. Valeria Bertucelli, one of the most prominent actresses in Argentina, talked about the violence she suffered from actor Ricardo Darin while working on a play together. Erica Rivas, who replaced Bertucelli in her role after she left the show, backed these claims. Darin is one of the most beloved male actors in Argentina; progressive and politically outspoken, he is a remarkable figure, and his wife led the Actresses Association. These were then two heavy lifters of the media. Shockingly, the leaders of the Actresses Association quickly turned their backs on Valeria. Darin did not conform to the image of the expected perpetrator, and many were not ready to put their relationships with him and his wife on the line (see also Cover; Newman & Haire, this collection). Bertucelli and Rivas were not just rejected; the same actresses that stood before Congress to defend abortion and equality of opportunities for women vilified them.

It is true that these episodes only provide anecdotal evidence of the ways in which the media and show business personalities reacted to sexual harassment claims. However, and regardless of the merits of each situation, the difference in reaction signals a lack of development of crucial theoretical aspects of anti-rape politics. Individual bonds and affinities prevailed over the recent political union of actresses. The structures of the entertainment industry were left intact that in many ways support and benefit from the exploitation and harassment of women, and power relations remained concealed behind the interpretation of these issues as personal problems in work relationships (see Loney-Howes, this collection). The abortion agenda took over, and in a context of scarce resources, actresses and the media were not going to become feminist advocates overnight.

Conclusion

The #MeToo movement that began in Hollywood set the stage for a watershed moment for anti-rape advocacy. In the US, it unveiled how structural discrimination and harassment in show business allow powerful men to place conditions on women's careers relating to their submission and silence about sexual abuse. Powerful, influential women revealed the long-standing experiences of harassment and discrimination perpetrated by the owners of the industry they have had to endure in order to become stars. Hollywood celebrities openly confronted these practices and gained unprecedented media attention. Their voices are being heard, and enthusiastic audiences from all around the world follow the news as 'gossip from the stars'. #MeToo sells.

By the time the windstorm of #MeToo arrived, feminist mobilization in Argentina was well equipped to profit from increased attention and quick to substitute the main claims of the movement. #MeToo prompted the media into a frenzy to inform the public on what was going on in Hollywood. In order to understand the anti-rape implications, the media had to reach out to 'specialists', a space that was filled by the feminist movement, providing them with mainstream media time. #NiUnaMenos, itself a local movement that was exported to other Latin American countries, has led social mobilization against gender violence and discrimination. Even though #NiUnaMenos originally focused on protesting against femicides, it quickly expanded its horizons to include historic feminist demands, such as the legalization of abortion.

In Argentina, the characteristics of the public sphere had historically obstructed the ability of women to influence public discourse and virtually vetoed the possibility of pushing Congress to discuss the Abortion Bill, which the women's movement had been promoting for years. Interestingly, the debate mobilized the population in ways that no one had anticipated. #MeToo also contributed to the movement for the legalization of abortion by inspiring actresses to unite and join their counterparts in North America, which amplified the visibility of the issue. They held public conferences, traveled around the country and lobbied for the law reform, and even agreed to wear green garments—the color that symbolizes the fight for abortion—to the most important awards gala in Argentina to express their support (Respighi, 2018). The actresses were calling themselves feminists and talking about other issues of sex discrimination, but they failed to condemn sexual harassment in show business. In fact, their union trembled when some of them started talking about sexual harassment, abuse and assault committed by some of the most important Argentine actors.

The #MeToo hashtag did not impact feminist mobilization in Argentina, especially because the cases where women looked for support in relation to workplace sexual harassment were not successful. Media plays a crucial role in shaping the public opinion and reflecting political sentiment (see Royal, this collection). #MeToo created a political opportunity aptly taken by the women's movement. In a context scarce of discursive resources and power, partly due to low access to mainstream media and politicians, the women's movement had invested in the most visible and extreme forms of gender-based violence and discrimination, focusing on physical harm and death, such as femicides and unsafe abortions. While #MeToo centers on anti-rape politics and sexual harassment, it created an opportunity to illuminate other essential but less visible aspects of women's subordination, despite these not being core claims or focal points of the movement.

The #MeToo uprising supplied Argentine feminists with new strategies and protagonists. The potential of the actresses' union as a relevant political group for the advancement of feminist agendas remains to be seen. However, the creation of this force is undoubtedly a promising repercussion of #MeToo. The Argentine case illuminates an understanding of #MeToo as a movement that provides a new arena for women's voices and new ways of organizing feminist mobilization. Ultimately, it reveals that the scope of #MeToo has the potential of offering a broader, more substantial agenda than just sexual harassment.

References

Adamovsky, E. (2015, July 6). "Ni Una Menos" feminism and politics in Argentina. *Telesur*. Retrieved December 20, 2018, from http://www.telesurtv. net/english/opinion/Ni-una-menos-Feminism-and-Politics-in-Argentina-20150706-0011.html.

Alcaraz, M. (2018). *Que sea ley. La lucha de los feminismos por el aborto legal.* Buenos Aires: Marea Editorial.

Bellucci, M. (2014). *Historia de una desobediencia, Aborto y Feminismo.* Buenos Aires: Capital Intelectual.

Bergallo, P. (2014). The struggle against informal rules on abortion in Argentina. In R. Cook, J. Erdman, & B. Dickens (Eds.), *Abortion law in transnational perspective: Cases and controversies* (pp. 143–165). Philadelphia: University of Pennsylvania Press.

Bergallo, P. (2016). Interpretando derechos: la otra legalización del aborto en América Latina. In C. Becerra, L. Lawson, & D. Squella-Narducci (Eds.), *Debates y reflexiones en torno a la despenalización del Aborto en Chile.* Udp Facultad de Derecho: Santiago de Chile.

Braslavsky, G. (2018, February 23). Nueva agenda de discusión Macri dio luz verde para que se abra el debate sobre el aborto en el Congreso. *Clarin.* Retrieved December 20, 2018, from https://www.clarin.com/politica/macri-dio-luz-verde-abra-debate-aborto-congreso_0_SJngdC3Pz.html.

Bukstein, G. (2012). A time of opportunities: The Piquetero movement and democratization in Argentina. *Coleccion Sur-Sur. CLACSO.* Retrieved from http://biblioteca.clacso.edu.ar/gsdl/collect/clacso/index/assoc/D5431.dir/8.buk.pdf.

Centera, M. (2018, February 7). El feminismo toma por asalto la televisión argentina. *El pais.* Retrieved December 20, 2018, from https://elpais.com/internacional/2018/02/06/argentina/1517952193_089718.html.

Clarin Diario (2018, October 10), El #MeToo cumple un año: qué pasó en Argentina y en el mundo con el movimiento que dijo basta al abuso sexual. *Lanacion.* Retrieved December 20, 2018, from https://www.lanacion.com.ar/2081509-calu-rivero-vivi-en-carne-propia-el-acoso.

Dillon, M. (2018, May 25). Clandestinidad Nunca Mas. *Pagina12.* Retrieved December 20, 2018, from https://www.pagina12.com.ar/116771-clandestinidad-nunca-mas.

Drovetta, I. (2015). Safe abortion information hotlines: An effective strategy for increasing women's access to safe abortions in Latin America. *Reproductive Health Matters, 23*(45), 47–57.

Frug, M. (1992). A postmodern feminist legal manifesto (An Unfinished Draft). *Harvard Law Review, 105*(5), 1045–1075.

Gamson, W., & Wolfsfeld, G. (1993). Movements and media as interacting systems. *The Annals of the American Academy of Political and Social Science, 528*, 114–125.

Goñi, U. (2016, October 20). Argentina's women joined across South America in marches against violence. *The Guardian.* Retrieved December 20, 2018, from https://www.theguardian.com/world/2016/oct/20/argentina-women-south-america-marches-violence-ni-una-menos.

Iglesias, M. (2015, June 4). Todo el país le dijo basta a los femicidios. Histórica marcha contra la violencia machista. *Clarin*. Retrieved December 20, 2018, from https://www.clarin.com/sociedad/violencia-genero-femicidios_0_BJEJPdYDQx.html.

Keck, M., & Sikkink, K. (1998). *Activists beyond borders, advocacy networks in international politics*. Ithaca: Cornell University Press.

Ministerio de Salud de la Republica Argentina (2016). *Analisis de la mortalidad materno infantil 2007–2016*. Ministerio de Salud de la Republica Argentina. Retrieved December 20, 2018, from http://www.msal.gob.ar/images/stories/bes/graficos/0000001229cnt-analisis-mmi-2007-2016.pdf.

Motta, R. (2015). Transnational discursive opportunities and social movement risk frames opposing GMOs. *Social Movement Studies, 14*(5), 576–595.

Ni Una Menos. (2016, May 9). El grito común. *Ni Una Menos*. Retrieved December 20, 2018, from https://www.niunamenos.org.ar/manifiestos/el-grito-comun.

O´Dwyer, M. (2016). #NiUnaMenos; standing up to femicides and "machismo" in Argentina. Retrieved December 20, 2018, from https://genderandpolitic-sucd.wordpress.com/2016/02/03/niunamenos-standing-up-to-femicides-and-machismo-in-argentina/.

Respighi, E. (2018, June 3). Hoy Martín Fierro se vestirá de verde. *Página12*. Retrieved December 20, 2018, from https://www.pagina12.com.ar/119012-hoy-martin-fierro-se-vestira-de-verde.

Russell, D., & Caputi, J. (1992). Femicide: Sexist terrorism against women. In J. Radford & D. Russell (Eds.), *Femicide: The politics of woman killing* (pp. 13–26). New York: Twayne.

Tarrow, S. (1994). *Power in movement: Social movements and contentious politics*. New York: Cambridge University Press.

Tarrow, S. (2005). *The new transnational activism*. Cambridge: Cambridge University Press.

Tarrow, S., & Tilly, C. (2007). Contentious politics and social movements. In C. Boix & S. Stokes (Eds.), *The oxford handbook of comparative politics*. Oxford: Oxford University Press.

Thalhammer, K., & Branigan, C. (2017). Fighting state terror and becoming the state: Argentina's human rights movement from mass mobilization to institutionalization. *Revista de Paz y Conflictos, 10*(1), 9–34.

Tsebelis, G., & Aleman, E. (2005). Presidential conditional agenda setting in Latin America. *World Politics, 57*(3), 396–420.

13

Shitty Media Men

Bridget Haire, Christy E. Newman,
and Bianca Fileborn

Could preventing sexual violence be as simple as circulating a Google Doc that named perpetrators and warned women about problem behavior?

In October 2017, inspired by the activism of the #MeToo movement sweeping the film and entertainment industry, a young woman put together a Google Doc spreadsheet for circulation among her peers. Dubbed the Shitty Media Men list, the document was intended as a mechanism for members of this peer group to share information about men in the media industry who had perpetrated some form of sexual misconduct and/or violence. It was open source, so any recipient could

B. Haire (✉)
The Kirby Institute, UNSW Sydney, Kensington, NSW, Australia
e-mail: b.haire@unsw.edu.au

C. E. Newman
Centre for Social Research in Health, UNSW Sydney, Kensington, NSW, Australia
e-mail: c.newman@unsw.edu.au

B. Fileborn
University of Melbourne, Parkville, VIC, Australia
e-mail: biancaf@unimelb.edu.au

© The Author(s) 2019
B. Fileborn, R. Loney-Howes (eds.), *#MeToo and the Politics of Social Change*,
https://doi.org/10.1007/978-3-030-15213-0_13

edit it, and its purported aim was to inform and warn women in the industry about potentially 'risky' men they might encounter—a form of informal justice-seeking, given that this strategy works to circumvent formal avenues for reporting and justice-seeking—in order to protect women from potential predators (see Fileborn, 2017). Women who were given access to the link in order to contribute were instructed to never name or 'out' an accuser, never show the list to a man and not to 'freak out' if they saw the name of a friend on this list. These admittedly flimsy rules were intended to limit the circulation of the list to women who had been and/or may become subjected to sexual predation by these men.

Making innovative use of contemporary digital platforms that in practice often blur distinctions between public and private, this list arguably represented a revamped form of the 'whisper network'—the process by which women have traditionally warned one another about predatory men (Meza, 2017; Tolentino, 2017). Headed by a disclaimer that the list contained allegations and rumors only, men listed as having perpetrated physical sexual violence (rape or sexual assault) by more than one woman were highlighted in red. Of the 72 names on the version of the list available at the time of writing, 15[1] were flagged in red (Wordpress, 2017).

Within hours of its release, the list became a viral Internet phenomenon. Despite the author taking it down after only 12 hours, a 'read-only' version moved quickly into circulation. A *Buzzfeed* journalist ran a story on the list several days after it had been taken down (Shafrir, 2017). Shortly afterward, right-wing blogger Mike Cernovich offered a $10,000 reward to anyone who would give him a copy, in a move described as the 'weaponizing' of the list. He obtained the list amidst claims of a journalistic coup and subsequently published two of the names on it: names that happened to be those of his so-called 'personal enemies' (Kircher, 2017). Seven men listed subsequently lost their jobs or resigned after investigations into misconduct were pursued by their employers (Jeong, 2018). Shortly afterward, *Harper's Magazine* commissioned a contrarian piece by Katie Roiphe, author of the 1990s 'backlash' tome *The Morning After*. Roiphe's article was rumored to be about 'outing' the creator of the list—a

---

[1] Interestingly, author Moira Donegan states that there were 14 red highlights. The version available on Wordpress has 15.

move that prompted former *New Republic* editor Moira Donegan to claim authorship (Donegan, 2018). A year after the publication of the list, Stephen Elliot, one of the men named in red as a Shitty Media Man, filed a lawsuit against Donegan (Canon, 2018).

The Shitty Media Men list generated a vast quantity of debate and commentary in both social and traditional media, despite the short amount of time it was actually available as an online Google Doc. From its inception, the list became the object of competing moral claims. Galvanized by the reporting of Harvey Weinstein's multiple acts of sexual violence, Donegan said she conceived of it as a way to share knowledge among potentially vulnerable women working in magazines and publishing that could empower them to avoid the situations or simply the men who had sexually harassed or assaulted others. Critics alleged the list represented a form of political zealotry, variously named as 'sex panic' (Gessen, 2017), 'McCarthyism' (Sullivan, 2018) or 'Trotskeyism' (Roiphe, 2018).

Clearly, Donegan's decision to create and share the list was a deeply divisive one and a move that raises a range of questions regarding the ethics of 'naming and shaming' perpetrators online, as well as the social, political and institutional contexts shaping the ways in which victim-survivors disclose or share experiences. In this chapter, we analyze responses to the Shitty Media Men list, including the claims put forth in the Elliot lawsuit, and consider how the conceptions of moral action contained within them operate to facilitate or constrain the reporting of sexual violence.

Jumbled Allegations

One of the key critiques of the Shitty Media Men list is that it placed allegations of rape and other forms of 'serious' sexual violence (e.g., 'non-consensual choking of a woman until she [loses] consciousness') alongside seemingly more trivial offenses (e.g., 'creepy af in the DM's'[2]; 'inappropriate conversation, unsolicited invitations to sex parties'). Katie Roiphe

---

[2] Translates as 'Creepy as fuck in the direct [text] messages'.

referred to this as a failure of proportionality, citing entries on the list referring to 'weird lunch dates', 'leering', 'flirting', 'violent language' and 'leading on multiple women online'—allegations she argued were not substantial enough to fit into the category of sexual misconduct (see Fileborn & Phillips, this collection, for a critique of this conceptualization of sexual violence). Andrew Sullivan was also indignant at what he called the 'chorus of minor offenses' sitting alongside what he deemed to be serious sexual violence, castigating the inclusion of offenses that have, he asserted, 'no claim of workplace misconduct at all' (Sullivan, 2018). Oddly, Sullivan seemed to regard non-consensual condom removal during sex as a trivial matter, despite being recognized as a significant betrayal of the conditions of consent and as a 'rape–adjacent' act (Brodsky, 2017). Sullivan also insisted upon a very narrow focus on the physical, 'real-life' workplace. However, such a conceptualization of the 'workplace' arguably no longer holds in an industry where workplaces have been transformed by technology, such that they are no longer limited to clearly physical and bounded spaces. Preoccupation with the workplace is also peculiar when considering the aims of the list—to warn women about men in the industry who might be perpetrators—whether sexual violence perpetrated by a work colleague occurs in a workspace or private context is clearly beside the point. Sullivan's emphasis on a physical workplace also precludes forms of harassment that occur online, such as cyberstalking and sending unwanted and unsolicited messages and pictures.

Similarly to Sullivan's and Roiphe's concerns about the mixing of allegations of different categories of behaviors, Daphne Merkin in *The New York Times* argued that there was a meaningful distinction to be preserved between harassment and assault and 'inappropriate conduct'. She suggested that harassment should contain an element of hostility, which she argued is not present with, say, an inappropriate kiss or sending an unwanted sexual image (Merkin, 2018). This critique echoed the views of an open letter responding to #MeToo authored by Sarah Chiche and signed by Catherine Deneuve and 98 other prominent French women, which was published in *Le Monde*. The *Le Monde* letter defended the right of men to 'pester' women in the name of eroticism (Chiche et al., 2018). It also sought to articulate a boundary between rape (recognized as a crime) and forms of 'machismo aggression' (within which they included flirting, 'stealing' kisses, men's hands on women's knees, etc.). Calling such behavior sexual harassment infantilizes women, the letter energetically claimed.

These critiques align the creation of the Shitty Media Men list with anti-eroticism rather than with anti-violence and implicitly suggest that women who call out sexual harassment are at best overreacting and, at worst, victimizing men. The context for the list's creation is lost in this reframing, where it is positioned as a public document that shames, as distinct from one that protects. This inversion is made possible by the 'viral' capacity of the Internet, where sharing in social networks can quickly lift communication from the limited private sphere into a seemingly boundless public one.

Whether Donegan was reasonable or, as Sullivan says, 'extremely naïve', to believe a list containing serious allegations against well-known media figures could remain 'private', the grab bag of complaints that the list contained did nonetheless align quite well with its self-description as 'only a collection of misconduct allegations and rumors' (Donegan, 2018). In the article with which she claimed her authorship, Donegan explained that one of the reasons she had thought the list would remain private was that no one would be interested in it. However, she acknowledged that it was short-sighted not to recognize that the list would become newsworthy, not simply because of the actions of the men named, but because of the potential impacts on those men of their naming (Donegan, 2018). The subsequent 'weaponizing' of the list by journalists also illustrated how women's efforts to utilize online platforms in order to protect others can be misappropriated. Certainly, the potential of such lists to be misused in this way was a key ethical challenge posed by what is essentially a form of online justice-seeking through informal reporting (see, for e.g., Fileborn, 2017; Salter, this collection). However, it is less clear that responsibility for this 'weaponization' lies with the list's authors, as opposed to those who chose to repurpose the list for their own means.

Lack of Verification and 'Due Process'

Many critiques of the list centered on issues of due process or the apparent lack thereof. One of the key claims that Elliot's lawsuit made was that the creators of the Shitty Media Men list—including, but not limited to, Moira Donegan—were negligent in the processes of verification that were asked of contributors. The lawsuit claimed that the list published defamatory allegations without any requirement for providing corroborating evidence (such as would be required, for example, by a media outlet) and without any means of assessing the credibility of the claimants. As an example of the kind of technical detail which became the focus of criticisms of these issues of 'process', journalist Sarah Jeong noted that while multiple serious allegations were highlighted in red, the lack of time stamps or links to corroborating detail made it impossible to know how many women had accused particular men (Jeong, 2018).

In an online essay in which he argued that he was innocent of the rape allegations outlined, Elliot wrote, 'Anyone—male or female—with access to the list could have added my name while it was online' (Elliot, 2018). The anonymity of the list, according to Donegan, was intended to free women from fears of 'retaliation, backlash and smearing' (Donegan, 2018). Without any power of enforcement, Donegan explained, women were freed from the adversarial processes required to prove sexual violence in a court of law. Further, the presumption of innocence required both legally and ethically when an accusation could result in legal consequences would not be necessary, she thought, if the aim was to warn not to punish, so the list would offer a non-adversarial tool through which to share intelligence (Donegan, 2018). The advice to 'take it all with a grain of salt' was an acknowledgment that the process was imperfect. While fact-checking processes are rarely possible in any open-sourced document or Wiki, critics of the list were particularly outraged about the lack of systematic verification of claims in this instance. This was primarily due to the potential damage to personal and professional reputations and the capacity for manipulation of the process (a single person using different aliases could report someone repeatedly, apparently, creating a fiction of verification)—all veiled by the anonymity of the accusers.

Elliot supported his claim of innocence in the essay with the revelation that he does not enjoy penetrating sexual partners and that his sexual practice is as a 'bottom' (submissive/receptive) in a BDSM context. Further, he claimed that his sexual practices were sufficiently well known, due to his public writing on the matter, and that therefore the allegations against him ought to have been known to be false. Elliot's claim framed sexual violence or misconduct as requiring penetrative sexual contact, rather than taking into account the broad spectrum of inter-related actions that can constitute sexual misconduct, harassment and assault (see Fileborn & Phillips, this collection). This is particularly pertinent given that at least three women have chronicled misconduct of Elliot's that they felt was demeaning and harassing (see Siegel, 2018; Lenz, 2018; Vaye Watkins, 2015).

Interestingly, while Katie Roiphe's article (as discussed earlier) was also critical of the lack of 'due process', many of the sources she cited as verification that the list lacked adequate process and a necessary sense of proportion were dubbed 'deeply anonymous'. Claims that the creation and dissemination of the list lacked due process again ignored that it was intended as a *private* document to be shared between women and was not proffered as legal evidence in the context of a criminal trial. While we should of course be concerned with the ethical principles guiding how shared disclosures and naming of perpetrators occur (see Salter, this collection), this does not mean that the safeguards in place to protect accused persons from the power of *the state* should be used in assessing the actions of private citizens (Gilmore, 2018). It is also notable that the men who faced serious consequences for their actions after being named on the list (such as having their employment terminated) incurred these consequences *after* a formal process (such as a workplace investigation) was followed (Jeong, 2018).

Sullivan invoked McCarthyism—another list, also anonymous—and rejected Donegan's claim that the list was intended to be consequence free, rather than a form of summary justice. Donegan refuted this, arguing that, as her list did not hold any enforcement power it did not need to meet normative evidentiary standards, particularly as its aim was to warn potential victims rather than punish reported perpetrators.

Donegan's claims reflect those made by victim-survivors who have engaged with other types of formal and informal justice-seeking: namely, to protect others from experiencing the same harms. For example, one study with victim-survivors who had gone through the criminal justice system found that 'community protection' was one key reason for doing so (Clark, 2010). Likewise, another study on street harassment victims' online disclosure practices similarly found that participants were motivated by the desire to act in solidarity with other victims and to work toward preventing this behavior (Fileborn, 2017). In contrast to the myth of the 'vengeful', 'scorned' woman, a range of factors motivate victim-survivors when they disclose (see also Franks, this collection). While retribution and punishment *can* be important, these are by no means the only reasons women name their perpetrators. What this research suggests is that victim-survivors often share experiences and information as a form of *collective* justice-seeking and protection.

A key element in critiques of the Shitty Media Men list was the presumption that if women want to complain about sexual misconduct and sexual violence, they should do so through formal institutional channels—the workplace human resources department or the police. Such claims, however, ignore the problematic ways in which these formal mechanisms have responded to sexual violence and harassment both in the past and contemporaneously (McGlynn, 2011). Moreover, cases of sexual violence face high levels of attrition—where they are 'filtered out' of the system, so that only a small number of cases reported to police proceed to court, while fewer still result in a successful conviction. Despite extensive legislative and procedural reform, survivors still describe the court system as 'retraumatizing', with the process frequently likened to a 'second rape' (Larcombe, 2011). Workplace sexual harassment does not fare much better in this regard, with those who report indicating that they face backlash, blame, stigmatization and outright retaliation in the workplace (AHRC, 2018). In short, to paraphrase Sara Ahmed, those who report to expose the problem of sexual harassment and violence become reframed as the cause of the problem (Ahmed, 2014). Claims that the authors of the Shitty Media Men list should have reported through 'socially accepted channels' ignore the extent to which these channels are themselves sites of injustice for victim-survivors. Indeed,

Sara Ahmed suggests that the use of 'official' complaints or reporting procedures can themselves be a way of *shutting down* a complaint, given that 'the gap between what is supposed to happen and what does happen is densely populated' (Ahmed, 2018, np). In other words, official complaint or reporting mechanisms can work as a means of silencing victims given the amount of red tape that complainants have to go through and the extent to which cases are filtered out of 'formal' mechanisms, while simultaneously giving the appearance that the right thing has been done.

The Ethics of 'Naming and Shaming'

As noted earlier, Elliot launched a lawsuit against Donegan in 2018. As the claimant, he also named 30 'Jane Does' in his suit—the as-yet unidentified women who contributed to the document, whose identities Elliot vowed to uncover by subpoenaing Google (Google has publicly stated this information no longer exists). Elliot's lawsuit, which made a claim of $1.5 million in damages for defamation, listed loss of income, loss of community standing and suicidal ideation as the personal and professional impacts of the publication. He argued that the publishers of the list—of which Donegan was the only person named—showed a reckless disregard for the truth, actively edited, organized, highlighted and published the information on the list and in doing so intentionally exposed him to contempt, aversion and vitriol. Elliot's claims largely center on the ethics (and legality) of 'naming and shaming' (alleged) perpetrators online.

Notably, the Elliot lawsuit against Donegan and the Jane Does appeared to treat the list as a public, rather than private, document and subsequently applied the standards of public broadcast to a document intended for sharing only among a select population. Arguably, it was the actions of Shafrir at *Buzzfeed* (who drew public attention to the list) that has allegedly caused reputational damage for Elliot. Yet, this action is not mentioned in the suit, nor is Cernovich's attempt, as mentioned earlier, to make the list public after it had been taken down. Donegan's role in 'publicizing' the list, however, is cited.

Five other men listed on the document did not support the legal action. These men, who spoke to Ruth Spencer for *The Cut* on the condition of anonymity, all said that Elliot's lawsuit brought the list back into the media spotlight, which for them was a bad outcome. Of the five, two stated that they did not do what they are accused of doing on the list, but one of these said that he clearly 'messed with' someone seriously enough to have been named. The others either admitted implicitly or explicitly that they had 'crossed a line' (with acts undefined). Of note, three of the men seemed to be quite protective of Donegan and opposed to the notion of punishing her or the other women who contributed (Spencer, 2018).

The contrast between the attitudes of the men in Spencer's article and Elliot raises a question: if some men named on the list did not perpetrate the actions it names, who is responsible for the damage to their reputations? Elliot's lawsuit clearly alleges that the fault lies not just with Donegan who has assumed 'first-author' responsibility, but with all of the women who contributed. There is a very stark ethical problem with assigning blame in this way: the list was not intended as a 'publication' but as an avenue to protect other women from sexual violence. The alleged responsibility could more reasonably be attached to those who made the publication public after Donegan had taken it down.

Arguably the punitive character of Elliot's lawsuit—in particular the targeting of the Jane Does who contributed to the list but have remained anonymous—could also be seen to be a vindictive and disproportionate response, as it targets women who were trying to keep other women safe, most of whom would have had nothing whatsoever to do with the claims made about Elliot and who were also victim-survivors. One of the anonymous sources in Spencer's article argues that these women—and specifically Donegan—should not be further victimized: 'And the idea that Moira or any of the contributors could be further exposed, or hurt, or damaged, makes me sick'. Another said: 'it makes you wonder if the point is to cause Moira pain or to make someone who contributed to the list afraid' (Spencer, 2018). These comments suggest that for some men at least, being named as some form of perpetrator is less significant than protecting those who have been damaged by sexual violence.

Aims and Limitations of Whisper Networks

'Whisper networks' are an age-old way that women have sought to keep each other safe, and the Shitty Media Men list is by no means the first time that complaints about men's sexual violence have been written and distributed by insider channels. Toilet walls and 'rape lists' in universities have sometimes operated in this way (The Cut, 2018). 'Ugly mug' publications, where sex workers share intelligence about violent clients, are a prime example of the genre, and these flourish where sex workers are collectivized. The purposes of 'ugly mug' publications and the Shitty Media Men list are closely aligned. The New South Wales (Australia) Sex Worker Outreach Program website through which submissions are compiled makes a similar disclaimer to Donegan's: 'The UML makes these reports available to help other sex industry workers avoid problem clients, and as an extension of the "word of mouth" warnings given by sex industry workers to each other. The UML makes no claims to the accuracy or legitimacy of the allegations, nor do we investigate the authenticity of the reports (provided in confidence by sex workers)' (SWOP, 2018). The integrity of such publications depends on them being distributed to the people whose interests they serve: closed networks, not available for casual voyeuristic consumption (Barnes, 2014). Notably, in the examples of both 'ugly mugs' and the Shitty Media Men list, these lists are generated in contexts of largely ineffective law enforcement responses and/or hostile relationships between police and these groups. This is not to conflate the experiences of sex workers and victim-survivors of sexual harassment and violence (while also noting that these groups are not mutually exclusive) but rather to highlight the ways in which grassroots protective mechanisms appear to flourish in the absence of safe and effective access to 'official' justice processes (see Ison, this collection, on this point in relation to the LGBTQIA community).

By their very nature, however, whisper networks *exclude*, and thus there are important questions to ask regarding who is included within particular networks: who is allowed to speak or disclose via these channels, and who is excluded. Operating as and through social networks, whisper networks tended to reproduce social inequities and thus women of color were prone to exclusion (Hobbs, 2018; Wortham, 2017; Donegan, 2018). Donegan also noted that whisper networks could be elitist, unreliable and insular and that the open-source digital product might democratize this, while still remaining essentially private—confined, as she imagined, to women in her social sphere (Donegan, 2018).

Exclusion is an issue documented in other informal feminist networks and digital justice practices. For example, Fileborn (2017) found similar issues with online disclosure through feminist sites such as *Hollaback!*, with some of her participants indicating that they experienced virtual exclusion and marginalization in these spaces. As a result, they were unable (or less able) to participate in these spaces. This suggests it is vitally important to consider who, precisely, is 'protected' through efforts to share information and the extent to which these seemingly protective networks may work to amplify or perpetuate other inequalities.

Donegan claimed that with its emphasis on the named perpetrator and the listed acts, the Shitty Media Men lists put the responsibility for sexual violence back onto men by making the perpetrator and his acts visible while securing anonymity for the complainant, which she saw as a radical action. In practical terms, however, this analysis is flawed, as once empowered with knowledge, the onus falls back on women to act: to prepare for and protect against male sexual violence. Thus, one interpretation of such lists is that they place a responsibility on women (or potential victims) to have read it and to then suitably 'protect' themselves when they interact with those named on the list. The mental, emotional and physical burden for protecting sexual violence is again placed on the (potential) victim. This 'responsibilizing' discourse (Newman, Persson, Miller, & Brown, 2016) may also be used to shift responsibility for sexual violence back on to women and be taken up as a form of victim-blaming. What happens, for instance, to someone who has read the list and is subsequently victimized by one of the named perpetrators? It is not difficult to see this being drawn on to argue that these women should have 'known better'. Of course, this is also challenging in the face of inadequate state, institutional and other responses to sexual violence, with women often placed in a context in which they have seemingly little choice but to bear the burden of sexual violence 'prevention' or, perhaps more appropriately, avoidance.

Conclusion

Despite the momentum of the #MeToo movement, with its focus on the stories of victim-survivors, the response to the Shitty Media Men list suggests that there is still no protected space for women to tell their stories if that includes the naming of perpetrators. The anonymity that the Google Doc appeared to offer was a mirage, at least as far as Donegan's identity was concerned, and the Elliot lawsuit demonstrates that what was intended as a limited, private communication may be subject to the rules that apply to communications intended for broadcast. While the outcome of the lawsuit is unknown at the time of writing, the fact that it is underway has had a chilling effect on the notional freedoms of cyber communication.

In the wake of the controversy over the form and distribution of the Shitty Media Men list, it is easy to lose sight of what it appeared to document: burdensome sexual harassment and endemic sexual violence in the magazine and publishing industry. As to why it took an anonymous, open-source spreadsheet to reveal this, Jia Tolentino commented, 'Women know how hard it is to connect male misconduct to real consequences. The most we generally hope for is to save other women some heartache and trauma and time' (Tolentino, 2017). Regarding the status of whisper networks in relation to due process, Jeong notes, 'Whisper networks certainly aren't due process, but they also don't bypass due process: they exist in a vacuum of due process'—a symptom of pervasive injustice and institutional failure.

References

Ahmed, S. (2014, February 17). The problem of perception. *Feminist Killjoys*. Retrieved October 20, 2018, from https://feministkilljoys.com/2014/02/17/the-problem-of-perception/.

Ahmed, S. (2018). *Complaint as diversity work*. University of Wollongong. Retrieved October 20, 2018, from https://www.sarahahmed.com/forthcoming-events/2018/10/25/complaint-public-lecture-wollongong-university.

Australian Human Rights Commission. (2018). *Everyone's business: Fourth national survey on sexual harassment in Australian workplaces*. Sydney: AHRC.

Barnes, L. (2014, August 19). Ugly mugs: 'An unacceptable breach of sex workers' privacy'. *The Conversation*. Retrieved December 19, 2018, from https://theconversation.com/ugly-mugs-an-unacceptable-breach-of-sex-workers-privacy-30615.

Brodsky, A. (2017). Rape-adjacent': Imagining legal responses to nonconsensual condom removal. *Columbia Journal of Gender and Law, 32*(2), 183–210.

Canon, G. (2018, October 13). Writer named on Shitty Media Men list sues its creator. *The Guardian*. Retrieved December 20, 2018, from https://www.theguardian.com/media/2018/oct/11/shitty-media-men-lawsuit-stephen-elliott-moira-donegan.

Clark, H. (2010). "What is the justice system willing to offer?" Understanding sexual assault victim/survivors' criminal justice needs. *Family Matters, 85*, 28–37.

Chiche, S., Millet, C., Robbe-Grillet, C., Sastre, P., Shalmani, A., et al. (2018, January 10). *World Crunch*. Retrieved October 20, 2018, from https://www.worldcrunch.com/opinion-analysis/full-translation-of-french-anti-metoo-manifesto-signed-by-catherine-deneuve.

Donegan, M. (2018, January). I started the Shitty Media Men list. *The Cut*. Retrieved December 19, 2018, from https://www.thecut.com/2018/01/moira-donegan-i-started-the-media-men-list.html.

Elliot, S. (2018, September 25). How an anonymous accusation derailed my life. Retrieved December 19, 2018, from https://quillette.com/2018/09/25/how-an-anonymous-accusation-derailed-my-life.

Fileborn, B. (2017). Justice 2.0: Street harassment victims' use of social media and online activism as sites of informal justice. *British Journal of Criminology, 57*(6), 1482–1501.

Gessen, M. (2017, November 14). When does a watershed become a sex panic? *New Yorker*. Retrieved December 19, 2018, from https://www.newyorker.com/news/our-columnists/when-does-a-watershed-become-a-sex-panic.

Gilmore, J. (2018, October 23). Presumption of innocence and the #MeToo backlash. *Sydney Morning Herald*. Retrieved December 19, 2018, from https://www.smh.com.au/lifestyle/life-and-relationships/presumption-of-innocence-and-the-metoo-backlash-20181019-p50aqw.html.

Hobbs, A. (2018, October 10). One year of #MeToo: The legacy of black women's testimonies. *New Yorker*. Retrieved December 19, 2018, from https://www.newyorker.com/culture/personal-history/one-year-of-metoo-the-legacy-of-black-womens-testimonies.

Jeong, S. (2018, February 21). When whisper networks let us down. *The Verge*. Retrieved December 19, 2018, from https://www.theverge.com/2018/

2/21/17035552/sexual-assault-harassment-whisper-network-reporting-failure-marquis-boire.

Kircher, M. M. (2017, October 27). The 'Shitty Men in Media' list has officially been weaponized. *New York Times*. Retrieved December 19, 2018, from http://nymag.com/intelligencer/2017/10/shitty-men-in-media-list-published-on-reddit-and-twitter.html.

Larcombe, W. (2011). Falling rape conviction rates: (Some) feminist aims and measures for rape law. *Feminist Legal Studies, 19*(1), 27–45.

Lenz, L. (2018). Twitter. Retrieved October 20, 2018, from https://www.trendsmap.com/twitter/tweet/1044702812616216577.

McGlynn, C. (2011). Feminism, rape and the search for justice. *Oxford Journal of Legal Studies, 31*(4), 825–842.

Merkin, D. (2018, January 5). Publicly, we say #MeToo. Privately, we have misgivings. *New York Times*. Retrieved December 19, 2018, from https://www.nytimes.com/2018/01/05/opinion/golden-globes-metoo.html?_r=0.

Meza, S. (2017, November 22). What is a whisper network? How women are taking down bad men in the #MeToo age. *Newsweek*. Retrieved December 19, 2018, from https://www.newsweek.com/what-whisper-network-sexual-misconduct-allegations-719009.

Newman, C. E., Persson, A., Miller, A., & Brown, R. J. (2016). "Just take your medicine and everything will be fine": Responsibilisation narratives in accounts of transitioning young people with HIV into adult care services in Australia. *AIDS Care, 28*(1), 131–136.

Roiphe, K. (2018, March). The other whisper network: How Twitter feminism is bad for women. *Harper's Magazine*. Retrieved December 19, 2018, from https://harpers.org/archive/2018/03/the-other-whisper-network-2/.

Sex Workers' Outreach Project. (2018). Report a mug. Retrieved October 20, 2018, from https://swop.org.au/report-a-mug.

Shafrir, D. (2017, October12). What to do with "Shitty Media Men"? *Buzzfeed*. Retrieved December 19, 2018, from https://www.buzzfeednews.com/article/doree/what-to-do-with-shitty-media-men.

Siegel, M. (2018, September 26). Firsthand. *The Rumpus*. Retrieved December 19, 2018, from https://therumpus.net/2018/09/firsthand.

Spencer, R. (2018, October 11). What 5 shitty media men think of Stephen Elliott's lawsuit against Moira Donegan. *The Cut*. Retrieved December 19, 2018, from https://www.thecut.com/2018/10/stephen-elliott-moira-donegan-men-respond.html.

Sullivan, A. (2018, January 12). It's time to resist the excesses of #MeToo. *New York Intelligencer*. Retrieved December 19, 2018, from http://nymag.com/intelligencer/2018/01/andrew-sullivan-time-to-resist-excesses-of-metoo.html.

The Cut. (2018, October 23). The anonymous list that started an uproar 28 years before 'Shitty Media Men. *The Cut*. Retrieved December 19, 2018, from https://www.gimletmedia.com/the-cut-on-tuesdays/hes-coming-after-us-a-list-and-a-lawsuit#episode-player.

Tolentino, J. (2017, October 14). The whisper network after Harvey Weinstein and "Shitty Media Men," *New Yorker*. Retrieved December 19, 2018, from https://www.newyorker.com/news/news-desk/the-whisper-network-after-harvey-weinstein-and-shitty-media-men.

Vaye Watkins, C. (2015, November 23). On pandering. *Tin House*. Retrieved December 19, 2018, from https://tinhouse.com/on-pandering/.

Wordpress. (2017, October 29). Shitty Media Men. *Wordpress*. Retrieved March 26, 2018, from https://shittymediamenlist.wordpress.com.

Wortham, J. (2017, December 13). We were left out. *The New York Times Magazine*. Retrieved December 19, 2018, from https://www.nytimes.com/interactive/2017/12/13/magazine/the-reckoning-women-and-power-in-the-workplace.html.

14

Journalist Guidelines and Media Reporting in the Wake of #MeToo

Kathryn Royal

Introduction

Media coverage was central in the development of the #MeToo movement and is significant in the reporting of sexual violence more widely. For those who have not experienced abuse, the media is a key source of information and understanding (Berns, 2004). How cases of sexual violence are reported on is therefore essential in informing the general public, and journalists have a unique opportunity to educate readers about the realities of sexual violence and have a responsibility for 'halting the perpetuation of myths' by educating not only the public, but also themselves (Meyers, 1997, p. 103). However, scholars Soothill and Walby (1991) suggest that media coverage of sexual violence is often inaccurate and sensationalist, and sexualizes victims of abuse, highlighting the damage done by media reporting.

Given the media frenzy that followed the allegations of sexual violence perpetrated by Harvey Weinstein, this chapter analyses four articles

K. Royal (✉)
Department of Sociology, Durham University, Durham, UK
e-mail: k.e.royal@durham.ac.uk

© The Author(s) 2019
B. Fileborn, R. Loney-Howes (eds.), *#MeToo and the Politics of Social Change*,
https://doi.org/10.1007/978-3-030-15213-0_14

covering the abuse committed by Harvey Weinstein published in UK newspapers; two when the allegations first came to light in October 2017, and two when he first appeared in court in June 2018. To do this, it uses guidelines produced for journalists when reporting violence against women. It highlights that reporting did not evenly follow the guidelines and therefore offers suggestions on improving the ways sexual violence is reported on and supporting journalists in this endeavour.

Media Guidelines for Reporting on Violence Against Women

Founded in 1907, the National Union of Journalists (NUJ) in the United Kingdom claims to be one of the largest journalist unions in the world (NUJ, 2018), and the guidelines published by the NUJ for reporting violence against women were used to analyse the four articles in this chapter. The guidelines offer advice for journalists reporting on a variety of forms of violence against women. As such, not all the guidelines were relevant for sexual violence, and so not all are included in the discussion here.

The Articles

Four articles were selected from *The Guardian* and *Daily Mail*, two UK-based publications that have a global reach. According to data published by the National Readership Survey, the *Daily Mail* is the most read news media across print, PC, and mobile platforms, and its readership is 53% female (NRS, 2017). Its online publication, also known as *mailonline.co.uk*, is well known for its 'sidebar of shame', which often includes 'stories' featuring—and shaming—female celebrities' bodies or clothing. *Daily Mail*'s website is the fifth most read news website in the world, third highest English-language news site globally, and second most popular news site in the United Kingdom (SimilarWeb, 2018a).

Meanwhile, *The Guardian* is the third most read news media across print, PC, and mobile in the United Kingdom and has an almost equal gender split readership (NRS, 2017). *The Guardian* is the third most read news website globally and first in the United Kingdom (SimilarWeb, 2018b). It was important to include publications that were UK based, so as to fit the scope of the NUJ guidelines, but that were also popular globally in order to speak to the global nature of the #MeToo movement. The first articles were published on 7 and 8 October 2017 (Hoby, 2017; Leonard, 2017) and discussed Weinstein's 'downfall', as it had emerged so far. The second articles were published on 5 June 2018 (Helmore, 2018; Spargo & Boyle, 2018) and covered Weinstein's appearance in court to enter his 'not guilty' pleas.

This sample is not intended to be representative of all articles published about Weinstein or #MeToo.[1] An analysis of broader media coverage is far beyond the scope of this chapter (for this, see Royal, 2019a). Rather, these articles are presented as case studies in order to highlight the mistakes journalists are making when reporting on gender-based violence and discuss how these could be rectified. The discussion of the guidelines is grouped into relevant themes, including: the presentation of victim-survivors, the presentation of perpetrators, the presentation of violence against women, and the need to provide information in order to better support survivors.

Presentations of Victim-Survivors

The presentation of victim-survivors in news media encompasses a number of guidelines. The first of these is to avoid the use of negative gender stereotypes:

> Have regard for women as individuals and avoid media reporting which reinforces negative gender stereotypes. (NUJ, 2013, p. 1)

---

[1] It should also be noted that the articles analysed in this chapter were reproduced in other popular news media outlets around the world.

Three of the four articles avoided using negative gender stereotypes, whilst one *Daily Mail* article did not.[2] The negative stereotypes found in the *Daily Mail* article often related to rape myths and discourses that sought to hold women responsible for the actions of Harvey Weinstein. For example:

> However, over the years, instead of criticising or refusing to work with him, scores of female stars—including Gwyneth Paltrow, Jennifer Lawrence, Meryl Streep and Judi Dench—have showered praise on him for championing their careers. (*Daily Mail*, 7/10/2017)

As evidenced in the quote above, the women who had appeared in Weinstein's films are shamed for not having brought his behaviour to light, positioning women (and not men) as responsible for the prevention of sexual violence. It is not these women's responsibility to blow the whistle, especially considering the power Weinstein exercised over their bodies and careers; moreover, no mention was made of the men who had worked with Weinstein and who could have criticized or refused to work with him.

The *Daily Mail* article also went on to comment:

> Long-time speculation over *which of those 'Harvey Girls' have succumbed to his sexual overtures* has inevitably been given new life by the latest revelations. (*Daily Mail*, 7/10/2017, my emphasis)

This paints Weinstein's abuse as women 'succumbing' to his advances, implying consent and sexualizing and sensationalizing decades of abuse committed by a man in a position of power. The women are therefore positioned as complicit in the abuse and responsible for their victimization.

This leads into the next guideline:

> Take care not to imply that a survivor of gender-based violence might be somehow, even partially, to blame for the violence she has experienced, nor

---

[2] It is worth noting the guidance does not offer specific advice around how to avoid perpetuating negative gender stereotypes.

assume or imply that any of her behaviour might have triggered the abuse or that 'she asked for it'. (NUJ, 2013, p. 2)

Only one article did not blame the victim-survivors. As with the use of gender stereotypes discussed above, this included referring to women who had worked with Weinstein as the so-called Harvey Girls. This was done with actresses Ashley Judd and Rose McGowan in one of the *Daily Mail* articles (7/10/2017), implying a mutually beneficial and consensual, rather than abusive, relationship with Weinstein. In doing so, the credibility of the women coming forward was undermined, with the journalist quoting from Weinstein's lawyer without challenging the comments he made:

His lawyer, Benjamin Brafman, has *challenged the credibility* of Weinstein's alleged victims and says his client is confident he will clear his name ... Brafman has called the rape allegations 'absurd', saying the accuser and Weinstein *had a decade-long consensual sexual relationship that continued after the alleged 2013 attack.* (*Guardian*, 5/06/2018, my emphasis)

Blaming victim-survivors of sexual violence is well documented in feminist scholarship, with many studies on the prevalence of rape myths—'prejudicial, stereotyped, or false beliefs about rape, rape victims and rapists' (Burt, 1980, p. 217). This includes blame in relation to behaviours such as alcohol consumption, clothing choices, and previous interactions with the rapist (Burt, 1980). Many victim-survivors experience victim-blaming—Ullman and Townsend (2007, p. 435), for example, found that 72% of their sample had experienced 'negative or revictimizing reactions, such as being blamed or disbelieved'. The media therefore has the opportunity to address and eliminate the victim-blaming levelled at victim-survivors of sexual violence, and to break down rape myths. However, as evidenced by these examples, the media routinely reinforces these attitudes and assumptions.

The next guideline relating to the presentation of victim-survivors discusses the sexualization of women:

Take care not to contribute to the sexualisation of women and girls in the media. (NUJ, 2013, p. 1)

Three articles did not sexualize women and girls, with the one that did being the *Daily Mail* article quoted above, speculating about 'Harvey Girls'. This sexualization also occurred elsewhere in the article:

Gwyneth Paltrow, a Weinstein favourite whom he propelled to Oscars glory in *Shakespeare In Love*, repaid him *by appearing in skimpy dominatrix gear* in his society magazine, Talk. (*Daily Mail*, 7/10/2017, my emphasis)

Here, Paltrow is implicated for being a 'Weinstein favourite', and, as discussed earlier, this responsibilizes her for his behaviour, whilst simultaneously sexualizing her. This sexualization, particularly when reporting upon sexual violence, is unacceptable and dangerous. As Soothill and Walby highlighted, news reporting of sexual violence often aims to squeeze 'all manner of sexual detail' into stories, with the sexual history of a woman legitimizing male violence, whilst sexual activity by the perpetrator is 'rarely seen as problematic' (1991, p. 58). Indeed, commenting on the way Paltrow was dressed in *Talk* magazine functions as a way to suggest that she was 'asking for it', that her sexual availability to Weinstein was the price of 'Oscars glory', and that Weinstein 'couldn't help himself'.

The final relevant guideline for how victim-survivors are presented relates to how they are referred to:

In the case of attack that has not resulted in murder, do not use the word 'victim' unless the woman self-identifies as one. If she has survived the attack, she is a 'survivor'. (NUJ, 2013, p. 1)

All four of the articles used inappropriate language to refer to the women being discussed. Whilst to see 'survivor' would have been surprising and 'victim' expected, given the ongoing criminal proceedings against Weinstein, the term 'accuser' was used in all four articles, reflected in the coverage of other high-profile cases of sexual violence (see Royal, 2019a). Examples in these articles include:

Brafman said in court on Tuesday that the two encounters which make up the indictment were consensual, not denying the fact that Weinstein engaged in sexual relations with the two *accusers*. (*Daily Mail*, 5/06/2018, my emphasis)

For years rumours surrounded the movie mogul … but now his *accusers* are going on the record alleging sex assaults. (*The Guardian*, 8/10/2017, my emphasis)

As I have argued elsewhere (Royal, 2019a), 'accuser' is a loaded term to use to refer to victim-survivors of sexual violence, and nor is it a legal term. 'Accuser' is problematic as it casts doubt onto the victim-survivor who has disclosed abuse, with the term heavily implying they are lying. It also focuses on their actions over those of the perpetrator of the abuse (Katz, 2015).

Presentations of Perpetrators

As with the presentation of victim-survivors, some of the guidelines also refer to how perpetrators should be portrayed in news stories. For example:

Avoid comments which could be interpreted as making excuses for the abuser, such as commenting on his remorse, or suggesting that the way women dress or behave incited the incident. (NUJ, 2013, p. 2)

All four articles excused Weinstein's behaviour in some way, either by creating sympathy for Weinstein or by referring to his career and family, sometimes all in one go:

Weinstein claims he has had *'really tough conversations' with his family, but that they are standing by him*. The tantalising question is *whether Hollywood will stand by him*, too. (*Daily Mail*, 7/10/2017, my emphasis)

Details of Weinstein's successful career were also featured in all four of the articles. One *Daily Mail* article included numerous references to films, many of which Weinstein or his company had been involved in, by using them as captions for photographs in the article (*Daily Mail*, 5/6/2018) in a way that created sympathy for Weinstein. These included *There Will Be Blood*, *Sweet Revenge*, *Last Chance Harvey* and *Inglorious Basterds*, reminding readers of Weinstein's achievements prior to the allegations coming to light.

A *Guardian* article referred to the 'fall' of Weinstein's career in the headline (8/10/2017), whilst both the *Daily Mail* and *The Guardian* articles from Weinstein's appearance in court discussed his appearance in a way that invoked sympathy:

> The former movie mogul looked *pale*, walking into New York Supreme Court in Manhattan with *a slight limp*. (*The Guardian*, 5/06/2018, my emphasis)
> The disgraced mogul arrived with his lawyer Ben Brafman and a bodyguard shortly before 10 am, *limping* as he walked into court. Weinstein, who did not shave and *looked ashen, outfitted himself in a suit jacket and tie* for his appearance. (*Daily Mail*, 5/06/2018, my emphasis)

However, one *Guardian* article did challenge this mode of representation when quoting Weinstein's lawyer, who had referred to him as an 'underdog', highlighting the power and control Weinstein possessed in Hollywood that made him almost untouchable:

> Bloom told the New York Post in July: 'It was just second nature to me that, of course; you have to fight for the underdog'. That term could in no way be applied to Weinstein, whose power is such that journalists have struggled to persuade his associates to speak on the record. (*The Guardian*, 5/06/2018)

Taking a sympathetic angle when representing perpetrators of violence in the media is not new. In fact perpetrators are often presented as victims (see Taylor, 2009). It is therefore unsurprising, but nonetheless troubling, that men who perpetrate violence against women have their behaviour routinely excused and deflected through focusing on their careers, family, and health, effectively positioning them as 'good men' (see Cover, this collection).

This suggests that the second guideline relating to the visibility of the perpetrator in news coverage was problematic in the reports on Weinstein's abuse. Specifically the guideline states:

Make the perpetrator visible in your report (e.g. women do not 'get themselves raped'). (NUJ, 2013, p. 2)

All four of the articles failed to make Weinstein visible, distancing him from the abuse, at some point within the article. This was apparent when articles did not make clear what Weinstein had done or did so passively:

Downfall of a sleazy tyrant: How Harvey Weinstein and his British wife are starring in their own disaster movie. (*Daily Mail*, 7/10/2017)

On the day before news officially broke of alleged sexual harassment stretching back decades, Harvey Weinstein, the 65-year-old movie mogul, offered this comment: 'The story sounds so good I want to buy the movie rights.' (*The Guardian*, 8/10/2017)

This is concerning as it is a form of linguistic avoidance, whereby perpetrators of such violence and abuse are rendered invisible, masking that this is a *structural*, not individual, problem (Romito, 2008), which ties in with a third relevant guideline pertaining to how perpetrators of abuse are referred to:

Do not refer to abusers as 'monsters', 'fiends', 'maniacs' or 'beasts' as this creates the myth that abusers are noticeably and substantially different from 'normal' men. (NUJ, 2013, p. 2)

Three of the articles used sensationalist language to refer to Weinstein, whilst one did not. Whilst the NUJ guidance refers to overtly negative language such as 'monster', one of *The Guardian* articles (8/10/2017) referred to Weinstein as 'God', drawing on comments made by Meryl Streep, which is not dissimilar to referring to Weinstein as a monster, as it positions him as 'noticeably and sustainably different' (NUJ, 2013, p. 2). Other examples of sensationalist language included calling Weinstein a 'sleazy tyrant' (*Daily Mail*, 7/10/2017). This sort of language, as the NUJ guidelines state, perpetuates the myth that abusers are markedly different from normal men (see Soothill & Walby, 1991; Cover, this collection). It has the effect of distracting the public from the reality that women are far more likely to experience sexual violence perpetrated by someone known to them and yet again places the responsibility back onto women to avoid these 'monsters'.

Presentations of Violence Against Women

Some of the guidelines relate to how violence against women more broadly should be presented, including that the abuse needs to be recognized as linked to gender inequality. Specifically, the guideline states:

> Frame violence against women and girls (VAWG) as a gender equality and human-rights abuses rather than as a 'mishap', a 'bad relationship' or as the consequence of women undertaking activities that would be unremarkable for men (walking alone, being out after dark, drinking in a bar, etc.). (NUJ, 2013, p. 1)

Of the four articles, only one framed Weinstein's abuse as violence against women. It did this by referring to and using quotes to highlight Weinstein's behaviour was not against an individual woman, but against *women*, although this was not asserted strongly:

> Harvey Weinstein said he was taking leave of absence from his company to get therapy for his *treatment of women*. (*Daily Mail*, 7/10/2017, my emphasis)

And:

> 'There is *a toxic environment for women at this company*,' she wrote. 'The balance of power is me: 0, Harvey Weinstein: 10.' She recounted how, a year earlier, Weinstein had summoned a woman called Emily Nestor, who had worked for just one day at his company as a temp, to the Peninsula Beverly Hills, and offered to advance her career if she accepted his sexual advances. (*Daily Mail*, 7/10/2017, my emphasis)

The above shows that even when Weinstein's abuse was framed as violence against women, this was with little attempt to link his behaviour to a culture where women are seen as objects and commodities. To not recognize these incidents as linked to men's violence against women more broadly misses an opportunity to join the 'dots' between forms of violence and their link to gender inequality (Westmarland, 2015, p. xv).

The second *Daily Mail* quote above hints at a culture that permits violence against women, and this is also recognized by the NUJ:

> Do not blame religion or culture for gender-based violence and do not assume that one religion or culture is more inclined than others. Represent gender-based violence as a cross-cultural phenomenon with no geographical or cultural boundaries. (NUJ, 2013, p. 2)

This chapter adopts a broader interpretation of 'culture' than the one suggested above, as articles included in this analysis referred to the culture around Hollywood, including that of the so-called 'casting couch', where those in a position of power (such as producers like Weinstein) use this power to demand sexual favours from those of a lower status. Using this understanding, three of the four articles blamed culture for the abuse Weinstein perpetrated. For example:

> Weinstein has attempted to justify his behaviour as having been a product of another Hollywood era. *'I came of age in the Sixties and Seventies when all the rules about behaviour and workplaces were different. That was the culture then,'* he claimed ... Hollywood insiders say it's easy to see why his reported victims were cowed into silence. As one commented yesterday, *Tinseltown had a very permissive culture for a long time, and Weinstein has been very powerful for a long time. (Daily Mail,* 7/10/2017, my emphasis)

The example above highlights that journalists need to be clear in critiquing the culture of the 'casting couch'. The blaming of culture detracts from the actions of Weinstein, presenting him as a product of the culture (instead of creating and reinforcing it), and normalizes the abuse he perpetrated.

Linked to the lack of framing of Weinstein's actions as violence against women, and the use of culture to excuse abuse, is how such abuse is named. This is also included in the NUJ guidelines:

> Name violence against women as violence against women (e.g. domestic violence is not a 'volatile relationship'). Do not use the word sex when you mean rape. (NUJ, 2013, p. 1)

None of the four articles accurately named the specific acts they were reporting upon consistently. Whilst the accurate titles for Weinstein's abuse were often used (particularly when reporting on his appearance in court in June 2018), inaccurate language was also used:

> The women were mostly in their 20s and alone with Weinstein when, they say he would appear either barely clothed or naked, *coercing them to massage him or watch him in the shower*… In at least one other instance, he allegedly *pressured a temporary assistant to have sex with him*. (*Daily Mail*, 7/10/2017, my emphasis)

This language does not call the acts what they are: sexual harassment and rape. To counter this, journalists should describe the act as above (although it is questionable whether the details are necessary), in conjunction with the legal term that applies, as one of *The Guardian* articles did:

> The former movie mogul looked pale, walking into New York supreme court in Manhattan with a slight limp, to answer one count each of first-degree rape and third-degree rape of one woman and one count of first-degree criminal sexual act (forcing another woman to perform oral sex). (*The Guardian*, 5/06/2018)

It is important to accurately name acts of sexual violence, as other language has been found to trivialize the violence being discussed (for example, Braber, 2014; Harrington, 2016) and can prevent women from identifying their experiences as sexual violence (Royal, 2019b).

Linked to this, and to the presentation of perpetrators as monsters, is an overrepresentation of rapes committed by strangers in news media, despite knowledge that these are rare occurrences. This is despite the NUJ guidelines seeking to challenge this position:

> In general, when presenting stories on rape keep in mind that stranger rapes are rarer than those involving people known to the survivor. (NUJ, 2013, p. 2)

None of the four articles reported stranger rapes as being rarer, and two of the articles reported Weinstein's lawyer actively challenging the possibility that a woman could be raped by someone she's been in a relationship with:

> 'This is an extraordinary case in my judgement where the only rape victim that Mr. Weinstein is accused of raping *is someone with whom he has had a 10-year consensual sexual relationship*—both before and after the alleged incident,' stated Brafman. (*Daily Mail*, 5/06/2018, my emphasis)
> Brafman has called the rape allegations 'absurd', saying the accuser and Weinstein *had a decade-long consensual sexual relationship that continued after the alleged 2013 attack*. (*The Guardian*, 5/06/2018, my emphasis)

These quotes highlight a lack of recognition around the reality of sexual violence, and previous research has highlighted how the media perpetuates the idea that sexual violence is committed by a stranger (Greer, 2003; Kitzinger, 2004; Soothill & Walby, 1991), playing into ideas about 'real rape' (Estrich, 1987).

Inform and Educate

A number of the guidelines relate to journalists' opportunity to inform and educate the public about sexual violence (Meyers, 1997). This includes their ability to signpost to support services:

Include helplines at the end of articles or broadcasts and include all juris-dictions information where appropriate (i.e. England, Scotland, Wales, Northern Ireland, etc.). (NUJ, 2013, p. 1)

However, none of the articles from either publication used in this case study included support information. This is an issue as we know that sexual violence can have a range of long-term consequences for victim-survivors, including flashbacks (WHO, 2013), and that news articles can be triggering for victim-survivors (Royal, 2019b). Research indicates that access to specialist support services can have a significant impact and improved outcomes for victim-survivors, such as feeling less distress when engaging with the legal system (Campbell, 2006), a reduction in experiences of flashbacks, panic attacks and suicidal feelings (Westmarland & Alderson, 2013). Including support information in news reporting is therefore crucial, as using a specialist support service can have a very real impact for victim-survivors, but they cannot access these services if they do not know they exist. The inclusion of support service information also works to normalize and encourage help-seeking behaviour, implicitly challenging the notion that sexual violence is a shameful or taboo topic that should not be discussed.

Additionally, the guidelines suggest that journalists have a responsibility to educate readers:

Include more informative and educational materials (e.g. challenging rape myths and misconceptions about the 'types' of victim). (NUJ, 2013, p. 1)

And

Use up-to-date statistics and do your research. (NUJ, 2013, p. 2)

None of the articles included educational materials or up-to-date statistics. Journalists, particularly those writing for newspapers such as the *Daily Mail* and *The Guardian*, have a unique opportunity to educate their readers about the reality of sexual violence given their widespread readership. However, in this instance, it would appear that the journalists have not met this responsibility.

Conclusion

This chapter has explored how four articles published by UK news publications that have a large global reach reported on the abuse committed by Harvey Weinstein and his initial court appearance. Whilst this sample is not representative of all media coverage, it highlights that coverage regularly fails to represent the reality and lived experience of sexual violence. Journalists are not following guidelines readily available to them and are therefore perpetuating inaccurate and damaging beliefs around the reality of sexual violence.

It is therefore recommended that editors and unions support journalists to utilize and follow these guidelines consistently. Journalists' unions therefore could be making these guidelines more widely available to their members and strongly encouraging their use. Offering training or more support for journalists to utilize the guidelines and involving specialist practitioners in this may also be beneficial. In addition, publications could adopt their own set of standards for reporting violence against women and make it a priority for their journalists and editors to follow these. Sexual violence and violence against women is reported in areas outside of crime (such as within sport and entertainment), and it is therefore key that *all* journalists and editors are aware of how sexual violence needs to be reported. In the wake of movements such as #MeToo, there are more public disclosures of sexual violence happening, and journalists need to be able to report on these sensitively and accurately. The media is a powerful force and frames our understanding of violence against women. By following guidelines such as those published by the NUJ, reporting could be much improved, and this would have wide-reaching implications not just for victim-survivors, but for all of us.

Suggestions for Journalists

This chapter has a number of suggestions for how journalists can implement these guidelines in their reporting of #MeToo and violence against women:

- Regarding signposting to support, a standard piece developed by each publication could be inserted into articles, listing websites that offer support for those who have experienced sexual violence. This could be national (so, for example, *The Guardian* and *Daily Mail* could include links to UK support, such as Rape Crisis England & Wales and Rape Crisis Scotland) or include international information for articles published online.
- In order to avoid negative gender stereotypes, journalists need to consider how they are framing the story being reported on and ensure they are avoiding holding women responsible for the actions of men.
- To avoid blaming victim-survivors journalists must recognize how these myths are potentially implied and reinforced through their writing.
- Journalists ought to ensure they use terms such as 'victim', 'survivor', or 'victim-survivor' or legal terms such as 'complainant' consistently when referring to victim-survivors.
- To avoid excusing perpetrators, journalists should ensure they are not including extraneous material and consider how details about a perpetrator, such as their family and career (particularly in cases with high-profile or celebrity perpetrators), may influence readers. Similarly, they should not passively quote from the defendant's legal team but rather interrogate their position.
- To make the perpetrator visible, journalists should ensure they are using the active voice, and that the perpetrator is the subject of their writing.
- Journalists should use statistics to highlight the reality of sexual violence (particularly around stranger rapes), educate the public, and ensure sexual violence is framed as violence against women.

References

Berns, N. (2004). *Framing the victim: Domestic violence media and social problems*. New York: Walter De Gruyter Inc.

Braber, N. (2014). Representation of domestic violence in two British newspapers, *The Guardian* and *The Sun*, 2009–2011. *English Language Research Journal, 1*, 86–104.

Burt, M. (1980). Cultural myths and supports for rape. *Journal of Personality and Social Psychology, 38*(2), 217–230.

Campbell, R. (2006). Rape survivors' experiences with the legal and medical systems: Do rape victim advocates make a difference? *Violence Against Women, 12*(1), 3–45.

Estrich, S. (1987). *Real rape*. Cambridge, MA: Harvard University Press.

Greer, C. (2003). *Sex crime and the media: Sex offending and the press in a divided society*. Cullompton: Willan.

Harrington, C. (2016). Feminist killjoys and women scorned: An analysis of news and commentary on the sexual violence allegations against Julian Assange. *Feminist Criminology, 13*(1), 87–111.

Helmore, E. (2018, June 5). Harvey Weinstein pleads not guilty on rape and criminal sex act charges. *The Guardian*. Retrieved December 20, 2018, from https://www.theguardian.com/us-news/2018/jun/05/harvey-weinstein-due-in-court-in-new-york.

Hoby, H. (2017, October 8). Harvey Weinstein: Fall of Hollywood player they once called 'God'. *The Guardian*. Retrieved December 20, 2018, from https://www.theguardian.com/film/2017/oct/08/harvey-weinstein-fall-of-hollywood-player-once-called-god.

Katz, J. (2015, January 21). Let's stop calling Bill Cosby's victims 'accusers'. *Women's E-News*. Retrieved November 17, 2018, from https://womensenews.org/2015/01/lets-stop-calling-bill-cosbys-victims-accusers/.

Kitzinger, J. (2004). *Framing abuse: Media influence and public understanding of sexual violence against children*. London: Pluto Press.

Leonard, T. (2017, October 7). Downfall of a sleazy tyrant: How Harvey Weinstein and his British wife are starring in their own disaster movie after he was accused of sexually harassing women in London and LA. *Daily Mail*. Retrieved December 20, 2018, from https://www.dailymail.co.uk/news/article-4957324/Harvey-Weinstein-having-disaster-movie.html.

Meyers, M. (1997). *News coverage of violence against women: Engendering blame*. London: Sage.

National Union of Journalists. (2013). NUJ guidelines for journalists reporting on violence against women. *National Union of Journalists*. Retrieved August 26, 2018, from https://www.nuj.org.uk/documents/nuj-guidelines-on-violence-against-women/.

National Union of Journalists. (2018). About. *National Union of Journalists*. Retrieved August 26, 2018, from https://www.nuj.org.uk/about/.

NRS. (2017). NRS October '16–September '17. Retrieved August 26, 2018, from http://www.nrs.co.uk/downloads/mobile-data/pdf/nrs_padd_mobile_standard_tables_oct_16_sept%2017.pdf.

Romito, P. (2008). *A deafening silence: Hidden violence against women and children*. Bristol: Policy.

Royal, K. (2019a). An analysis of a high profile rape trial: The case of UK footballer Ched Evans. *Journal of Gender Based Violence. 3* (1), 83–99.

Royal, K. (2019b). *'It's like wallpaper': Victim-blaming, sexual violence and the media*. Doctoral Thesis. Durham University.

SimilarWeb. (2018a). *dailymail.co.uk*. Retrieved August 26, 2018, from https://www.similarweb.com/website/dailymail.co.uk#overview.

SimilarWeb. (2018b). *theguardian.com*. Retrieved August 26, 2018, from https://www.similarweb.com/website/theguardian.com.

Soothill, K., & Walby, S. (1991). *Sex crime in the news*. London: Routledge.

Spargo, C., & Boyle, L. (2018, June 5). Scruffy Harvey Weinstein pleads not guilty to two counts of rape and one count of criminal sexual assault after limping into court for his arraignment wearing baggy jeans. *Daily Mail*. Retrieved December 20, 2018, from https://www.dailymail.co.uk/news/article-5808187/Harvey-Weinstein-pleads-not-guilty-two-counts-rape-one-count-criminal-sexual-assault.html.

Taylor, R. (2009). Slain and slandered: A content analysis of the portrayal of femicide in crime news. *Homicide Studies, 13*(1), 21–49.

Ullman, S. E., & Townsend, S. M. (2007). Barriers to working with sexual assault survivors: A qualitative study of rape crisis center workers. *Violence Against Women, 13*(4), 412–443.

Westmarland, N. (2015). *Violence against women: Criminological perspectives on men's violences*. New York: Routledge.

Westmarland, N., & Alderson, S. (2013). The health, mental health, and well-being benefits of rape crisis counselling. *Journal of Interpersonal Violence, 28*(17), 3265–3282.

WHO. (2013). *Guidelines for medico-legal care for victims of sexual violence*. Geneva: World Health Organisation.

15

'A Reckoning That Is Long Overdue': Reconfiguring the Work of Progressive Sex Advice Post #MeToo

Christy E. Newman and Bridget Haire

Introduction

The metaphor of a 'reckoning'—defined as 'the avenging or punishing of past mistakes or misdeeds' (Oxford University Press, 2018), with overtones of the Last Judgement of the Abrahamic religions—has become familiar in both scholarly and popular commentary on gender relations in the twenty-first century (e.g., Messerschmidt, Messner, Connell, & Yancey Martin, 2018). In the months following the emergence of the #MeToo movement, a number of sex and relationships 'advice' writers took up this metaphor in seeking to mobilize their audiences to engage with the political and ethical implications of this movement.

C. E. Newman (✉)
Centre for Social Research in Health, UNSW Sydney,
Kensington, NSW, Australia
e-mail: c.newman@unsw.edu.au

B. Haire
The Kirby Institute, UNSW Sydney, Kensington, NSW, Australia
e-mail: b.haire@unsw.edu.au

© The Author(s) 2019
B. Fileborn, R. Loney-Howes (eds.), *#MeToo and the Politics of Social Change*,
https://doi.org/10.1007/978-3-030-15213-0_15

In this chapter, we analyze three of the key themes observed in this material, focusing on those advice writers we characterize as influential in shaping a 'progressive' approach to sexuality and relationships, meaning they adopt a rights-based perspective that acknowledges sexual and gender diversity and questions heteronormative and patriarchal assumptions (Rasmussen, 2010). This approach contrasts with the advice provided in mainstream 'sex media' cultures (Attwood, 2018), which have been critiqued for remaining largely organized around understanding and satisfying the sexual subjectivities of men (Lulu & Alkaff, 2018).

Analyzing Sex Advice in the Left-Wing Media

Sex and relationships advice has been a feature of media publications from the earliest periodicals to the newest digital forms (Boynton, 2015), as well as across diverse geographies and cultures (Lulu & Alkaff, 2018). While the format has remained remarkably stable, typically following a Q&A, audience-anonymized, 'agony aunt' format in newspapers and magazines (Kurtz, 2014), digital transformation is driving increasing expectations of a more 'relational' exchange between advisor and audience (Baym, 2015). Building on the work of UK-based sexuality and media researchers Barker, Gill, and Harvey, we view those who write and speak sex advice today as 'socialising agents for life in neoliberal society' (2018, p. 15), as well as being subject, themselves, to the vagaries of social and technological change.

Among the examples of responses to #MeToo that we collated for this analysis, five advice columns/platforms stood out as most energetically engaging with the political and ethical implications of this movement: Dan Savage (*Savage Love* column and podcast), Cheryl Strayed and Steve Almond (*Dear Sugars* column and podcast), Daniel Mallory Ortberg (*Dear Prudence* column and podcast), Heather Havrilevsky (*Ask Polly* column), and Tristan Taormino (*Sex Out Loud* podcast). While this is only a small selection of the many sex advice 'experts' actively working today, and a very small proportion of the number of public commentators on #MeToo, the combination of their texts spans the main platforms through which advice-giving is made accessible online today, specifically free-to-access online magazines, such as *Slate*, paywall-protected traditional media, such as *The New York Times*, and audio podcasts. This selected group of sex and relationships advisors also share a number of socio-political attributes: they are all US based, they all present as educated, middle-class White professionals, they are all publicly identified with a feminist, progressive, left-leaning politics, and all incorporate personal stories into their advice about sex and relationships.

Distinguishing this group of sex and relationships advisors as 'progressive' in their politics is important, because popular media researchers have argued that mainstream advice-giving, even across incredibly diverse cultural contexts, consistently privileges both heterosexuality and men's sexual pleasure, even while spruiking women's sexual 'empowerment' (e.g., Lulu & Alkaff, 2018). Mainstream approaches to sex and relationships advice-giving also do not have a strong record of addressing issues of sexual violence, coercion, and abuse in the depth that many argue is necessary (Barker et al., 2018). While Petra Boynton, a sexual health researcher and agony aunt, believes that she and others working in this field have seen an increase in questions about sexual abuse, which 'may be a reflection of a greater awareness of abuse as a problem and of young people's ability to recognize and report sexual abuse' (2009, p. 117), there is little empirical evidence that this has led to increased attention to issues of consent and communication in mainstream sex and relationships advice.

Barker et al. (2018) hold up the online BDSM and kink communities as representing best practice in approaches to negotiating and communicating consent. Two of the ways in which these kink-positive sexual cultures achieve this are through cultivating 'cultures of consent', which extends the responsibility for successfully securing consent from individuals to communities, and recognizing the intersections and influence of various forms of social power and position (Barker, 2013). However, inspired by academic Mary-Lou Rasmussen's critical analysis of the notion of 'progressive' approaches to sexuality education (Rasmussen, 2017), we want to avoid reproducing an assumed binary distinction between the 'mainstream' and these more sex-positive communities with regard to sexual ethics. Instead, our analysis deliberately focuses in on understanding the 'particular sets of ideas [which] produce and reference the "taken-for-granted" understandings' (Rasmussen, 2017, p.116) we saw repeated throughout sex advice discussions and responses to the #MeToo movement, among advice writers who explicitly identify with left-wing, inclusive understandings of sexuality and relationships.

In this chapter, we have headed each of the key thematic sections with a stylized question to capture the ethos of discussions we observed happening in response to #MeToo. Within these themes, we consider how these sex advisors contribute to promoting a progressive representation of how to live in a post-#MeToo world.

Do I Need to Change How I Live?

The sex advice we analyzed engaged explicitly with the subject of the #MeToo movement in responding to questions asked by audience members and in providing their own forms of commentary and opinion on the significance of this social movement for reframing life experiences. As might be expected of this genre of sex advice, much of this material was engaged with the question of whether and how to change the way one goes about one's daily life in response to the issues raised by #MeToo. This was particularly evident in relation to the sense of obligation and impact of sharing personal stories of survival.

The first example comes from Daniel Mallory Ortberg, who writes the 'Dear Prudence' column for online magazine *Slate* and publishes an audio podcast of the same name in conversation with selected guests. Daniel publicly announced his gender transition in February 2018 (see Havrilesky, 2018), but the material quoted here was published prior. Interviewed by a journalist about whether #MeToo was influencing sex advice, Ortberg described this as a turning point in the history of gender relations, inspiring many to think differently about their own relationships and actions:

> I'm starting to hear from people who are becoming aware of this conversation for the first time [...] I have started hearing from some people, especially men, who are just now thinking, 'Oh, maybe I should actually give some thought to this. Maybe I should consider the interiority of my female

co-workers and employees and think about how they may have felt histori-cally.' And that's been fascinating [...] We live in a really sexist society, and it's a reckoning that is long overdue. (Ortberg, interviewed in: Coaston, 2017)

In the final months of 2017, Ortberg also answered a few audience questions about #MeToo, both of which reveal some of the private con-sequences of this very public movement. For example, one letter writer said:

I don't know how to deal with #MeToo as a rape survivor [...] Social media is a big part of my job, so I can't just turn it off all day, but [...] I keep find-ing myself going to the bathroom and sobbing.

Ortberg's reply was to make clear that

[y]ou are not obligated to share your own trauma simply because there is a social media campaign going on [and] you do not ever have to share your story unless you feel safe and comfortable doing so, and *you want to share your story.* (2017, emphasis in original)

There was a dual role for the sex advisor being enacted here as both facilitator and custodian of the highly intimate, and often deeply upset-ting, stories of non-consensual sexual experiences, which were circulating post #MeToo. Readers were being encouraged to be supportive of this outpouring of personal stories and to be brave if they felt they had the capacity and desire to share their own stories. However, it was also recog-nized that for some, feeling an obligation to share may not be experi-enced positively and may even contribute to additional trauma.

Other advisors focused on the collective power of sharing stories and the need to work together to maintain momentum and achieve lasting change. For example, Heather Havrilevsky writes the 'Ask Polly' column for online magazine *The Cut*: a standalone site targeting women readers of *The New York Magazine*. However, she is also a book and article author, and most of her contributions that explicitly engaged with #MeToo were in other online formats. This included an article for *The Cut* which sought to incite an intense, collective pushback against the powerful men who were being outed as serial perpetrators, which she saw as the most important outcome of #MeToo. Subsequently, she described this as the opportunity for a collective 'coming out' about personal histories of abuse:

> What's most shocking of all right now might be the chorus of voices saying 'We knew all along, and wondered when the truth would come out!' The truth doesn't come out until someone is very brave. In this, the Year of the Sociopathic Baby-Man, we have no more excuses […] We all have to be brave now, and speak the truth to power. (Havrilesky, 2017)

Similar entreaties to take up the opportunity to share collective stories were evident in 'Dear Sugars'. Cheryl Strayed and Steve Almond, both writers (particularly high profile in the case of Strayed, who wrote the best-selling memoir 'Wild', subsequently made into a successful Hollywood movie), co-author an advice column in *The New York Times* and an audio podcast (which published its final season in 2018), both using this name. In March 2018, they released a three-part series of podcasts explicitly focused on exploring issues relating to consent in the aftermath of the #MeToo movement. The following extracts are from a podcast called 'Working in the Gray', which focused on sexual harassment in workplaces. It is Cheryl Strayed who is speaking in the following extract:

> The reason that #MeToo feels vital is because everybody who suffered this kind of abuse is realising that they're trying to isolate us. They're trying to create a situation where we feel we're alone and powerless, up against the whole office […] And so we all are collectively responsible for making sure that men understand there *are* consequences and that we're able to collectively create those consequences. No one woman should be responsible for creating them on her own. I mean the laws have existed for many, many years that make this behaviour illegal but clearly men do not feel that it is […] And so we need to make it clear that time is up. (Strayed & Almond, 2018b)

In contrast to the description of mainstream sex advice as focused on understanding and responding to the needs of men, these examples are clearly seeking to establish a new repertoire of collective action and cultural healing in a post-#MeToo era. The vitality of this movement is celebrated, and there is energy in their attempts to mobilize their audiences, particularly but not only women, to continue to demand justice and change, in response to this 'long overdue reckoning' (Ortberg, interviewed in: Coaston, 2017).

Could I Have Been a Perpetrator, Too?

A second theme in the material was worried men asking for advice about whether or not their past behaviors fit with a retrospective narrative of 'perpetration'. In some cases, advisors suggested that the sheer number of testimonies being generated through #MeToo had created conditions in which, for the first time, men might feel they *have* to look at their own lives and the sexual culture they contribute to differently:

> Women are speaking enough in significant enough numbers and with enough kind of collective weight behind them that men have to actually give it credence now. And once they do, it is very, very obvious when something is wrong. And they don't like that, and it's painful, and it's uncomfortable, and it makes a lot of them think, 'Holy shit, I might have done this myself, even though I'm not a monster like Harvey Weinstein,' or, 'Wow, if this is harassment, then almost every man I know has committed harassment.' And then answer to that is, unfortunately, hell yeah. (Ortberg, interviewed in: Coaston, 2017)

Cheryl Strayed constructed a similar narrative of psychological and social resistance to doing this work of interrogating the self and others as 'potential past perpetrators'. Although she begins by focusing only on men, she expands this as she speaks into an argument about the entire social system being invested in maintaining the status quo:

> I think there are plenty of men who are hearing this conversation and resisting it because they think 'Well, if that's true then I've hurt people'. And it's very deeply human to, just on a psychological level, resist integrating

any new information that goes against deeply-held beliefs such as 'I'm a decent person who doesn't hurt anyone'. (Strayed & Almond, 2018a)

Steve Almond's contribution was to then perform a kind of public self-reckoning himself, sharing that he had been rethinking a particular event in his own life: sitting in a hot tub with friends at a high school party, a younger girl had sat on his lap, which he had loved. Looking back, he wondered if she had really wanted to do that or felt she had no choice. Steve claimed to feel appalled that it had never occurred to him to ask this question before #MeToo (Strayed & Almond, 2018a).

Steve was providing a moral template in this podcast to guide the post #MeToo 'work' of men reflecting on their sexual histories. Both Steve and Cheryl, and Daniel, quoted earlier, welcomed this practice of critical self-refection, supporting the efforts of (some) men to willingly place themselves alongside the cultural image of the perpetrator, while also contributing to a reconfiguring of that image to become much broader than the archetypal 'rapist' representations of the past. However, they also made clear that they believed much was at stake for men who engage in this process of self-reckoning, at a time when abusive or coercive sexual behavior was becoming more culturally shameful and indeed, more socially and professionally perilous.

What was unclear from the above examples, however, is what men were being advised to do *after* they had completed this process of critical self-reflection (see Cover; Flood, this collection). Dan Savage suggested some additional steps in his response to a letter entitled '#MeThough'. Arguably one of the most well known of the progressive sex advisors at the time of this analysis, Dan Savage had published his LGBTQ-friendly advice column 'Savage Love' in the alternative newspaper *The Stranger* since 1991, also syndicated across North America, and produced a weekly call-in advice podcast, 'Savage Lovecast', since 2006. The following advice was published in 'Savage Love' on 18 October 2017, just as the #MeToo hashtag was gaining traction. The reader had written in questioning his actions earlier in life, describing an instance of having 'guilted' a friend he was having a sexual relationship with into having sex with him. While the reader acknowledged his behavior was problematic, he was unsure as to how he should proceed: should he contact the friend to apologize? Dan replied:

> #MeToo, like everything else, has its critics. Some argue it may ask too much of survivors [...] I often hear from people who want to reach out and apologize for past wrongs [...] I usually advise people in your situation to leave it/them alone. It's not her job—and it's almost always a her that was wronged—to make the person who used, abused, or sexually assaulted her feel better [...] [But] I think you should discuss this with your ex-FWB/current friend [...] She's still a part of your life and you're still a part of hers [...] Apologize to her sincerely and then listen just as sincerely to whatever she wants or needs to say. But even if she doesn't remember it the way you did [...] a woman with a different history and different fears—could've experienced the same behavior as coercive and/or rapey [...] All women are socialized to defer to men, all women have experienced sexual harassment, and far too many have been victims of sexual assault [...] So don't beg, don't plead, don't guilt. Ask. If the answer is no, the answer is no. (Savage, 2017)

A number of intersecting representations of the perpetrator were revealed through this exchange. This young man was engaged in the 'self-reckoning' we have described. He recognized that one particular encounter may have been experienced as coercive by his partner, and was seeking some kind of absolution, while also accepting he didn't necessarily get to secure that. Dan answered by contradicting his 'usual' advice and suggesting this is one of the few cases in which it is justifiable to take this possible-perpetrator narrative further and to directly apologize to his friend for his past behavior. Although the letter writer was advised to change how he goes about securing consent in future, Savage's response also maintained space for this man to move on from that past, precisely because he was seeking to rethink that history and to understand how he should then act as a result.

An interview conducted with Dan Savage in March 2018 provided some additional insights into the reasoning behind this response:

> 'Most guys aren't monsters and don't want to act in a way that violates someone,' he says, "but a lot of guys are really clueless [...] Some men, like

Harvey Weinstein, are predatory monster shitbags. I'm not talking about those guys; I'm talking about this muddy middle [...] There needs to be some path to redemption,' he continues. 'If you're creating new social norms [...] You have to allow people who "sinned" to become converts.' (Lunney, 2018)

Clearly, Dan Savage, one of the most prominent progressive voices in the sex and relationships field in the US, was making room here for those who have 'sinned' in the crafting of a post-#MeToo sexual culture. However, he, and the other advice writers, were also insisting that this involves a comprehensive challenge to and remaking of masculine sexual entitlement. Yet, there was little evidence in these particular texts that men were being encouraged to go further than simply engaging in an internal process of 'rethinking' their sense of themselves as good, feminist men, with the potential for expanding this to include good, feminist but *clueless* men. There remains a sense that the serious perpetrators are othered as 'predatory monsters' like Harvey Weinstein, while these men remain on the side of the hapless but are not really that dangerous. The 'monster' trope diverts attention from the ways that aspects of normative masculinity can produce sexual violence.

Is It Even Possible to Create a Safe Sexual Culture?

#MeToo was celebrated in sex advice material when it was seen to be exposing sexual cultures in which harassment, coercion, and violence were widespread and unseating the rich and powerful 'Sociopathic Baby-Men', as Havrilevsky put it (2017). However, there was also recognition, as seen in the past two sections, that these issues were apparent across *all* of the sexual cultures to which these expert commentators were connected, including those represented as more progressive, inclusive, and ethical (see Cover, this collection). Indeed, in some comments, as in the following quote from Cheryl Strayed, we saw a desire to create a shared sexual culture that was safer for all, including for those who are not cis-gender or heterosexual in orientation:

Myself and other people are out there trying to advocate for that change so that we'll have just a more human, caring kind of sexual culture, right, and not one that posits men as the aggressor and women as sort of the passive object. And never mind how heteronormative that whole model is, right? (Strayed & Almond, 2018a)

While this quote reveals its progressive politics, even if only through the use of the queer theory keyword of 'heteronormative', a different kind of reckoning was conceptualized in discussions which presumed a distinction between the mainstream and a range of minority and alternative sexual cultures, including 'sex-positive' (Nodulman, 2016) communities.

Tristan Taormino, an influential sex and relationships educator, author, and pornographer, explicitly advocates for the kind of progressive sexual ethics we have been discussing throughout this chapter: inclusive of sexual and gender diversity, supportive of ethical, alternative relationship frameworks, and invested in the creation of sexual cultures which are safe for all who commit to contributing to them with insight, honesty, and openness (Taormino, 2018b). It was particularly interesting, therefore, to see a three-part podcast series produced by Taormino in March 2018, called 'Me Too in sex-positive communities', which asked some very challenging questions about this ideal, through the format of a community panel. She described her own interest in this topic at the start:

I think that there's this idea that sex-positive, sex educator, polyamorous, kinky, queer folks talk about consent a lot [...] [But] we're not, we're no longer in a sex-positive bubble, right? [...] I know for me that when things happen within the community, I have an expectation that it's gonna go differently than it does. But then all of a sudden [...] we see [...] people who are blaming victims and survivors. We see people apologising for perpetrators, 'cause that person is, 'They're just so nice and I met them once. And they were super-cool.' [...] So I for one want us to kind of stop seeing ourselves as exceptional [...] I wanna know how we make space to confront these issues in our communities, how we make space for accountability and justice. (Taormino, 2018a)

We see here a similar valuing of the 'potential past perpetrator' narrative, as well as a range of propositions for new ways of living in a post-#MeToo era, particularly in paying more attention to, and making room for accountability for, experiences of coercion, harassment, and the transgression of the ethical ideals within sex-positive communities.

A key phrase in the above extract is 'stop seeing ourselves [the LGBTQIA community] as exceptional', which is indeed one of the most complex challenges for those working to promote progressive understandings of sexuality and relationships. Are these alternative sexual communities truly able to prevent sexual violence, simply because of their deliberate separation from what they view as 'mainstream' sexual culture (see Ison, this collection, for a critique of #MeToo in relation to the LGBTQIA community)? And is it possible to achieve a shared sense of what it means to practice these ethics in a progressive manner, given the multiple differences and differentials shaped by social and structural conditions? Tristan concluded the podcast by arguing that even though there were many issues in presuming the #MeToo reckoning applies mainly to the 'mainstream', there is much to be said about the fact that these issues are being deliberately raised within sexual sub-cultures:

> We are having conversations. We are trying to, you know, put forth our missions. We are trying to create safer spaces. [And] I think that that gives us a leg up in that like we're not, we're not ignoring what's happening. (Taormino, 2018a)

Whether it will be enough for those participating in and promoting the ethics and politics of progressive sexual cultures to simply be engaging in this conversation is yet to be seen.

Conclusion

We saw the quasi-religious metaphor of a 'reckoning' deployed frequently in the sex advice material collated for this analysis, which we see as a deliberately dramatic rendering within this 'discourse community' (Little, Jordens, & Sayers, 2003) of self-described 'progressive' sex and relationships writers, speakers, and educators to rethink gender relations and to challenge cultures of sexual violence, coercion, and abuse (Mendes,

Ringrose, & Keller, 2018). What we can learn from analyzing their responses to letters and discussions about #MeToo is therefore how a particular set of ideas about the 'agentic subjects' (Maxwell & Aggleton, 2013) of progressive sexual cultures are being co-produced through the relational labor now required of sex advisors, and others working in the cultural industries today, in 'cultivating audiences that function as affectively engaging communities' (Baym, 2015, p. 20), and in this process, co-producing a particular set of ideas about community and subjective norms.

In the material we analyzed, this included thinking relationally about how to live in a post-#MeToo world, including how to take care of the self or others who may have their own survivor stories, but also how to build and maintain the sense of collective safety that is permitted when a multitude of such stories are shared. We also saw attention invested in encouraging a relatively new form of confessional narrative among progressive communities: the possible past perpetrator. This work of revisiting sexual histories was framed as a process of taking accountability for one's actions, even if the stories themselves may be located within the more 'nebulous' realms of sexual consent (Beres, 2007), compared with the clear cases of violence exposed through the more high-profile #MeToo cases. This public confessional work potentially provides an avenue for redemption—a way for perpetrators to perform the role of the morally progressive, feminist man, which may be protective of their own positions as the fallout of #MeToo continues to unfold (see also Cover, this collection). Whether this self-reckoning is truly transformative, or whether it merely enables perpetrators to save face, rather than take full legal and ethical responsibility, remains to be examined.

While there is no doubt that a kind of exceptionalism is being performed within these examples of progressive sex advice, positioning this way of thinking about sex and relationships as more ethical and insightful than the 'mainstream'—as literally further 'progressed' from normative understandings of sexual and gender relations—we also saw a turning in to look directly at particular sexual sub-cultures, including those typically held up as employing best practice approaches to securing consent. There was at least some recognition in these texts that these sub-cultures can also struggle to accept that violence, coercion, and harassment can happen within ethical, sex-positive communities and relationships and in some ways, that an investment in representing a culture or community as 'progressive' may make this even more complex to address. We look forward to seeing how these issues continue to be explored, relationally, across the range of sex and relationships advice which continues to proliferate online, as the implications of #MeToo unfold over the coming years.

References

Attwood, F. (2018). *Sex media*. Cambridge, UK: Polity.

Barker, M. (2013). Consent is a grey area? A comparison of understandings of consent in Fifty Shades of Grey and on the BDSM blogosphere. *Sexualities, 16*(8), 896–914.

Barker, M. J., Gill, R., & Harvey, L. (2018). *Mediated intimacy: Sex advice in media culture*. Cambridge: Polity.

Baym, N. K. (2015). Connect with your audience! The relational labor of connection. *The Communication Review, 18*(1), 14–22.

Beres, M. A. (2007). 'Spontaneous' sexual consent: An analysis of sexual consent literature. *Feminism & Psychology, 17*(1), 93–108.

Boynton, P. M. (2009). Whatever happened to Cathy and Claire?: Sex, advice and the role of the Agony Aunt. In F. Attwood (Ed.), *Mainstreaming sex: The sexualization of western culture* (pp. 111–128). London: IB Tauris.

Boynton, P. M. (2015). Agony, misery, woe: A new role for media advice columns. *The Lancet Psychiatry, 2*(3), 203–204.

Coaston, J. (2017, January 22). Giving advice in the #MeToo era. *Vox*. Retrieved December 20, 2018, from https://www.vox.com/culture/2018/1/22/16906122/sex-harassment-advice-metoo.

Havrilesky, H. (2017, October 6). Don't call it 'toxic masculinity.' They're sociopathic baby-men. *The Cut*. Retrieved December 20, 2018, from https://www.thecut.com/2017/10/this-isnt-toxic-masculinity-its-sociopathic-baby-men.html.

Havrilesky, H. (2018, March 13). 'Mallory is not gone': Daniel Mallory Ortberg on coming out as trans. The beloved internet writer talks to Heather Havrilesky about his new identity. *The Cut*. Retrieved December 20, 2018, from https://www.thecut.com/2018/03/daniel-mallory-ortberg-interview-heather-havrilesky.html.

Kurtz, I. (2014). *My life in agony: Confessions of a professional Agony Aunt*. London: Alma Books.

Little, M., Jordens, C. F., & Sayers, E.-J. (2003). Discourse communities and the discourse of experience. *Health: An Interdisciplinary Journal for the Social Study of Health, Illness and Medicine, 7*(1), 73–86.

Lulu, R. A., & Alkaff, S. N. H. (2018). Of lust and love: A cross-cultural study of sex and relationship advice articles in women's magazines. *Sexuality and Culture, 22*(2), 479–496.

Lunney, T. (2018, March 22). Dan Savage on #metoo redemption, the normalcy of odd sex, and butt plug question nostalgia. *Citypages*. Retrieved December 20, 2018, from http://www.citypages.com/arts/dan-savage-on-metoo-redemption-the-normalcy-of-odd-sex-and-butt-plug-question-nostalgia/477552353.

Maxwell, C., & Aggleton, P. (2013). Middle-class young women: Agentic sexual subjects? *International Journal of Qualitative Studies in Education, 26*(7), 848–865.

Mendes, K., Ringrose, J., & Keller, J. (2018). #MeToo and the promise and pitfalls of challenging rape culture through digital feminist activism. *European Journal of Women's Studies, 25*(2), 236–246.

Messerschmidt, J. W., Messner, M. A., Connell, R., & Yancey Martin, P. (Eds.). (2018). *Gender reckonings: New social theory and research*. New York, USA: New York University Press.

Nodulman, J. A. (2016). 'Put me in, coach, I'm ready to play': Sexuality education for adults at Good Vibrations. *Sex Education, 16*(6), 649–662.

Ortberg, M. (2017, December 28). More than a hashtag. *Slate*. Retrieved December 20, 2018, from http://www.slate.com/articles/life/dear_prudence/2017/10/dear_prudence_dealing_with_social_media_as_a_survivor.html.

Oxford University Press. (2018). *English Oxford living dictionaries*. Oxford University Press. Retrieved July 17, 2018, from https://en.oxforddictionaries.com/definition/reckoning.

Rasmussen, M. L. (2010). Secularism, religion and 'progressive' sex education. *Sexualities, 13*(6), 699–712.

Rasmussen, M. L. (2017). Faith, progressive sexuality education, and Queer secularism: Unsettling associations. In L. Allen & M. L. Rasmussen (Eds.), *The Palgrave handbook of sexuality education* (pp. 115–135). London: Palgrave Macmillan UK.

Savage, D. (2017, October 18). Savage love letter of the day: #MeThough. *The Stranger*. Retrieved December 20, 2018, from https://www.thestranger.com/slog/2017/10/18/25476992/savage-love-letter-of-the-day-methough.

Strayed, C., & Almond, S. (2018a, March 10). Consent part 1: Into the gray—With Jaclyn Friedman. *Dear Sugars*. WBUR. Retrieved December 20, 2018, from http://www.wbur.org/dearsugar/2018/03/10/consent-part-1-into-the-gray-with-jaclyn-friedman.

Strayed, C., & Almond, S. (2018b, March 24). Consent part 3: Working in the gray. *Dear Sugars*. WBUR. Retrieved December 20, 2018, from http://www.wbur.org/dearsugar/2018/03/24/consent-part-3-working-in-the-gray.

Taormino, T. (2018a, April 20). MeToo in sex positive communities, part 1. *Sex Out Loud*. Voice America. Retrieved December 20, 2018, from https://www.voiceamerica.com/episode/106714/metoo-in-sex-positive-communities-part-1.

Taormino, T. (2018b). Tristan Taormino: Feminist. Author. Educator. Activist. Retrieved July 13, 2018, from http://tristantaormino.com/.

Part IV

Ethical Possibilities and the Future of Anti-sexual Violence Activism

16

Consent Lies Destroy Lives: Pleasure as the Sweetest Taboo

Cyndi Darnell

Introduction

My years in adult sex education and private psychotherapy have illustrated to me how discussions of sex and pleasure have become misappropriated by dialogs of violence and abuse—an important but in some respects different issue. This is, in part, due to our collective and cultural discomfort in discussing sex and the visceral realities of pleasure (Allen, 2004). While discussions of sex (in all its forms) for pleasure and eroticism remain subordinate to conversations about sex and violence (particularly when discussing women's sexuality), our efforts to work toward *truly* consensual (and pleasurable) sex will stagnate (Carmody, 2005). In a culture still deeply uncomfortable with women's ownership of eroticism, the current obsession with yes/no versions of consent leaves women with few avenues to experience pleasure, eroticism and power (over self and others) on their terms, men with little incentive nor methods to explore sex outside of the aggressor/initiator role, while those outside the

C. Darnell (✉)
New York City, NY, USA
e-mail: cyndi@cyndidarnell.com

© The Author(s) 2019
B. Fileborn, R. Loney-Howes (eds.), *#MeToo and the Politics of Social Change*,
https://doi.org/10.1007/978-3-030-15213-0_16

gender binary are rendered invisible (Carmody, 2005; see also Matthews, this collection). The shame of discussing pleasure, what turns us on and how we might make sex satisfying rather than terrifying, erases the issues we need to consider in order to transform sex for ourselves and future generations.

One of the 'hottest' aspects of sex for many of the people I have worked with over the years is the exchange of power between partners—whether we look at power in its relationship to vitality (e.g. 'I feel strong, healthy and empowered') or its relationship to control (of self or others) and validation. Statements such as:

- 'I like feeling desirable'
- 'Feeling desirable makes me feel validated'
- 'Your wanting *me* turns *me* on'
- 'I want to make you feel X, Y, Z'
- 'I want you to like me' or
- 'I want to *have* you' and so on

reflect the eroticism associated with the exchange or power in sexual encounters, and it is this exchange that is often at the core of our incentive to engage sexually with one another.

The trouble is that historically in feminist circles, power in all its forms is generally only discussed in the context of men and patriarchy, and thus, as something bad, dangerous and undesirable. We are uncomfortable discussing power's relationship to eroticism and the exchange of desires. Yet, if it were not for this interactive element of sex, most of us would be satisfied with masturbation alone (of course some are, and this is perfectly fine). By omitting women and non-binary folk from the conversation of protagonists in power and eroticism, or placing women only as victims who lack agency, we maintain the illusion that sex does not belong to us. Thus, our reductive conversations about consent, focused solely on violence prevention and not on our erotic motivations, ignore this exciting yet crucial dynamic. And, as scholars such as Moira Carmody (2005) have suggested, focusing on negotiating pleasure may actually *help* us to reduce sexual violence anyhow.

Human interactions, both professional and personal, frequently depend upon power exchange to mobilize and motivate us in many of life's most valuable endeavors. Power and its acquisition or exchange provides an incentive to throw ourselves into something, whether it be self-empowerment or social collateral. From employment and scholarly pursuits, to acquiring wealth and friendships, or divisions of domestic labor between partners and children alike, we recognize an exchange of power is crucial to ensuring life runs smoothly. Power in this sense is understood as mutual exchange and reciprocity, rather than something exercised over others as a mechanism of control and punishment (see Foucault, 2008 [1978]).

Somehow, sex gives us a public excuse to rage against the perceived and actual power imbalances we often otherwise accept. We acquiesce to professional deadlines in the name of teamwork, making a sale or climbing the corporate ladder, but we do not allow ourselves (nor men) the same graces when it comes to sex. From this position, I'd argue that it's not only power (and the misuse of power) that truly irks us—it's sex. To be clear, I am not suggesting women, nor anyone, should acquiesce to sex against their will *ever*. I am, however, suggesting we need to look at our erotic motivations and behaviors more honestly and the role(s) that an exchange of power may play in shaping these, despite the discomfort they may bring us.

As a sex therapist, I spend my entire professional life facilitating this discussion for people wanting more from their sex lives and wondering how to access it. Being distracted from these uncomfortable truths by focusing on *what's going wrong*, rather than *how to do it right*, and ignoring the role of power as an erotic imperative between partners overlooks any exploration of the centrality of power in shaping and producing sexual desire and pleasure. Instead, antiquated tales of sex and relationships from conservatives and feminists alike being solely about love, babies, penis-in-vagina privilege and doing it for the 'right' reasons (Rubin, 1992; see also Matthews, this collection) perpetuate the stigma associated with nuanced, mature discussions of sex that centralize our complex, varied and sometimes 'unsavory' motivations for sex.

Without a willingness to look at why we have sex, who gets what from it and what makes it *hot*, we are shortchanging ourselves and preventing the opportunity for sex education that allows for an inclusive and honest discussion of how to make sex better for everyone. Instead I propose a model that holds consent dear by privileging honesty, mutual pleasure and 'hotness' and reducing the stigma that derails so many well-intentioned, but poorly executed, yes/no conversations about consent.

The Trouble with Consent as a Yes-No Binary Conversation

The cultural sanctioning of women's sexual subjectivity as passive, how we are both positioned by omission on social media or position ourselves through the absence of pleasure in women's health initiatives (that focus solely on disease and reproduction) as sexual gatekeepers rather than sexual agents, means we have zero examples of women or feminist public figures that embody sexual agency without scrutiny.

None.

We pay lip service to consent and women as empowered, liberated sexual agents but in reality do not encourage its practice, nor seek out or amplify the positions of those who do.

We don't like the thought of women *really* being vocal about sex.

We certainly don't like women flaunting their bodies.

We don't like women having multiple partners.

We don't like women using sex for business or profit.

We insist that sex and love are the same or at least preferable, yet wonder why *low libido* is such an issue for women worldwide.

We are uncomfortable discussing pleasure and strongly favor *vagina* as a catch-all for words we'd prefer not to say like *clitoris*, *vulva*, *labia* and *engorgement*, which are central to female pleasure in ways 'vagina' is simply not.

We tolerate discussions about sex when tied to fertility and monogamy when our anatomy loses its eroticism completely to become the *birth canal*, while the *penis* remains rigid (pun intended), whether for fornication or procreation.

We don't like to admit that consensual, pleasurable sex can be tricky when lust, emotions, vulnerability and power collide.

While we are unable to discuss the complexity of sexuality without tying it to violence or love, we all remain subordinate and ashamed. Consent in a yes/no format is too frequently discussed like a magical ointment. A balm that once rubbed on the infection that is 'sexual violence' will make everything magically better because the boundaries of what constitutes consensual and non-consensual sex are supposedly rendered clear. Except, it's not that easy. We need to offer ourselves the time and space to discuss sex in the context of what we want from it, how we want it and who benefits from it, without being derailed by moral discussions of how it 'should' be (Allen, 2004; Rubin, 1992).

Part of the reason yes/no sex conversations don't work is because they ignore our motivations for sex and collapse the complexities of sexual communication into a simple 'yes' or 'no'. The way we *want* to feel becomes secondary when our capacity for sexual negotiation is cut short by the anxiety of discussing sex in favor of 'just doing it and hoping for the best'. As illustrated in a public discussion about 'touch' I facilitated in New York City in 2018, the idea I proposed of discussing likes and dislikes with prospective and current partners *before* engaging in sex was met with resistance by some attendees. Liza,[1] for example, stated:

---

[1] Not her real name.

I don't want to have to say what I like. It's a distraction, it takes me out of the moment. I just want him to take me on a journey. I want him to be the man.

This position, while understandable and very popular, sits at the core of everything that's wrong with consent conversations that only teach yes/no processes. When women feel that 'consent' only requires them to lie back and say yes or no (and men expect this of them), there is no room for thickening our narratives of sex and gender (Wiederman, 2005).

A further illustration of our discomfort at discussing pleasure is reflected in the now infamous Ansari case, in which the #TimesUp poster boy royally screwed up by repeatedly asking Grace '*where* [she] wanted to be fucked', rather than *what* she wanted to do or *how* she wanted to do it. What he got wrong was not the dirty talk, the unbridled enthusiasm nor the alleged 'porno' moves, but that his conversation wasn't as direct as it needed to be. His questions were a good start, but they were not the *right* questions and, more notably, he wasn't listening to the answers. He didn't account for the power differential between himself as a celebrity and Grace as an infatuated fan, nor did he (allegedly) display any knowledge of how to even touch a pussy! This case was a watershed moment in distinguishing differing degrees of sexual violations and how more systemic issues are at play that keep all of us from getting closer to the crux of the problem 'consent' as a lone strategy is attempting to resolve. While the pendulum swings only between *sexual liberation* and *sexual coercion* we omit reverence for the role of the erotic—from the sacred to the profane.

Most discussions of consent continue to reduce otherwise rich conversation to damage control. A discussion that focused on mutual sexual pleasure and desire, rather than yes/no consent, may have created a different ending to the Grace and Ansari story:

- He could have asked her what she wanted and she *may* have felt emboldened enough to tell him.
- She could have asked him what he wanted if their power dynamic had been acknowledged.

- She may have felt comfortable masturbating in front of him to show him how she liked to be touched.
- He may have observed her and thought how great it was that she was so comfortable with her sexuality and not for a second thought that she was a slut or felt emasculated by her relationship to erotic abandon.
- Both of them could have been operating from a place of curiosity rather than shame.
- He could have kept his attention *on her* rather than his own desires.

However, all these alternatives would require a degree of comfort most of us struggle with regardless of gender identity, and this is a massive problem if we are actually trying to remodel consent beyond the yes/no binary.

The Inconvenient Truth

When anxiety and shame are a more familiar state than erotic honesty, we know we have lost our way. This is because satisfying sex is about so much more than our ability to say simply 'Yes' or 'No!' An embodied 'Yes!' and textured 'Maybes' with descriptions are something most lovers dare not discuss with each other. The current consent framework is heterosexually inclined and leaves men, boys and masculine folk as the controllers responsible for asking and initiating sex (Beasley, 2008). If they are too afraid, awkward, avoidant or uncomfortable, it shifts the entire responsibility onto girls, women and femmes to do the heavy lifting without addressing the concept of mutuality at all (Wiederman, 2005). Seeking permission is important, but alone it tells us nothing about pleasure, nor invites us to share anything about how we like sex to be.

When we repeatedly hear that sex hurts women, or women don't enjoy sex or that he can't control himself and that he needs it more than women, that the prerogative is only on women to give consent or that intercourse is 'real' sex and non-heteronormative sex is not, an exploration of how we might do sex differently is erased. When men are told 'women don't experience much pleasure from sex', there's no incentive to learn how to create pleasurable contexts for them.

In therapy, I regularly see that men are taught to focus on themselves, not explicitly but by omitting the information they need to be good lovers: to practice listening, to practice asking, to practice negotiating touch and to recognize they can be receivers too. Instead they focus specifically on their pleasure to minimize the anxiety of discussing sex and in responding to what they've been taught about consent (because most do want to be good and kind), seek it in yes/no format. Women are taught to focus on being kind and certainly not upsetting a man, and as a result, a woman doesn't know what she wants or how to speak up so she says nothing. The man doesn't know how to ask, doesn't listen well or doesn't know what to do even if she were to respond! Sexual negotiation demands for a degree of explicit conversation, both speaking and listening about *what* sex is even *for*. It demands we also consider *who* it's for. Getting real about what turns us on when it comes to sex is crucial, even if it's a little inconvenient or uncomfortable.

By acknowledging and teaching such innate longings within us as 'normal', like Ansari's passion and Liza's desire to relinquish power and be taken on a 'journey', we make room for nuanced discussions of pleasure to exist beyond yes/no conversations. Instead we can consider what will make sex between partners hot and potentially 'fairer'. Describing what we'd like to do, have done to us or hope to feel allows partners to opt in and out, to add caveats and feel like they are participating in something that includes them too, rather than being strung along or surprised when accused of the 'journey' not working out as hoped in our fantasy. It insists we get to the business of discussing sex in ways that uphold its majesty while simultaneously acknowledging its complexity. In allowing us to remain honest about our motivations and desires, we describe what needs to happen to make sex mutually pleasurable and consensual. It insists we step past our discomfort to a place of integrity that makes us simultaneously aroused, present *and* accountable—communicating our hopes, expectations and willingness to try something new while knowing we can stop or change at any time.

Herein, I aim to describe a vision for a cultural shift, equally as seismic as the #MeToo movement, but one that centers eroticism instead of violence at its heart. In other words, imagine if we were equally as comfortable discussing pleasure as we are discussing violence! And we already have the same tools to do it as the birthing of the #MeToo movement—social media. Except that most social media platforms that allow discussions of sexual violence, including rape, ban discussions of pleasurable sex, the very ingredient we need to create a cultural shift.

This is no accident. As renowned black feminist Audre Lourde explains:

> In order to perpetuate itself, every oppression must corrupt or distort those various sources of power within the culture of the oppressed that can provide energy for change. For women, this has meant a suppression of the erotic as a considered source of power and information within our lives. (1984, p. 53)

If speaking of 'hot sex' out loud remains a taboo, we cannot even imagine what erotic integrity might feel like, let alone entail. Yet, as a result of many social media platforms' 'community guidelines', we cannot even establish conversations about good sex without allegedly causing offence. Our silences embolden the stigma of speaking truthfully about sex, particularly when it involves women's pleasure. We have yet to envisage nor embody a world where 'better sex' is a ritual we practice on a regular basis. The omission of 'better sex' is deliberate. It's what's not said about pleasure that makes room for sexual violations to flourish.

Ideas into Action—How Honesty Can Teach Us About Consent

Sex education and consent isn't just for kids. In fact, it's often adults who struggle with sex the most, particularly when discussing it with others (especially given sex education in schools was often—and continues to be—poorly developed and delivered, and may have been entirely absent for older generations. See Fileborn et al., 2016). When we struggle to discuss our bodies in ways that reflect how we feel about ourselves and what we want, it can be hard to imagine describing that to a partner or lover. As a beginning course of action, if you are interested in sex, getting comfortable using language that describes *your* body on *your* terms can be helpful. Whether it's erotic, sexy or simple is up to you, but practicing saying those words out loud is a great place to start. Whether you like clinical/anatomically accurate words, X-rated words or even made-up words, it helps to be able to define a set of language you are OK with practicing saying out loud—to yourself and then to others.

Recall some of the words you have enjoyed hearing being used to describe your body or you have enjoyed hearing in places you go for erotic inspiration. If you don't have any, ask your friends what words *they* use. Whether it's erotic literature, feminist porn, tube porn, Tumblr (RIP)[2] or anywhere else, see which words you are drawn to as an indication of the kinds of words you might like to use or hear. (Remember, the core themes of romance/erotic literature *and* porn are *both* about power, yet class definitions determine that one is more refined than the other.)

Next consider the *doing* words—the acts you'd like to do or have done to you/with you. Surrender, control, desire and validation are among the most popular incentives for sex. These are the incentives that sit at the center of the #MeToo movement also. Power lies at the core of consent. This is not about making what we like wrong, it's about being curious about what turns us on and making space for that.

Are you more in tune with language that errs toward romance? Or perhaps you like bolder, more graphic language to describe the acts you want or like? Taking ownership of your body by saying these words out loud can be challenging, but this is also part of the fun. Getting used to talking about sex is precisely where change needs to happen to embody the shift #MeToo aims to create.

It's helpful to discuss what you like *before* you are engaged in a sexual activity. On a date, in a text message or wherever you can, negotiate what happens and with whom. Discussing sex when you are not in the midst of it is often a great way to get the conversation rolling and feel less vulnerable because you're likely clothed and likely not inserting or being inserted into at the time. This was precisely what was omitted from Ansari's date. He didn't ask until it was too late *and* he didn't listen to the response. Talk through an ideal scenario with your current (or prospective)

---

[2] During the writing of this chapter, Tumblr announced that it would no longer permit 'adult content' on the site.

partner about what you *think* might happen in sex and how you'd like to feel.

One of the common misconceptions about consent—and one perpetuated in some of the backlash against #MeToo—is the idea that it's an interruption to be asking every 30 seconds. For example:

'Can I touch your leg?'
'Can I suck your neck?'
'Will you go down on me?'

However, setting up the contexts for sex to happen is *part of sex.* Whether via text, emoji, phone, Instagram or face to face, there are a plethora of ways to get talking about sex and the kind of sex you want to have to make sure that everyone is on the same page.

Having this conversation when you're halfway through is far more awkward and more likely to take you out of the moment. Having the chance to discuss what you like or are curious about beforehand means getting to the event is less likely to go awry—and you're both already confident in your ability to discuss what's on the menu and actually hear each other's responses to it.

During sex, try throwing the pre-negotiated ideas into a 'Sex Sandwich'—a variation on the Compliment Sandwich (two compliments as the bread with the filling [sex request] in the middle—except it's sexier):

'I love the way you suck my clit'.
'I want you to keep sucking it'. 'Yes, Just like that. That's how I like it'.
'You're so damn good at that'.

During sex it's also useful to check in with what's happening by asking questions that require more than 'yes' or 'no' answers. It needn't be a non-stop narration, but being present to the experience of yourself and your partner, and communicating this by speaking and listening is helpful. Some say that planning what you're going to do ruins the mood. However, planning what kinds of activities you like and how you like them can be part of the seduction. Nothing says 'I am really into this' more than a discussion about what you like and how you like it, no matter how long you've known your partner. It needn't be X rated, but it does need to be considered and shared to relieve the burden of one side only doing the asking and the other side only doing the telling. Listening and sharing ideas is a huge part of establishing consent, including being able to say 'yes' and 'no' to the things you like, might like or definitely don't like—and also *how* you want to do them.

And use your senses. Look, listen and touch. If your partner *looks* uncomfortable, they probably are. If they're saying something, listen to them—don't go racing ahead to avoid the anxiety of slowing down. Just slow it down. Good sex experiences peaks and troughs, so use the slow-downs to rebuild tension again. If you're experiencing dryness, redness, soreness, STOP. Add lube. Take a break. All these things are parts of consent that get skimmed over by couples in their teens through to their 80s. Don't skim. Stay with it.

Equality for All—Except in Bed

The risks involved in sexual miscommunication are very real and varied in relation to gender, sexuality and race. For women and non-binary people, the greatest risk *is* in speaking up about what we want or do not want sexually. To be clear: explicit and honest descriptions about our erotic longings sit firmly in contrast with what it means to be feminine, desirable and attractive, and therefore validated (Allen, 2004). Dominant social and cultural norms mean that we lose social collateral if women are perceived as demanding or in control of our sexual pleasure and put our own needs front and center. Simultaneously, this opens us up to shame and ridicule both from our partners and from broader society, and is amplified if one is not white or cis-gender. Traditionally, women who embody and facilitate their sexual joy are sluts, whores and candidates asking to be raped, abused and even murdered. For even the most progressive and educated women on the planet this is a very real, familiar and visceral threat that transcends cognition and operates as a default of self-preservation.

In contrast, the risk for men is in *not* speaking out about their pleasures and desires, and simply taking them by force at worst or coercion at best rather than communicating them. In doing so, they risk not only acting outside of the parameters of consent and open themselves up to becoming predators and rapists, but like Ansari, being self-absorbed, inattentive and generally 'bad in bed', with all options on a spectrum from 'getting away with it' to 'utterly devastating'. Until recently, being deemed 'a predator' didn't lose men much social collateral. In many cases, they didn't lose anything at all, especially if they were not caught. Likewise there has been no incentive for men to explore the ramifications of 'not speaking up' before and during erotic encounters, and simply bypassing the anxiety of discussing sex by just doing it and avoiding the consequences later. What the Ansari case has illustrated is that while taking the low road of being a negligent partner doesn't necessarily make one a rapist, it can still result in problematic and harmful sexual experiences—the very thing the #MeToo movement is drawing attention to. It demands our only recourse is to get comfortable communicating about sex frankly and transforming the social and cultural conditions that make openly talking about sex and pleasure an anxiety-producing endeavor (if not one we are actively punished for) for many of us.

While public organizations depend upon funding from governments and institutions that only fund violence, fertility and disease programs, we reinforce the idea that sex is something dangerous or merely functional. A reaction. An afterthought. Not something that is a visceral human way of connecting, integral to our health like breathing and drinking water. As members of the public we can demand more from our legislators and ourselves to examine a paradigm that centers sex and pleasure the same way we center economics—crucial to longevity rather than emergency response. When pleasure occupies space the way violence does, the impact on our labor, resources and minds will be enormous.

Conclusion

In all my years working in human sexuality, I have come to the definitive conclusion that consent is not just a 'yes' or a 'no'. Rather, it is something you actively communicate and embody. We all must become comfortable with this. While we collectively avoid discussing eroticism as a public health issue, prioritizing its avoidance by distracting ourselves with how to avoid violence rather than how to finger someone, we are simply paying lip service to consent. Without getting comfortable with explicit, meaningful discussions about sex, pleasure, eroticism and who benefits from a sexual transaction—anything else is simply a circus. Instead of leaving the burden of consent to women and girls alone, let's expand the conversation to include information about exactly who is doing what to whom, how it feels and who gets what from it. When we can speak as freely of our achievements in negotiating pleasurable sex as we can about celebrating our sporting expertise, we will be closer to a workable version of nuanced consent.

Until then, giddy up!

References

Allen, L. (2004). Beyond the birds and the bees: Constituting a discourse of erotics in sexuality education. *Gender and Education, 16*(2), 151–167.

Beasley, C. (2008). The challenge of pleasure: Re-imagining sexuality and sexual health. *Health Sociology Review, 17*(2), 151–163.

Carmody, M. (2005). Ethical erotics: Reconceptualizing anti-rape education. *Sexualities, 8*(4), 465–480.

Fileborn, B., Lyons, A., Hinchliff, S., Brown, G., Heywood, W., & Minichiello, V. (2016). Learning about sex in later life: Sources of education and older Australian adults. *Sex Education*, online first.

Foucault, M. (2008) [1978]. *The history of sexuality: Volume I*. Camberwell, VIC: Penguin Books.

Lourde, A. (1984). *Sister outsider*. New York: Crossing Press.

Rubin, G. (1992). Thinking sex: Notes for a radical theory of politics of sexuality. In C. S. Vance (Ed.), *Pleasure and danger: Exploring female sexuality* (pp. 267–319). London: Pandora.

Wiederman, M. (2005). The gendered nature of sexual scripts. *The Family Journal, 13*, 496–502.

17

#MeToo as Sex Panic

Heidi Matthews

Introduction

This chapter seeks to refocus our analysis on the 'sex' part of the wave of sexual violence allegations currently leveled at male celebrity figures in the wake of the #MeToo movement. To do so requires us to put sex back on the table as a part of an analytic frame that is irreducible to power. In other words, sexual violence must be analyzed from within the framework of 'pleasure and danger,' as a real threat that women must negotiate as part of their daily sexual lives. Re-centering sex in this way rejects a core commitment of much of the recent mainstream writing on the topic of #MeToo, which contends that '[o]ur conflict is not over sex, or with men in particular or in general, but over power' (Grant, 2017, n.p.). In doing so, it recognizes the complexity, nuance, and ambivalence of women's lived experience, positioning their desires along a spectrum

H. Matthews (✉)
Nathanson Centre on Transnational Human Rights, Crime and Security,
Osgoode Hall Law School, York University, Toronto, ON, Canada
e-mail: hmatthews@osgoode.yorku.ca

© The Author(s) 2019
B. Fileborn, R. Loney-Howes (eds.), *#MeToo and the Politics of Social Change*,
https://doi.org/10.1007/978-3-030-15213-0_17

wherein their pleasure and pain, their emancipation, and their victimization can be articulated in sexual terms.

Refocusing our attention on the sexual part of violence and harassment also allows us to productively deploy the analytic of the 'sex panic,' reclaiming it from the right and using it to emphasize the ambivalent and oftentimes internally contradictory concept of sexual consent. Analytically reducing sexual harassment to power is a profoundly conservative political move. The frame of the 'sex panic' is useful because it allows us to unpack the political costs of feminist activism in the post-Harvey Weinstein 'moment' in explicitly sexual terms. Sexualities scholar Carole Vance lays out the idea of a sex panic thus: these panics 'mobilize fears of social pollution in an attempt to draw firm boundaries between legitimate and deviant individuals and forms of sexuality' (Vance, 1993, p. 295). To be clear: the fact that sex panics generally result in conservative policy shifts highlights that the creation, fueling, and dissemination of material that leads to a sex panic is a profoundly right-wing endeavor. The left therefore needs to take care to note that when it deploys the language of 'sex panic,' it does so in the mode of political analysis, so as to better understand and combat the right. It is in this sense that I am using the sex panic framework.

A quick word about what this chapter is not doing. A full leftist reckoning with the current moment necessitates a labor-focused frame as well as a sex-focused frame. Socialist feminist Barbara Ehrenreich (2017) has already noted that we have been hearing '[t]oo much about actresses and not enough about housekeepers' (see also Kagal, Cowan & Jawad, this collection). While not the primary focus of this chapter, the labor frame, and its intersections with the sex frame, needs to be constantly borne in mind.

This chapter does not aim to silence, object to, or in any other way devalue the voices of those women (and many men) who have come forward in the thousands with their stories of sexual, physical, and emotional misconduct, abuse, harassment, and assault at the hands of powerful men. It is not skeptical of the truthfulness of these women's stories. It does not seek put them back in the closet, or to analyze them within a totalizing frame. Instead, I am concerned with studying the way these stories are told, and retold, in media and scholarly accounts. For ease of reference throughout, I use the '#MeToo movement' as shorthand for these accounts.

My goals in this chapter are threefold. Firstly, I describe the current wave of sexual violence allegations against famous and powerful men within the framework of a sex panic. Secondly, I argue that this sex panic is of a piece with larger conservative sex-skeptical public policy movements that have taken root over roughly the past decade across English-speaking Western liberal democratic states. And thirdly, I show how much of the mainstream media and scholarly reaction to the panic follows a set of narrative tropes that inscribe questions of desire and sexual consent in binary terms (see also Darnell, this collection), thus reading out the potential for a more open-textured and nuanced analysis of the pleasure/danger dialectic.

A Watershed Moment?

On October 5, 2017, the *New York Times* published an article alleging a nearly 30-year-long history of sexually inappropriate conduct perpetrated by Harvey Weinstein against women in various positions and career stages in the film and media industry. According to the *Times*, these allegations 'share a common narrative: Women reported to a hotel for what they thought were work reasons, only to discover that Weinstein, *who has been married for most of three decades*, sometimes seemed to have different interests' (Kantor & Twohey, 2017, n.p.—my emphasis). The severity of the alleged sexually inappropriate encounters ranged widely from asking women to watch him bathe to allegations of non-consensual sex (in other words, what would amount in the United States or United Kingdom to rape and in Canada to sexual assault). In the days after the initial revelations, allegations against Weinstein multiplied. Public condemnation was swift and unforgiving. He was fired from the board of his company (although he still reportedly owns nearly a quarter of its stock), suspended from the British Academy of Film and Television Arts, and expelled from the Academy of Motion Picture Arts and Sciences and the Producers Guild of America. He was criminally charged in New York in May 2018 with offenses including a criminal sexual act, rape, and predatory sexual assault.

In the time since all of this began, hundreds of famous and influential men in the media industry, politics, sports, journalism, and academia have been the subject of allegations of sexual misconduct, again to varying degrees of severity. Some of these men have lost their jobs, and all have been publicly disgraced. Others, like Weinstein, vociferously denied the allegations against them. A small handful, like comedian Louis C.K., issued apologies.

The current moment has been described in the popular discourse as marking a sea change in the way that 'we'—presumably middle-class (white) women and men in Western liberal countries—see, hear, and react to sexual violence in all its myriad forms. We are, we are told, in the midst of a 'national reckoning' (O'Hehir, 2017), a 'profound episode' (Flanagan, 2017), a 'watershed' (Gessen, 2017), and 'a movement' which is 'revolutionary' (Gilbert, 2017). Following their naming of the 'Silence Breakers' as the 2017 Person of the Year, *TIME* wrote that the #MeToo moment 'unleashed one of the highest-velocity shifts in our culture since the 1960s' and *Merriam-Webster* named 'feminism' its word of 2017.[1]

The link between the '#MeToo movement' and concrete justice gains is, however, far from straightforward. The analytic of the sex panic can help us unpack the ways in which the #MeToo movement might come with a host of political costs that we have, as yet, barely anticipated, and that we should not accept. Sex panics—a version of moral panic—describe persistent conflicts over sex with recurrent, structural features. Janice Irvine (2006, p. 82) summarizes the stages of a panic as:

> Following a natural cycle, progressing through several stages. First, a group, person, or issue emerges to become defined as a social threat. Media representations then stylize this alleged threat in a simplistic and stereotypical way, fueling intense public concern. Next, moral entrepreneurs of various types devise coping mechanisms and solutions. The perceived threat eventually diminishes and the panic recedes. The group or condition may have vanished or simply dropped from public interest. Finally, the panic may simply be forgotten or it may generate political changes. Repressive legislation and policies are common legacies of moral panics, rendering them mechanisms of social control against their folk devil targets.

---

[1] https://www.merriam-webster.com/words-at-play/word-of-the-year-2017-feminism.

Using this frame, we can see here how Weinstein figures as a social threat, one that triggers a panic because it touches a third rail: it makes visible something we knew was there all along; the widespread structural shielding of sexually inappropriate conduct by powerful men in certain industries. We can also see how #MeToo fulfils the role of moral entrepreneur, presenting society with a coping mechanism, which may or may not generate actual social change when the panic recedes.

Situating #MeToo as Sex Panic

I now turn to the second part of the chapter, which seeks to contextualize the #MeToo movement within a set of policy debates and developments that have emerged, over the past three decades, around the regulation of sex. Taken together with recent local and global debates about sex trafficking and sex work, campus sexual assault, sexting, and revenge porn constitute a wider sex panic, the culmination of which might turn out to be the #MeToo movement.

#MeToo itself, as a cultural sensibility, did not begin with Harvey Weinstein. Since at least 2015, high-profile figures were being outed as sexual predators, abusers, and violators in a way that already challenged the 'culture of silence' around powerful men and institutions. We have seen Bill Cosby, arguably at least as famous and powerful as Weinstein in his day, acquitted of sexual assault pre-#MeToo and convicted post-#MeToo. The NFL and corporate sponsors dropped several American football players for domestic violence, and in 2014, the League instituted a new policy on domestic violence. Donald Trump had his 'grab 'em by the pussy' moment, which arguably increased his popularity among white voters (including white women). In Canada, there was the Ghomeshi affair, where a beloved CBC program host was accused and tried for sexual assault. He was eventually acquitted of one set of allegations due to unreliable witness testimony; however, the judgment, sound in legal principle, became the focus of a huge 'feminist' backlash (Gollom, 2016). Rather than a singular cataclysmic event reducible to the Weinstein allegations, what we really see today is the emergence of a generalized concern with sexual harassment and assault in situations where the alleged perpetrators are shielded by large wealthy institutions from either social or legal accountability (see Loney-Howes, this collection, for a related discussion).

Recent heightened attention to campus sexual assault has foreshadowed some of the conservative potential embedded in the #MeToo sex panic. Universities and colleges in Anglo-American jurisdictions, concerned with maintaining their reputations, competitiveness in varsity sports, and their position vis-à-vis powerful private clubs and funders, have historically under-investigated and under-reported instances of campus sexual assault. In 2011, under the Obama Administration, the Department of Education's Office for Civil Rights instructed American universities and colleges on how to reform their sexual assault policies, threatening to end federal funding for failure to comply. In response, American campuses rewrote their policies, introducing elements that were previously not considered essential for compliance with federal law. These new policies have long been considered by liberal and left legal academics as fundamentally unfair to the accused and sometimes also the complainant (see Gruber, 2016). A memo on behalf of four Harvard Law School professors, written in August 2017, contends, among other things, that:

> [d]efinitions of sexual wrongdoing on college campuses are now seriously overbroad. They go way beyond accepted legal definitions of rape, sexual assault, and sexual harassment. They often include sexual conduct that is merely unwelcome, even if it does not create a hostile environment, even if the person accused had no way of knowing it was unwanted, and even if the accuser's sense that it was unwelcome arose after the encounter. The definitions often include mere speech about sexual matters. (Bartholet, Gertner, Halley, & Suk-Gersen, 2017, p. 2)

The campus sexual assault 'panic' has traveled to Canada, my home jurisdiction (as well as the UK, Australia, and elsewhere). In 2016 the Ontario legislature passed Bill 132, the 'Sexual Violence and Harassment Action Plan Act' (Supporting Survivors and Challenging Sexual Violence and Harassment), which requires all universities and colleges in the province to have formal policies and procedures to deal with sexual violence.

Notably, Bill 132 radically expands the purview of conduct that schools have the jurisdiction to regulate. Instead of using the language of 'sexual assault,' it refers to 'sexual violence,' defined as:

[a]ny sexual act or act targeting a person's sexuality, gender identity or gender expression, whether the act is physical or psychological in nature, that is committed, threatened or attempted against a person without the person's consent.

Ontarian institutions have subsequently adopted a swath of new policies widely described as 'survivor-centric' in character yet suffer from many of the same due process and fairness considerations as the American policies.

One high-profile conservative backlash against the introduction of these policies has been the Lindsay Shepherd affair at Wilfred Laurier University in Ontario (Choise, 2018). In the fall of 2018, while a teaching assistant for an undergraduate English language class, Shepherd introduced a tutorial discussion on the politics of evolving trends in the use of pronouns by playing a video clip of the University of Toronto Psychology Professor Jordan Petersen. Petersen has come under attack by transgender rights groups for his very public opposition to using gender-neutral pronouns. When the course instructor discovered Shepherd's tutorial content, she was called in for an inquisition-style meeting with him and other University officials. In the meeting, which she audio recorded and subsequently posted online, officials intimate that Shepherd may be in violation of Laurier's campus Gendered and Sexual Violence Policy on the grounds that she targeted students on the basis of their gender identity. In the fallout that has ensued, conservative, 'anti-political correctness' groups have appropriated Shepherd's story, making it the centerpiece of a 'free speech' platform geared toward reducing the influence of 'the left' on university campuses. Shepherd has been referred to as the 'alt-right's new hero on campus' and has herself garnered an enormous and influential Twitter following (at the time of writing, she had over 76,000 followers).

It seems that the socio-legal and cultural pump was primed sometime well before the 'Weinstein moment' to be receptive to—or perhaps more accurately, generative of—a 'social movement' against what has been referred to by some feminists as 'rape' and/or 'porn culture' (see Fileborn & Loney-Howes, this collection). Back in March 2017, Martha Nussbaum gave a lecture titled 'Accountability in an Era of Celebrity.' In it, she noted that 'it isn't as if these things are new events: it's the climate of their reception' (2017, p. 8). Accountability in a 'culture of celebrity' that sustains rape culture through the silencing of women's voices, according to Nussbaum, is 'likely to prove elusive—unless the public rises up […] outrage is useful only if it leads to a real project: really hearing women's voices' (2017, p. 25).

Sophie Gilbert has encapsulated the mainstream understanding of #MeToo, which sees its power in the idea 'that it takes something that women had long kept quiet about and transforms it into a movement.' Writing for *the Guardian's* Family column, Georgina Lawton (2017) notes that the 'campaign took off because it is real.' Lawton combines personal anecdote with a call to action. Because of the 'goosepimple-inducing' empowerment of the #MeToo movement, she writes that she will now:

> [b]e asking my younger brother and my male friends and colleagues how they really behave on nights out, what they would do if they saw something inappropriate, and what they think constitutes sexual harassment. (Lawton, 2017, n.p.)

The idea here is that by contributing their voices women can, *one by one*, 'change a global culture of [male] sexual entitlement' (see Lawton, 2017, n.p.).

The Continuum of Consent: Making Space for Pleasure and Danger

The sort of social change that the #MeToo movement is generating, however, is sexually repressive in disturbing ways. I argue that a core component of #MeToo—as well as the campus sexual assault policy reform movement—is women's mass identification with membership in the movement through the mode of victimhood. The public narration of #MeToo follows the sexual script envisaged for campus sexual violence complainants, wherein sex is too often reduced to an initiator/respondent structure. Sex is seen as something that *happens to* women (see Darnell, this collection). In the face of the clear necessity of some law to deal with the heightened danger women face in sexual situations, legal feminism has played along with this construction of consent, pretending that its absence—a material element of the criminal offense of rape and sexual assault—actually exists as a social fact, out there to be found by the trier of fact. In reality, however, sexual encounters take place along a complicated spectrum of pleasure and danger, and rape law's binary, 'on/off' approach to consent is highly problematic. Sexual consent is therefore a legal fiction designed to help us navigate principled, proportionate legal responses to sexual assault. It does not describe the complex reality of consent between men and women in daily life (see Darnell, this collection).

The public narration of the #MeToo movement combines two worrying assumptions about consent to sex. On one hand, it adopts the 'governance feminist' sexual ideology, wherein true consent is never *really* possible because of women's inescapable entanglement in social structures of male domination (see Halley, Kotiswaran, Rebouché, & Shamir, 2018). On the other, it adopts the framework of the neoliberal carceral state, focusing on punishment and retribution not just for alleged instances of rape, but for a wide range of objectionable—but not criminally actionable—behavior, ranging from making off-color jokes to placing an unwanted hand on a women's back to persistent sexual threats to violent rape. In the logic of the contemporary sex panics, the terminology of sexual violence has come to color nearly the whole spectrum of sexual encounters as dangerous, threatening to flatten out the range of sexual experience, desire, and erotic possibility open to women (see Darnell, this collection).

Mainstream public discourse around the #MeToo movement has facilitated this hollowing out of sexual perspective. In this discourse, feminists reject the claim that the Weinstein moment is actually part of a larger war on sex. In a recent piece in *The Atlantic*, titled 'To hell with the witch-hunt debate,' Caitlin Flanagan (2017, n.p.) writes that '[s]aying there's a sex panic on the grounds that women don't like having their asses grabbed is the 2017 way of calling women frigid.' What, exactly, is going on here? Of course there is a very real sense in which it is *true* that it would be preposterous to claim that women should be ok with having their asses grabbed (presumably in a non-consensual context, but Flanagan doesn't specify). But surely it must *also* be true that some women, some of the time, might like having their asses grabbed without also thereby being whores. What Flanagan is implying is that the only permissible space for female desire lies at the far end of the consent spectrum, away from the grey zone of innuendo and nuanced, often non-verbal, communication about the shifting boundaries of sexual expression. This is, of course, the sexually conservative implication of Flanagan's statement: if this second scenario—which reflects a more complicated, non-binary understanding of male-female desire—were thinkable, then not only would the sex panic piece fall away, but so too would the universalizability of women's reasonable desire. The opposite of the frigid woman is, after all, the slut. There is no room in Flanagan's account for context and ambiguity, where a woman might reasonably entertain a host of complex moving desires related to her ass being grabbed. No room for the woman who one day, based on contextually derived information but without affirmative con-sent, actually *wants* her ass to be grabbed by a stranger. The dominant #MeToo discourse structurally precludes this woman from having *her* voice heard.

A certain conservative narrative pattern is also identifiable in #MeToo contributions. In her King's College lecture, Nussbaum includes her own detailed personal story of sexual assault. She tells us how in 1968, when she 'was an enterprising twenty-year-old,' she ended up in bed with a 40-something famous actor. While she 'intended to consent to intercourse,' she 'did not consent to […] the gruesome, violent, and pain-ful assault that he substituted for intercourse.' Nussbaum further explains that part of the reason she consented to the sexual encounter at all was because she had 'decided to be daring, since it was the late 60's and I felt that I should join the culture' (specifically the sexual liberation culture of the 1960s and 1970s). She continues: 'So what did I do? After my inju-ries faded, I decided not to "join the culture." I met a lovely man my own age, *settled down into a monogamous life, married, and soon had a child*' (2017, pp. 2–3—my emphasis).

Let us juxtapose this personal story, told as part of an academic talk, to part of the *New York Times* article that exposed Louis C.K.'s infractions. One of C.K.'s five accusers was an anonymous woman who was the recipient of repeated requests to masturbate in front of her. The story explains:

> She was in her early 20s and went along with his request, but later questioned his behavior.
>
> 'It was something that I knew was wrong,' said the woman, who described sitting in Louis C.K.'s office while he masturbated in his desk chair during a workday, other colleagues just outside the door. 'I think the big piece of why I said yes was because of the culture,' she continued. (Ryzik, Buckley, & Kantor, 2017, n.p.)

Unlike Nussbaum's story, the *Times* doesn't reveal whether this woman ever eventually 'settled down' or 'had a child.' There are, however, other common narrative tropes at play here. Both Nussbaum and the Woman were in their early 20s. Both had encounters with powerful men significantly older than them. Both reflected on the meaning of their respective experiences differently years later. Both associated being placed in a situation that would lead to their assaults with participation in a certain sexual 'culture.' Explicitly for Nussbaum—and perhaps implicitly for the Woman—their experiences of violation led them to reject said sexual 'culture.'

I want to be clear: for all its familiarities with the Woman's story, Nussbaum is narrating an initially consensual encounter that later turned violent and non-consensual. The Woman's story is told to us, on the other hand, as a situation in which consent may have been vitiated or attenuated by the coercive environment in which she found herself. That being said, both these accounts speak to the issue of consent in other important ways. We see the women's judgment impliedly affected by their young age and associated lack of sexual experience. Their emplacement within a libertine sexual environment is not a product of their fully informed choice. With the rejection of the more permissive sexual culture in Nussbaum's case, we see the reinscription of 'true' consent within the safety of the marital and procreative bond; in her monogamous coupling, sex is now domesticated, rather than recreational. For the Woman, we see her troubled consent—the fact that she 'went along' with something that she 'knew was wrong'—superimposed on her initial experience through an act of remembering inflected by the political commitments of #MeToo.

I now want turn to what we do not see and hear in the Woman's story—to what is left unsaid and is rendered somehow unsayable. As opposed to reading her encounter with Louis C.K. solely in the register of violation, I want to suggest that it could be read in the register of 'bad sex.' I'm drawing here on the short story 'Cat Person' published in the *New Yorker* (Roupenian, 2017). The story recounts the fraught 'courting' of Margot and Robert, which transpires mostly via text. Their awkward first date eventually culminates in, variously, humiliating, disgusting, yet also, at points, titillating sex. Margot is alternately turned on by the thought of Robert's arousal by her and disgusted by his slopping kissing and too-big belly. She vacillates between 'changing her mind' and carrying on more than once, and in the end considers the encounter not as an assault but as merely 'bad sex.'

'Cat Person' produced, in the same vein as #MeToo, thousands of responses on social media, with women revealing their own 'bad sex' stories. The *Guardian* reports it as 'the short story that launched a thousand theories' (Cain, 2017). *Vice* promptly published a piece called the '"Cat Person" Problem,' which recounts four women's experiences of their own personal 'cat people' (Faj, 2017). Consider Daphne's story:

> When I was 19, at university, I was doing what they call 'living my best life'. After my first year exams I invited this guy from back home I'd been flirting with to come down to visit my uni accommodation. He was older—31, if my memory serves me correctly. He wasn't my 'type'—he was sort of on the short side and he was a little fluffy, but he had a really handsome face. He was a father, but he owned his own barber's, so on one hand I didn't see anything serious happening with a man with children, but on the other he seemed to have his life together.
>
> Anyway, he came down, we Netflix-and-chilled before Netflix existed, and then he put the moves on me. I was going with the flow and then I changed my mind, mid-third base. It felt a little rude to tell him I wasn't in the mood any more, so I just let him thrust himself inside of me. I just laid there, thinking about when to call my dad to drive down to collect me and my things for the summer holidays. (Faj, 2017, n.p.)

Here yet another young woman is narrated as having 'gone along' with sex with an older, slightly ugly, and overweight man.

What makes the 'bad sex' and attenuated #MeToo consent stories similar? Certainly, there are distinctions, not least of which is the lack of power imbalance in the former. But in terms of similarities, both *genres* narrate sex as something that is done *to* women. (The viral response to 'Cat Person' is particularly surprising to me, since while we can admit that women suffer sexual violence disproportionately, it is simply unsustainable to claim that men do not encounter bad sex at similar rates to women). Critically, both the #MeToo and bad sex narratives *read out* the malleability of consent that *is so recognizably present* in 'Cat Person.' In effect, the bad sex responses have very little to do with the kind of sexual complexity mapped out in Roupenian's story and look much more like watered-down versions of #MeToo. In other words, they amount to the radical extension of the reach of #MeToo to virtually the entirety of human sexual experience.

Suddenly, what looks like a progressive social movement ends up restrained by dangerously conservative ideas about sexual culture. Here we find ourselves back again at Flanagan's *Atlantic* essay, where she writes: 'Saying there's a sex panic is a fancy way of saying that women's bodies don't completely belong to them *the way their cars do*.' She goes on by pointing out that '[y]ou learn early on, if you're female, that your body mostly belongs to you [...] But in a small way a little bit of it belongs to the men of the world' (2017, n.p.). While Flanagan is aghast at her own seemingly inextricable conclusion, I am more sympathetic to its potential relational quality.

To make this point clear, I am going to playfully interact with the #MeToo and 'bad sex' narrative genre but with a twist: I am going to pursue the confessional gesture without the wrap-around neoliberal move—the one that cloaks the emancipatory sexual moment in the affirmative consent paradigm and the securitization of home life and traditional family values, to the exclusion of less mainstream forms of women's sexual self-actualization. I am going to tell a story that could easily figure as a #MeToo installment.

Two years ago, in the middle of the night, I invited a stranger I met on Tinder to my flat in Camden Town (at that time I lived in London). I knew nothing about this man other than that he was, supposedly, an American fine artist who was somewhat, though not drastically, older than me. I consented (not affirmatively, but through a series of verbal and non-verbal cues) to sexual activity with him short of intercourse. Neither of us was entirely sober. At some point things got rough, which I was ok with. He began lightly choking me. I was seated on my couch and he was standing over me. Judging from his physique, he was several times stronger than me. No one knew where I was or that I was with him. The choking became more intense, which I signaled I was also ok with. It continued until, for the smallest fraction of a second, I became actually frightened. He was watching my face the whole time. Seeing the rawness of my fear, he relented. We continued and eventually had intercourse.

I consider this encounter to have been consensual. *More than that*, it was one of the sexiest moments of my life. Yet by any standard definition of sexual violence, this man assaulted me. It would have been easy to interpret or re-read the episode as such, to add it to the chorus of #MeToo stories. For me, however, the sensation of full-on fear—such as I had never experienced with a man before—created an opening, a suddenly new and free space of wanting, needing, having, and being had. We both shared in the production of the fear and the recognition of what it had allowed to pass between us, which was fleeting, *liminal trust* (relatedly, see Cover, this collection, in regard to the recognition of vulnerability as vital for the prevention of violence). In that moment I belonged, for one split second, to this man.

The sexually conservative thrust of the #MeToo movement to date is incompatible with this kind of story. The fluidly of consent, danger, and desire contained in my story does not translate into neoliberal feminist discourses. What is more, the spectrum approach to sexual consent makes it much more difficult to determine and cast out the 'folk devil' male villains. It is also not conducive to a straightforward policy project. In short, focused as we are on sexual danger, we are losing the ability to positively theorize 'liminal trust' as a core concept in the sexual encounter. The #MeToo movement posits women and men as intensely individuated, self-responsible actors, the one demanding something of the other, *ostensibly* without regard for the other's will, desire, or sexual self-actualization.

In order to rescue—if indeed this is possible—#MeToo from total conservative co-optation, we need to be able to open up space within its storylines to see the nuance, the affective folding and weaving, and the relational creation of meaning in highly ambiguous sexual moments.

References

Bartholet, E., Gertner, N., Halley, J., & Suk-Gersen, J. (2017, August 21). Fairness for all students under Title IX. *Harvard Law School*. Retrieved January 8, 2019, from https://dash.harvard.edu/handle/1/33789434.

Cain, S. (2017, December 14). Cat person: The story that launched a thousand theories. *The Guardian*. Retrieved January 8, 2019, from https://www.theguardian.com/books/2017/dec/13/cat-person-short-story-that-launched-thousand-theories.

Choise, S. (2018, April 5). Documents reveal new details in Lindsay Shepard-Wilfrid Laurier University Saga. *The Globe and Mail*. Retrieved January 8, 2019, from https://www.theglobeandmail.com/canada/article-documents-reveal-new-details-in-lindsay-shepherd-wilfrid-laurier/.

Ehrenreich, B. (2017, November 10). *Twitter*. Retrieved January 8, 2019, from http://twitter.com/B_Ehrenreich/status/928633359521083393.

Faj, R. (2017, December 13). The 'cat person' problem—Four women share their real-life stories. *Vice*. Retrieved January 8, 2019, from https://www.vice.com/en_asia/article/qvzvvp/the-cat-person-problem-four-women-share-their-real-life-stories.

Flanagan, C. (2017, November 22). To hell with the witch-hunt debate: The post-Weinstein moment isn't a war on sex. It's a long-overdue revolution. *The Atlantic*. Retrieved January 8, 2019, from https://www.theatlantic.com/entertainment/archive/2017/11/to-hell-with-the-witch-hunt-debate/546713/.

Gessen, M. (2017, November 14). When does a watershed become a sex panic? *The New Yorker*. Retrieved January 8, 2019, from https://www.newyorker.com/news/our-columnists/when-does-a-watershed-become-a-sex-panic.

Gilbert, S. (2017, October 16). The movement of #MeToo: How a hashtag got its power. *The Atlantic*. Retrieved January 8, 2019, from https://www.theatlantic.com/entertainment/archive/2017/10/the-movement-of-metoo/542979/.

Gollom, M. (2016, March 24). Jian Ghomeshi found not guilty on choking and all sexual assault charges. *CBC News*. Retrieved January 8, 2019, from https://

www.cbc.ca/news/canada/toronto/jian-ghomeshi-sexual-assault-trial-ruling-1.3505446.

Grant, M. (2017, December 8). "The unsexy truth about harassment." *The New York Review of Books*. Retrieved January 8, 2019, from https://www.nybooks.com/daily/2017/12/08/the-unsexy-truth-about-harassment/.

Gruber, A. (2016). Anti-rape culture. *University of Kansas Law Review, 64*(4), 1027–1056.

Halley, J., Kotiswaran, P., Rebouché, R., & Shamir, H. (2018). *Governance feminism: An introduction*. Minneapolis: University of Minnesota Press.

Irvine, J. (2006). Emotional scripts of sex panics. *Sexuality Research & Social Policy, 3*(3), 82–94.

Kantor, J., & Twohey, M. (2017, October 5). Harvey Weinstein paid off sexual harassment accusers for decades. *New York Times*. Retrieved January 8, 2019, from https://www.nytimes.com/2017/10/05/us/harvey-weinstein-harassment-allegations.html.

Lawton, G. (2017, October 28). #MeToo is here to stay. We must challenge all men about sexual harassment. *The Guardian*. Retrieved January 8, 2019, fromhttps://www.theguardian.com/lifeandstyle/2017/oct/28/metoo-hashtag-sexual-harassment-violence-challenge-campaign-women-men.

Nussbaum, M. (2017, March 9). Accountability in an era of celebrity. *Inaugural lecture at the Dickson Poon Law Centre, Kings College London*, pp. 1–26.

O'Hehir, A. (2017, November 18). Is this a "sex panic" or a national moment of reckoning? Can it be both? Salon. Retrieved January 8, 2019, from https://www.salon.com/2017/11/18/is-this-a-sex-panic-or-a-national-moment-of-reckoning-cannot-it-be-both/.

Roupenian, K. (2017, December 11). Cat person. *The New Yorker*. Retrieved January 8, 2019, from https://www.newyorker.com/magazine/2017/12/11/cat-person.

Ryzik, M., Buckley, C., Kantor, J. (2017, November 9). Louis C.K. is accused by 5 women of sexual misconduct. *The New York Times*. Retrieved January 8, 2019, from https://www.nytimes.com/2017/11/09/arts/television/louis-ck-sexual-misconduct.html.

Vance, C. S. (1993). More danger, more pleasure: A decade after the Barnard sexuality conference. *New York Law School Law Review, 38*, 289–317.

Legislation

Bill 132, Sexual violence and harassment action plan Act—Supporting survivors and challenging sexual violence and harassment. (2016). Retrieved January 8, 2019, from https://www.ola.org/en/legislative-business/bills/parliament-41/session-1/bill-132.

18

Men and #MeToo: Mapping Men's Responses to Anti-violence Advocacy

Michael Flood

Men's responses to #MeToo, and other forms of feminist advocacy on rape and sexual harassment, range from enthusiastic support to hostile backlash. There are common forms of resistance among men to these campaigns, including defensive denials that men's violence is routine, a focus on 'other' men, and complaints that #MeToo has 'gone too far' (see Fileborn & Phillips, this collection). And for many men, there is simply mute discomfort. Masculinity is implicated directly in men's perpetration of rape and sexual harassment, but also in men's widespread inaction or complicity in the face of men's violence against women. At the same time, #MeToo has prompted valuable public scrutiny of the narrow and dangerous ideals of masculinity which inform men's violence toward women.

#MeToo's call to action among men comprises three key tasks. First, #MeToo asks men to listen to women, in order to recognize men's violence against women as common, serious, and wrong. Second, #MeToo asks that men reflect on and change their own behavior and everyday relations with women and other men. Third, #MeToo asks that men

M. Flood (✉)
Queensland University of Technology, Brisbane, QLD, Australia
e-mail: m.flood@qut.edu.au

© The Author(s) 2019
B. Fileborn, R. Loney-Howes (eds.), *#MeToo and the Politics of Social Change*,
https://doi.org/10.1007/978-3-030-15213-0_18

contribute to social change, both by challenging other men and by contributing to wider efforts to shift the systemic gender inequalities that form the foundation of sexual harassment and abuse. For each, this chapter assesses to what extent men have taken up this task and the common forms of resistance many men show. The chapter thus traces the contours of men's responses to #MeToo: what we know about how #MeToo has produced change and how it has not.

The data with which to assess #MeToo's impact are limited. Although #MeToo certainly has significant cultural presence and grassroots mobilization in a wide variety of countries (see Garibotti & Hopp; Zeng, this collection), most of the available surveys on awareness of the campaign come from the Global North and particularly the US. Even less is known about how #MeToo's impact plays out among intersections of gender, ethnicity, class, and other forms of social difference and inequality (see Kagal, Cowan & Jawad; Ryan; Ison, this collection). Note that, while #MeToo has prompted public attention also to the harassment *of men*, which is largely by other men, in reviewing men's responses to #MeToo, I focus here on men's violence against women and on responses among men related to this.

Men: Listen to Women

For #MeToo to have affected men's awareness of sexual harassment and other forms of violence against women, men themselves must have heard of the campaign. We should not overestimate #MeToo's reach among men. In a US survey of men aged 18–55, close to half (41%) had never heard of #MeToo (Editors of GQ, 2018), while in another, nearly one-quarter of employed men said that they had not heard of #MeToo (Koeze & Barry-Jester, 2018). In a UK survey among adults over August–September 2018, more than half (57%) had not heard of the movement (Fawcett Society, 2018).

One sign that a campaign or movement is contributing to social change is if people discuss it or the issues it raises among their peers. Yet, research from the US and the UK finds that most men have not had conversations about #MeToo or sexual harassment despite having heard of

#MeToo. In a US survey of men aged 18–55, 47% of men had not discussed #MeToo, with anyone, ever (Editors of GQ, 2018). In a UK survey, only 28% of men had had conversations about sexual harassment with a same-sex other, compared to 34% of women, and only 31% of men had done so with a woman. Young men in the UK were more likely than older men to have had conversations with their peers: 54% of men aged 18–34 had done so, compared to 27% of those 35–54 and only 16% of those aged 55 and older (Fawcett Society, 2018).

Despite men's levels of ignorance of #MeToo, the campaign does seem to have prompted greater awareness of sexism and gender inequalities. In one US survey, close to half of men (44%) agreed that recent stories about sexual harassment have changed their view about how women are treated in society (NBC News and the Wall Street Journal, 2017). #MeToo's effects here may be greater among younger men. Among young men aged 18–25, 61% said they have thought about how society enables sexist behavior among men since the initiative began, and 59% said the movement has made them think about how difficult the world is for women (MTV News, 2018).

There are signs of shifts in social norms in terms of what behaviors are perceived as acceptable or unacceptable. In a UK survey, a little over half of men (53%) agreed that 'In the last 12 months there has been a change in what behavior other people think is and isn't acceptable'. In contrast to other findings, agreement here was not higher among younger cohorts, with similar levels of agreement among younger and older men (Fawcett Society, 2018). However, while older men in the UK felt that there had been a change in *other* people's ideas about what is and isn't acceptable, they were far less likely than younger men to say that *they* themselves thought differently about such things.

If the task is to listen to and believe women, there are numerous forms of resistance to this. Men may recognize only the bluntest forms of violence, emphasize that harassment is perpetrated by a deviant minority, raise concerns about false allegations, and protest that #MeToo has 'gone too far'. Such responses reflect typical gender gaps in understandings of gender and violence. Men's understandings of men's violence against women are consistently poorer than women's, as international surveys of community attitudes document (Herrero, Rodríguez, & Torres, 2017).

While many men agree that sexual harassment is unacceptable, often they recognize only the bluntest and most grotesque abuses of power. This is similar to perceptions of sexual assault, where assaults by a stranger, in a public location, using a weapon, and involving serious injury dominate the community's perceptions of 'real rape'. Sexual harassment can be classified into three forms: (1) sexual coercion (sexual blackmail, threats aimed at receiving sexual cooperation, or physical attacks), (2) unwanted sexual attention (unwelcome sexual advances, touching, explicit sexual remarks), and (3) gender harassment (telling sexist jokes, offensive gendered commentary, exposing pornographic materials at work, etc.) (Holland, Rabelo, Gustafson, Seabrook, & Cortina, 2016; Maass, Cadinu, & Galdi, 2013). Gender harassment is the most common form of sexual harassment, but also the least likely to be viewed as such (Holland et al., 2016). Instead, men (and women) are more likely to recognize the first two forms as sexual harassment, involving unwanted sexual advances and particularly those comprising quid-pro quo coercion, in which an individual who holds power provides advantages (e.g., hiring) or withholds disadvantages (e.g., firing) in exchange for sexual favors. One journalist, referring to Harvey Weinstein, the film producer whose perpetration of sexual coercion and harassment sparked the #MeToo mobilization, describes:

> the Weinstein problem: the fact that many harassers see harassment as limited to grotesque abuses of power, whereas their own actions can be excused as merely a case of misread signals, inept attempts at seduction, harmless flirting. They hear the Weinstein stories and think: Oh, I'm not so deviant after all. And anyway, that guy is worse. (Lewis, 2017)

Many men also mistakenly see violence against women as perpetrated by only a tiny minority of deviant men. 'Not all men!', they say, in what is a common rallying cry for those who feel that feminist critiques unfairly tarnish all men. Indeed, '#NotAllMen' was a popular hashtag in 2014–2015, with some women responding '#YesAllWomen'—that is, that all women deal with sexism and violence on a daily basis (Plait, 2014). Similar responses are visible in countries across the world, such as 'Don't accuse men!' in Denmark (MÄN, 2018). The statement 'Not all men' can express men's rejection of the feminist insight that perpetration and perpetrators are common in society but also a more personal rejection of the request that they critically examine their own behavior. I return to the latter below.

Men's willingness to listen to and believe victims and survivors is stymied by pervasive narratives of women as false accusers (see Franks, this collection). It has long been asserted and assumed that women 'cry rape'—that women often invent allegations of rape for malicious, vengeful, and other motives (Lisak, Gardinier, Nicksa, & Cote, 2010). The reality is, instead, that false reports of sexual assault are rare, as a series of studies and examinations of crime data have shown (Kelly, 2010; Lisak et al., 2010). Despite this, there is widespread support for the idea that women often make false allegations, of both rape and domestic violence. For example, in Australia, a 2017 national survey found that 33% of men agreed with the statement that 'many allegations of sexual assault made by women are false', while just under half of men (49%) agreed that 'Women going through custody battles often make up or exaggerate claims of domestic violence in order to improve their case' (Webster et al., 2018).[1] In a US survey of 6251 adults in early 2018, one-third (31%) agreed that women falsely claiming sexual harassment or assault is a 'major problem', and close to half (45%) agreed that it is a 'minor problem', with only 22% seeing it as 'not a problem' (Pew Research Centre, 2018). At the same time, close to half (46%) agreed that women not being believed is a 'major problem' and one-third (34%) saw it as a 'minor problem'.

There is a troublingly widespread concern about young men, in particular, being the victims of false allegations. A survey among US adults in October 2018 found that more than half were *equally* concerned for victimized women and falsely accused men, while one in six were *more* concerned about falsely accused men. Of all adults, 57% reported that they were equally concerned about young women and the sexual harassment and assault they could suffer and young men and the false allegations of sexual harassment or assault they could suffer, 15% were more concerned about the latter, and only 17% about the former (Morning

---

[1] The figures for women were 23% and 37%, respectively.

Consult, 2018). This focus on men's subjection to false allegations received endorsement from the highest political figure in that country, with US President Donald Trump commenting in October 2018 that it is 'a very scary time for young men in America, when you can be guilty of something that you may not be guilty of'. Yet, false allegations of violence and abuse are far less common than false denials of perpetration (Jaffe, Johnston, Crooks, & Bala, 2008). Indeed, men are far more likely to be sexually assaulted themselves—230 times as likely, according to the UK numbers—than they are to be falsely accused of sexual assault (Lee, 2018).

#MeToo does not seem to have dented men's belief in false allegations. If anything, this belief has worsened over the past year, at least in the US. An Ipsos poll in 2018 found that men's agreement that 'Those who report being the victims of sexual harassment should be given the benefit of the doubt until proven otherwise' declined from 74% to 68% over the 10 months from December 2017 to October 2018 (while women's higher levels of agreement remained steady). Similarly, a YouGov poll found that agreement that 'False accusations of sexual assault are a bigger problem than unreported assaults' increased over November 2017–September 2018, from 16% to 20% among men and 13% to 18% among adults (YouGov, 2018). In October 2018, Ipsos found that over half of men (57%) agreed that, 'False accusations of sexual harassment against men are very common', as did half (48%) of women. One-third of men (36%) reported worrying that they will be unfairly accused of sexual harassment, while close to one-third of women (30%) reported worrying that a man they care about will be unfairly accused. Republican voters had consistently more harassment-supportive attitudes than Democrat voters (Ipsos, 2018).

The belief that men are often the victims of women's false allegations of harassment and assault contributes to the wider perception that #MeToo has 'gone too far'. Popular and social media commentary includes common claims that #MeToo has brought a repressive and unjust regime of sexual McCarthyism, a 'sex panic', a 'police state', a 'witch-hunt', and so on (Garber, 2018). Men's perceptions here are one expression of backlash, a response by members of a dominant group who feel threatened by challenges to their privilege by disadvantaged groups

(Flood, Dragiewicz, & Pease, 2018; Rosewarne, this collection). This also can be seen as a form of 'aggrieved entitlement', an effort to restore traditional, patriarchal forms of manhood as men's experiences of unquestioned entitlement come under challenge (Kimmel, 2013).

It should not surprise us that significant numbers of men see themselves as the victims of an unjust #MeToo regime, given the prevalence of anti-feminist beliefs in male disadvantage. For example, in a national survey of Australians aged 16 and above in March 2018, 41% of males (and 23% of females) agreed that 'Political correctness gives women an advantage in the workplace', while 42% of males (and 23% of females) agreed that 'Men and boys are increasingly excluded from measures to improve gender equality' (Evans, Haussegger, Halupka, & Rowe, 2018). Lest one assume that these anti-feminist beliefs were concentrated only among older men in Australia, Millennial young men in their mid-20s to late 30s had some of the highest levels of agreement. Similar findings come from the US. For instance, a survey of 777 young men aged 11–24 undertaken in early 2017 demonstrated substantial levels of agreement with the ideas that 'men/boys are held to a higher standard than women/girls' (43% agreed, 31% neutral), 'men/boys are punished just for acting like men/boys today' (32% agreed, 32% neutral), and 'women/girls receive special treatment' (37% agreed, 30% neutral) (Joyful Heart Foundation, 2018).

Men: Put Your Own House in Order

#MeToo also asks men to 'put their own house in order': to reflect on their own behavior and to ensure that they behave in respectful and gender-equitable ways. The campaign thus asks that men consider the impact and meaning of their behavior *for women*. Certainly, there are signs that some men are doing this, from four US surveys:

- Half of men (49%) said that recent stories about sexual harassment had made them think about their own behavior around women (while half disagreed) (NBC News and the Wall Street Journal, 2017). Higher proportions had done so among younger than older men, and among Democrat than Republican men.

- Among men aged 18–55, over one-third of men (38%) said that #MeToo had made them re-evaluate their past sexual experiences (Editors of GQ, 2018).
- Among young men aged 18–25, one-third agreed that, 'I'm worried something I've done could be seen as sexual harassment' (MTV News, 2018).
- Among men who had heard of #MeToo, one in three said they thought about their behavior at work differently as a result (Koeze & Barry-Jester, 2018).

Re-evaluating one's behavior is one thing, but actually changing it is another. Around one-quarter to one-third of men in the US, depending on the survey, report having altered their dating and romantic behaviors in the wake of #MeToo:

- In a US survey, one-quarter (24%) of men said they had changed their behavior in romantic relationships in the wake of the movement, while three-quarters (86%) had not (Koeze & Barry-Jester, 2018).
- In another US survey, one-third (35%) of men had changed their dating habits in response to MeToo, and 59% of those who had heard of MeToo (Editors of GQ, 2018).
- In a 2017 survey among US young men aged 18–25, 40% said that #MeToo had changed the way they act in potential romantic relationships. One in four (25%) agreed that 'since the #MeToo movement, I have noticed that the guys around me have changed their behavior' (MTV News, 2018).

While these statistics appear promising, there are four limitations to these reports of change. First, most men—over half to two-thirds—report that they *have not* re-evaluated or changed their behavior in the wake of #MeToo. Second, we do not know *how* such men have changed their behavior, and the changes they have in mind may be trivial or inappropriate. Third, to the extent that there was change, it is self-reported change, and it may be shaped by social desirability bias and either exaggerated or misguided. Finally, it is also clear that large numbers of men continue to endorse the norms of male sexual entitlement and sexism which structure men's sexual harassment and coercion of women.

Still, sizeable minorities of men report some kind of reassessment and reworking of their sexual and dating behavior. Anecdotal media reports offer some corroboration here. For example, journalist and social commentator Laurie Penny writes of 'otherwise well-meaning male friends who are frantically reassessing their sexual history', and notes:

> That's where a lot of men and boys I know are at right now. Bewildered. Uncomfortable. Wrestling with the spectre of their own wrongdoing. Frightened, most of all, about how the ground rules for being a worthwhile person are changing so fast. (Penny, 2017, n.p.)

As some men take stock of their pasts in light of #MeToo, and as some realize their past wrongs, some try to make amends (see also Newman & Haire, this collection). A wave of spontaneous apologies from men to women, over email, text, and Facebook, apparently has followed in the wake of #MeToo (Schneider, 2017).

Some sense of the confusion among men about how to interact with women comes too from a large survey among adults in the US conducted in February–March 2018. Over half of men (55%) agreed that the increased focus on sexual harassment and assault has made it harder for men to know how to interact with women in the workplace, as did close to half (47%) of women (Pew Research Centre, 2018).

At the same time, there is profound resistance among men to #MeToo's call for them to address their own behavior and interactions. A common reaction among men is the sense that violence against women is a 'women's issue', and not one of direct concern to them. Even if they acknowledge that domestic and sexual violence against women are pervasive social problems, many men see addressing them as women's work (Crooks, Goodall, Hughes, Jaffe, & Baker, 2007). In what one can think of as 'dominant group deflection', they shift responsibility for preventing and reducing violence away from themselves and toward women (Rich, Utley, Janke, & Moldoveanu, 2010).

A related response among men is that violence against women is a problem of 'other' men. Men may insist that 'not all men' are violent, and that they are one of the 'good guys' (see Cover, this collection). Many men portray batterers and rapists as 'the other', diminishing their own accountability for violence against women in a violence-supportive culture (Rich et al., 2010). Some men disavow responsibility by using racist stereotypes of perpetrators (PettyJohn, Muzzey, Maas, & McCauley, 2018; see also Kagal, Cowan & Jawad, this collection), drawing on well-established racialized narratives in media and popular culture (Pepin, 2016). Indeed, even men involved in anti-violence advocacy are not immune to such comforting distinctions between themselves and those 'other', violent men (Macomber, 2012).

This means that when men *are* asked to address their own potential perpetration of violence against women or their complicity in this, many are disinterested or reluctant, and some react with hostility. In a survey of male students about a proposed rape prevention program on a US university campus, half did not want to attend, and 10% had a visceral, hostile response, expressing anger, outrage, and offense (Rich et al., 2010). Likewise, when a social media effort aimed at men and based on the hashtag #HowIWillChange began in October 2017 in the wake of #MeToo, one stream of response centered on men's indignant resistance to the proposal that they should examine their own role in the perpetuation of rape culture (PettyJohn et al., 2018).

Men: Smash the Patriarchy

Beyond changing their own abusive behavior, #MeToo asks men to challenge the abusive behavior of other men and the attitudes and behaviors which sustain this. That is, #MeToo invites men to be pro-social bystanders who take action to prevent and reduce harm, including by strengthening the conditions that prevent initial perpetration or victimization (Powell, 2011).

Polls taken in the wake of #MeToo show increases in men's (and women's) self-reported likelihood of and reports of bystander intervention. In a US poll conducted in October 2017, 77% of men said that they are now more likely to speak out if they see a woman treated unfairly (NBC News and the Wall Street Journal, 2017). In a UK survey among adults between August and September 2018, 35% of men and women agreed that, 'In the last 12 months I have been more likely to challenge behavior or comments I think are inappropriate'. Focusing on men, this was far stronger among younger men, in that proportions agreeing were 58% of those aged 18–34, 32% of those aged 35–54, and only 24% of those aged 55 and older (Fawcett Society, 2018).

#MeToo, finally, asks men to take collective action to address the social and structural roots of men's violence against women. Mobilizing men is not a new idea, and men's collective anti-violence advocacy already had a presence in countries around the world. Anti-sexist and anti-violence men's groups began amidst the second wave of feminism in the early 1970s, and there is now a range of national and international men-focused organizations and networks (Flood, 2018). Efforts to prevent and reduce men's violence against women have, over the past three decades, included an increasing emphasis on the need to engage men as agents of change (McGann, 2014). Reflecting this, #MeToo commentary has included appeals to men to take action against men's sexual harassment, just as earlier hashtag campaigns such as #NotOkay did (Maas, McCauley, Bonomi, & Leija, 2018).

There are several signs of organized responses to #MeToo among men, from both within and outside established anti-violence men's networks. Men's networks and organizations have held roundtables, issued discussion papers, and offered reflections on #MeToo's significance (MÄN, 2018; MenEngage, 2017; White Ribbon Trust, 2018). There is at least one country where #MeToo prompted a significant increase in men's participation in anti-violence advocacy. In Sweden, the feminist organization MÄN (1993–) developed a guide for #AfterMeToo discussion groups in late 2017, leading to an upsurge of interest in the organization, a tripling in member numbers, and the formation of 30 groups at the time of writing in 2018 (MÄN, 2018).

#MeToo has also prompted new initiatives among men. A group of film industry and anti-violence men launched #AskMoreOfHim in March 2018, just before the Oscars movie awards, to challenge men to use their privilege and platforms for good in addressing sexual harassment, abuse, and assault (Katz & Newsom, 2018). Australian writer Benjamin Law initiated a hashtag campaign directed at men, #HowIWillChange, in October 2017 as an effort to involve men and boys in reflection on how they perpetuate rape culture and how they intend to change this (PettyJohn et al., 2018). #MeToo also may have raised the bar for what it means to be a 'male ally' or male 'feminist', given the visibility of feminist critiques of tokenistic and hypocritical displays among men.

Still, we have yet to see any major international increase in men's collective anti-violence advocacy in response to #MeToo. Such efforts remain relatively small, although they are growing in their political and practical sophistication (Flood, 2018).

Conclusion

#MeToo asks three tasks of men: to listen to women, to change their own sexist and harassing behavior, and to take collective action to prevent and reduce violence and abuse. In order to do so, men must overcome their socialized deafness to women's experiences, take on the issue of men's violence against women as of personal relevance and concern, and develop gender-equitable skills and habits.

#MeToo instigated a public outpouring of women's stories of victimization, and research demonstrates that hearing women's stories is a key path to men's sensitization to violence against women (Flood, 2018). The data reviewed in this chapter do suggest that #MeToo has prompted some shifts—albeit slight or uneven in some cases—in men's attitudes and behaviors. The campaign certainly is likely to have contributed to some slight weakening of the social norms underpinning men's sexual violence against women. #MeToo is likely to have informed increases in awareness of men's violence and in the perceived credibility and legitimacy of victims' allegations. More widely, it may have prompted some level of rethinking of patriarchal forms of flirting, dating, and interaction.

Yet #MeToo, like other feminist efforts to address men's violence against women, is up against well-established and well-rehearsed defenses of men's violence and privilege. The data in this chapter also demonstrate the extent of men's silence about and collusion with other men's violence and sexism.

To transform violence-supportive cultures, we will need intensified public attention to male privilege, male sexual entitlement, and alternatives to sexist manhood (The Men's Project & Flood, 2018). We will need focused challenges to the particular constructions of masculinity and male sexuality that sustain some men's perpetration—and many men's perpetuation—of violence against women. And we will need to mobilize men themselves, as educators, leaders, and activists, to join with women in collective struggles for gender justice.

References

Crooks, C. V., Goodall, G. R., Hughes, R., Jaffe, P. G., & Baker, L. L. (2007). Engaging men and boys in preventing violence against women: Applying a cognitive-behavioral model. *Violence Against Women, 13*(3), 217–239.

Editors of GQ. (2018, May 30). What 1,147 men think about #MeToo: A glamour X GQ survey. *GQ*. Retrieved December 20, 2018, from https://www.gq.com/story/metoo-and-men-survey-glamour-gq.

Evans, M., Haussegger, V., Halupka, M., & Rowe, P. (2018). *From girls to men: Social attitudes to gender equality issues in Australia*. Canberra: 50/50 by 2030 Foundation, University of Canberra.

Fawcett Society. (2018). *#Metoo one year on—What's changed?* London: The Fawcett Society.

Flood, M. (2018). *Engaging men and boys in violence prevention*. Palgrave Macmillan.

Flood, M., Dragiewicz, M., & Pease, B. (2018). *Resistance and backlash to gender equality: An evidence review*. Brisbane: Crime, Justice and Social Democracy Research Centre, Queensland University of Technology (QUT).

Garber, M. (2018, February 11). The selective empathy of #Metoo backlash. *The Atlantic*. Retrieved December 20, 2018, from https://www.theatlantic.com/entertainment/archive/2018/02/the-selective-empathy-of-metoo-backlash/553022/.

Herrero, J., Rodríguez, F. J., & Torres, A. (2017). Acceptability of partner violence in 51 societies: The role of sexism and attitudes toward violence in social relationships. *Violence Against Women, 23*(3), 351–367.

Holland, K. J., Rabelo, V. C., Gustafson, A. M., Seabrook, R. C., & Cortina, L. M. (2016). Sexual harassment against men: Examining the roles of feminist activism, sexuality, and organizational context. *Psychology of Men and Masculinity, 17*(1), 17–29.

Ipsos. (2018). *Ipsos Npr examine views on sexual harassment and assault.* Washington, DC: Ipsos Public Affairs.

Jaffe, P. G., Johnston, J. R., Crooks, C. V., & Bala, N. (2008). Custody disputes involving allegations of domestic violence: Toward a differentiated approach to parenting plans. *Family Court Review, 46*(3), 500–522.

Joyful Heart Foundation. (2018). *Defining manhood for the next generation: Exploring young men's perceptions of gender roles and violence.* New York, NY: Joyful Heart Foundation.

Katz, J., & Newsom, J. S. (2018, March 2). How Hollywood men can lead #Askmoreofhim campaign. *The Hollywood Reporter.* Retrieved December 20, 2018, from https://www.hollywoodreporter.com/news/how-hollywood-men-can-lead-askmoreofhim-campaign-guest-column-1090128.

Kelly, L. (2010). The (in)credible words of women: False allegations in European rape research. *Violence Against Women, 16*(12), 1345–1355.

Kimmel, M. (2013). *Angry white men: American masculinity at the end of an era.* New York, NY: Nation Books.

Koeze, E., & Barry-Jester, A. M. (2018, June 20). What do men think it means to be a man? *FiveThirtyEight.* Retrieved December 20, 2018, from https://fivethirtyeight.com/features/what-do-men-think-it-means-to-be-a-man/.

Lee, G. (2018, October 12). Fact check: Men are more likely to be raped than be falsely accused of rape. Retrieved December 20, 2018, from https://www.channel4.com/news/factcheck/factcheck-men-are-more-likely-to-be-raped-than-be-falsely-accused-of-rape.

Lewis, H. (2017, October 17). The Harvey Weinstein allegations are monstrous but it's not just monsters who harass women. *New Statesman.* Retrieved December 20, 2018, from https://www.newstatesman.com/politics/uk/2017/10/harvey-weinstein-allegations-are-monstrous-it-s-not-just-monsters-who-harass.

Lisak, D., Gardinier, L., Nicksa, S. C., & Cote, A. M. (2010). False allegations of sexual assault: An analysis of ten years of reported cases. *Violence Against Women, 16*(12), 1318–1334.

Maas, M. K., McCauley, H. L., Bonomi, A. E., & Leija, S. G. (2018). "I was grabbed by my pussy and it's #Notokay": A Twitter backlash against Donald

Trump's degrading commentary. *Violence Against Women.* https://doi.org/10.1177/1077801217743340

Maass, A., Cadinu, M., & Galdi, S. (2013). Sexual harassment: Motivations and consequences. In M. K. Ryan & N. R. Branscombe (Eds.), *The Sage handbook of gender and psychology* (pp. 341–358). Thousand Oaks, CA: Sage.

Macomber, K. (2012). *Men as allies: Mobilizing men to end violence against women.* Raleigh, North Carolina: North Carolina State University.

MÄN. (2018). *Men, masculinity and #Metoo.* Stockholm: MÄN.

McGann, P. (2014). *Current practices and challenges with engaging men on campus.* Washington, DC: The Department of Justice Office on Violence Against Women.

MenEngage. (2017). *Summary report, virtual roundtable dialogue: Roles and responsibilities of men and boys in response to #Metoo.* Washington, DC: MenEngage.

Morning Consult. (2018). *A year into #Metoo, public worried about false allegations.* New York, NY: Morning Consult.

MTV News. (2018, January 29). The #Metoo movement is affecting men too. *MTV News.*

NBC News and the Wall Street Journal. (2017, October 30). Nbc/Wsj Poll: Nearly half of working women say they've experienced harassment. *NBC News.* Retrieved December 20, 2018, from https://www.nbcnews.com/politics/first-read/nbc-wsj-poll-nearly-half-working-women-say-they-ve-n815376.

Penny, L. (2017, October 10). The horizon of desire. *Longreads.* Retrieved December 20, 2018, from https://longreads.com/2017/10/10/the-horizon-of-desire/.

Pepin, J. R. (2016). Nobody's business? White male privilege in media coverage of intimate partner violence. *Sociological Spectrum, 36*(3), 123–141.

PettyJohn, M. E., Muzzey, F. K., Maas, M. K., & McCauley, H. L. (2018). #Howiwillchange: Engaging men and boys in the #MeToo movement. *Psychology of Men & Masculinity.* https://doi.org/10.1037/men0000186

Pew Research Centre. (2018). *Sexual harassment at work in the era of #Metoo.* Washington, DC: Pew Research Centre.

Plait, P. (2014). #Yesallwomen. *Slate.* Retrieved December 20, 2018, from http://www.slate.com/blogs/bad_astronomy/2014/05/27/not_all_men_how_discussing_women_s_issues_gets_derailed.html.

Powell, A. (2011). *Review of bystander approaches in support of preventing violence against women*. Melbourne: Victorian Health Promotion Foundation (VicHealth).

Rich, M. D., Utley, E. A., Janke, K., & Moldoveanu, M. (2010). "I'd rather be doing something else": Male resistance to rape prevention programs. *Journal of Men's Studies, 18*(3), 268–288.

Schneider, K. (2017, July 17). When men decide it's time to say sorry. *The Cut*. Retrieved December 20, 2018, from https://www.thecut.com/2018/07/when-men-decide-its-time-to-say-sorry.html.

The Men's Project, & Flood, M. (2018). *The man box: A study on being a young man in Australia*. Melbourne: Jesuit Social Services.

Webster, K., Diemer, K., Honey, N., Mannix, S., Mickle, J., Morgan, J., … Ward, A. (2018). *Australians' attitudes to violence against women and gender equality: Findings from the 2017 National Community Attitudes towards Violence against Women Survey (NCAS)*. Sydney, NSW: ANROWS.

White Ribbon Trust. (2018). *Report on how White Ribbon New Zealand can align with the #Metoo movement*. Auckland, New Zealand: White Ribbon Trust.

YouGov. (2018, October 15). After a year of #Metoo, American opinion has shifted against victims. *The Economist*. Retrieved December 20, 2018, from https://www.economist.com/graphic-detail/2018/10/15/after-a-ye.

19

Understanding Anger: Ethical Responsiveness and the Cultural Production of Celebrity Masculinities

Rob Cover

Introduction

The #MeToo movement is a phenomenon consisting of multiple causes, discourses, articulations and ways of responding to contemporary social conditions related to gender, sexuality, vulnerability, workplace and interpersonal relations. For example, the #MeToo movement has emerged simultaneously alongside the growth of a particular kind of populism that disavows the role of older institutions, such as courts and policing, to 'decide' on what constitutes a violation of another person's body, space or dignity. At the same time, it is a product of digital media's 'call-out' culture in which interactive engagement on sites such as Twitter enables actors to articulate their grievances without recourse to the gatekeeping of more traditional media forms such as print newspapers. #MeToo is also a reconfiguring of older assumptions about the culture of North American film production, including shifting the idea of the Hollywood

R. Cover (✉)
School of Social Sciences [M257], The University of Western Australia, Crawley, WA, Australia
e-mail: rob.cover@uwa.edu.au

© The Author(s) 2019
B. Fileborn, R. Loney-Howes (eds.), *#MeToo and the Politics of Social Change*,
https://doi.org/10.1007/978-3-030-15213-0_19

301

'casting couch' from a topic of mirth to one of scandal through the open communication of real-life experiences directly to a popular audience. By extension, we can shift the critique generated through #MeToo into the culture of other performing arts, particularly theater, which has long been assumed to be a space of liberal and libertine camp, mutual care and alternative masculinities. In both 'celebrity' settings, what has been revealed is that these spaces, supposedly made 'safe' by the exclusion of traditional hypermasculine dominance, are indeed marked by experiences in which senior male figures have articulated a sense of sexual ownership over women and junior co-stars and crew (Ford, 2018, p. 51).

One way of making sense of the #MeToo movement as a form of cultural change involves recognizing the shift in the public understanding of what kinds of masculinities are implicated in sexual harassment, assault and violence. Connected with these other aspects driving #MeToo is a shift that involves a loss of faith not only in liberal institutions or contemporary legal approaches to preventing sexual violence, but in the *value* and *veracity* of 'new masculinities' as liberal, gender-equitable, 'softer', elite, transnational, aware of and opposed to power imbalances, 'safe' and so on (see also Newman & Haire, this collection). That is, the #MeToo movement is an expression of outrage that such new masculinities are not necessarily good at dealing with gender relationality or responsibly respecting the rights and equities of women and other minorities, but prove often to be no better than the kinds of hypermasculinities represented typically—albeit not necessarily correctly—in lower class performativities of masculine gender or in highly homosocial institutional settings of hypermasculinity such as sporting teams (Waterhouse-Watson, 2011; Cover, 2015), the military (Flood, 2007) and fraternities (Anderson, 2008).

In this chapter, I address some of the ways we can make sense of the #MeToo phenomenon through an idea of 'anger' or 'disappointment' in the failure of new masculinities (or, at least, those masculinities operating outside the more traditional hypermasculine contexts) to provide settings that ensure gender relationality is enacted without vulnerabilization, assault, violence or lacking in an ethical responsibility of care of the other. I do so by first working through the ways hypermasculinity has become the 'recognized norm' of sexual assault stories, producing a binary arrangement in which men who are sexually aggressive possess 'bad' masculine qualities, while men who appear to be 'non-violent' are positioned as 'good'. I then discuss what kinds of hegemonic (or dominant) masculinities operate today in a way that has tended to obscure or offset the risk of public scrutiny over sexual harassment and assault. Finally, I address how #MeToo can be understood as an outrage over the failure of new masculinities in the context of its failure to recognize vulnerability as an ethical framing of relationality. To do so, I discuss an ethical alternative to #MeToo's *anger* by using the work of North American philosopher and gender theorist Judith Butler (2004, 2009) who pointed to how vulnerability can be understood as a social condition that is universally shared but undemocratically distributed. In her work, vulnerability, if thought through alternative approaches, can be articulated as a means of producing non-violence through recognition of its mutuality. That is, while the #MeToo phenomenon is problematic in that it oversimplifies and dehistoricizes masculinities, collapsing them into a single 'patriarchy', it has value in providing a new framework through which contemporary masculinities, that are sometimes seen as 'untouchable' (Ford, 2018, p. 44), can be understood as vulnerable and thus potentially capable of recognizing the vulnerability of others—particularly women and younger or more junior men and boys. This, I suggest, can be helpful in producing a more ethical gender and sexual relationality—at least in celebrity workplaces.

Hypermasculinity as an Outdated Representation of the Problem

One of the most significant shortcomings of much writing about #MeToo and its responses to celebrity sexual assaults is that these are understood through an ahistorical lens. For example, feminist public commentator Clementine Ford (2018) argued that the sexual perpetration highlighted by #MeToo Twitter announcements are reflective of a singular phenomenon of women being silenced by rapists, continuous since Homer's *Odyssey* 3000 years ago, through Ovid, Shakespeare and up to the revelations about Harvey Weinstein in late 2017. Ford argued that these are all products of the same misogynistic 'system that enforces patriarchal social order' across time (2018, pp. 49–50). What is articulated in such assumptions is not the more-nuanced fact that there are a variety of ways of *speaking* and ways of *silencing* that have been strategically deployed to empower men in very different cultural, institutional and historical circumstances across the years, but that men and masculinity are always the same, repeating the same stories again and again without change. Indeed, to see experiences of sexual violence shared through #MeToo and men more generally as conditioned singularly by 'patriarchy', as Ford (2018, p. 51) has argued, is to radically oversimplify the complex mechanisms and frameworks of gender performativity and gender relationality. This is to misread or ignore the vast changes in expected and recognized intelligibilities of masculine performativity in contemporary culture, particularly in celebrity and corporate settings. That is, it is a misapprehension to assume masculinity represents a singularity rather than a multiplicity of performativities, expectations, practices and ways of being (Connell, 2005, pp. 106–108), and types of masculinities that assert dominance or sexual rights over women and minors result automatically in scandal rather than acceptance (Cover, 2015).

In other words, patriarchal hypermasculinity is an outdated 'model' of masculinity that no longer presents itself as masculinity's norm in everyday settings. In previous writings (e.g., Cover, 2013, 2015), I have addressed some of the ways in which the persistence of hypermasculinity in certain institutional settings, such as elite sporting teams, are implicated in sexual scandals—particularly group sexual assault and gang rape. Hypermasculine machismo is a particular framework of the performativity of gender relations (Buchbinder, 1994, p. 1). It is best understood to be symbolically represented and fetishized through attempts at dominance via competitiveness and heroism (Mohr, 1992, pp. 163–164), muscled bodies, roughness and ruggedness (Clarkson, 2006, p. 187) and testosterone-driven sexuality (Cover, 2004, p. 87), potentially (but not always) lacking in sexual self-control and capable of becoming violent (Lunny, 2003, p. 316). These are no longer the visual, performative or intelligible markers of the kind of masculinity that is at stake in the #MeToo sexual assault and harassment articulations.

Nevertheless, stereotypes of hypermasculinity persist in the popular imaginary, and this has real implications as the backdrop for the ways in which masculinities are produced, understood and articulated in the context of scandal and critique. A stereotype links an identity category to a set of attributes (Rosello, 1998). Although critiqued in scholarship, popular culture, various feminisms and through public scrutiny that emerges in scandal (Cover, 2015), hypermasculinity is a powerful and popular stereotype that links a hypermasculine identity to the attribute of sexual perpetrator, or the disposition of ownership of women and others. Sometimes, it is framed as men whose drives and ruggedness combine to produce behaviors seen to be out of control and unable, without intervention, to resist opportunities for harassment, assault, articulations of superiority or violent behavior. Pointing to the stereotype is not to say that such critical perspectives are necessarily wrong but are problematic in that the stereotype of this particular form of masculinity risks exonerating *other* kinds of masculinities that are deemed to be less violent, less 'dangerous' in the context of sexual relationality, having for a long time protected them from being seen as performances that risk perpetration, particularly in workplaces. In other words, hypermasculinity serves as a 'lightning rod' to distract from the potentialities of new masculinities as potentially based on gender dominance in public discourse, resulting in a form of 'forgetting' and hence surprise, anger and scandal when they are indeed revealed as problematic. This can be seen, for example, in the Aziz Ansari case, in which accusations of sexual misconduct were countered with arguments that the controversy over his treatment of women trivialized more serious sexual assault cases. Arguably, Ansari's representation as a gentler, non-hypermasculine subject framed the controversy in a way which allows debate on sexual perpetration based on the extent to which a perpetrator performs masculinity rather than on the act itself or the relational engagement between perpetrator and complainant.

Hegemonic Masculinity and Transnational Capitalism

Although it is the case that there are multiple masculinities, and these are not equally valued, there have also been articulations over the past two decades that masculinity is in crisis. For instance, anti-feminist groups have argued that women and others who question masculine dominance have effectively feminized men and/or wounded men to the point that a sense of masculine dignity has been lost. These claims have been made concurrent with calls for a return to 'traditional' or 'authentic' masculinity. Both anti-feminist and actors within the #MeToo movement claims assume that highly patriarchal forms of masculine identity are timeless and ahistorical—the former seeing them as 'right' and the latter as problematic (Buchbinder, 1997, pp. 30, 46). This includes the production of new masculinities which, although participating in the subordination and/or marginalization of women, are a softer, less-ostensibly harmful form of masculine identity and correlative behaviors. They include what has increasingly come to usurp older ideals of masculinity: what David Buchbinder (1994) has referred to as the *new man*, a subject who is 'less convinced of the authority and rightness of traditional male logic, and more amenable to alternative ways of thinking' (p. 2). The disavowal of machismo and the increasing reification of pro-feminist, queer-affirmative discourses (Buchbinder, 1997, pp. 21–25), the repudiation of blatant misogyny (Flood, 2007, p. 11) and the increasingly outright opposition to male violence and sexual violence in public sphere discourse also form part of this more recent shift in what is considered a more *accountable* masculinity.

By the early 2000s, the increasingly dominant, hegemonic and expected form of masculinity marked by a stronger interest in self-grooming, a disavowal of trade and risky sports, and a supposed greater interest in sexual consent was becoming closely aligned with the formation that has been termed *metrosexuality*. This concept represents the heterosexual, fashion-conscious, grooming-conscious urban male according to Mark Simpson, who coined the term in 1994. He describes this representative formation of masculine identity as follows:

The typical metrosexual is a young man with money to spend, living in or within easy reach of a metropolis—because that's where all the best shops, clubs, gyms and hairdressers are. He might be officially gay, straight or bisexual, but this is utterly immaterial because he has clearly taken himself as his own love object and pleasure as his sexual preference. Particular professions, such as modeling, waiting tables, media, pop music and, nowadays, sport, seem to attract them. (Simpson, 2002)

Much like Buchbinder's description of the new male, this softer, 'safer' masculinity is produced through a supposed disavowal of misogyny and sexism, physical violence and aggression—in the case of metrosexuality through a turning of attention to consumption and the self; in the case of others in corporate settings through compliance with workplace equity policies. However, while the figuration of new masculinity differs from older hypermasculine performances of misogynistic dominance and exclusiveness, it never attempted to disguise the continuation of attitudes of competition and subordination of others in other frameworks. What #MeToo reveals, of course, is that it may not have shaken off misogyny and sexual exploitation either.

This figure of new masculinity is marked by the motifs of transnational capitalist dominance in one respect, but also performances and performativities of gentleness, care, corporate social responsibility, gender equity and inclusiveness (Beasley, 2008). The visual image of the suit as differentiated from the sports shorts of the footballer, the dirty high-vis safety jacket of the worker on a building site, the casual wear of the fraternity member or the fatigues of the soldier in the ranks is significant. As Clementine Ford (2018) notes in her summary of the meaning of the #MeToo movement, there is a connection between a man wearing a suit and the idea that this man is 'to be considered a feminist superhero' (p. 45). The performativities of the visual, the clothing, the demeanor, the right kinds of touches and the disavowal of the wrong kinds in public view are markers of new masculinity tied to transnational capital—which is not to suggest that such masculinities are themselves inclusive of transnationality but are marked by cosmopolitanism and mobility, themselves the markers of class. Of course this is not necessarily to indicate that an ethical framing of relationality through genuine inclusivity, equality, care and responsibility becomes the norm, but to say that at the surface level of new masculinity this is articulated and avowed even if the reality is not achieved. This is apparent if one looks, for example, at the publicity images of the figures who have appeared at the center of #MeToo scandals. Harvey Weinstein may at times appear in the media as rugged and unshaven, but for the most part, his image incorporates the key signifiers of transnational capitalist masculinity: suited, groomed, surrounded by international celebrities, appearing at major 'red carpet' events and associated with the 'business' of film production. By appearance alone, there is nothing that is indicative of hypermasculinity, sexual violence or rape. Likewise, Kevin Spacey—groomed, suited, known as gay prior to his coming out, associated with the kind of softer non-domineering (if dominant) masculinity that is signified in stereotypes of non-heterosexuality as well as theater acting. Matt Lauer, former host of the NBC *Today Show*, spent years performing 'new masculinity', discussing issues beyond politics and culture to encompass those that are indicative of women's lives and traditional domestic lives, alongside his women co-hosts, with the flair of cosmopolitan sophistication.

It is notable here too that whiteness is part of the signification of new masculinity, and it is perhaps alarming that a figure, such as African-American actor Bill Cosby who was found guilty of sexual assault, does not appear on at least one of the growing lists of men accused of being perpetrators in the context of the #MeToo movement (Berkowitz, 2017). Indeed, very few of the men depicted in the many compiled images of male perpetrators in the #MeToo context are anything but white. What we have experienced in contemporary Western culture is a shift in what constitutes *hegemonic* masculinity as the forms of masculinity which, while dominating, are consented to socially across a range of institutions from the legal to the political, to that found in entertainment media and thereby deemed socially acceptable and not 'risks' of being sexual perpetrators. Yet, conversely, sexual perpetration and violence has throughout the 2000s and until very recently been associated with the hypermasculinity of the figure of the sportsplayer, the working class, the underclass and other figures of masculinity's otherness (in the Australian context, for example, the problematic representation of Lebanese migrant gangs as rapists, resulting in outrage that obscures the reality of sexual violence among middle-class white subjects in domestic spheres; see Evers, 2008; Poynting, Noble, Tabar, & Collins, 2004, p. 6).

The cultural shift in the West between dominant, traditional masculinities and hypermasculinities marked by performances that can be described as patriarchal and—since the late 1990s or early 2000s—the gentler, transnational 'new masculinity' performed as a set of codes of sophistication, gentleness, embracing of gender equality and women's dignity and respect is one not of a radical change or a reference to two sets of tribes. Rather, it is a shift in dominant cultural expectations for men's behavior among the upper-middle classes such that the new form of masculinity becomes hegemonic in place of the hypermasculine, the aggressive and the violent. Such a shift, however, is underwritten by both continuities and disjunctures. What #MeToo might be described as being very angry about is that while there has been a disjuncture in the theatrics of masculinity to embrace respect for women, juniors, minorities and others alongside corporate and celebrity moves toward surface-level social responsibility claims, the understanding that women, younger men and others are still perceived as 'available' for sexual gratification and the idea of a 'right' or 'entitlement' to such gratification is continuous. The #MeToo phenomenon is a production of cultural anger—not necessarily conscious nor individual but affective and collective—in the 'discovery' that sexual violence has been continuous despite the surface-level shift from the theatrics of hypermasculine dominance to the transnational 'new masculinity'. This anger is therefore directed at the *betrayal* of the promise of new masculinity as providing a space of safety, respect and responsibility toward women and younger men in workplaces and creative contexts.

Pivoting the Debate: Toward an Ethics of Mutuality, Vulnerability and Care

The #MeToo debate arises, as I have been describing, in part through the widespread anger at the failure of 'new masculinity' or 'transnational hegemonic masculinity' to deliver the sorts of gender equities, care,

responsibility and mutual respect it offered through the surface significa-
tions of class-derived gentleness, the discourses of corporate social responsibility (Benn, Todd, & Pendleton, 2010) and its refiguring of power
relations via codings that are different from more traditional masculine-
feminine performances of dominance. This occurs alongside (or perhaps
partly as a result of) a sense of betrayal in which a man who boasts of
sexual assault is able to become president of the United States—betrayal,
because it feels as though the promise that basic decency is the core ingredient of individual career success is utterly and permanently broken
(Ford, 2018, p. 46). Anger is productive, and the role that the emergence
of such anger might bring in refiguring dominant structures of feeling in
relation to gender relationality has both potential for change and an
unknowability (Williams, 1977). Alongside, however, the problem that
#MeToo obscures the broad social problems of intimate partner violence
occurring among those who are not white, upper-middle-class celebrities,
and the focusing of public debate on the needs of Hollywood celebrities
who are arguably less vulnerable than those with no media or financial
empowerment (see also Kagal, Cowan & Jawad; Rosewarne, this collection), what the #MeToo movement lacks in its articulation of anger over
the treatment of celebrity women is an ethical solution *beyond* the expression of anger.

Butler's (2004, 2009) approach to ethical reflexivity here can be useful
by pointing the way to a gender relationality of non-violence built on
recognizing the self and other as sharing a vulnerability common to
humanity, life and being as embodied subjects in the social world. Reliant
on a concept of recognition, Butler has argued that an ethics of non-
violence can be grounded in a conceptual understanding that all humans
are vulnerable in our exposure to one another; that is, all life is precarious,
all bodies are easily harmed and, from the very beginning of life, we are
all dependent upon relationality with others for the ongoingness of life
and bodies (Butler, 2004, p. 44). Through perceiving the commonality of
vulnerability for ourselves and for the other whom we encounter, we are
compelled to engage with others in ways which are responsible and
responsive to that vulnerability; that is, in relations of non-violence. This
ethics is not simply a moral or policy injunction to *behave* in a particular
way, but a framework in which non-violence underwrites the encounter

between subjects. In conceptual terms, when a man in a position of power is engaged in an encounter with a less powerful woman, he is obliged to consider how to treat that woman in the context of sexual behavior. It is at a moment of fundamental vulnerability that recognition becomes necessary, possible and self-conscious, and this form of recognition is a reciprocal state of being *for the* other or *given over to* the other (Butler, 2000). This encounter requires opening oneself to having one's identity reconfigured in ways which acknowledge the mutual vulnerability of each party. Understanding all subjects, whether men or women, to have vulnerability in common is not, of course, to assume that vulnerability is evenly distributed. Rather, it is unevenly distributed among bodies according to a broad range of factors, gender being one as reflected in the high rates of sexual violence but also along the lines of differentiation between different masculinities. As I have argued above, hypermasculine men stereotypically associated with sexual violence are not necessarily themselves less vulnerable or more dominant than the softer, gentler, socially responsible representations of celebrity, white masculinities represented by figures such as Kevin Spacey, Harvey Weinstein, Geoffrey Rush or others who have been alleged to have perpetrated violence against women through the #MeToo movement.

This ethics differs significantly from the dominant approach taken by #MeToo, which utilizes social media to 'call out' in a game of punishments. An ethical encounter, however, can be described as a 'struggle over the claim of nonviolence without any judgment about how the struggle finally ends' (Butler, 2007, p. 187). It does not resolve the ethical problem it raises, but opens the *possibility* for subjects to recognize the vulnerability of others through understanding it in terms of their own vulnerability and thereby initiating a struggle one must undertake with one's own violence (Butler, 2007, p. 181). It is, therefore, as Angela McRobbie puts it, a discourse capable of 'intervening to challenge, interrupt and minimize aggressive retaliation' (2006, p. 82). In the context described here, a sexual ethics based on recognizing the mutual vulnerability of all subjects requires reconceptualization for those in dominant positions to recognize their own vulnerability rather than, in more simplistic terms, seeing their women co-workers on the Hollywood set or in the theater as victims.

In the context of this ethics, just as hypermasculine sports stars can become the product of an ethics of vulnerability when able to recognize their own vulnerability to loss (of the match), injury (of the body), fragmentation (of the team), or reputation (in both on-field and off-field contexts), the new masculine transnational figure can—through the #MeToo discourse—come to recognize the potential for loss. Weinstein, Spacey and others have all suffered considerable losses when it was revealed through #MeToo that their sexual utilization of others was a failure to recognize the vulnerability of the other. The value of #MeToo in this context is that it brings about a possibility for the new masculine figure to see himself otherwise: not merely as being 'at risk' of reputational damage, but as always to begin with vulnerable to losses of career, dignity, respect, financial security or other kinds of loss. In the case of Spacey, that loss is not only the possibility that a productive opus of creative work on stage and screen for many years suffers damage, nor only the loss of possible future income as he becomes less palatable to those who would otherwise have hired him, but the actual erasure from film as he is literally CGI'd or reshot out of films that were thought to have been complete.

One of the reasons why this framing of vulnerability has been difficult to come to socially is due to the fact that, even among men performing new masculinities, aspects of gender inequality have been difficult to understand (Bacchi, 2005). Indeed, arguably, the framework of gender equity that is prescribed to as part of the performativity of new masculinity may actively obscure the reality of vulnerabilities among women and others. It is not solely a lack of awareness on the part of some men, as if they are a blank slate waiting to be given the right information for the right kind of attitude. Rather, this is the result of the relationship between masculine identity, homosocial institutions, the obscuring practices of new masculinities in organizational settings and the cultural or perceptual frames which present situations, personages or attributes as normative and intelligible. For Butler, interpretative frames are that which socially and politically constitute formations that 'allocate recognition differentially' (Butler, 2009, p. 6). These are implicated in the cultural production of some subjects as recognizable and others as more difficult to recognize as vulnerable or worthy of protection from vulnerability

(Butler, 2009, pp. 5–6). That is, the capacity to understand and recognize the other as a life is 'dependent on norms that facilitate that recognition' (Butler, 2009, pp. 3–4). Critical disruption is the key to beginning to make sense of how norms and frames set the conditions for reactions to particular scenes, visualities, texts, images or knowledges (Butler, 2009, p. 11). Arguably, while #MeToo is problematic in providing solutions to gender-based sexual violence and has limited itself to the expression of anger, it may serve a subsidiary value in providing an instant of critical disruption that can open subjects to look differently at how relationalities are normalized and how alternative, non-violent practices might replace those norms, or indeed, open questions on what might constitute sexual violence in the first place (see also Fileborn & Phillips, this collection).

Conclusion

The #MeToo movement is arguably problematic in its failure to articulate an ethical alternative to gender-based sexual violence in the celebrity workplace and has limited itself to the open expression of anger and an unproductive retaliation. A number of commentators have misapprehended #MeToo as being a movement that speaks of having had enough of 'patriarchy' in a timeless, ahistorical sense, although this has failed to see how #MeToo is a reaction to the failure of new masculinities to incorporate gender equity and sexual nonownership of women and others despite the other changes and developments it has brought in superseding older, dominant hypermasculinities to become the expected norm of masculine intelligibility in the workplace. By drawing out the distinction in different kinds of masculinities, it is possible to understand what it is that sets the conditions for the emergence of #MeToo as a response at this particular time.

Although I am critical of a politics that disavows the potential utility of existing institutions of justice in favor of a retaliatory 'call-out' culture, it remains true that the phenomenon has potential for disrupting normative interpretative frameworks that have permitted new masculinities to get away with not being associated with sexual violence in the way marginal hypermasculinities and certain non-white masculinities are over-associated with violence and sexual assault. By drawing attention to this and to the complex arrangement of distinctions, the conditions are potentially set for a more ethical gender relationality that calls upon all subjects to recognize vulnerability as a corporeal trait of livability and hence obliges them to act without violence, which includes the violences of domination, ownership, exploitation and sexual abuse that have marked this scandal.

References

Anderson, E. (2008). Inclusive masculinity in a fraternal setting. *Men and Masculinities, 10*(5), 604–620.

Bacchi, C. (2005). Affirmative action for men: 'A test of common sense'? *Just Policy, 36*, 5–10.

Beasley, C. (2008). Rethinking hegemonic masculinity in a globalizing world. *Men and Masculinities, 11*(1), 86–103.

Benn, S., Todd, L. R., & Pendleton, J. (2010). Public relations leadership in corporate social responsibility. *Journal of Business Ethics, 96*(3), 403–423.

Berkowitz, J. (2017, November 1). Here's the complete list of men accused of sexual harassment since Harvey Weinstein. *Fast Company*. Retrieved October 13, 2018, from https://www.fastcompany.com/40489989/heres-the-ever-growing-list-of-men-accused-of-sexual-harassment-since-weinstein.

Buchbinder, D. (1994). *Masculinities and identities*. Melbourne: Melbourne University Press.

Buchbinder, D. (1997). *Performance anxieties: Re-producing masculinity*. St Leonards, NSW: Allen & Unwin.

Butler, J. (2000). Longing for recognition. *Studies in Gender and Sexuality, 1*(3), 271–290.

Butler, J. (2004). *Precarious life*. London: Verso.

Butler, J. (2007). Reply from Judith Butler to Mills and Jenkins. *Differences: A Journal of Feminist Cultural Studies, 18*(2), 180–195.

Butler, J. (2009). *Frames of war: When is life grievable?* London and New York: Verso.

Clarkson, J. (2006). 'Everyday Joe' versus 'pissy, bitchy queens': Gay masculinity on straightacting.com. *The Journal of Men's Studies, 14*(2), 191–207.

Connell, R. W. (2005). *Masculinities* (2nd ed.). Crow's Nest, NSW: Allen & Unwin. [Orig. 1995].

Cover, R. (2004). Bodies, movements and desires: Lesbian/gay subjectivity and the stereotype. *Continuum: Journal of Media & Cultural Studies, 18*(1), 81–98.

Cover, R. (2013). Suspended ethics and the team: Theorising sportsplayers' group sexual assault in the context of identity. *Sexualities, 16*(3–4), 300–318.

Cover, R. (2015). *Vulnerability and exposure: Footballer scandals, masculine identity and ethics.* Crawley, WA: UWA Publishing.

Evers, C. (2008). The Cronulla race riots: Safety maps on an Australian beach. *South Atlantic Quarterly, 107*(2), 411–429.

Flood, M. (2007). Men, sex, and homosociality: How bonds between men shape their sexual relations with women. *Men and Masculinities, 10*(3), 339–359.

Ford, C. (2018). The turning point: One man's downfall, #MeToo, and the rising up. *Meanjin, 77*(2), 40–52.

Lunny, A. M. (2003). Provocation and 'homosexual' advance: Masculinized subjects as threat, masculinized subjects under threat. *Social & Legal Studies, 12*(3), 311–333.

McRobbie, A. (2006). Vulnerability, violence and (cosmopolitan) ethics: Butler's Precarious life. *The British Journal of Sociology, 57*(1), 69–86.

Mohr, R. (1992). *Gay ideas: Outing and other controversies.* Boston: Beacon Press.

Poynting, S., Noble, G., Tabar, P., & Collins, J. (2004). *Bin Laden in the suburbs: Criminalising the Arab other.* Sydney: Sydney Institute of Criminology.

Rosello, M. (1998). *Declining the stereotype: Ethnicity and representation in French cultures.* Hanover, NH: University Press of New England.

Simpson, M. (2002, July 22). Meet the metrosexual. *Salon.* Retrieved January 22, 2018, from http://www.salon.com.

Waterhouse-Watson, D. (2011). (Un)reasonable doubt: A 'narrative immunity' for footballers against sexual assault allegations. *M/C Journal, 14*(1). Retrieved December 12, 2012, from http://journal.media-culture.org.au.

Williams, R. (1977). *Marxism and literature.* Oxford: Oxford University Press.

20

Online Justice in the Circuit of Capital: #MeToo, Marketization and the Deformation of Sexual Ethics

Michael Salter

Social media has emerged as a powerful mechanism for the circulation of counter-hegemonic and feminist discourses of sexual violence (Salter, 2013). There is now a burgeoning amount of scholarship on the utility of social media for survivors and social movements against gendered violence (Fileborn, 2016; Keller, Mendes, & Ringrose, 2018; Loney-Howes, 2018). However, social media does not merely facilitate political communication. Through its architecture and embedded incentives, it *produces* sociality and shapes political discourses and practices in specific ways (Milan, 2015). Using the example of #MeToo, this chapter explores how social media directs online justice-seeking in a manner conducive to its underlying commercial interests, generating contradictions and moments of rupture in social movements. Adapting Dean's (2005) conceptualization of 'communicative capitalism', the chapter examines three allegations of sexual misconduct that departed in significant ways from #MeToo's prior focus on seeking justice for victims and survivors of sexual violence and harassment. The analysis suggests that market imperatives

M. Salter (✉)
University of New South Wales, Sydney, NSW, Australia
e-mail: m.salter@unsw.edu.au

© The Author(s) 2019
B. Fileborn, R. Loney-Howes (eds.), *#MeToo and the Politics of Social Change*,
https://doi.org/10.1007/978-3-030-15213-0_20

had a significant role to play in undermining and contradicting #MeToo's promotion of ethical sexuality, and argues that online social movements should develop a more strategic orientation toward social media and networked technology.

The Development of the #MeToo Media Template

Kitzinger (2000) coined the term 'media templates' to describe the way in which key events become journalistic 'shorthand' for a specific construction of social problems. In the case of #MeToo, the paradigmatic 'media template' was undoubtedly the revelation that Hollywood mogul Harvey Weinstein, well known for his support of progressive politics and Democratic candidates, was credibly accused by multiple women of sexual misconduct including rape (see Garibotti & Hopp, this collection, for a discussion about a similar situation in Argentina). The broader context to Weinstein's alleged offending was his outsized influence in the film industry as founder of the entertainment company Miramax. Women's resistance to Weinstein's advances and assaults could curtail or destroy an acting career, while acquiescence and silence could secure career advancement. Weinstein's behavior was an open secret in Hollywood where the tradition of the 'casting couch'—in which female talent is expected to trade sexual favors for roles—has been public knowledge since the early twentieth century.

The call to join #MeToo was expressly in sympathy with the women victimized by Weinstein, in which social media users were encouraged to identify their own experiences with the features of the case. While evincing a general concern about the ubiquity of sexual threats in women's lives, the #MeToo media template emphasized four key interrelated elements: (1) sexual harassment/assault typically involving (2) men exploiting a superior position in a workplace or industry in which (3) resistance or acquiescence had career implications for the victim and (4) a lack of consequences for the perpetrator, often due to institutional complicity or a failure to investigate. The #MeToo media template has had the effect of highlighting the commonalities of sexual harassment across a diverse set of experiences, from the comparably wealthy women of Hollywood to the everyday social media user or fast food attendant (Orleck, 2018). Unlike other political hashtag phenomena such as Occupy or the Arab Spring, #MeToo did not generate its own mass protests, but instead politicized individual experiences of sexual harassment and leant momentum to efforts to combat sexual violence and discrimination across the globe.

The Corporate Choreography of Online Activism

The taken-for-granted role of Facebook and Twitter in #MeToo demonstrates the naturalization of a relatively recent phenomenon, namely how contemporary political activism is 'shamelessly appropriating corporate social networking sites like Facebook or Twitter' (Gerbaudo, 2012, p. 2). Reflecting on the impact of social media on the Egyptian revolution of 2011, Gerbaudo (2012) describes the role of social media in political activism in terms of a 'choreography of assembly'. He defines this choreography as 'a process of symbolic construction of public space', specifically 'an emotional space within which collective action can unfold' (p. 5). This is an apt descriptor of the effects of #MeToo, in which participation via Twitter, Facebook and other platforms generated feelings of solidarity, recognition and outrage (Mendes, Ringrose, & Keller, 2018; see also Mendes & Ringrose, this collection). Not only did social media host this 'emotional space', but it also directed public attention to particular examples of harassment and inequality. Emanating from #MeToo were calls for men accused of sexual misconduct to be sacked or otherwise professionally and socially exiled, intended as informal substitutes for the formal sanctions that are rarely applied in such cases.

Capturing attention is, as Tucekci (2017) observes, key to the success of both social media and social movements. Social movements can gain attention and support on social media with unprecedented speed, making social media an indispensable forum for contemporary activism. However, social media is not a neutral platform for public discourse. In accordance with the underlying business model of Web 2.0, which commodifies the data produced through user-generated content and interaction, social media platforms are built to incentivize users to seek attention and engagement on as wide a scale as possible (Van Dijck, 2013). Social media users who adapt their political claims and activities in accordance with social media mechanics and incentives will therefore potentially find greater 'success' (i.e. a heightened public profile, reach and influence) than those who do not. Processes by which some social media contributions are ignored and others amplified exert an implicit effect over online discourse and practice, as users are disciplined to adopt those discursive frames and positions that 'rate' on social media and discard alternative forms of expression. In this process, users and platforms mutually benefit, since platforms profit directly from the spikes in activity that result from highly salient online phenomena, simultaneously boosting profit and user profile and connectedness.

The effect on political discourse is considerable, denying visibility to forms of political expression that do not stimulate quantifiable metrics and lack advertiser salience. Indeed, social media platforms can suppress political phenomena that are deemed to be insufficiently advertising friendly in favor of other social movements with a more commercial flavor (Tucekci, 2017). Thus, the 'choreography of assembly' (Gerbaudo, 2012) on social media is not self-determined by the activists and users involved, but rather it is channeled in particular ways that conform to the corporate nature of the platform. This effect is obscured by a prevailing techno-utopianism that posits social media as the solution to complex social problems. Claims about the democraticizing and socially transformative effects of the Internet and social media that attend outbreaks of online political activism, whether it be Occupy, the Arab Spring or #MeToo, are coterminous with the corporate interests and self-perceptions of the technology industries. As Dean (2009, p. 9) notes, 'new media activists celebrate, even fetishize, the latest communication gadgets, unaware that their message is indistinguishable from Apple's'. However, close analyses of social media political movements over the past ten years have consistently revealed their fragility. The amassing of large, spontaneous online 'collectives' has not reliably translated into durable movements capable of opposing entrenched interests (Fuchs, 2014; Gerbaudo, 2012; Salter, 2017; Tucekci, 2017).

Communicative Capitalism and #MeToo

In her account of 'communicative capitalism', Dean (2005) emphasizes the disconnection between 'politics circulating as content and official politics' (p. 53). She suggests that the proliferation of political debate and discussion online appears robustly democratic but is, in fact, disconnected from institutionalized power and questions of political economy. Key to communicative capitalism is the exclusion of the very means of online communication from the horizon of political analysis. That is to say, within the mythos of e-democracy, online platforms are characterized as neutral or democratically orientated, rather than services delivered by for-profit engines of global capital. Moreover, she argues that the diversity of online communicative opportunities may disperse the energies necessary for alternative political formations:

> Instead of engaged debates, instead of contestations employing common terms, points of reference, or demarcated frontiers, we confront a multiplication of resistances and assertions so extensive that it hinders the formation of strong counterhegemonies. The proliferation, distribution, acceleration, and intensification of communicative access and opportunity, far from enhancing democratic governance or resistance, results in precisely the opposite, the postpolitical formation of communicative capitalism. (Dean, 2005, p. 53)

Dean's (2005) contribution is focused on the apparent gap between the online political discourse and the democratic politics of the early 2000s. This gap was particularly apparent between the robust anti-war sentiment online and the zeal with which the American government and allies pursued catastrophic military interventions in Iraq and Afghanistan. That gap has arguably narrowed although not closed, as governments and corporations have become selectively responsive to online discourse. However, her concept of 'communicative capitalism' in which 'the market, today, is the site of democratic aspirations, indeed, the mechanism by which the will of the demos manifests itself' (Dean, 2005, p. 54) captures how commercial prerogatives, embedded in online metrics and architecture, continue to shape political discourse as 'spectacle', delimiting reflection on material relations and economic conditions.

Drawing on the theoretical perspectives outlined above, the following sections analyze three case studies of sexual misconduct allegations associated with #MeToo to illustrate the complex but pervasive effects of market forces on the movement. The case studies emphasize the disciplining of online politics and political subjectivities by the entangled commercial prerogatives of social and mass media, which shape the efforts of journalists, social media users and political activists to gain and hold mass attention. The chapter suggests that the corporate choreography of #MeToo has been particularly problematic since it has generated moments of ethical contradictions, co-options and failures in a movement that is ostensibly in support of sexual ethics.

Aziz Ansari

In January 2018, the previously obscure website *Babe.net* published an online article describing an alienating sexual encounter between a young woman called Grace (a pseudonym) and US comedian Aziz Ansari. At this point, the #MeToo media template had been sustained on mass and social media with a high degree of coherence, foregrounding multiple examples of high-profile men who had sexually coerced or assaulted women (and some men) over whom they wielded considerable power. The *Babe.net* article maintained some aspects of this media template but disposed with others. While Ansari was certainly famous and wealthy, he was not exploiting a position of formal power over Grace, and the ethical status of his conduct was arguably more ambiguous. Unlike previous contributions to #MeToo, the article did not describe a *prima facie* case of sexual wrongdoing. Instead, the article's narrative conformed to a familiar heterosexual 'sexual script' (see Gavey, 2005), characterized by Ansari's eagerness for sexual intercourse and Grace's discomfort and uncertainty.

Grace was clear to *Babe.net* that she felt violated by her encounter with Ansari. Yet, while initial responses on social media insisted that, if Grace felt she had been raped, then she had been, these quickly gave way to assessments that the article did not describe criminal sexual misconduct. The details provided in the article suggested that Ansari had been persistent but responsive to Grace when she declined sexual intercourse. In their discussion of the case, social media users and journalists explored the spectrum between 'awkward sexual encounter' and 'sexual assault'—a spectrum that has long been the subject of feminist analysis (e.g. Kelly, 1988; Russell, 1984; see also Fileborn & Phillips, this collection). These discussions maintained their focus on the content of the *Babe.net* article and elaborated upon the fraught issues of consent and mutual desire, but generally avoided rehabilitating Ansari or defending him from the significant reputational damage caused by the article.

In contrast, a parallel stream of responses questioned the legitimacy of the article and its consequences for Ansari, pointing to *Babe.net*'s journalistic and editorial practices as evidence that the site was motivated by a desire for profile and profit (Bunch, 2018; Framke, 2018; Tiffany, 2018). It emerged that Grace did not approach *Babe.net*, but that *Babe.net* had heard rumors about Ansari and spoke to several people in their efforts to find Grace and convince her to speak publicly (Stelter, 2018). The interview and fact-checking of the story took place within the same week that the article was published, and Ansari was only given six hours to respond before publication (Framke, 2018). The haste of publication and *Babe.net*'s efforts to capitalize on the #MeToo groundswell was spectacularly successful, with over 2.5 million people reading the story within two days of it going online (Stelter, 2018). The website then leveraged the attention garnered by the Ansari piece to launch its first email newsletter, promising subscribers more details about the story.[1]

These facts remained persistently outside the mainstream of #MeToo discourse. Writing in the Guardian, Solemani (2018) characterized the controversy over the *Babe.net* article as a conflict between those who normalize or trivialize male sexual wrongdoing and the proponents of a 'bigger, brighter historical movement' toward gender inequality. For

---

[1] https://twitter.com/elenimitzali/status/95266149889106329.

Solemani, the reputational destruction of men such as Ansari was just 'collateral damage' in pursuit of a better future. In this framing of the debate, discussion of the underlying commercial imperatives of the publicization of the allegations against Ansari were irrelevant at best, and politically suspect at worst—a veiled form of anti-feminist attack. This refusal or inability to acknowledge the media production processes underlying the Ansari article produced a moment of ethical contradiction within #MeToo, in which a movement for sexual ethics lacked the collective will or conceptual resources to address its vulnerability to questionable or potentially unethical journalistic practice. Indeed, when Babe.net folded in early 2019, it became evident that female journalists had significant concerns about the sexualised culture within the media outlet, including sexual attention and contact from senior men in the company (Davis, 2019).

Junot Diaz

In May 2018, at the Sydney Writers Festival, the Dominican American novelist Junot Diaz was on stage when he was asked by writer Zinzi Clemmons about his treatment of her six years ago (Alter, Engel Bromwich, & Cave, 2018). She later wrote, on Twitter, that she had invited him to a workshop, and Diaz had forcibly kissed her as they left together, and that she is 'far from the only one he's done this 2'.[2] Clemmons' foreshadowing of further allegations was in accordance with the broader #MeToo narrative. Rumor and accounts of questionable behavior had preceded major revelations about Weinstein and others. In Diaz's case, however, subsequent reports were limited to reports of conflicts with Diaz at professional or social events. On Facebook, author Monica Byrne described being shouted at by Diaz at dinner (Grady, 2018a). On Twitter, author Carmen Maria Machado claimed that Diaz had subjected her to 'a blast of misogynist rage' at a literary event after she asked him about his characters' 'pathological' relationships with women.[3]

---

[2] https://twitter.com/zinziclemmons/status/992299032562229248.
[3] https://twitter.com/carmenmmachado/status/992318613494218753?lang=en.

Following the allegations, Diaz was suspended and placed under investigation by his employers at the Massachusetts Institute of Technology (MIT) and the *Boston Review*, and was forced to stand down from various professional responsibilities. However, he was reinstated to MIT and the *Boston Review* after the conclusion of separate investigations into his conduct did not uncover evidence of wrongdoing (Grady, 2018a). Some social media users interpreted the fact that he was not sanctioned for his actions as exemplary of the lack of accountability for perpetrators of sexual harassment. However, it is not entirely clear what, precisely, Diaz should have been punished for. Clemmons' description of an unwanted kiss from Diaz is the only public allegation that approaches sexual misconduct, although Diaz has categorically denied that this kiss took place, and Clemmons has chosen not to elaborate upon the circumstances (Flood, 2018). Clemmons, Machado and Byrne have all intimated that they have heard worse allegations against Diaz, but none have been forthcoming.

To support their claims, Byrne and Machado have argued that their personal disagreements with Diaz are indicative of his propensity for sexually aggressive violence. Byrne characterized Diaz's tone at a dinner party as an example of 'verbal violence', characterized by 'aggression and violence and anger and hate coming at you that is meant to produce fear, to silence to you. It has that effect, and it's deliberate' (Grady, 2018b). Byrne is reportedly compiling a dossier of first- and secondhand accounts of his misconduct, including a tweet from a man who claimed that Diaz belittled his manuscript in a writing workshop. When queried by a journalist on whether such an account describes a 'sexual abuser or a jerk', Byrnes responded by asking, 'What is the difference?' (Shanahan & Ebbert, 2018).

Machado's report of being publicly humiliated by Diaz was contested when an audio recording of their encounter was published on Twitter. The recording shows that Diaz was calm if somewhat exasperated in his discussion with her. Machado defended her account of his 'misogynist rage' but went on to describe their conversation as a 'weird interaction', and one that did not rise to the level of 'abuse' (Shapiro, 2018). Much of Machado's stated concern about Diaz relates to his treatment of women in his novels (Shapiro, 2018), which she derided as 'misogynist trash'.[4]

---

[4] https://twitter.com/carmenmmachado/status/992318615004172288?lang=en.

When Machado claimed on Twitter that Diaz has 'treated women horrifically in every way possible',[5] many assumed she was referring to acts of sexual misconduct and assault; however, the comment may refer to his *fictional* portrayal of women.

The allegations against Diaz were not brokered by any media outlet in particular, but rather they were made in person (Clemmons) or on social media (Byrne and Machado), garnering press and social media circulation. However, the linking of these complaints to #MeToo, and their subsequent framings of those allegations on social media, reflect similar logics to those deployed by *Babe.net* in an effort to garner as wide an audience for the Ansari story as possible. The allegations against Diaz were a poor fit within the #MeToo media template, painting a picture of a conflicted and volatile literary figure rather than a sexual offender. However, key interlocutors strategically sought to blur the boundaries between upsetting personal interactions, criticisms of Diaz's fiction and sexually aggressive misogyny. An uncomfortable public debate became a 'blast of misogynist rage', a disagreement at a dinner party became 'verbal violence' and the distinction between sexual assault and 'horrific' fictional portrayals of women became unclear. On the facts presented, the allegations might have struggled for public purchase. It was only through a metaphorical association between speech, writing and violence that the link to #MeToo was maintained, buttressed by Clemmon's reference to an unwanted kiss.

The notion that a lack of courtesy or manners may be symptomatic of underlying prejudice, justifying public shaming and other acts of retaliation, has been popularized with the rise of social media (Ronson, 2015). Outright calls for Diaz to lose his employment and face banishment from literary circles on the basis of the transgressions described above can be situated firmly within so-called 'call-out culture'. Nagle (2017) connects the pervasiveness of this milieu online with the hierarchical competition for attention, reach and impact on social media, which has normalized outsized responses to individual impropriety in a manner that has had major impacts on progressive political organizing. By its very architecture, social media privileges simplistic but shocking claims and mass 'pile-ons' in a manner that has, Nagle (2017) suggests, shifted contemporary political culture as a whole. However, the economic and technological

---

[5] https://twitter.com/carmenmmachado/status/992318618032455686.

conditions underlying the form that online politics takes is almost inevitably beyond the grasp of that politics. Much like the case of Aziz Ansari, many #MeToo advocates took the widespread circulation of these allegations against Diaz as the de facto evidence of their truth. Social media now hosts ongoing claims that Diaz is a 'rapist' and 'predator' although he was never accused of such.

Cory Booker

Dean (2005) describes utopian visions of online political discourse as a 'disavowal of a more fundamental political disempowerment or castration' (p. 61). In techno-utopianism, the persistence of political conflict, and pervasive feelings of powerlessness, are mystified by fantasies of 'unity, wholeness, or order' (p. 63). Rather than approach technology as a mode of action, or in terms of its production via historical, social and economic contingency, technology is instead reified as a discrete material object or system invested with fantasies of power and completeness. In this process, 'the complexities of politics—of organization, struggle, duration, decisiveness, division, representation, etc.—are condensed into one thing, one problem to be solved and one technological solution' (Dean, 2005, p. 63). However, the political naivety of techno-utopianism is actively promoted by the technology industries and operates as a legitimizing mechanism for its extractive business practices. This utopianism was evident in the widespread belief animating #MeToo that the more women disclosed sexual harassment and assault on social media, and the more pressure that was applied to employers and others to sack abusive men, then the greater the rebalancing of gender inequality would be.

The sexual assault allegations made against US senator Cory Booker in late 2018 suggest a far more complex picture, in which institutionalized power not only ignores the pressure exerted by online sexual assault disclosures but can actively repurpose and subvert them. Booker is well known as a prominent supporter of progressive causes, including lesbian, gay, bisexual, transgender, intersex and queer (LGBTIQ) rights and gender equality, and he is reviled in conservative circles. This acrimony only increased during the September 2018 nomination process of conservative judge Brett Kavanaugh to the US Supreme Court, when Christine Blasey Ford, a psychology professor, alleged that she had been sexually assaulted by a drunken Kavanaugh when they were both teenagers (Stolberg & Fandos, 2018). Shortly after her report was made public, two other women came forward to describe being subject to sexual misconduct by Kavanaugh when he was a young man. The allegations were firmly rejected by Kavanaugh and his advocates, who claimed there was a political conspiracy afoot among progressives and Democrats to block his nomination (Shabad, 2018). In the press and online, the allegations against Kavanaugh were widely situated within the #MeToo 'moment'. Vocal in his support of Kavanaugh's accusers, Booker actively sought to prevent Kavanaugh's nomination through his role on the Senate Judiciary Committee. When Ford testified to the Committee, Booker personally delivered her coffee while she was speaking, becoming one of her most visible supporters.

On October 20, three weeks after Ford testified against Kavanaugh, an anonymous allegation of sexual misconduct perpetrated by Booker was widely circulated on Twitter, garnering over 6000 'retweets' and 8000 'likes'.[6] The tweet linked to a four-page statement on a Google Drive document. The statement was purportedly written by a gay man who described Booker locking him in a toilet and sexually assaulting him in 2014. The piece sought to accuse Booker of sexual assault and hypocrisy, given his support for Ford, and indicted the #MeToo movement for bias on the basis of 'gender, sexual orientation or political affiliation'. While the author goes to some lengths to characterize himself as a 'liberal', the statement is riddled with right-wing sentiment, including claims of discrimination against Republicans, gratuitous use of right-wing shibboleths such as 'safe spaces' and 'triggering', and pejorative references to the Kavanaugh allegations as a 'debacle'.

The allegation was then popularized on the fringe far-right blog, the Gateway Pundit. The Gateway Pundit, it should be noted, was also implicated in an alleged attempt to solicit false allegations of sexual harassment against Robert Mueller, in order to derail ongoing investigations into Russian interference in the US election (Darcy, Scannell, & Shortell, 2018). The anonymous and uncorroborated allegation against Booker was widely shared through conservative circles on Twitter,

---

[6] https://twitter.com/TheeDeepThroat/status/1053521823843811328.

Facebook, YouTube and conservative podcasts, and was discussed on the right-wing *Fox News* television channel. While the allegation did not break through to mainstream media, its repetition in right-wing circles only further added to ongoing online attacks on Booker and the #MeToo movement as a whole, which was widely blamed among conservatives for encouraging and supporting Ford's allegation against Kavanaugh.

The use of false allegations to discredit the movement against sexual violence is not a new tactic, nor is it unique to social media. Australian feminist Anne Summers has recently described how, in the mid-1990s, false claims were circulated in the mass media that she was to be charged with sexual harassment (Summers, 2018). Summers had a high-profile role in drafting and tightening Australian sexual harassment laws, and she attributes the false allegations to a 'calculated and orchestrated attack' designed to discredit her and her work. However, with the advent of social media, Tucekci (2017) argues that inundating audiences with false information has become a new form of censorship:

> In the networked public sphere, the goal of the powerful often is not to convince people of the truth of a particular narrative or to block a particular piece of information from getting out (that is increasingly difficult), but to produce resignation, cynicism, and a sense of disempowerment amongst people. (p. 228)

In the aftermath of #MeToo, the promotion of false allegations of assault appears to have become an automated tactic for conservative and right-wing operatives. During Kavanaugh's nomination process, automated Twitter accounts known as 'bots' actively circulated false allegations of sexual assault against Booker and other politicians (de Haldevang, 2018). The availability of this strategy signals that neither disclosures of sexual violence nor their circulation on social media are inherently liberatory or transformative, but rather they are operative within the broader economic, political and social relations and structures. Social and political conflicts are dynamic, as the strategic use of systems such as social media by political actors *shifts* in response to their opponent's own adaptive movements. Hence, the political impact of social media is not static but rather evolves over time, reflecting changes in the socio-technical arrangements that contextualize and shape social media use. Just as oppressive state authorities adapted to the use of social media by opposition forces, developing effective strategies to neutralize online dissent (Tufecki, 2017), so too have right-wing and conservative forces proven adept at using mimicry and vexatious complaints to parody and confuse feminist claims of victimization (Nagle, 2017). The techno-utopianism that has driven online movements such as #MeToo assigns a fixed political meaning and utility to social media that is in the interests of social media platforms and advertisers, but mystifies the production and application of technology within economic and political antagonisms.

Conclusion

In their research with women who have disclosed sexual assault as part of online activism, Mendes et al. (2018, p. 238) emphasize the 'complex terrain of emotions' and 'sleepless nights' that accompanied participation in movements like #MeToo. They also described the positive role of online validation and support that can accompany online sexual assault disclosures (p. 239). The 'emotional space' and feelings of solidarity and support extended to innumerable participants in #MeToo have been powerful and, in the history of anti-rape activism, unprecedented in scope. In turn, this has catalyzed an increased political consciousness of sexual violence as well as individual and collective action, including formal complaints to authorities and community and workplace organizing. However, this chapter has illustrated how deeply felt, shared aspirations for justice and social change are 'choreographed' by social and mass media companies to maximize profit in ways that can profoundly reshape and compromise those movements, bringing online justice into the circuit of capital.

Online politics does not operate externally to or against 'communicative capitalism' (Dean, 2005) and yet struggles to take its own political and economic context into account. The convergence of profit motives in online political activism and discourse thus potentiates a kind of 'spectacle' (Debord, 1998) or 'hyper-reality' (Baudrillard, 1988), in which the appearance of political activism obscures, rather than analyzes or seeks to transform, the very conditions of its emergence and possibility. Opposing the fetishization of social media as a neutral tool or democratic instrument, the chapter emphasizes the importance of attending to the dynamism of socio-technical arrangements in online political activism. It is apparent that social media movements such as #MeToo can evoke powerful emotion and debate, contribute momentum to collective action and exert influence over institutions with formal, decision-making power. However, the commercial mediation of the relationship between social media and institutional power requires critical analysis by movements for gender equality.

A movement for ethical sexuality, such as #MeToo, is potentially imperiled by the objectifying and instrumental tendencies of social media platforms, which are built to commodify user interaction, enable micro-targeted advertising and direct public attention en masse in profitable directions. Mass outrage and grief over sexual violence can be hijacked by 'old' and 'new' media companies seeking to redirect and rework political movements to profitable ends. Indeed, such strategies are so pervasive on social media that they are internalized and reworked by individual social media users in their own efforts to assert their political claims, reproducing forms of political discourse that mirror commercial imperatives. The need for online movements to interrogate the complex interdependence between public discourse and its socio-technological conditions is made only more urgent by the evident availability of social media for anti-feminist and anti-democratic aims. Communicative capitalism is fundamentally amoral in its orientation, and without a critique of this amorality, movements such as #MeToo risk their own ethical integrity.

References

Alter, A., Engel Bromwich, J., & Cave, D. (2018, May 4). The writer Zinzi Clemmons accuses Junot Diaz of forcibly kissing her. *New York Times*. Retrieved December 20, 2018, from https://www.nytimes.com/2018/05/04/books/junot-diaz-accusations.html.

Baudrillard, J. (1988). *The ecstasy of communication*. New York: Semiotext(e).

Bunch, S. (2018, January 15). Babe's Aziz Ansari piece was a gift to anyone who wants to derail #MeToo. *Washington Post*. Retrieved December 20, 2018, from https://www.washingtonpost.com/news/act-four/wp/2018/01/15/babes-aziz-ansari-piece-was-a-gift-to-anyone-who-wants-to-derail-metoo/?utm_term=.2d739ada45ce.

Darcy, O., Scannell, K., & Shortell, D. (2018, November 1). How a right-wing effort to slime Mueller with a sexual assault allegation fell apart. *CNN*. Retrieved December 20, 2018, from https://edition.cnn.com/2018/10/31/media/gateway-pundit-robert-mueller-false-allegations/index.html.

Davis, A. (2019, June 23). The rise and fall of Babe.net. *The Cut*. Retrieved from https://www.thecut.com/2019/06/babe-net-aziz-ansari-date-rise-and-fall.html.

de Haldevang, M. (2018, October 3). Russian trolls and bots are flooding Twitter with Ford-Kavanaugh disinformation. *Quartz*. Retrieved December 20, 2018, from https://qz.com/1409102/russian-trolls-and-bots-are-flooding-twitter-with-ford-kavanaugh-disinformation/.

Dean, J. (2005). Communicative capitalism: Circulation and the foreclosure of politics. *Cultural Politics, 1*(1), 51–74.

Dean, J. (2009). *Democracy and other neoliberal fantasies: Communicative capitalism and left politics*. Durham and London: Duke University Press.

Debord, G. (1998). *Comments on the society of the spectacle*. London: Verso.

Fileborn, B. (2016). Justice 2.0: Street harassment victims' use of social media and online activism as sites of informal justice. *British Journal of Criminology, 57*(6), 1482–1501.

Flood, A. (2018, July 2). Junot Diaz says alleged sexual harassment 'didn't happen'. *The Guardian*. Retrieved from https://www.theguardian.com/books/2018/jul/2002/junot-diaz-says-sexual-harassment-allegations-didnt-happen-zinzi-clemmons.

Framke, C. (2018, January 18). The controversy around Babe.net's Aziz Ansari story, explained. *Vox*. Retrieved December 20, 2018, from https://www.vox.com/culture/2018/1/17/16897440/aziz-ansari-allegations-babe-me-too.

Fuchs, C. (2014). *OccupyMedia!: The occupy movement and social media in crisis capitalism*. Winchester: Zero Books.

Gavey, N. (2005). *Just sex? The cultural scaffolding of rape*. New York and London: Routledge.

Gerbaudo, P. (2012). *Tweets and the streets: Social media and contemporary activism*. London: Pluto Press.

Grady, C. (2018a, June 19). A month after accusations of sexual misconduct, Junot Diaz is more or less unscathed. *Vox.* Retrieved December 20, 2018, from https://www.vox.com/culture/2018/6/19/17478886/junot-diaz-sexual-misconduct-mit-boston-review.

Grady, C. (2018b, May 7). Pulitzer winner Junot Diaz has been accused of forcibly kissing a woman and berating 2 others. *Vox.* Retrieved December 20, 2018, from https://www.vox.com/culture/2018/5/4/17318668/junot-diaz-sexual-misconduct-accusation.

Keller, J., Mendes, K., & Ringrose, J. (2018). Speaking 'unspeakable things': Documenting digital feminist responses to rape culture. *Journal of Gender Studies, 27*(1), 22–36.

Kelly, L. (1988). *Surviving sexual violence.* Oxford: Blackwell.

Kitzinger, J. (2000). Media templates: Patterns of association and the (re)construction of meaning over time. *Media, Culture and Society, 22*(1), 61–84.

Loney-Howes, R. (2018). Shifting the rape script: "Coming out" online as a rape victim. *Frontiers: A Journal of Women Studies, 39*(2), 26–57.

Mendes, K., Ringrose, J., & Keller, J. (2018). # MeToo and the promise and pitfalls of challenging rape culture through digital feminist activism. *European Journal of Women's Studies, 25*(2), 236–246.

Milan, S. (2015). From social movements to cloud protesting: The evolution of collective identity. *Information, Communication & Society, 18*(8), 887–900.

Nagle, A. (2017). *Kill all normies: Online culture wars from 4Chan and Tumblr to Trump and the Alt-Right.* Alresford: Zero Books.

Orleck, A. (2018, September 20). #MeToo and McDonalds. *Jacobin.* Retrieved December 20, 2018, from https://www.jacobinmag.com/2018/2009/mcdonalds-strike-metoo-sexual-harassment-organizing.

Ronson, J. (2015). *So you've been publicly shamed.* Riverhead: Picador.

Russell, D. H. (1984). *Sexual exploitation: Rape, child sexual abuse, and workplace harassment.* Thousand Oaks, CA: Sage.

Salter, M. (2013). Justice and revenge in online counter-publics: Emerging responses to sexual violence in the age of social media. *Crime, Media, Culture, 9*(3), 225–242.

Salter, M. (2017). *Crime, justice and social media.* London and New York: Routledge.

Shabad, R. (2018, September). An angry, emotional Kavanaugh accuses Democrats of 'search and destroy'. *NBC News.* Retrieved December 20, 2018, from https://www.nbcnews.com/politics/congress/christine-blasey-ford-tells-senate-memories-brett-kavanaugh-assault-have-n913531.

Shanahan, M., & Ebbert, S. (2018, June 30). Junot Diaz case may be a #MeToo turning point. *Boston Globe*. Retrieved December 20, 2018, from https://www.bostonglobe.com/metro/2018/06/30/junot-diaz-case-may-be-metoo-turning-point/3TMFseenE4Go1eVsqbFSxM/story.html.

Shapiro, L. (2018, June). Misogyny is boring as hell. *Vulture*. Retrieved December 20, 2018, from https://www.vulture.com/2018/06/misogyny-is-boring-carmen-maria-machado.html.

Solemani, S. (2018, January 22). The Aziz Ansari furore isn't the end of #MeToo. It's just the start. *The Guardian*. Retrieved December 20, 2018, from https://www.theguardian.com/commentisfree/2018/jan/21/aziz-ansari-metoo-sexual-equality.

Stelter, B. (2018, January 16). Babe editor stands by Aziz Ansari story. *CNN Business*. Retrieved December 20, 2018, from https://money.cnn.com/2018/01/15/media/aziz-ansari-babe-editor-interview/index.html.

Stolberg, S. G., & Fandos, M. (2018, September 23). Christine Blasey Ford reaches deal to testify at Kavanaugh hearing. *New York Times*. Retrieved December 20, 2018, from https://www.nytimes.com/2018/09/23/us/politics/brett-kavanaugh-christine-blasey-ford-testify.html.

Summers, A. (2018, October 26). The fragility of feminist progress and why rage is a luxury we can't afford. *The Guardian*. Retrieved December 20, 2018, from https://www.theguardian.com/world/2018/oct/26/the-fragility-of-feminist-progress-and-why-rage-is-a-luxury-we-cant-afford..

Tiffany, K. (2018, January). The Aziz Ansari story is a mess, but so are the arguments against it. *The Verge*. Retrieved December 20, 2018, from https://www.theverge.com/2018/1/17/16893896/babe-aziz-ansari-sexual-misconduct-new-journalism-millennials-platform-reporting.

Tucekci, Z. (2017). *Twitter and tear gas: The power and fragility of networked protest*. New Haven and London: Yale University Press.

Van Dijck, J. (2013). *The culture of connectivity: A critical history of social media*. Oxford: Oxford University Press.

21

Conclusion: 'A New Day Is on the Horizon'?

Rachel Loney-Howes and Bianca Fileborn

When renowned media personality Oprah Winfrey accepted the Cecil B. De Mille Award at the 2018 Golden Globe Awards, she triumphantly declared that 'a new day is on the horizon' on account of the public reckoning that was playing out, thanks to #MeToo. Though we lack the bold certainty that Winfrey displayed in her rousing speech, we are cautiously optimistic about what #MeToo has achieved and how anti-sexual violence activism might progress moving forward.

In this collection, we have attempted to bring together a diverse range of perspectives and interpretations of the #MeToo movement. Rather than aiming to reach some kind of consensus as to the impact, influence and shortcomings of the movement, we instead sought to embrace the (perhaps uncomfortable, messy, and less satisfying) position of resisting 'easy' answers and neat, fully resolved conclusions about #MeToo.

R. Loney-Howes (✉)
University of Wollongong, Wollongong, NSW, Australia
e-mail: rlhowes@uow.edu.au

B. Fileborn
University of Melbourne, Parkville, VIC, Australia
e-mail: biancaf@unimelb.edu.au

© The Author(s) 2019   **335**
B. Fileborn, R. Loney-Howes (eds.), *#MeToo and the Politics of Social Change*,
https://doi.org/10.1007/978-3-030-15213-0_21

Indeed, if there is a key 'take-away' point from the contributions to this book, it is that the #MeToo movement is a deeply complex and multi-faceted one, brimming with points of tension, contradiction, and polarization.

The ability to reach any kind of definitive conclusions about the movement (to the extent that this is *ever* possible, or even desirable) is further hindered by the fact that #MeToo is still a live activist movement—a 'work in progress', if you will. During the writing process, the speed at which the ground shifted made keeping up with new developments in the movement challenging, with new disclosures of sexual harassment and assault regularly emerging alongside backlash and critique. Indeed, in the days before we commenced writing this chapter, actor Yael Stone of *Orange Is the New Black* fame made a public disclosure of sexual harassment and misconduct allegedly perpetrated by the 'internationally acclaimed' actor Geoffrey Rush. While Rush (perhaps unsurprisingly) denies these and other claims made against him, this development generated fresh debate regarding the roles of power, celebrity, and institutional structures in facilitating sexual violence and silencing survivors.

Thus, we are heartened by the momentum generated by #MeToo and the continuous stream of stories in news media about sexual violence, consent, and gender. If the past is anything to go by, then the #MeToo movement may soon find itself in the annals of history, another chapter in a long trajectory of activism seeking to keep sexual harassment and violence on the public agenda. Yet, far from becoming *just* another hashtag, #MeToo seems to have engrained itself in popular discourse—a shortcut to positioning oneself as a survivor and to act in solidarity with survivors—in a way that previous forms of activism arguably have not.

However, as we flagged earlier, we wish to conclude this collection with caution. Although #MeToo has been successful at putting sexual harassment and violence on the public policy agenda in some capacity, as Lauren Rosewarne has argued, consciousness-raising alone does not equate to social, cultural, and political change. Giving voice to one's story—and having that story believed and validated—can be vitally important for survivors. Indeed, as both Mendes and Ringrose, and Gleeson and Turner highlighted in their contributions, engaging in online disclosure via movements such as #MeToo can provide an inroad to further political awakening and the formation of activist identities. The collective storytelling and consciousness-raising facilitated by #MeToo is a necessary starting point, but is not *sufficient* in generating social, cultural, and structural change. Indeed, the exposure of *personal* stories of sexual harassment and assault is often at the cost of addressing the *political* causes of that violence. We must be careful not to allow widespread discussion and discursive engagement alone to act as a smoke screen giving the *appearance* of more substantive change.

Moreover, we must continue to question and challenge whose interests are served by any resultant changes from the momentum of #MeToo and to what extent they perpetuate the same parameters of inclusion/exclusion that have dogged anti-harassment and anti-violence efforts since the 1970s, as illustrated in Loney-Howes' chapter. Relatedly, advocates for institutional and structural reforms must continue to interrogate the foundations of those systems lest they continue to reinforce the very power structures activists are seeking to critique. Yet, even less formal and institutionalized structures are constrained by the contexts in which they operate, as Haire, Newman, and Fileborn illustrated in their chapter about the circulation of the 'Shitty Media Men' list. The backlash against those who contributed to and circulated the list—despite the well-intended and preventative nature that sat behind the list's creation—demonstrates the risks associated with women speaking out in counter-public spaces. Subsequently, activists and advocates must be mindful of the platforms and mechanisms they utilize in advancing their cause: as Michael Salter has illustrated, how we undertake activist work has the potential to perpetuate systems of inequality and ethically questionable practices, even if inadvertently.

This potential for #MeToo to perpetuate power structures and inequalities which delimit the recognition of survivors has been echoed by contributors who expressed concern over the continued failure to acknowledge the experiences of women of color (Kagal, Cowan and Jawad; Ryan) and members of the lesbian, gay, bisexual, transgender/transsexual, queer/questioning, intersex, and asexual (LGBTQIA) communities (Ison). There are numerous other groups and individuals whose experiences have been further marginalized or failed to be adequately acknowledged in the confines of #MeToo whom we have unfortunately not been able to address in detail in this collection. This includes, but is certainly not limited to, sex workers, women with disabilities, older women, and men who are victim-survivors of sexual violence. In this sense, we are also complicit, despite our best intentions, in perpetuating some boundaries and limiting the scope for these individuals to speak out. It is, likewise, important, to acknowledge the impossibility of representing all experiences and perspectives. As Jess Ison astutely pointed out in her chapter, the language we have available to us simultaneously includes and excludes, and we cannot speak of any coherent and all-encompassing experience or perspective of the #MeToo movement. Thus, the discussions initiated here are inevitably partial and incomplete (and perhaps even more so, given the evolving nature of #MeToo), further highlighting the need for this conversation to be an ongoing and broadly inclusive one.

In this sense, we interpret #MeToo as a *rupture* in public discussions and perceptions about sexual harassment and violence. This rupture can be viewed as an opportunity to *intervene* in broadening the parameters of recognition, but also in generating critical discussions about the socio-political causes of violence and the possibility of response and prevention. However, as both Fileborn and Phillips, and Rosewarne cautioned, these moments of rupture and progress can readily be undone: they are contested, fluid, and unstable. Numerous contributors have highlighted how feminist activism and survivor speech are consistently met with backlash and resistance. As such, any apparent gains made in the wake of #MeToo should not be taken for granted. It is therefore particularly pertinent to heed Mary Anne Franks' warning about #MeToo: women who deign to speak out against men's violence have been silenced, both historically and contemporaneously. While this signals the power and danger of women's speech, it remains to be seen whether we will once again 'ignore them at our peril' (Franks).

Further, any apparent achievements of the movement should not be overstated. The gains of #MeToo have been largely discursive in nature, as both Franks and Rosewarne argued. Michael Flood's discussion on #MeToo in relation to men similarly indicated that any influence in progressing men's attitudes and behavior has been limited and uneven at best. Finally, while the movement may be conceived of as a rupture and an opportunity to intervene, that is not to say that it has consistently been presented that way. Mainstream media representations, for example, continued to construct sexual violence in limited ways through reporting on #MeToo, as Kathryn Royal demonstrated. Such discursive acts function to reaffirm rape myths and misconceptions (therefore delimiting, rather than opening up, the possibilities for recognition) and elide opportunities for critical, transformative discussion. Additionally, as Heidi Matthews argued, dominant discourses surrounding #MeToo may serve conservative, rather than progressive, sexual agendas. However, as Christy E. Newman and Bridget Haire note, some authors of pop-culture media channels, such as progressive online sex advice columns, offer more complex and nuanced representations and understandings of sexual relationships and sexual violence. Of course, the parameters of the platforms where sexual violence is being discussed constrain or enable what can be expressed, and this points to the potential of non-traditional forms of media to initiate more critical conversations about sexual violence, consent, and ethical relationships. Yet, this is not an excuse for traditional media outlets to perpetuate myths and stereotypes about gender-based violence.

It is also important that we are attentive to the local and microlevel impacts of #MeToo. Certainly, these can also be problematic and contentious. As Tess Ryan's chapter illustrated, the #MeToo movement in Australia has been implicated in ongoing colonial projects of oppression and silencing of the voices and experiences of Aboriginal women. In a similar vein, Kagal, Cowan, and Jawad provided an insightful critique of the inability of #MeToo to be inclusive of Muslim women as well as Indian women involved in the informal economy. Conversely, both Jing Zeng and Garibotti & Hopp's work demonstrated the ways in which transnational campaigns can be taken up by local activists and put to work in ways perhaps not intended or envisaged; creatively adapted to the needs and circumstances of women and other survivors in particular contexts, places, and socio-political moments in time. While we must remain mindful and cautious of the limitations of a movement initiated by and for White, wealthy, Western women, neither should we make sweeping claims nor assumptions about the impacts (or lack thereof) of the movement for women and survivors outside of this privileged context.

From #MeToo to #NoMore: Where to from Here?

In closing, we would like to reflect on some potential avenues for future anti-sexual violence activist work. Whether this work occurs under the banner of #MeToo remains an open question. While the movement has been a robust one to date, it is also in many respects a deeply flawed and contentious one, as has been illustrated throughout the collection. In this respect, the potential demise and/or evolution of #MeToo is not necessarily inherently problematic. Indeed, it may be a necessary step in generating space for more responsive, inclusive, and ethical forms of anti-sexual violence activism. Regardless of the form this ongoing activism takes, contributions to this collection point to a number of issues that future activist and violence prevention work must navigate.

The first of which is the ethics of discursive representations of sexual violence, particularly in media reporting on sexual harassment and assault, but also representations of sexual violence in popular culture more broadly (something we haven't specifically touched on in this collection). Modes of representation have the capacity to draw boundaries around who constitutes a victim-survivor worthy of public support, who constitutes a perpetrator or offender, and what 'counts' as sexual violence. Although a focus on discursive representations of sexual violence is in some respects limited (as our earlier discussion highlighted), shifting the language available to represent and construct sexual violence is nonetheless vitally important as it broadens the scope for *all* survivors to label and express their experiences as sexual violence (if they so choose). If we can't make it visible, we can't respond to it (Ison, this collection). This focus on language and discourse, however, should not be at the expense of examining the structural and institutional patterns, practices, and power relations that continue to exclude and oppress women and others who are in subordinate social and political positions. Indeed the limitations surrounding the discursive construction of sexual harassment and assault are inherently political ones that seek to maintain the illusion that sexual violence is rare, random, and perpetuated by a stranger in order to keep women in a constant state of fear.

Secondly, we need to evolve how we think about sexual ethics and consent. While the extent to which sexual violence is a product of 'sex' or 'power' has been heavily contested in scholarship and activism on sexual violence, contributions to this collection suggest that sexual violence, sex, power, and gender (and other forms of identity) are deeply intertwined and co-inform one another. This suggests that in moving forward, activists must be attentive to the interplay between these factors. As Cyndi Darnell and Heidi Matthews advocated, in progressing our sexual politics and practices to preclude the possibility of sexual violence, we must pay heed to sexual pleasure and danger. Rather than focusing solely on avoiding sexual violence, achieving substantive change requires us to rethink our approach to sexual pleasure, desire, and communication. Yet, creating the space for this to occur likewise necessitates a restructuring of our gendered norms and expectations when it comes to sex.

This leads into a third area regarding the need to evolve gendered norms and relations. As Rob Cover and Michael Flood articulated in their chapters, norms of masculinity create the conditions from which sexual violence can emerge, but also influence men's responses to, or sense of responsibility for the prevention of, sexual violence. Both authors suggest the need to deconstruct and open up opportunities for 'doing' masculinity differently—not just making surface-level changes, as Cover highlighted in his discussion of 'new' masculinities. Cover points to the possibilities for doing so through generating an ethic of care and vulnerability that may facilitate, in turn, a process of recognition predicated on nonviolence and an understanding of the operation of power. However, such an approach requires a structural and cultural shift that enables men to recognize (and respect) the vulnerability of those with less power than themselves. In doing so, we might begin to address the systematic ways in which men are social, politically and sexually privileged, and engage in a more productive dialogue about developing an agenda for change.

As Tarana Burke has stated, we have to 'talk about what happens after' we say #MeToo—the hard, 'unglamorous', grinding work of generating change (Brockes, 2018). This is the path we must take so that we no longer have to say 'me too'.

Reference

Brockes, E. (2018, January 15). #MeToo founder Tarana Burke: 'You have to use your privilege to serve other people'. *The Guardian*. Retrieved December 20, 2018, from https://www.theguardian.com/world/2018/jan/15/me-too-founder-tarana-burke-women-sexual-assault.

Index[1]

---

[1] Note: Page numbers followed by 'n' refer to notes.

© The Author(s) 2019
B. Fileborn, R. Loney-Howes (eds.), *#MeToo and the Politics of Social Change*,
https://doi.org/10.1007/978-3-030-15213-0

CPSIA information can be obtained
at www.ICGtesting.com
Printed in the USA
LVHW081454080320
649322LV00018B/2539